SCHOLASTIC
★ KID'S ★
ALMANAC
for the 21st Century

WRITTEN BY
Elaine Pascoe
and Deborah Kops

ILLUSTRATED BY
Bob Italiano
and David C. Bell

A BLACKBIRCH GRAPHICS BOOK

SCHOLASTIC
REFERENCE

New York • Toronto • London • Auckland • Sydney
Mexico City • New Delhi • Hong Kong

CREATED AND PRODUCED BY BLACKBIRCH GRAPHICS, INC.

Blackbirch Graphics Staff
Bruce Glassman, Executive Editor
Calico Harington, Design and Production
Jenifer Corr Morse, Assistant Editor

Scholastic Reference Staff
Wendy Barish, Editorial Director
Mary Varilla Jones, Assistant Editor
David Saylor, Creative Director
Nancy Sabato, Art Director

Library of Congress Cataloging-in-Publication Data

Scholastic Kid's Almanac for the 21st Century / Blackbirch Graphics, Inc.
p.   cm.
ISBN 0-590-30723-1 (hc)
ISBN 0-590-30724-X (pb)
1. Encyclopedias and dictionaries. I. Blackbirch Graphics, Inc.
AG6 .S36 1999 • 031—dc21 98-48739 • CIP • AC

10 9 8 7 6 5 4 3 2 1   9/9 0/0 01 02 03
Printed in the U.S.A.   23
First edition, July 1999

CONTENTS

AEROSPACE

Aerospace includes the atmosphere, the blanket of air that surrounds Earth, and endless space beyond. Air travel was not possible for people until the twentieth century. But today air travel is routine, and satellites and spacecraft orbit Earth.

The aerospace era began when Orville and Wilbur Wright's simple airplane made the first successful powered flight at Kitty Hawk, North Carolina, in 1903. Today, jet airplanes carry people higher, faster, and farther than the Wright brothers could have imagined. Rockets travel even farther—into space. Space exploration began in 1957, when the Soviet Union put a satellite called *Sputnik 1* into orbit. Just 12 years later, U.S. astronauts Neil Armstrong and Edwin "Buzz" Aldrin walked on the moon, more than 250,000 miles (400,000 km) from Earth.

In the United States, space travel has been guided by the National Aeronautics and Space Administration (NASA). In recent years, nations around the world have pooled their resources and knowledge, working together. The aerospace industry employs thousands of people worldwide. They range from research scientists and engineers, who design new aircraft and spacecraft, to factory workers, who produce the craft.

Since the Apollo moon missions of the 1960s and early 1970s, American astronauts have not traveled so far. Instead, they have carried out research aboard space shuttles and orbiting space stations. Unmanned space probes have explored the far reaches of our solar system, and even traveled beyond. Will people one day visit these distant regions? Aerospace scientists believe that it's only a matter of time.

Yearbook

December 17, 1903 The Wright brothers pilot the first powered, heavier-than-air craft.

October 4, 1957 The Soviet Union launches *Sputnik* 1, the first human-made satellite to orbit in space.

July 20, 1969 Astronauts Armstrong, Collins, and Aldrin land on the moon aboard the *Apollo* 11.

December 23, 1986 Pilots Yeager and Rutan set a world record for nonstop flight around the world.

• Notables •

Amelia Earhart (1897–1937) First woman to cross the Atlantic in an airplane.

Yuri Gagarin (1934–1968) Russian; first human to orbit in space.

Robert H. Goddard (1882–1945) American physicist; fired the first liquid fuel-propelled rocket in 1926.

Charles Lindbergh (1902–1974) Made the first nonstop solo airplane flight across the Atlantic.

Shannon Lucid (1943–) U.S. astronaut; woman who has spent most time in space.

Joseph-Michel (1740–1810) and Jacques-Etienne (1745–1799) Montgolfier First humans to ascend into the sky in 1783; in a hot air balloon.

Igor Sikorsky (1889–1972) Aeronautical engineer; developed the first practical helicopter in 1939.

Charles Yeager (1923–) First person to fly faster than the speed of sound.

KEY IDEAS

aerodynamics The study of the behavior of air in motion, particularly when air encounters a solid body, such as an airplane or a car.

airship A large, balloonlike aircraft powered by engines.

aviation The science of building and flying aircraft.

payload The load carried by a spacecraft, such as passengers or instruments, or the weight of this load.

rocket A type of engine that produces more power for its size than any other type of engine; also the vehicle driven by a rocket engine.

satellite A spacecraft sent into orbit around Earth, the moon, or around another heavenly body.

space probe Vehicles without people that are sent to space so that scientists can gather data.

space shuttle A reusable spacecraft designed to transport people and cargo between Earth and space. They carry payloads of up to 65,000 pounds (29,500 kilograms).

5

EXPLORING SPACE

(number of satellites and space probes launched, by country, 1957–1997)

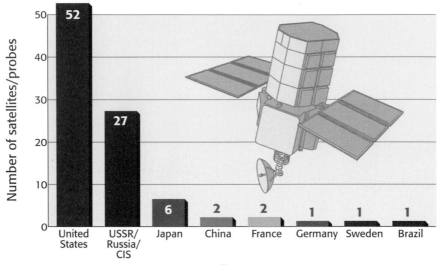

Number of satellites/probes (y-axis)

Country (x-axis): United States 52, USSR/Russia/CIS 27, Japan 6, China 2, France 2, Germany 1, Sweden 1, Brazil 1

Source: NASA

Note: CIS = Commonwealth of Independent States

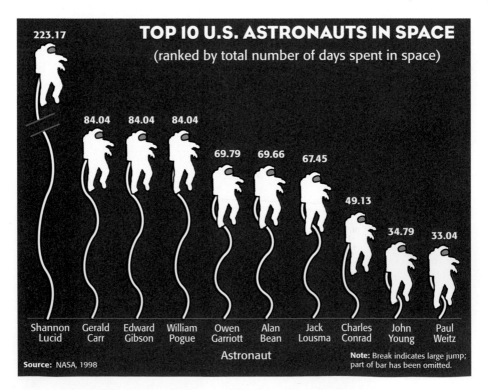

TOP 10 U.S. ASTRONAUTS IN SPACE

(ranked by total number of days spent in space)

Astronaut	Days
Shannon Lucid	223.17
Gerald Carr	84.04
Edward Gibson	84.04
William Pogue	84.04
Owen Garriott	69.79
Alan Bean	69.66
Jack Lousma	67.45
Charles Conrad	49.13
John Young	34.79
Paul Weitz	33.04

Astronaut

Source: NASA, 1998

Note: Break indicates large jump; part of bar has been omitted.

Flight	Orbiter	Launch date
STS-102	*Atlantis*	November 4, 1999
STS-103	*Columbia*	December 2, 1999
STS-104	*Discovery*	January 13, 2000
STS-105	*Endeavour*	February 10, 2000
STS-106	*Atlantis*	March 23, 2000
STS-107	*Columbia*	May 4, 2000
STS-108	*Endeavour*	June 22, 2000
STS-109	*Atlantis*	August 10, 2000
STS-110	*Endeavour*	November 9, 2000
STS-111	*Discovery*	December 7, 2000
STS-112	*Atlantis*	January 18, 2001
STS-113	*Columbia*	February 22, 2001
STS-114	*Discovery*	May 3, 2001
STS-115	*Atlantis*	June 14, 2001
STS-116	*Discovery*	September 13, 2001
STS-117	*Endeavour*	November 1, 2001
STS-118	*Atlantis*	December 6, 2001
STS-119	*Discovery*	February 7, 2002
STS-120	*Endeavour*	April 18, 2002
STS-121	*Atlantis*	May 23, 2002
STS-122	*Discovery*	June 27, 2002
STS-123	*Columbia*	August 8, 2002

Key

Atlantis

Discovery

Columbia

Endeavour

Source: NASA

TOP 10 LONGEST SPACE SHUTTLE MISSIONS

(ranked by number of days in orbit)

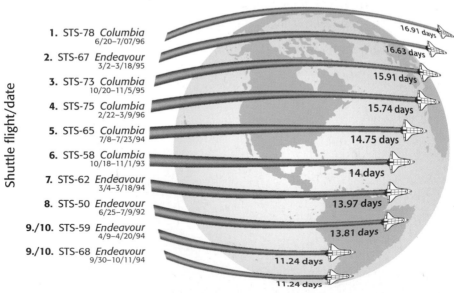

Shuttle flight/date

1. STS-78 *Columbia*
   6/20–7/07/96
2. STS-67 *Endeavour*
   3/2–3/18/95
3. STS-73 *Columbia*
   10/20–11/5/95
4. STS-75 *Columbia*
   2/22–3/9/96
5. STS-65 *Columbia*
   7/8–7/23/94
6. STS-58 *Columbia*
   10/18–11/1/93
7. STS-62 *Endeavour*
   3/4–3/18/94
8. STS-50 *Endeavour*
   6/25–7/9/92
9./10. STS-59 *Endeavour*
   4/9–4/20/94
9./10. STS-68 *Endeavour*
   9/30–10/11/94

16.91 days
16.63 days
15.91 days
15.74 days
14.75 days
14 days
13.97 days
13.81 days
11.24 days
11.24 days

Source: NASA

TOP 10 LONGEST FLIGHTS EVER RECORDED
(ranked by miles [kilometers] traveled in the air)

Pilot(s)/craft

1. Boeing 747
San Francisco to San Francisco, Oct. 28–31, 1977 — 26,382 (42,457)

2. Two U.S. Army airplanes
Seattle to Seattle, 1924 — 26,103 (42,000)

3. Max Conrad (solo)
Miami to Miami, Feb. 28–Mar. 8, 1961 — 25,946 (41,755)

4. *Hindenburg Zeppelin* (H. R. Ekins)
Lakehurst, NJ, to Lakehurst, Oct. 19, 1936 — 25,654 (41,285)

5. Trevor K. Bougham
Darwin, Australia, to Darwin, Aug. 5–10, 1972 — 24,800 (39,911)

6. Three U.S. Air Force B-52 Stratofortresses
Merced, CA, to Merced, Jan. 15–18, 1957 — 24,325 (39,146)

7. USAF B-50 *Lucky Lady II*
Forth Worth, TX, to Fort Worth, Mar. 2, 1949 — 23,452 (37,741)

8. A. Godfrey, R. Merrill, F. Austin, K. Keller
New York to New York, Jun. 4–7, 1966 — 23,333 (37,550)

9. Globester, U.S. Air Transport Command
Washington, DC, to Washington, DC, Oct. 4, 1945 — 23,279 (37,463)

10. Robert and Joan Wallick
Manila, Phillipines, to Manila, June 2–7, 1966 — 23,129 (37,221)

0   4,000   8,000   12,000   16,000   20,000   24,000   28,000

Miles traveled

Source: Civil Aviation and Aeronautics Association

TOP COUNTRIES TO PUT PEOPLE IN SPACE
(ranked by number of individuals sent into orbit)

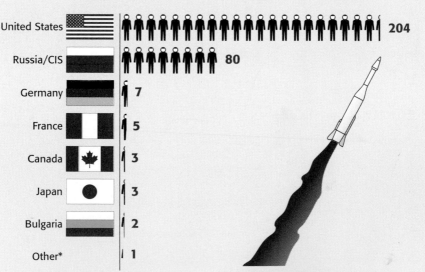

United States — 204

Russia/CIS — 80

Germany — 7

France — 5

Canada — 3

Japan — 3

Bulgaria — 2

Other* — 1

*Afghanistan, Austria, Belgium, Cuba, Czechoslovakia, Hungary, India, Italy, Mexico, Mongolia, Netherlands, Poland, Romania, Saudi Arabia, Switzerland, Syria, United Kingdom, and Vietnam have each sent one individual into space.

Source: Congressional Research Service, 1997

IMPORTANT U.S. PLANETARY MISSIONS

Spacecraft	Launch date	Mission	Highlights
Mariner 2	Aug. 27, 1962	Venus	Passed within 22,000 mi. of Venus 12/14/62; contact lost 1/3/63 at 54 million mi.
Mariner 5	Jun. 14, 1967	Venus	In solar orbit; closest Venus fly-by 10/19/67
Mariner 6	Feb. 24, 1969	Mars	Came within 2,000 mi. of Mars 7/31/69; sent back data, photos
Mariner 7	Mar. 27, 1969	Mars	Came within 2,000 mi. of Mars 8/5/69
Mariner 9	May 30, 1971	Mars	First craft to orbit Mars 11/13/71; sent back more than 7,000 photos
Mariner 10	Nov. 3, 1973	Venus, Mercury	Passed Venus 2/5/74; arrived Mercury 3/29/74. First time gravity of one planet (Venus) used to whip spacecraft toward another (Mercury)
Viking 1	Aug. 20, 1975	Mars	Landed on Mars 7/20/76; did scientific research, sent photos; functioned 6½ years
Viking 2	Sep. 9, 1975	Mars	Landed on Mars 9/3/76; functioned 3½ years
Voyager 1	Sep. 5, 1977	Jupiter, Saturn	Encountered Jupiter 3/5/79, provided evidence of Jupiter ring; passed near Saturn 11/12/80
Voyager 2	Aug. 20, 1977	Jupiter, Saturn, Uranus, Neptune	Encountered Jupiter 7/9/79; Saturn 8/5/81; Uranus 1/24/86; Neptune 8/25/87
Pioneer Venus 1	May 20, 1978	Venus	Entered Venus orbit 12/4/78; spent 14 years studying planet; ceased operating 10/19/92
Magellan	May 4, 1989	Venus	Orbited and mapped Venus; monitored geological activity on surface; first planetary spacecraft to lower its orbit by using planet's atmosphere (aerobraking) 5/25/93–8/3/93; ceased operating 10/12/94
Titan IV	June 14, 1989	Orbit Earth	First of 41 such rockets whose primary purpose is defense
Galileo	Oct. 18, 1989	Jupiter	Used Earth's gravity to propel it toward Jupiter; encountered Venus Feb. 1991; launched robot to Jupiter 7/13/95
Mars Observer	Sep. 25, 1992	Mars	Communication was lost 8/21/93

Source: NASA

SPEED OF SOUND TIMELINE
(Mach 1 = speed of sound)

1947 Chuck Yeager pilots Bell X-1, first aircraft to fly faster than the speed of sound. Aircraft reached Mach 1.015.

1953 F100 Super Sabre becomes first jet-powered aircraft to exceed the speed of sound in level flight. Aircraft reached Mach 1.17.

1967 The world's fastest aircraft, the X-15, reaches Mach 6.72, powered by rockets.

1969 Powered by four turbojets, the Concorde offers commercial flights at Mach 2.2.

1976 The spy jet aircraft SR-71 *Blackbird* reaches Mach 3.3, which is the record for jet aircraft.

Source: NASA; Smithsonian Institution/Air and Space Museum

THE NASA BUDGET, 1997: HOW MONEY WAS SPENT
Total Budget: $13.8 billion

Mission Support
- Safety testing
- Communications
- Research
- Facility construction

Human Space Flight
- Space station
- Russian cooperation
- Space shuttle
- Payload and utilization operations

Science, Aeronautics, and Technology
- Space science
- Aeronautic research
- Academic programs
- Mission to planet Earth

19%

39%

42%

NASA

Source: NASA; *Budget Summary, 1996 and 1997*

FLYING FIRSTS TIME LINE

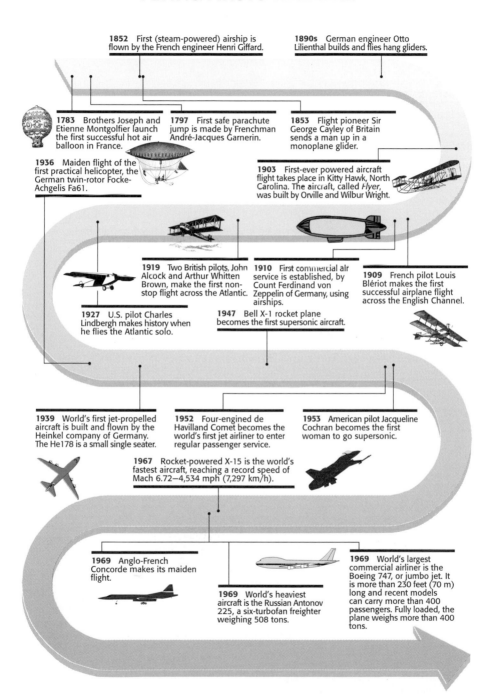

1852   First (steam-powered) airship is flown by the French engineer Henri Giffard.

1890s   German engineer Otto Lilienthal builds and flies hang gliders.

1783   Brothers Joseph and Etienne Montgolfier launch the first successful hot air balloon in France.

1797   First safe parachute jump is made by Frenchman André-Jacques Garnerin.

1853   Flight pioneer Sir George Cayley of Britain sends a man up in a monoplane glider.

1936   Maiden flight of the first practical helicopter, the German twin-rotor Focke-Achgelis Fa61.

1903   First-ever powered aircraft flight takes place in Kitty Hawk, North Carolina. The aircraft, called *Flyer*, was built by Orville and Wilbur Wright.

1919   Two British pilots, John Alcock and Arthur Whitten Brown, make the first non-stop flight across the Atlantic.

1910   First commercial air service is established, by Count Ferdinand von Zeppelin of Germany, using airships.

1909   French pilot Louis Blériot makes the first successful airplane flight across the English Channel.

1927   U.S. pilot Charles Lindbergh makes history when he flies the Atlantic solo.

1947   Bell X-1 rocket plane becomes the first supersonic aircraft.

1939   World's first jet-propelled aircraft is built and flown by the Heinkel company of Germany. The He178 is a small single seater.

1952   Four-engined de Havilland Comet becomes the world's first jet airliner to enter regular passenger service.

1953   American pilot Jacqueline Cochran becomes the first woman to go supersonic.

1967   Rocket-powered X-15 is the world's fastest aircraft, reaching a record speed of Mach 6.72—4,534 mph (7,297 km/h).

1969   Anglo-French Concorde makes its maiden flight.

1969   World's heaviest aircraft is the Russian Antonov 225, a six-turbofan freighter weighing 508 tons.

1969   World's largest commercial airliner is the Boeing 747, or jumbo jet. It is more than 230 feet (70 m) long and recent models can carry more than 400 passengers. Fully loaded, the plane weighs more than 400 tons.

ANIMALS

If you were to name your favorite animals, you might list dogs or cats or gerbils. You probably wouldn't include worms or flies—but they are animals, too. You might not think of humans, either. But people also belong to the animal kingdom.

An animal is a living thing that can move and eat. Animals live in all parts of the world. There are more than 1.2 million known kinds, or species, of animals. Many more may yet be identified.

Animals are classed in two main groups: vertebrates (animals with backbones) and invertebrates (without backbones). Scientists divide these groups into many subgroups. Invertebrates include worms, jellyfish, shellfish, insects, crustaceans, and spiders. There are more kinds of insects than any other animal, about 800,000 species. Vertebrates include fish, reptiles, amphibians, birds, and mammals.

About 10,000 years ago, dogs began to be domesticated, or kept and bred by humans. Later, along with domestic cats, they became pets. Other animals are important to humans as well. Domestic animals—sheep, cattle, pigs, and poultry—are raised for food. Horses provide transportation, and wild animals are hunted for food.

Animals have lived on Earth for hundreds of millions of years. During that time, many species have died out, or become extinct. Today a number of people worry that the rate of extinction is increasing, and more animals are dying out. A major cause is the destruction of animal habitats, the natural areas where animals live. The answer is conservation—protecting natural areas, so that wildlife can survive.

Yearbook

7000 B.C. In Egypt and parts of Europe, dogs have become pets.

circa A.D. 1600 Spanish missionaries bring horses to the Southwest—the first to appear in the present-day United States.

July 1, 1874 America's first zoo opens in Philadelphia, Pennsylvania.

December 22, 1938 A coelacanth, a fish that was thought to be extinct, is caught near the coast of South Africa.

1966 The first U.S. Endangered Species Act is passed.

1990s Once endangered, more than 1,000 peregrine falcons are in the United States.

• Notables •

John James Audubon (1785–1851) Ornithologist; painted portraits of live birds.

Charles Darwin (1809–1882) English naturalist; published *On the Origin of Species* in 1859; considered the founder of evolutionary science.

Konrad von Gesner (1516–1565) Swiss naturalist; his encyclopedia on animals is regarded as the beginning of modern biology.

Jane Goodall (1934–) English naturalist; studies African chimpanzees and saved them from extinction.

John Ray (1627–1705) English naturalist; suggested fossils are the remains of ancient animals.

Theodore Roosevelt (1858–1919) U.S. president; championed the beginning of the National Wildlife Refuge System.

KEY IDEAS

extinct A living thing has become extinct when no more individuals of its species exist.

fossil The preserved traces or remains of an animal or plant that lived millions of years ago.

naturalist Someone who studies animals and plants in their natural habitats.

natural selection A concept popularized by Charles Darwin; a process that results in the survival of individuals or groups of living things that have adjusted best to their environment.

ornithology The study of birds.

species A group of related animals or plants. Animals of the same species can reproduce, but animals of different species cannot.

wildlife Wild animals living in their natural habitats.

zoology The study of animal life.

BIOLOGICAL KINGDOM OF ANIMALS

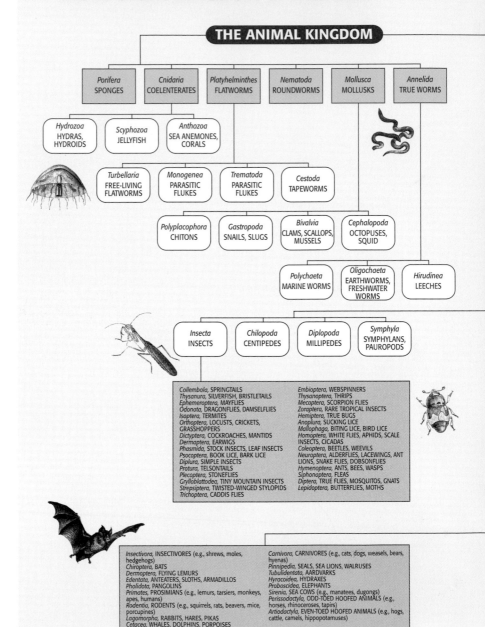

THE ANIMAL KINGDOM

| *Porifera* SPONGES | *Cnidaria* COELENTERATES | *Platyhelminthes* FLATWORMS | *Nematoda* ROUNDWORMS | *Mollusca* MOLLUSKS | *Annelida* TRUE WORMS |

Cnidaria:
- *Hydrozoa* HYDRAS, HYDROIDS
- *Scyphozoa* JELLYFISH
- *Anthozoa* SEA ANEMONES, CORALS

Platyhelminthes:
- *Turbellaria* FREE-LIVING FLATWORMS
- *Monogenea* PARASITIC FLUKES
- *Trematoda* PARASITIC FLUKES
- *Cestoda* TAPEWORMS

Mollusca:
- *Polyplacophora* CHITONS
- *Gastropoda* SNAILS, SLUGS
- *Bivalvia* CLAMS, SCALLOPS, MUSSELS
- *Cephalopoda* OCTOPUSES, SQUID

Annelida:
- *Polychaeta* MARINE WORMS
- *Oligochaeta* EARTHWORMS, FRESHWATER WORMS
- *Hirudinea* LEECHES

Arthropoda:
- *Insecta* INSECTS
- *Chilopoda* CENTIPEDES
- *Diplopoda* MILLIPEDES
- *Symphyla* SYMPHYLANS, PAUROPODS

Insecta

Collembola, SPRINGTAILS
Thysanura, SILVERFISH, BRISTLETAILS
Ephemeroptera, MAYFLIES
Odonata, DRAGONFLIES, DAMSELFLIES
Isoptera, TERMITES
Orthoptera, LOCUSTS, CRICKETS, GRASSHOPPERS
Dictyptera, COCKROACHES, MANTIDS
Dermaptera, EARWIGS
Phasmida, STOCK INSECTS, LEAF INSECTS
Psocoptera, BOOK LICE, BARK LICE
Diplura, SIMPLE INSECTS
Protura, TELSONTAILS
Plecoptera, STONEFLIES
Grylloblattodea, TINY MOUNTAIN INSECTS
Strepsiptera, TWISTED-WINGED STYLOPIDS
Trichoptera, CADDIS FLIES

Embioptera, WEBSPINNERS
Thysanoptera, THRIPS
Mecoptera, SCORPION FLIES
Zoraptera, RARE TROPICAL INSECTS
Hemiptera, TRUE BUGS
Anoplura, SUCKING LICE
Mallophaga, BITING LICE, BIRD LICE
Homoptera, WHITE FLIES, APHIDS, SCALE INSECTS, CICADAS
Coleoptera, BEETLES, WEEVILS
Neuroptera, ALDERFLIES, LACEWINGS, ANT LIONS, SNAKE FLIES, DOBSONFLIES
Hymenoptera, ANTS, BEES, WASPS
Siphonaptera, FLEAS
Diptera, TRUE FLIES, MOSQUITOS, GNATS
Lepidoptera, BUTTERFLIES, MOTHS

Mammalia

Insectivora, INSECTIVORES (e.g., shrews, moles, hedgehogs)
Chiroptera, BATS
Dermaptera, FLYING LEMURS
Edentata, ANTEATERS, SLOTHS, ARMADILLOS
Pholidota, PANGOLINS
Primates, PROSIMIANS (e.g., lemurs, tarsiers, monkeys, apes, humans)
Rodentia, RODENTS (e.g., squirrels, rats, beavers, mice, porcupines)
Lagomorpha, RABBITS, HARES, PIKAS
Cetacea, WHALES, DOLPHINS, PORPOISES

Carnivora, CARNIVORES (e.g., cats, dogs, weasels, bears, hyenas)
Pinnipedia, SEALS, SEA LIONS, WALRUSES
Tubulidentata, AARDVARKS
Hyracoidea, HYDRAXES
Proboscidea, ELEPHANTS
Sirenia, SEA COWS (e.g., manatees, dugongs)
Perissodactyla, ODD-TOED HOOFED ANIMALS (e.g., horses, rhinoceroses, tapirs)
Artiodactyla, EVEN-TOED HOOFED ANIMALS (e.g., hogs, cattle, camels, hippopotamuses)

Source: *Our Living World*, Blackbirch Press, 1994

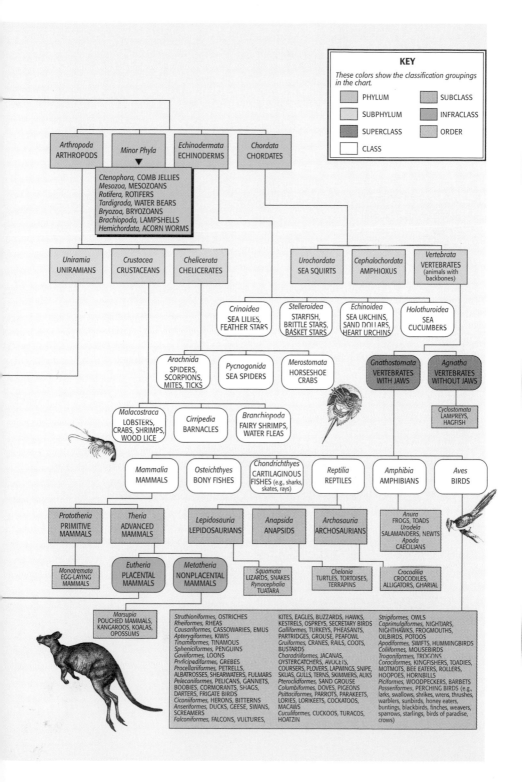

KEY

These colors show the classification groupings in the chart.

- PHYLUM
- SUBPHYLUM
- SUPERCLASS
- CLASS
- SUBCLASS
- INFRACLASS
- ORDER

Arthropoda ARTHROPODS

Minor Phyla ▼

Ctenophora, COMB JELLIES
Mesozoa, MESOZOANS
Rotifera, ROTIFERS
Tardigrada, WATER BEARS
Bryozoa, BRYOZOANS
Brachiopoda, LAMPSHELLS
Hemichordata, ACORN WORMS

Echinodermata ECHINODERMS

Chordata CHORDATES

Uniramia UNIRAMIANS

Crustacea CRUSTACEANS

Chelicerata CHELICERATES

Urochordata SEA SQUIRTS

Cephalochordata AMPHIOXUS

Vertebrata VERTEBRATES (animals with backbones)

Crinoidea SEA LILIES, FEATHER STARS

Stelleroidea STARFISH, BRITTLE STARS, BASKET STARS

Echinoidea SEA URCHINS, SAND DOLLARS, HEART URCHINS

Holothuroidea SEA CUCUMBERS

Arachnida SPIDERS, SCORPIONS, MITES, TICKS

Pycnogonida SEA SPIDERS

Merostomata HORSESHOE CRABS

Gnathostomata VERTEBRATES WITH JAWS

Agnatha VERTEBRATES WITHOUT JAWS

Malacostraca LOBSTERS, CRABS, SHRIMPS, WOOD LICE

Cirripedia BARNACLES

Branchiopoda FAIRY SHRIMPS, WATER FLEAS

Cyclostomata LAMPREYS, HAGFISH

Mammalia MAMMALS

Osteichthyes BONY FISHES

Chondrichthyes CARTILAGINOUS FISHES (e.g., sharks, skates, rays)

Reptilia REPTILES

Amphibia AMPHIBIANS

Aves BIRDS

Prototheria PRIMITIVE MAMMALS

Theria ADVANCED MAMMALS

Lepidosauria LEPIDOSAURIANS

Anapsida ANAPSIDS

Archosauria ARCHOSAURIANS

Anura FROGS, TOADS
Urodela SALAMANDERS, NEWTS
Apoda CAECILIANS

Monotremata EGG-LAYING MAMMALS

Eutheria PLACENTAL MAMMALS

Metatheria NONPLACENTAL MAMMALS

Squamata LIZARDS, SNAKES *Rynocephalia* TUATARA

Chelonia TURTLES, TORTOISES, TERRAPINS

Crocodilia CROCODILES, ALLIGATORS, GHARIAL

Marsupia POUCHED MAMMALS, KANGAROOS, KOALAS, OPOSSUMS

Struthioniformes, OSTRICHES
Rheiformes, RHEAS
Casuariformes, CASSOWARIES, EMUS
Apterygiformes, KIWIS
Tinamiformes, TINAMOUS
Sphenisciformes, PENGUINS
Gaviiformes, LOONS
Podicipediformes, GREBES
Procellariiformes, PETRELLS, ALBATROSSES, SHEARWATERS, FULMARS
Pelecaniformes, PELICANS, GANNETS, BOOBIES, CORMORANTS, SHAGS, DARTERS, FRIGATE BIRDS
Ciconiiformes, HERONS, BITTERNS
Anseriformes, DUCKS, GEESE, SWANS, SCREAMERS
Falconiformes, FALCONS, VULTURES,

KITES, EAGLES, BUZZARDS, HAWKS, KESTRELS, OSPREYS, SECRETARY BIRDS
Galliformes, TURKEYS, PHEASANTS, PARTRIDGES, GROUSE, PEAFOWL
Gruiformes, CRANES, RAILS, COOTS, BUSTARDS
Charadriiformes, JACANAS, OYSTERCATCHERS, AVOCETS, COURSERS, PLOVERS, LAPWINGS, SNIPE, SKUAS, GULLS, TERNS, SKIMMERS, AUKS
Pteroclidformes, SAND GROUSE
Columbiformes, DOVES, PIGEONS
Psittaciformes, PARROTS, PARAKEETS, LORIES, LORIKEETS, COCKATOOS, MACAWS
Cuculiformes, CUCKOOS, TURACOS, HOATZIN

Strigiformes, OWLS
Caprimulgiformes, NIGHTJARS, NIGHTHAWKS, FROGMOUTHS, OILBIRDS, POTOOS
Apodiformes, SWIFTS, HUMMINGBIRDS
Coliiformes, MOUSEBIRDS
Trogoniformes, TROGONS
Coraciformes, KINGFISHERS, TOADIES, MOTMOTS, BEE EATERS, ROLLERS, HOOPOES, HORNBILLS
Piciformes, WOODPECKERS, BARBETS
Passeriformes, PERCHING BIRDS (e.g., larks, swallows, shrikes, wrens, thrushes, warblers, sunbirds, honey eaters, buntings, blackbirds, finches, weavers, sparrows, starlings, birds of paradise, crows)

ANIMALS WITH MOST KNOWN SPECIES

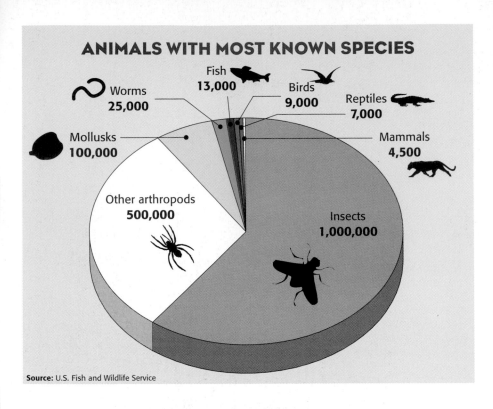

Worms
25,000

Fish
13,000

Birds
9,000

Reptiles
7,000

Mollusks
100,000

Mammals
4,500

Other arthropods
500,000

Insects
1,000,000

Source: U.S. Fish and Wildlife Service

TOP 10 LONGEST-LIVED ANIMALS

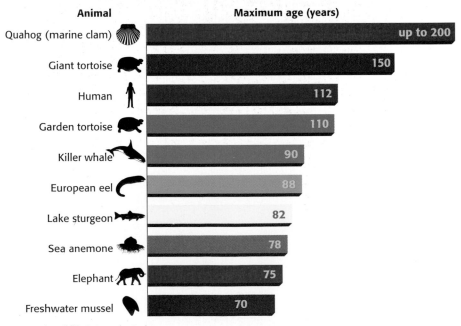

Animal	Maximum age (years)
Quahog (marine clam)	up to 200
Giant tortoise	150
Human	112
Garden tortoise	110
Killer whale	90
European eel	88
Lake sturgeon	82
Sea anemone	78
Elephant	75
Freshwater mussel	70

Source: The Wildlife Conservation Society

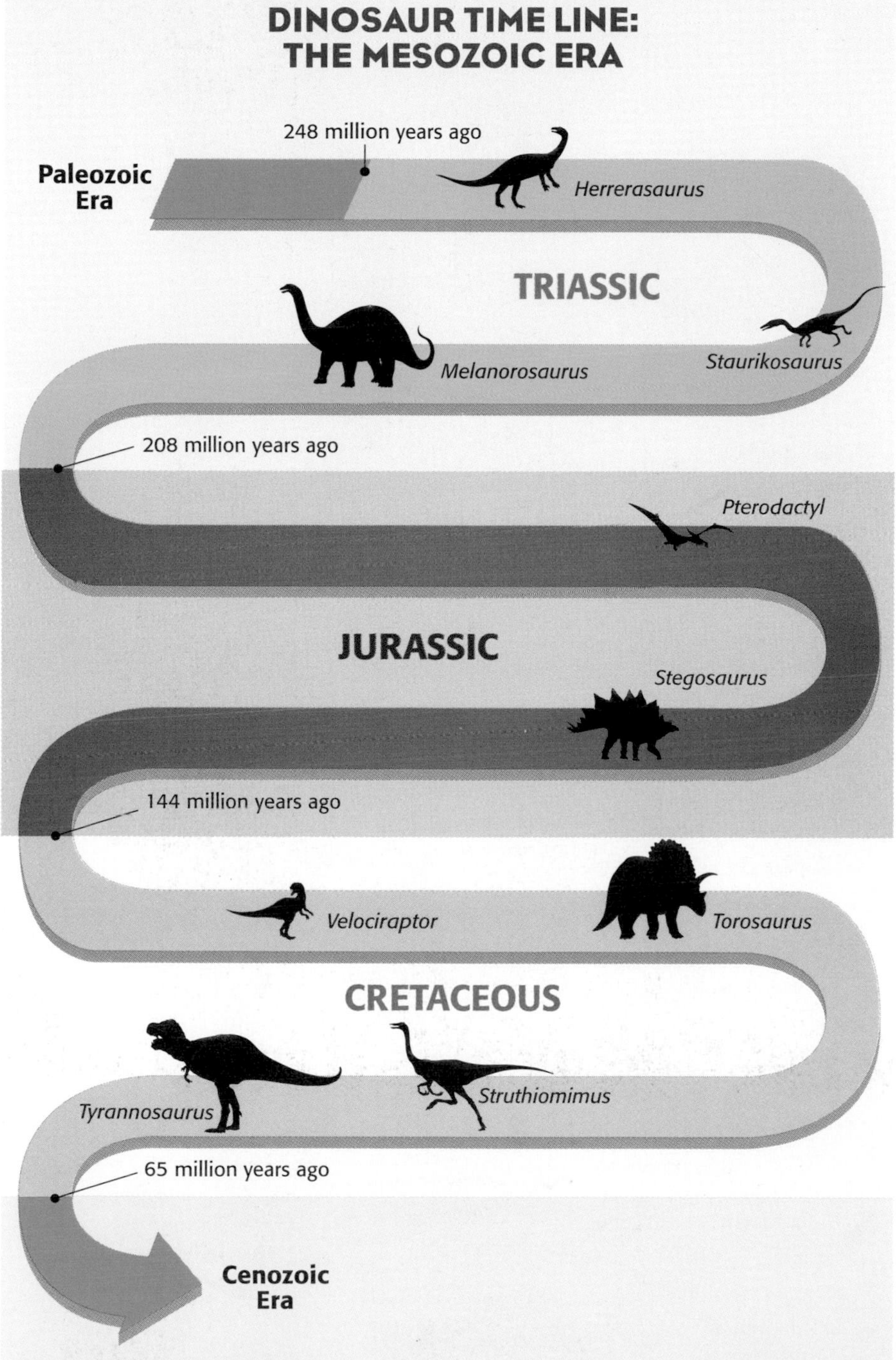

DINOSAUR TIME LINE:
THE MESOZOIC ERA

248 million years ago

Paleozoic
Era

Herrerasaurus

TRIASSIC

Melanorosaurus

Staurikosaurus

208 million years ago

Pterodactyl

JURASSIC

Stegosaurus

144 million years ago

Velociraptor

Torosaurus

CRETACEOUS

Tyrannosaurus

Struthiomimus

65 million years ago

Cenozoic
Era

Source: Denver Museum of Natural History

SELECTED ENDANGERED SPECIES OF THE WORLD

NORTH AMERICA

SOUTH AMERICA

NORTH AMERICA

MAMMALS
Bear, polar
Cougar, Florida
Prairie dog, Utah
Puma, eastern
Wolf, gray
Wolf, red

BIRDS
Albatross, short-tailed
Crane, whooping
Pelican, brown
Woodpecker, ivory-billed

REPTILES
Crocodile, American

OCEANS

MAMMALS
Whale, blue
Whale, humpback

SOUTH AMERICA

MAMMALS
Cat, little-spotted
Deer, marsh
Monkey, spider
Puma, Costa Rican
Sloth, maned

BIRDS
Condor, Andean
Falcon, peregrine
Parrot, red-browed
Pelican, brown

REPTILES
Crocodile, American

AFRICA

MAMMALS
Cheetah
Chimpanzee, W. African
Gorilla, mountain
Zebra, Cape mountain

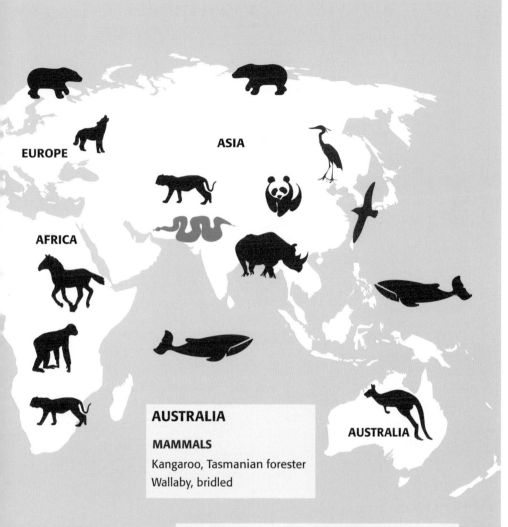

AUSTRALIA

MAMMALS
Kangaroo, Tasmanian forester
Wallaby, bridled

ASIA

MAMMALS
Bear, polar
Bear, brown
Cheetah
Dolphin, Chinese river
Elephant, Asian
Elephant, Indian
Leopard, snow
Lion, Asiatic
Panda, giant
Rhinoceros
Tiger
Wolf, gray

BIRDS
Albatross, short-tailed
Stork, oriental

REPTILES
Python, Indian

EUROPE

MAMMALS
Bear, polar
Lynx, Spanish
Wolf, gray

Source: Data compiled by World Conservation Monitoring Center

TOP 10 HEAVIEST LAND MAMMALS

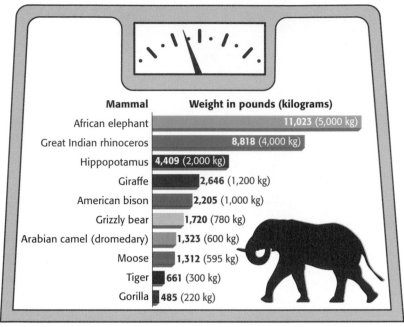

Mammal	Weight in pounds (kilograms)
African elephant	11,023 (5,000 kg)
Great Indian rhinoceros	8,818 (4,000 kg)
Hippopotamus	4,409 (2,000 kg)
Giraffe	2,646 (1,200 kg)
American bison	2,205 (1,000 kg)
Grizzly bear	1,720 (780 kg)
Arabian camel (dromedary)	1,323 (600 kg)
Moose	1,312 (595 kg)
Tiger	661 (300 kg)
Gorilla	485 (220 kg)

Source: The Wildlife Conservation Society

TOP 10 HEAVIEST MARINE MAMMALS

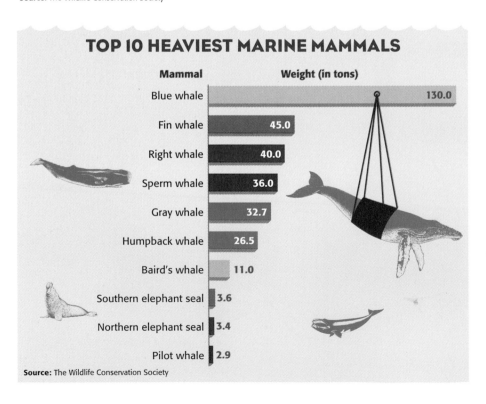

Mammal	Weight (in tons)
Blue whale	130.0
Fin whale	45.0
Right whale	40.0
Sperm whale	36.0
Gray whale	32.7
Humpback whale	26.5
Baird's whale	11.0
Southern elephant seal	3.6
Northern elephant seal	3.4
Pilot whale	2.9

Source: The Wildlife Conservation Society

TOP 10 SMALLEST MAMMALS

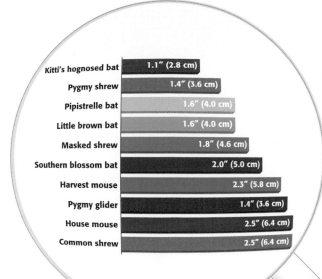

Mammal	Size
Kitti's hognosed bat	1.1" (2.8 cm)
Pygmy shrew	1.4" (3.6 cm)
Pipistrelle bat	1.6" (4.0 cm)
Little brown bat	1.6" (4.0 cm)
Masked shrew	1.8" (4.6 cm)
Southern blossom bat	2.0" (5.0 cm)
Harvest mouse	2.3" (5.8 cm)
Pygmy glider	1.4" (3.6 cm)
House mouse	2.5" (6.4 cm)
Common shrew	2.5" (6.4 cm)

Source: The Wildlife Conservation Society

PACKS AND PRIDES: ANIMAL MULTIPLES

ants: colony
baboons: tribe
bears: sleuth, sloth
bees: grist, hive, swarm
birds: flight, volery
cattle: drove
cats: clutter, clowder
chicks: brood, clutch
clams: bed
cranes: sedge, seige
crocodiles: congregation
crows: murder
dolphins: pod
doves: dule
ducks: brace, team
elephants: herd
elks: gang
finches: charm
fish: school, shoal, drought
foxes: leash, skulk

geese: flock, gaggle, skein
gnats: cloud, horde
goats: trip
gorillas: band
hares: down, husk
hawks: cast
hens: brood
hogs: drift
horses: pair, team
hounds: cry, mute, pack
kangaroos: troop
kittens: kindle, litter
larks: exaltation
lions: pride
locusts: plague
magpies: tidings
mules: span
nightingales: watch
oxen: yoke
oysters: bed
parrots: company

partridges: covey
peacocks: muster, ostentation
pheasants: nest, bouquet
pigs: litter
ponies: string
quail: bevy, covey
rabbits: nest
seals: pod
sheep: drove, flock
sparrows: host
storks: mustering
swans: bevy, wedge
swine: sounder
toads: knot
turkeys: rafter
turtles: bale
vipers: nest
whales: gam, pod
wolves: pack, route
woodcocks: fall

Source: The Wildlife Conservation Society

Animals • 21

NAMES FOR ANIMAL MALE, FEMALE, AND YOUNG

Animal	Male ♂	Female ♀	Young
Bear	Boar	Sow	Cub
Cat	Tom	Queen	Kitten
Cattle	Bull	Cow	Calf
Chicken	Rooster	Hen	Chick
Deer	Buck	Doe	Fawn
Dog	Dog	Bitch	Pup
Donkey	Jack	Jenny	Foal
Duck	Drake	Duck	Duckling
Elephant	Bull	Cow	Calf
Fox	Dog	Vixen	Cub
Goose	Gander	Goose	Gosling
Horse	Stallion	Mare	Foal
Lion	Lion	Lioness	Cub
Rabbit	Buck	Doe	Bunny
Sheep	Ram	Ewe	Lamb
Swan	Cob	Pen	Cygnet
Swine	Boar	Sow	Piglet
Tiger	Tiger	Tigress	Cub
Whale	Bull	Cow	Calf
Wolf	Dog	Bitch	Pup

Source: The Wildlife Conservation Society

TYPES OF PETS IN THE U.S.

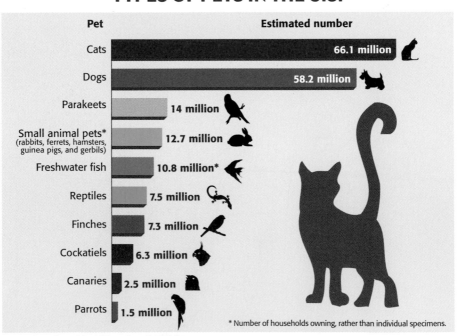

Pet	Estimated number
Cats	66.1 million
Dogs	58.2 million
Parakeets	14 million
Small animal pets* (rabbits, ferrets, hamsters, guinea pigs, and gerbils)	12.7 million
Freshwater fish	10.8 million*
Reptiles	7.5 million
Finches	7.3 million
Cockatiels	6.3 million
Canaries	2.5 million
Parrots	1.5 million

* Number of households owning, rather than individual specimens.

Source: Pet Industry Joint Advisory Council, 1998 data

TOP 10 REGISTERED U.S. DOG BREEDS

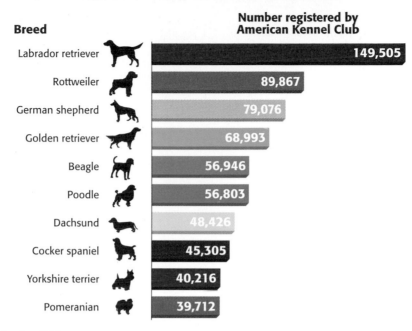

Breed

Number registered by American Kennel Club

Breed	Number registered
Labrador retriever	149,505
Rottweiler	89,867
German shepherd	79,076
Golden retriever	68,993
Beagle	56,946
Poodle	56,803
Dachsund	48,426
Cocker spaniel	45,305
Yorkshire terrier	40,216
Pomeranian	39,712

Source: American Kennel Club

TOP 10 REGISTERED U.S. CAT BREEDS

Breed **Number registered**

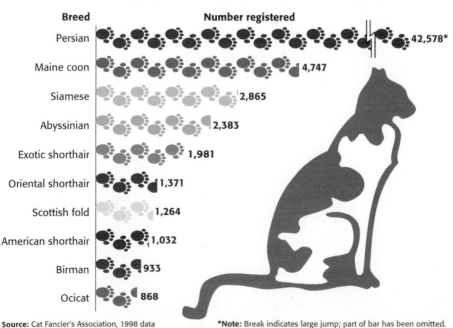

Breed	Number registered
Persian	42,578*
Maine coon	4,747
Siamese	2,865
Abyssinian	2,383
Exotic shorthair	1,981
Oriental shorthair	1,371
Scottish fold	1,264
American shorthair	1,032
Birman	933
Ocicat	868

Source: Cat Fancier's Association, 1998 data   ***Note:** Break indicates large jump; part of bar has been omitted.

ARTS AND MUSIC

It's hard to imagine life without the arts—without music, poetry, dance, or painting. They enrich our lives in many ways. They offer pleasure and entertainment. And they provide insights into human nature, helping people understand their own and other cultures.

People often divide the arts into these broad categories:

The visual arts include the forms people usually think of as "art"—drawing, painting, architecture, and sculpture. Visual arts create their effects through the careful balancing of certain elements: line, form, color, space, light, and shade.

The literary arts include all kinds of writing—poetry, novels, essays, and short stories. Even cultures without written language have had literature. Their stories and legends were passed down orally from one generation to the next. Spoken or written, the literary arts move us through the power of words.

The performing arts include dance, drama, and music, all of which are performed in front of an audience. Often the performing arts rely on the talents of many people. An opera, for example, brings together a composer, a librettist (who writes the text), musicians, singers, a conductor, a director, costume and set designers, and many others who work behind the scenes.

Every culture has developed its own creative styles and forms. In the United States, the arts grew out of traditions that began largely in Europe. But today influences from many parts of the world are helping to shape everything from popular music to serious literature.

Yearbook

circa 20,000 B.C. (or earlier) Humans paint about 300 images of animals on the walls of a cave in France.

circa 800 B.C. Homer is said to have written the epic poem, the *Odyssey*.

1508–1512 Michelangelo paints frescoes in the Sistine Chapel in Rome.

1600–1601 Shakespeare's *Hamlet* is published.

1770 Chamber music is developed.

1907–1908 Pablo Picasso paints *Les Demoiselles d'Avignon*.

1960s The Beatles become the most popular rock group of the century.

• Notables •

Jane Austen (1775–1817) English novelist; wrote *Pride and Prejudice*, *Emma*, and other works.

Johann Sebastian Bach (1685–1750) German composer; widely popular.

Ludwig von Beethoven (1770–1827) German composer; considered by many to have been the world's greatest composer.

Charles Dickens (1812–1870) English novelist; author of *Oliver Twist*, *A Christmas Carol*, *David Copperfield*, and many more.

Wolfgang Amadeus Mozart (1756–1791) Austrian composer; wrote about 650 compositions during his life.

Georgia O'Keeffe (1887–1986) American painter; inspired by the deserts.

Pablo Picasso (1881–1973) Spanish painter and sculptor; created more than 20,000 works.

Elvis Presley (1935–1977) American singer; known as "King of Rock and Roll."

KEY IDEAS

a cappella Choral music that is sung without any instruments as accompaniment.

alto The highest adult male voice or lowest female voice.

bass The lowest male voice or the lowest part in a musical composition.

chord Three or more tones that are played together.

concerto A composition for solo instruments, usually accompanied by an orchestra.

key A series of notes that form a scale.

scale A series of tones that are arranged in rising pitches so that each one is higher than the tone before it.

soprano The highest female or boy's voice.

symphony A composition for an orchestra, usually in four movements, or parts.

tone A sound that has a definite duration and pitch—high or low.

CLASSIFICATION OF INSTRUMENTS

The basic classification of instruments—now accepted by musicologists all over the world—is derived from the system published in 1914 by Erich von Hornbostel and Curt Sachs. Under this system instruments are categorized according to the way in which sound is produced.

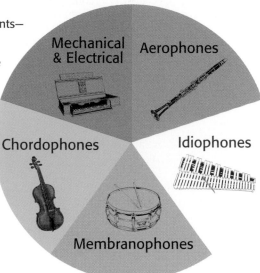

Mechanical & Electrical
Aerophones
Chordophones
Idiophones
Membranophones

Mechanical & Electrical

Radio-electric instruments
Electric organs
Electromechanical instruments
Electric guitars
Mechanical organs
Automatic pianos
Mechanical music makers
Carillons and chimes
Music boxes

Chordophones

Pianoforte
Clavichord
Dulcimer
Spinet
Virginal
Harpsichord
Psaltery
Long zithers
Stick zithers
Raft zithers
Tube zithers
Trough zithers
Ground zithers
Fiddles
Fretted lutes
Flat-backed lutes
Round-backed lutes
Frame harps
Angle harps

Bow harps
Bowl lyres
Box lyres
Multiple bows
Mouth bows
Resonated bows
Simple bows

Membranophones

Mirlitons
Friction drums
Frame drums
Vessel drums
Long drums
Footed drums
Goblet drums
Waisted drums
Barrel drums
Conical drums
Cylindrical drums

Idiophones

Plucked idiophones
Scraped idiophones
Concussion idiophones
Metallophones
Lithophones
Xylophones
Vessels
Gongs
Struck bells

Clapper bells
Pellet bells
Jingles
Rattles
Stamped idiophones
Stamping idiophones

Aerophones

Organs
Buzzers
Bull-roarers
Harmoniums
Concertinas/accordions
Mouth organs
Horns
Trumpets/trombones
Bagpipes
Bassoons
Oboes
Shawms
Saxophones
Clarinets
Flageolets
Recorders
Whistle flutes
Whistles
Panpipes
Multiple flutes
Vessel flutes
Nose flutes
Side-blown flutes
End-blown flutes

TYPICAL ORCHESTRA SEATING PLAN

In the usual orchestral seating plan, instruments of the four "families"—woodwinds, brass, percussion, and strings—are positioned in groups. This arrangement offers the best blending of tones of individual instruments and helps the musicians play together in their groups.

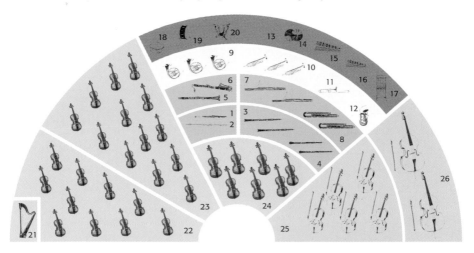

Woodwind
1 Piccolo
2 Flutes
3 Oboes
4 Cor anglais
5 Clarinets
6 Bass clarinet
7 Bassoons
8 Contrabassoon

Percussion
13 Tam-tam
14 Cymbals
15 Xylophone
16 Glockenspiel
17 Tubular bells
18 Side drum
19 Bass drum
20 Timpani

Brass
9 Horns
10 Trumpets
11 Trombones
12 Tuba

Strings
21 Harp
22 1st violins
23 2nd violins
24 Violas
25 Cellos
26 Double basses

MOST EXPENSIVE PAINTINGS EVER SOLD AT AUCTION

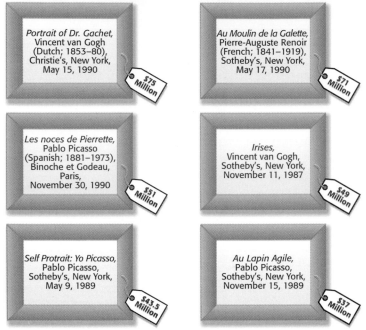

Portrait of Dr. Gachet,
Vincent van Gogh
(Dutch; 1853–80),
Christie's, New York,
May 15, 1990
$75 Million

Au Moulin de la Galette,
Pierre-Auguste Renoir
(French; 1841–1919),
Sotheby's, New York,
May 17, 1990
$71 Million

Les noces de Pierrette,
Pablo Picasso
(Spanish; 1881–1973),
Binoche et Godeau,
Paris,
November 30, 1990
$51 Million

Irises,
Vincent van Gogh,
Sotheby's, New York,
November 11, 1987
$49 Million

Self Protrait: Yo Picasso,
Pablo Picasso,
Sotheby's, New York,
May 9, 1989
$43.5 Million

Au Lapin Agile,
Pablo Picasso,
Sotheby's, New York,
November 15, 1989
$37 Million

Source: Based on data from Sotheby's, New York and Christie's, New York

TOP 10 BEST-SELLING BOOKS OF ALL TIME

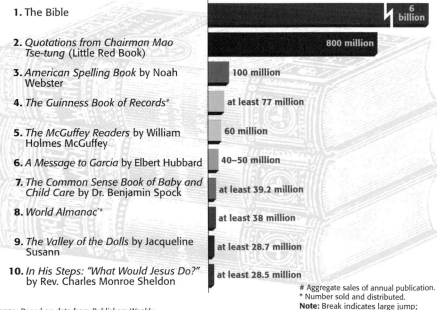

1. The Bible — 6 billion
2. *Quotations from Chairman Mao Tse-tung* (Little Red Book) — 800 million
3. *American Spelling Book* by Noah Webster — 100 million
4. *The Guinness Book of Records*[#] — at least 77 million
5. *The McGuffey Readers* by William Holmes McGuffey — 60 million
6. *A Message to Garcia* by Elbert Hubbard — 40–50 million
7. *The Common Sense Book of Baby and Child Care* by Dr. Benjamin Spock — at least 39.2 million
8. *World Almanac*[*#] — at least 38 million
9. *The Valley of the Dolls* by Jacqueline Susann — at least 28.7 million
10. *In His Steps: "What Would Jesus Do?"* by Rev. Charles Monroe Sheldon — at least 28.5 million

Source: Based on data from *Publishers Weekly*

[#] Aggregate sales of annual publication.
[*] Number sold and distributed.
Note: Break indicates large jump; part of bar has been omitted.

THE BEST-SELLING ALBUMS OF ALL TIME (WORLDWIDE)

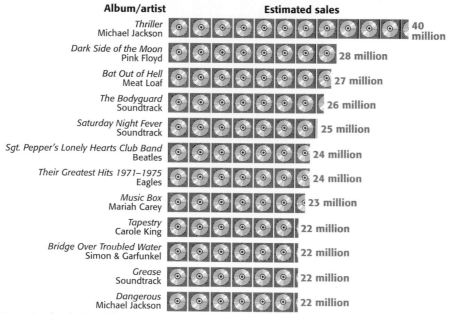

Album/artist	Estimated sales
Thriller Michael Jackson	40 million
Dark Side of the Moon Pink Floyd	28 million
Bat Out of Hell Meat Loaf	27 million
The Bodyguard Soundtrack	26 million
Saturday Night Fever Soundtrack	25 million
Sgt. Pepper's Lonely Hearts Club Band Beatles	24 million
Their Greatest Hits 1971–1975 Eagles	24 million
Music Box Mariah Carey	23 million
Tapestry Carole King	22 million
Bridge Over Troubled Water Simon & Garfunkel	22 million
Grease Soundtrack	22 million
Dangerous Michael Jackson	22 million

Source: Based on data from *Billboard*, 1996

TOP 5 LONGEST-RUNNING BROADWAY PLAYS OF ALL TIME

On June 19, 1997, *Cats* staged its 6,138th performance, putting it ahead of *A Chorus Line* as the longest-running Broadway show in history.

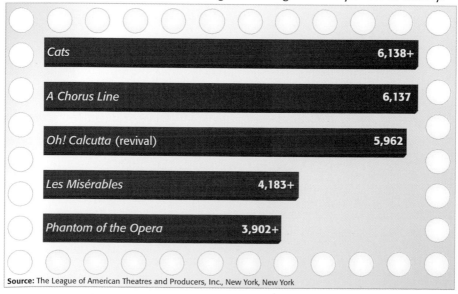

Play	Performances
Cats	6,138+
A Chorus Line	6,137
Oh! Calcutta (revival)	5,962
Les Misérables	4,183+
Phantom of the Opera	3,902+

Source: The League of American Theatres and Producers, Inc., New York, New York

ASTRONOMY

How did the universe begin? How do stars form? Is there life on other planets? These are just a few of the questions astronomers seek to answer. Astronomy is a branch of science with a truly enormous subject—nothing less than the universe and everything it contains.

Astronomy began in ancient times. In lands as far apart as China and Mesopotamia, people watched the movements of the stars and planets in the night sky. Most people then believed that Earth stood at the center of the universe, and that everything—the sun, other planets, the stars—revolved around it. Nicolaus Copernicus, a Polish scientist, challenged that idea in 1543. He recognized that Earth revolves around the sun. But it was not until 1608, when the Italian astronomer Galileo Galilei made his first telescope, that scientists had firm evidence that Copernicus was right.

Today astronomers use sophisticated tools to peer ever deeper into space. High-tech instruments search for radio waves and X rays from distant space. And unmanned spacecraft have transmitted close-up views of distant planets in our solar system.

One of the most amazing new tools is the Hubble Space Telescope (HST), placed in orbit above Earth in 1990. The HST has taken pictures of stars being born in clouds of gas. It has shown that there may be 50 billion galaxies, each one made up of billions of stars. Such discoveries have made astronomers rethink old ideas and ask new questions about the nature of the universe.

Yearbook

1543 Copernicus's landmark book, *De Revolutionibus Orbium Coelestium* (*On the Revolutions of Celestial Bodies*), marks the birth of modern astronomy.

1687 Isaac Newton publishes his *Principia*, which includes a theory of gravitational pull and provides a theoretical basis for the ideas of Copernicus.

1950s Development of radio astronomy (transmission of sound waves) enables scientists to probe the universe and shows that our known universe is twice the size previously believed.

• Notables •

Tycho Brahe (1546–1601) Danish astronomer; observed stars, comets, and novas; made important calculations about distances and brightness that helped develop modern astronomical theories and concepts of the universe.

Nicolaus Copernicus (1473–1543) Polish astronomer; first to propose a heliocentric (sun-centered) theory of the solar system.

Galileo Galilei (1564–1642) Italian astronomer and inventor; used a homemade telescope to observe the heavens and proved through observation that Copernicus's theories were right.

Johannes Kepler (1571–1630) German astronomer; theorized that planets revolve around the sun in elliptical orbits; an observation that contributed to Newton's theory of gravity.

KEY IDEAS

asteroid A tiny planetlike body in orbit; often clustered together in large groups.

comet Often called "dirty snowballs" of ice and dust, comets orbit the sun or other large bodies. As a comet approaches the sun, it appears brighter.

galaxy A large group of stars bound by gravity. Our solar system is part of the Milky Way galaxy, which is part of the Local Group of galaxies. The Andromeda galaxy is the largest in the Local Group.

meteor A bright streak of light that occurs when cosmic particles of metal and rock enter and vaporize in Earth's atmosphere.

solar system Our system is called "solar" because the sun is at its center. Within our solar system, all planets, moons, comets, and asteroids are kept in orbit by the gravitational pull of the sun. Our solar system includes at least nine planets and is more than 4.65 trillion miles across.

star A large body of burning gases—often hydrogen, helium, nitrogen, oxygen, iron, nickel, and silicon.

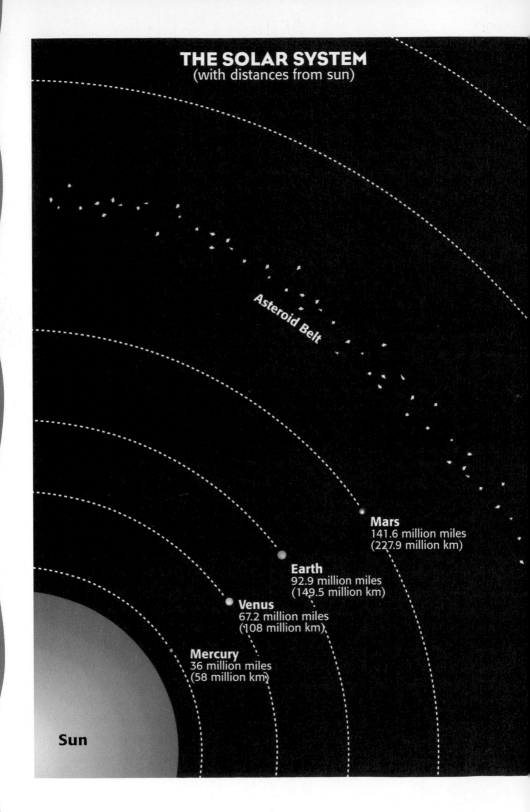

THE SOLAR SYSTEM
(with distances from sun)

Asteroid Belt

Mars
141.6 million miles
(227.9 million km)

Earth
92.9 million miles
(149.5 million km)

Venus
67.2 million miles
(108 million km)

Mercury
36 million miles
(58 million km)

Sun

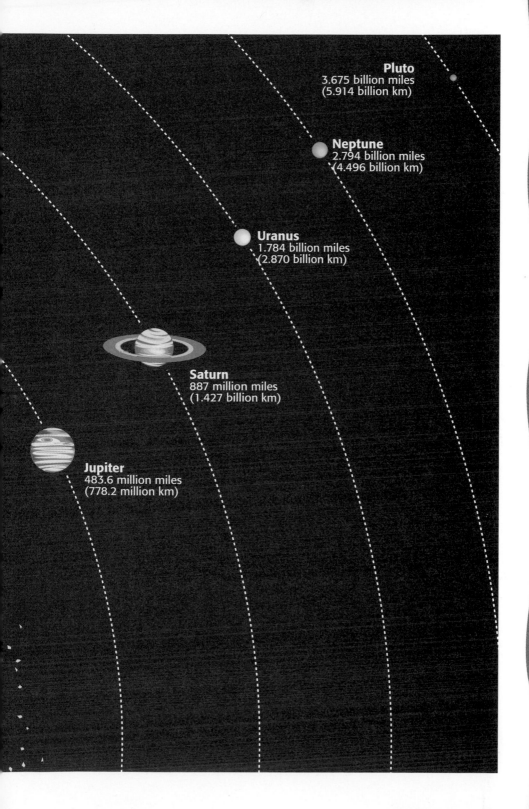

Pluto
3.675 billion miles
(5.914 billion km)

Neptune
2.794 billion miles
(4.496 billion km)

Uranus
1.784 billion miles
(2.870 billion km)

Saturn
887 million miles
(1.427 billion km)

Jupiter
483.6 million miles
(778.2 million km)

BASIC FACTS ABOUT THE PLANETS IN OUR SOLAR SYSTEM

	Average distance from sun	Rotation period (hours)	Period of revolution (in Earth days)	Diameter relative to Earth	Average surface temperature	Planetary satellites (moons)
Mercury	35,900,000 miles (57.8 mil. km)	1,407.6 hours	88 days	38.2%	332°F (166°C)	None
Venus	67,200,000 miles (108.1 mil. km)	-5,832.2* hours	224.7 days	94.9%	854°F (456°C)	None
Earth	92,960,000 miles (150 mil. km)	23.9 hours	365.26 days	100%	59°F (15°C)	1 moon
Mars	141,600,000 miles (227.9 mil. km)	24.6 hours	687 days	53.2%	-67°F (-55°C)	2 moons
Jupiter	483,600,000 miles (778.2 mil. km)	9.8 hours	4,332.6 days	1,121%	-162°F (-108°C)	16
Saturn	886,700,000 miles (1.43 bil. km)	10.2 hours	10,759.2 days	941%	-208°F (-133°C)	18
Uranus	1,783,000,000 miles (2.87 bil. km)	17.2 hours	30,685.4 days	410%	-344°F (-207°C)	15
Neptune	2,794,000,000 miles (4.5 bil. km)	16.1 hours	60,268 days	388%	-365°F (-220°C)	8
Pluto	3,666,100,000 miles (5.9 bil. km)	-153* hours	90,950 days	18%	-355°F (-215°C)	1

Source: NASA   *Retrograde rotation; rotates backwards, or in the opposite direction from most other planetary bodies.

BASIC FACTS ABOUT THE SUN

Position in solar system	center
Mean distance from Earth	92,955,600 mi. (150 mil. km)
Distance from center of Milky Way galaxy	27,710 light-years
Period of rotation	27 days on average
Equatorial diameter	864,930 mi. (1.4 mil. km)
Diameter relative to Earth	109 times
Temperature at core	27,000,000°F (15,000,000°C)
Temperature at surface	8,700°F (4,811°C)
Main components	hydrogen and helium
Expected life of hydrogen fuel supply	6.4 billion years

Source: NASA

TOP 10 LARGEST BODIES IN THE SOLAR SYSTEM
(ranked by size in diameter)

7. Venus
7,520 mi.
(12,101 km)

2. Jupiter
88,846 mi.
(142,979 km)

8. Mars
4,222 mi.
(6,794 km)

3. Saturn
74,898 mi.
(120,533 km)

1. Sun
864,930 mi.
(1.4 million km)

4. Uranus
31,763 mi.
(51,116 km)

5. Neptune
30,778 mi.
(49,531 km)

9. Ganymede
(moon of Jupiter)
3,274 mi.
(5,268 km)

6. Earth
7,926 mi.
(12,755 km)

Source: NASA

10. Titan (moon of Saturn) 3,200 mi. (5,149 km)

ASTRONOMY TERMS AND DEFINITIONS

	Light-year (distance traveled by light in one year)	5,880 billion miles (9,462 billion km)
	Velocity of light (speed of light)	186,281.7 miles/sec. (299,782 km/sec.)
	Mean distance, Earth to moon	238,860 miles (384,397 km)
	Equatorial radius of Earth (distance around middle of Earth)	3,963.34 miles (6,378 km)
	Polar radius of Earth (distance around top to bottom)	3,949.99 miles (6,357 km)
	Earth's mean radius (how far around, averaged)	3,958.89 miles (6,371 km)
	Earth's mean velocity in orbit (how fast it travels)	18.5 miles/sec. (29.8 km/sec.)

THE MILKY WAY GALAXY

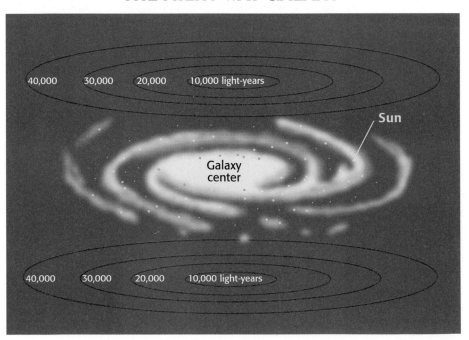

40,000 30,000 20,000 10,000 light-years

Sun

Galaxy center

40,000 30,000 20,000 10,000 light-years

TOP 10 MOST FREQUENTLY SEEN COMETS

Comet	Orbit period (years)

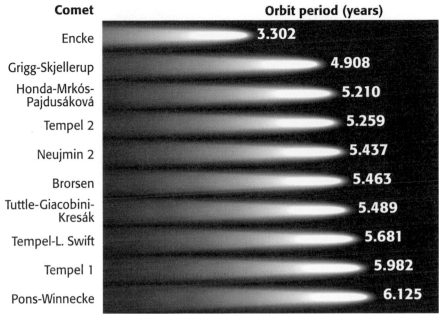

Comet	Orbit period (years)
Encke	3.302
Grigg-Skjellerup	4.908
Honda-Mrkós-Pajdusáková	5.210
Tempel 2	5.259
Neujmin 2	5.437
Brorsen	5.463
Tuttle-Giacobini-Kresák	5.489
Tempel-L. Swift	5.681
Tempel 1	5.982
Pons-Winnecke	6.125

Source: NASA

TOP 10 CLOSEST COMET APPROACHES TO EARTH
(ranked by distance in miles/kilometers)

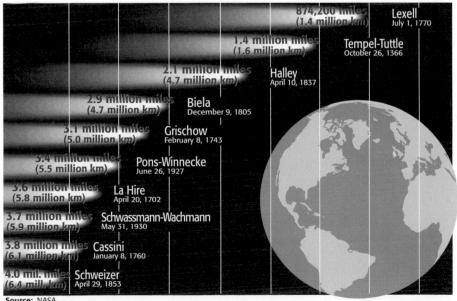

874,200 miles
(1.4 million km) — Lexell — July 1, 1770

1.4 million miles
(1.6 million km) — Tempel-Tuttle — October 26, 1366

2.1 million miles
(4.7 million km) — Halley — April 10, 1837

2.9 million miles
(4.7 million km) — Biela — December 9, 1805

3.1 million miles
(5.0 million km) — Grischow — February 8, 1743

3.4 million miles
(5.5 million km) — Pons-Winnecke — June 26, 1927

3.6 million miles
(5.8 million km) — La Hire — April 20, 1702

3.7 million miles
(5.9 million km) — Schwassmann-Wachmann — May 31, 1930

3.8 million miles
(6.1 million km) — Cassini — January 8, 1760

4.0 mil. miles
(6.4 mill. km) — Schweizer — April 29, 1853

Source: NASA

MAJOR CONSTELLATIONS
Here is a table of selected major constellations
and their English names

Latin	English	Latin	English
Andromeda	Andromeda	Lepus	Hare
Aquarius	Water Bearer	Libra	Scales
Aquila	Eagle	Lupus	Wolf
Aries	Ram	Lynx	Lynx
Camelopardalis	Giraffe	Lyra	Harp
Cancer	Crab	Microscopium	Microscope
Canes Venatici	Hunting Dogs	Monoceros	Unicorn
Canis Major	Big Dog	Musca	Fly
Canis Minor	Little Dog	Orion	Orion
Capricornus	Goat	Pavo	Peacock
Cassiopeia	Cassiopeia	Pegasus	Pegasus
Centaurus	Centaur	Phoenix	Phoenix
Cetus	Whale	Pictor	Painter
Chameleon	Chameleon	Pisces	Fish
Circinus	Compass	Piscis Austrinus	Southern Fish
Columba	Dove	Sagitta	Arrow
Corona Australis	Southern Crown	Sagittarius	Archer
Corona Borealis	Northern Crown	Scorpius	Scorpion
Corvus	Crow	Sculptor	Sculptor
Crater	Cup	Scutum	Shield
Crux	Southern Cross	Serpens	Serpent
Cygnus	Swan	Sextans	Sextant
Delphinus	Dolphin	Taurus	Bull
Dorado	Goldfish	Telescopium	Telescope
Draco	Dragon	Triangulum	Triangle
Equuleus	Little Horse	Triangulum Australe	Southern Triangle
Gemini	Twins	Tucana	Toucan
Grus	Crane	Ursa Major	Big Bear
Hercules	Hercules	Ursa Minor	Little Bear
Horologium	Clock	Virgo	Virgin
Lacerta	Lizard	Volans	Flying Fish
Leo	Lion	Vulpecula	Little Fox
Leo Minor	Little Lion		

TOP 10 CLOSEST STARS TO EARTH
(ranked by distance in light-years*, excluding the sun)

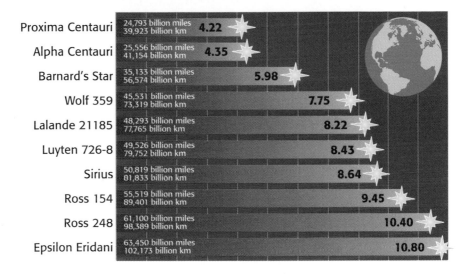

Star	Distance	Light-years
Proxima Centauri	24,793 billion miles / 39,923 billion km	4.22
Alpha Centauri	25,556 billion miles / 41,154 billion km	4.35
Barnard's Star	35,133 billion miles / 56,574 billion km	5.98
Wolf 359	45,531 billion miles / 73,319 billion km	7.75
Lalande 21185	48,293 billion miles / 77,765 billion km	8.22
Luyten 726-8	49,526 billion miles / 79,752 billion km	8.43
Sirius	50,819 billion miles / 81,833 billion km	8.64
Ross 154	55,519 billion miles / 89,401 billion km	9.45
Ross 248	61,100 billion miles / 98,389 billion km	10.40
Epsilon Eridani	63,450 billion miles / 102,173 billion km	10.80

Source: NASA

*Note: One light-year = 5,880 billion miles/9,462 billion kilometers, which is the distance light travels in one year.

THE WORLD'S TOP 10 LARGEST REFLECTING TELESCOPES

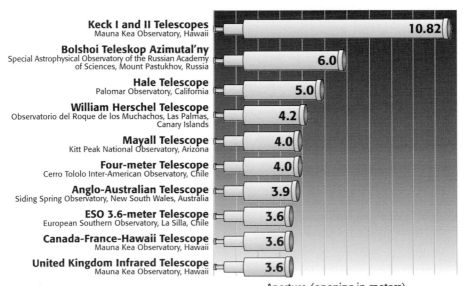

Telescope	Aperture
Keck I and II Telescopes — Mauna Kea Observatory, Hawaii	10.82
Bolshoi Teleskop Azimutal'ny — Special Astrophysical Observatory of the Russian Academy of Sciences, Mount Pastukhov, Russia	6.0
Hale Telescope — Palomar Observatory, California	5.0
William Herschel Telescope — Observatorio del Roque de los Muchachos, Las Palmas, Canary Islands	4.2
Mayall Telescope — Kitt Peak National Observatory, Arizona	4.0
Four-meter Telescope — Cerro Tololo Inter-American Observatory, Chile	4.0
Anglo-Australian Telescope — Siding Spring Observatory, New South Wales, Australia	3.9
ESO 3.6-meter Telescope — European Southern Observatory, La Silla, Chile	3.6
Canada-France-Hawaii Telescope — Mauna Kea Observatory, Hawaii	3.6
United Kingdom Infrared Telescope — Mauna Kea Observatory, Hawaii	3.6

Aperture (opening in meters)

Source: NASA

BUILDINGS, BRIDGES, DAMS, AND TUNNELS

When the Great Pyramid was completed in Egypt around 2600 B.C., this remarkable structure stood 481 feet (147 m) tall. (The outer layer of stone was later removed, so the pyramid is shorter now.) Workers had cut and moved every one of its huge blocks of stone by hand. Built as the tomb of an Egyptian king, the pyramid today is a monument to the skills of its builders.

Since ancient times, people have been engineers, designing and constructing bridges, dams, tunnels, and buildings of all kinds. These projects serve a purpose: A dam contains water. A bridge spans a river or a ravine. A tunnel lets people go through a mountain or under water. A building provides shelter. But great construction projects do more. They are important in their own right—for their beauty, for their daring, sometimes for their sheer size.

Every age has had its engineering marvels. The Romans were the most famous builders of ancient times. They constructed roads, bridges, amphitheaters, and aqueducts (to carry water) throughout their empire. In medieval Europe, the tall spires of cathedrals rose over major towns. Today city skyscrapers dwarf those spires.

Modern builders have materials such as steel that were not available in ancient times. They have machines to do hard work. They have computers to aid in planning and design. With these tools, they have been able to construct taller buildings, bigger dams, and longer bridges and tunnels than ancient people could have imagined.

Yearbook

2600 B.C. The Great Pyramid, a 481-foot (147 m)-high tomb is completed in Egypt.

A.D. 1100 The 800-room Pueblo Bonito is built in Chaco Canyon, New Mexico.

1883 The Brooklyn Bridge is completed.

1931 New York's Empire State Building is constructed in one year and 45 days.

1941 The Grand Coulee Dam is completed on the Columbia River in Washington State.

1973 Chicago's Sears Tower is completed, rising 1,454 feet (443 m) high.

1994 The 31-mile (50 km) Channel Tunnel opens below the English Channel.

• Notables •

Deinokrates (dates unknown)
Macedonian architect; laid out the city of Alexandria along the Nile in 331 B.C.

Buckminster Fuller (1895–1983)
American engineer; inventor best known for the geodesic dome.

Thomas Jefferson (1743–1826)
Third U.S. president; noted architect who designed his own home, called Monticello.

Andrea Palladio (1508–1580)
Leading architect of the Italian Renaissance.

Eero Saarinen (1910–1961)
American architect; designs include the Gateway Arch, St. Louis, Missouri.

Frank Lloyd Wright (1867–1959)
American architect; known for original designs; key figure in American Prairie school of architecture.

KEY IDEAS

amphitheater A large round or oval-shaped building that is open to the air and has many rows of seats surrounding an arena.

aqueduct A structure for transporting large quantities of water from a source to the place where it is distributed. Ancient Romans built tall aqueducts to move water across a valley.

architecture The process of designing buildings, or the style in which they are built, such as Colonial architecture.

curtain-wall construction A method of constructing a building so that the outside walls are not supported by a steel skeleton; they hang like a curtain.

engineer Someone who designs and supervises the construction of a bridge, road, dam, or other structure; some engineers design engines.

post-and-beam construction The use of horizontal beams supported by vertical posts to construct a building. This method was used by ancient Egyptians and Greeks and is still used today.

MILESTONES IN MODERN ARCHITECTURE TIME LINE

1884 First modern metal-frame skyscraper, Chicago's 10-story Home Insurance Building, is designed by U.S. architect William Jenney (1832–1907). It features metal skeleton of cast-iron columns and nonsupporting curtain walls, which become characteristic of modern design.

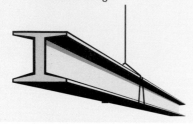

1900 U.S. architect Frank Lloyd Wright (1867–1959) becomes famous for designing houses in Prairie style, characterized by low, horizontal lines and use of natural earth colors. Wright believes buildings should complement settings.

1919 Walter Gropius (1883–1969) founds Bauhaus, German school of design, to combine arts and architecture with modern industrial technology. Bauhaus styles are notable for geometric lines and use of steel, glass, and concrete.

1928 Noted American architect (Richard) Buckminster Fuller (1895–1983) designs self-contained "4-D" technological house. Fuller becomes known for his "Dymaxion" principle of trying to get most from least amount of material and energy.

1937 Ludwig Mies van der Rohe (1886–1969) emigrates to United States and becomes leader in glass-and-steel architecture. He pioneers rectangular lines in design, including cubelike brick structures, uncovered steel columns, and large areas of tinted glass.

1951 Finnish-born American architect Eero Saarinen (1910–1961) becomes known for innovative designs for various buildings in United States. His sweeping style features soaring roof lines, extensive use of glass, and curved lines.

1970 New York's World Trade Center opens. Its tubular design eliminates steel skeleton of previous skyscrapers. Exterior tubular walls, achieved by exterior columns built close together and/or diagonal bracing, are strong enough to withstand wind and other pressure.

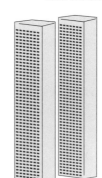

CONSTRUCTION TIMELINE OF IMPORTANT EARTHWORKS, DAMS, AND CANALS

1718   Elaborate system of earthen levees is built along Mississippi River at New Orleans, LA, to control floodwaters.

1825   United States opens NY's Erie Canal, linking Great Lakes with New York City by way of Hudson River. It leads to increased development of western NY State.

1869   Suez Canal, 100 miles (161km) long, is completed, built by French engineer Ferdinand de Lesseps (1805–1894) to connect Mediterranean and Red Seas. It is enlarged in 1980 to enable passage of supertankers.

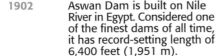

1902   Aswan Dam is built on Nile River in Egypt. Considered one of the finest dams of all time, it has record-setting length of 6,400 feet (1,951 m).

1904–1914   Panama Canal across Isthmus of Panama connects Atlantic and Pacific Oceans. It is built by U.S. military engineers on land leased from Republic of Panama. Canal Zone is returned to Panama in 1978.

1941   Grand Coulee Dam, built for electric generation and irrigation, is completed on Columbia River in WA. At 550 feet (168 m) high and 4,173 feet (1,272 m) long, dam is world's largest concrete structure.

1944   World's longest tunnel, Delaware Aqueduct, is completed. It is 105 miles (169 km) long and supplies water to New York City.

1959   United States and Canada complete construction of St. Lawrence Seaway. It provides access to Lake Ontario for oceangoing traffic by way of St. Lawrence River.

1970   Aswan High Dam, on Nile River in Egypt, is complete. Dam is 364 feet (111 m) high and 12,565 feet (3,830 m) long.

1985   Construction on world's longest railroad tunnel is completed in Japan. Almost 33.5 miles (54 km) long, tunnel connects islands of Hokkaido and Honshu.

THE SEVEN WONDERS OF THE MODERN WORLD

Wonder/Location

Description

Channel Tunnel
England and France

The 31-mile (50 km) Channel Tunnel (Chunnel) is actually three concrete tubes, each 5 ft. (2 m) thick, which plunge into the earth at Coquelles, France, and burrow through the English Channel. They re-emerge at Folkstone, behind the white cliffs of Dover. Through two of the tubes rush the broadest trains ever built—double-decker mega-trains 14 ft. (4 m) across that travel close to 100 mph (161 kph).

CN Tower
Toronto

The world's tallest free-standing structure soars 1,815 ft. (553 m) above the sidewalks of Toronto, three times the height of its better-known cousin, the Seattle Space Needle. Designed with the aid of a wind tunnel, the CN Tower can withstand 260-mph (418-kph) gusts.

Empire State Building
New York City

At 1,250 ft. (381 m), the Empire State Building is the best-known skyscraper in the world and was by far the tallest building in the world for more than 40 years. Construction was completed in only one year and 45 days, without requiring overtime. Ironworkers set a breathtaking pace, riveting the 58,000-ton (53,000 metric tons) frame together in 23 weeks.

Golden Gate Bridge
San Francisco

The world's tallest suspension bridge, it hangs from two 746-ft. (227 m)-high towers, its cables—each a yard thick—are the biggest ever to support a bridge. In fact, the Golden Gate Bridge contains enough cable to encircle the earth three times.

Itaipu Dam
Brazil/Paraguay

Five miles (8 km) wide and requiring enough concrete to build five Hoover Dams, the main dam, as high as a 65-story building, is composed of hollow concrete segments, while the flanking wings are earth and rock fill. Some 160 tons (145 metric tons) of water per second pour onto each turbine, generating 12,600 megawatts—enough to power most of California.

Netherlands North Sea Protection Works
Netherlands

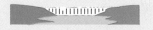

Unique in the world, this vast and complex system of dams, floodgates, storm surge barriers, and other engineered works literally allows the Netherlands to exist. The North Sea Protection Works also includes a 19-mile (31 km)-long enclosure dam that is 100 yards (91 m) thick at the waterline and the Delta Project, which controls the treacherous area where the mouths of the Meuse and Rhine Rivers become a delta.

Panama Canal
Panama

One of civil engineering's greatest triumphs, the Panama Canal employed 42,000 workers who dredged, blasted, and excavated from Colón to Balboa. They moved enough earth and rubble to bury the island of Manhattan to a depth of 12 ft. (4 m)—or enough to open a 16-ft. (5 m)-wide tunnel to the center of the earth.

Source: International Engineering Society

THE SEVEN WONDERS OF THE ANCIENT WORLD

Wonder/Location	Description
Colossus of Rhodes Harbor of Rhodes, in Aegean Sea, off coast of Turkey	Huge bronze statue of sun god Helios, erected in harbor by people of Rhodes at end of year-long siege; took 12 years to build; about 105 feet (35 m) tall; destroyed by earthquake 224 B.C.
Hanging Gardens of Babylon ancient city of Babylon (now near Baghdad, Iraq)	Series of landscaped terraces along banks of the Euphrates River, connected by marble stairways amd planted with many trees, flowers, and shrubs. Probably built by King Nebuchadnezzar for his wife.
Mausoleum of Halicarnassus ancient city of Halicarnassus, now Turkish town of Bodrum	A monumental, expansive marble tomb built by the widow of Mausolus, king of Anatolia in 353 B.C.
Pharos (lighthouse) Pharos Island off coast of Alexandria, Egypt	Built around 270 B.C., it was the world's first important lighthouse. It stood in the harbor for 1,000 years until it was destroyed by earthquake; also prototype for all others built by Roman Empire.
Pyramids of Egypt Giza, Egypt	The oldest pyramid, Cheops, was built with more than two million limestone blocks and stands more than 480 feet (146 m) high. The only one of the ancient wonders still in existence. 
Statue of Zeus Olympia, Greece	A huge, ornate statue of the god on his throne that reached almost 60 feet (18 m) high.
Temple of Artemis ancient Greek city of Ephesus, now in Turkey near Selcuk	Built in the sixth century B.C. to honor goddess Artemis; one of the largest Greek temples ever built; famous for its artistic decoration and use of marble.

Source: International Engineering Society

WORLD'S TOP 10 HIGHEST DAMS

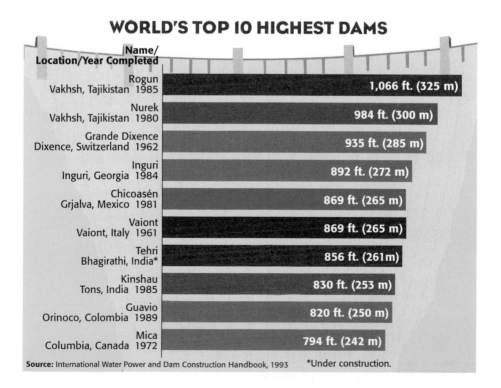

Name/Location/Year Completed	Height
Rogun Vakhsh, Tajikistan 1985	1,066 ft. (325 m)
Nurek Vakhsh, Tajikistan 1980	984 ft. (300 m)
Grande Dixence Dixence, Switzerland 1962	935 ft. (285 m)
Inguri Inguri, Georgia 1984	892 ft. (272 m)
Chicoasén Grjalva, Mexico 1981	869 ft. (265 m)
Vaiont Vaiont, Italy 1961	869 ft. (265 m)
Tehri Bhagirathi, India*	856 ft. (261m)
Kinshau Tons, India 1985	830 ft. (253 m)
Guavio Orinoco, Colombia 1989	820 ft. (250 m)
Mica Columbia, Canada 1972	794 ft. (242 m)

Source: International Water Power and Dam Construction Handbook, 1993   *Under construction.

TOP 10 LONGEST SUSPENSION BRIDGES

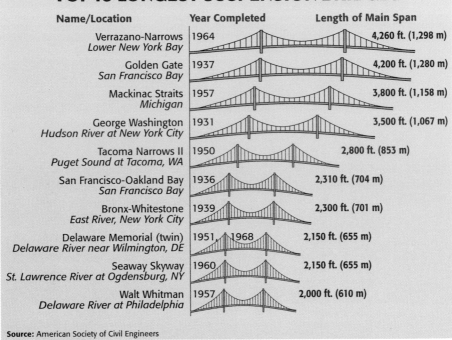

Name/Location	Year Completed	Length of Main Span
Verrazano-Narrows *Lower New York Bay*	1964	4,260 ft. (1,298 m)
Golden Gate *San Francisco Bay*	1937	4,200 ft. (1,280 m)
Mackinac Straits *Michigan*	1957	3,800 ft. (1,158 m)
George Washington *Hudson River at New York City*	1931	3,500 ft. (1,067 m)
Tacoma Narrows II *Puget Sound at Tacoma, WA*	1950	2,800 ft. (853 m)
San Francisco-Oakland Bay *San Francisco Bay*	1936	2,310 ft. (704 m)
Bronx-Whitestone *East River, New York City*	1939	2,300 ft. (701 m)
Delaware Memorial (twin) *Delaware River near Wilmington, DE*	1951 1968	2,150 ft. (655 m)
Seaway Skyway *St. Lawrence River at Ogdensburg, NY*	1960	2,150 ft. (655 m)
Walt Whitman *Delaware River at Philadelphia*	1957	2,000 ft. (610 m)

Source: American Society of Civil Engineers

WORLD'S TOP 10 LONGEST ROAD TUNNELS

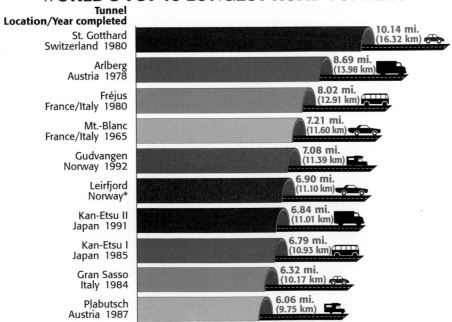

Tunnel Location/Year completed	
St. Gotthard Switzerland 1980	10.14 mi. (16.32 km)
Arlberg Austria 1978	8.69 mi. (13.98 km)
Fréjus France/Italy 1980	8.02 mi. (12.91 km)
Mt.-Blanc France/Italy 1965	7.21 mi. (11.60 km)
Gudvangen Norway 1992	7.08 mi. (11.39 km)
Leirfjord Norway*	6.90 mi. (11.10 km)
Kan-Etsu II Japan 1991	6.84 mi. (11.01 km)
Kan-Etsu I Japan 1985	6.79 mi. (10.93 km)
Gran Sasso Italy 1984	6.32 mi. (10.17 km)
Plabutsch Austria 1987	6.06 mi. (9.75 km)

Source: American Society of Civil Engineers and Bridge and Turnpike Association

*Under construction.

WORLD'S TOP 10 CITIES WITH MOST SKYSCRAPERS*

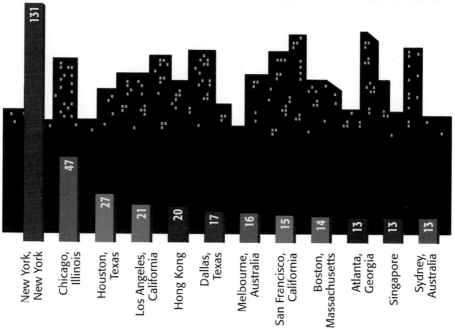

New York, New York	131
Chicago, Illinois	47
Houston, Texas	27
Los Angeles, California	21
Hong Kong	20
Dallas, Texas	17
Melbourne, Australia	16
San Francisco, California	15
Boston, Massachusetts	14
Atlanta, Georgia	13
Singapore	13
Sydney, Australia	13

Source: Based on data from Council on High Buildings and Urban Habitat   *Habitable buildings of over 500 ft./152 m.

THE TOP 10 TALLEST BUILDINGS IN THE WORLD

Petronas Tower 1	Kuala Lumpur, Malaysia	1,476 ft. (450 m)
Petronas Tower 2	Kuala Lumpur, Malaysia	1,476 ft. (450 m)
Sears Tower	Chicago, Illinois	1,454 ft. (443 m)
Jin Mao Building	Shanghai, China	1,379 ft. (421 m)
World Trade Center, North	New York, USA	1,368 ft. (417 m)
World Trade Center, South	New York, USA	1,362 ft. (415 m)
Empire State Building	New York, USA	1,250 ft. (381 m)
Central Plaza	Hong Kong, China	1,227 ft. (374 m)
Bank of China Tower	Hong Kong, China	1,209 ft. (369 m)
Tuntex and Chien-Tai Tower	Kaoshiung, Taiwan	1,140 ft. (348 m)

Source: Council on High Buildings and Urban Habitat, Lehigh University (1995)

BUSINESS AND MONEY

"The business of America is business," President Calvin Coolidge said in 1925. By "business" he meant all the ways that people produce, buy, and sell goods and services.

Something as simple as buying a pair of jeans can involve many people. First, a manufacturer buys equipment and supplies. Factory workers cut and stitch the jeans, and a trucking company ships them to a store. An advertising agency creates a campaign to sell them. Banks, accounting firms, and others help at every step.

Each firm hires workers, so your jeans help provide jobs for many people. Each firm makes a profit on its part in the process, benefiting the owners of the firm. They may be a few individuals or many stockholders—people who have bought shares in the company. People use their earnings (from wages or profits) to buy other goods or make new investments, and that keeps business growing.

If a company can't sell enough of its products, profits fall. It may let workers go or even shut down. In a business recession (or a more severe depression), hard times spread, and unemployment rises.

Today business often crosses national borders. A company may ship raw materials to one country for assembly and to yet another country for sale. That's where exchange rates and international currencies affect the profitability of many goods.

Yearbook

A.D. 900 China uses paper money.

1789 The Industrial Revolution begins in the United States.

1908 Henry Ford builds his Model T car, using an assembly line.

1913 The Federal Reserve System is established.

1929 The Great Depression begins following the stock market crash.

1950 The first credit card is introduced.

1980s Japan is a world financial center.

1990s The Asian economy falters and effects ripple across the world.

• Notables •

Andrew Carnegie (1835–1919)
Scottish immigrant; built an empire in U.S. steel industry.

Thomas Edison (1847–1931)
American; founded what would become General Electric.

William (Bill) Gates III (1955–   )
American; cofounder of the Microsoft Corporation; second wealthiest person in the world.

J.P. Morgan (1837–1913) American banker and financier.

John D. Rockefeller (1839–1937)
Founder of the Standard Oil Company.

Robert Edward (Ted) Turner III (1938–   ) American; founded cable network CNN.

Eli Whitney (1765–1825) American; invented the cotton gin.

KEY IDEAS

corporation A business or an institutional organization that can own property and make legal contracts as if it were a person.

credit An amount of money put at a person's disposal by a bank, or the time given for payment for goods and services.

currency The form of money used in a country.

franchise Permission given by a company to sell its services or distribute its products in a particular place.

market A place where people meet for the purpose of buying and selling goods. Also a geographical area of demand for a good or service, or a category of potential buyers.

monopoly The complete control of something, especially a service or the supply of a product.

philanthropist Someone who sets aside money for the benefit of society.

profit The amount of money left after all of the costs of running a business are subtracted from all of the money earned.

TOP 10 LARGEST CORPORATIONS IN THE U.S., 1997

(by annual sales)

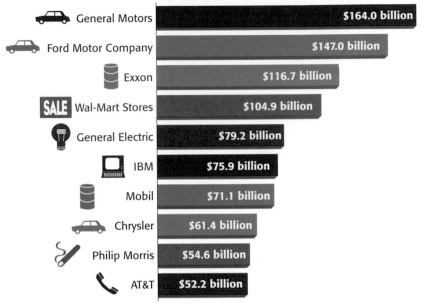

General Motors — $164.0 billion
Ford Motor Company — $147.0 billion
Exxon — $116.7 billion
Wal-Mart Stores — $104.9 billion
General Electric — $79.2 billion
IBM — $75.9 billion
Mobil — $71.1 billion
Chrysler — $61.4 billion
Philip Morris — $54.6 billion
AT&T — $52.2 billion

Source: Based on data from www.forbes.com/*Forbes* magazine

WORLD'S RICHEST BILLIONAIRES, 1997

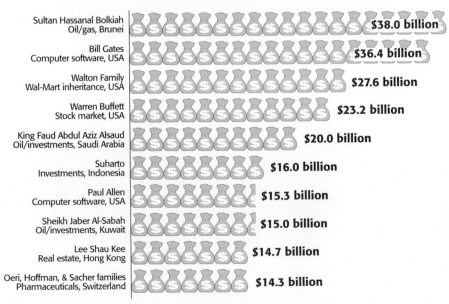

Sultan Hassanal Bolkiah
Oil/gas, Brunei — $38.0 billion

Bill Gates
Computer software, USA — $36.4 billion

Walton Family
Wal-Mart inheritance, USA — $27.6 billion

Warren Buffett
Stock market, USA — $23.2 billion

King Faud Abdul Aziz Alsaud
Oil/investments, Saudi Arabia — $20.0 billion

Suharto
Investments, Indonesia — $16.0 billion

Paul Allen
Computer software, USA — $15.3 billion

Sheikh Jaber Al-Sabah
Oil/investments, Kuwait — $15.0 billion

Lee Shau Kee
Real estate, Hong Kong — $14.7 billion

Oeri, Hoffman, & Sacher families
Pharmaceuticals, Switzerland — $14.3 billion

Source: Based on data from www.forbes.com/*Forbes* magazine

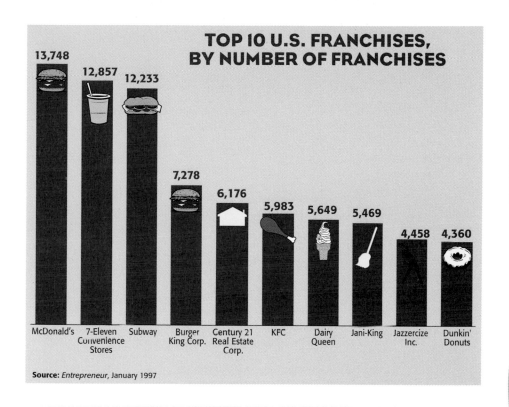

TOP 10 U.S. FRANCHISES, BY NUMBER OF FRANCHISES

McDonald's	13,748
7-Eleven Convenience Stores	12,857
Subway	12,233
Burger King Corp.	7,278
Century 21 Real Estate Corp.	6,176
KFC	5,983
Dairy Queen	5,649
Jani-King	5,469
Jazzercize Inc.	4,458
Dunkin' Donuts	4,360

Source: *Entrepreneur*, January 1997

TOP 10 LEADING U.S. COMPANIES IN MARKET VALUE, 1997

Market value

Company	Market value
General Electric Co.	$169.4 billion
Coca-Cola Co.	$147.6 billion
Exxon Corp.	$125.6 billion
Microsoft	$118.6 billion
Intel	$113.2 billion
Merck & Co.	$106.6 billion
Morris (Philip) Co.	$104.6 billion
Procter & Gamble	$85.4 billion
Johnson & Johnson	$77.1 billion
IBM	$73.0 billion

Source: Based on data from www.forbes.com/*Forbes* magazine.

EARNING INTEREST

Simple Interest

Simple interest is computed on the amount of principal of a loan. That principal is multiplied by the rate of interest: the resulting figure is then multiplied by the time over which the loan will be repaid.

Simple Interest on a $100 Loan

Time	Annual Rate			
	5%	10%	15%	20%
1 month	$0.42	$0.83	$1.25	$1.67
6 months	$2.50	$5.00	$7.50	$10.00
12 months	$5.00	$10.00	$15.00	$20.00
24 months	$10.00	$20.00	$30.00	$40.00
36 months	$15.00	$30.00	$45.00	$60.00

Compound Interest

Compound interest is computed by multiplying the sum of the principal and the accrued interest by the rate of interest. The calculation must be refigured each time the principal is compounded.

Compound Interest on $100 Principal, Compounded Annually

Time	Annual Rate			
	5%	7.5%	10%	12.5%
6 months	$2.50	$3.75	$5.00	$6.25
1 year	$5.00	$7.50	$10.00	$12.50
2 years	$10.25	$15.56	$21.00	$26.56
3 years	$15.76	$24.23	$33.10	$42.38
4 years	$12.55	$33.55	$46.41	$60.18
5 years	$27.63	$43.57	$61.05	$80.20

Source: U.S. Department of Commerce

GLOSSARY OF BANKING TERMS

Backed To be able to exchange one asset for another; for many years our money was backed or exchangeable for gold and silver.

Bankruptcy When a person or a business declares they are unable to pay their bills and other debts.

Beneficiary The person designated to receive the income from an account held in trust for that person.

Bond An IOU issued by a corporation, a municipality, or the U.S. government. The issuer promises to pay the bondholder, who has made the loan, a specified rate of interest for a certain period of time. When that time period is up, the bond matures and the bondholder receives the full face value back, i.e., the amount loaned.

Bounced check One that is not paid because of insufficient funds in the account.

Central bank A government bank for banks that is generally responsible for national monetary policy.

Collateral Specific property that a borrower pledges as security against repayment of a loan. The lender can sell the collateral if the borrower fails to repay the loan.

Compound Interest paid upon the principal plus the interest already earned.

Endorsement One's signature, by which the endorser transfers the money represented by a check to someone else.

Estate All the things one owns at the time of death. An estate can consist of real estate, stocks, bonds, money, a business or part of a business, furniture, jewelry, paintings, cars, and so forth. One's estate is distributed to heirs and others according to directions left in a will or, if there is no will, by court ruling.

Face value Sometimes called par value. The dollar value of a bond, note, or motgage as stated on its certificate.

Federal Trade Commission (FTC) A federal agency established in 1914 that fosters free and fair business competition and at the same time protects consumers.

Interest The cost of using money; when you borrow money from a bank you must pay the bank for that money. The amount you pay is called interest and is expressed as a percent, such as 8 percent.

Legal tender Money that the government requires a creditor to accept in discharge of debts.

Liquidity Refers to the assets that can easily and quickly be converted into cash, without substantial loss, such as savings and checking account deposits.

Loan Letting out or renting of money by a lender to a borrower with the understanding that the money will be paid back.

Maturity Date on which the principal amount of a bond (the amount the bondholder loaned the issuer) becomes due and must be paid back to the bondholder.

Mint A place where legal coins are manufactured.

Mortgage A loan made by an institution to a homeowner; the homeowner pledges his or her home as collateral against the loan. The lender, usually a bank, may take possession of the home if the borrower does not pay back the loan as agreed.

Mutual fund An investment company in which thousands of dollars from individual shareholders are pooled together to purchase stocks, bonds, and other investments. This money is managed by a professional portfolio manager.

Periodic Payments made over time, usually but not necessarily at fixed intervals, such as the first of every month.

Principal The amount invested as distinguished from interest or profits.

Quarter A three-month period of the year. The first quarter consists of January, February, and March.

Specie Coined money as opposed to paper money.

Stock Ownership in a corporation that is represented by a stock certificate.

Stop payment A request by a depositor to the bank to refuse to pay a certain check when it is returned to the bank.

Treasuries Bonds, notes, and bills issued by the U.S. government and backed by its full faith and credit. These securities are considered the safest and highest quality available.

Trust A legal relationship in which a person, called the trustee, holds property, investments, or money for someone else, called the beneficiary.

Yield Rate of return earned on a deposit or security.

GLOSSARY OF STOCK MARKET TERMS

Bear market A market in which stock prices are declining. Opposite of *Bull market*.

Big board A popular term for the New York Stock Exchange.

Blue chip Common stock in a company known nationally for the quality of its products or services and for its ability to make money and pay dividends in good times and bad.

Broker One who executes orders as an agent for others and receives a commission, as distinct from *dealer*.

Bull market A market in which stock prices are rising. Opposite of *Bear market*.

Common stock Securities that represent an ownership interest in a corporation. If the company has also issued preferred stock, both common and preferred have ownership rights, but the preferred normally has prior claim on dividends and, in the event of liquidation, on assets.

Stock dividend A dividend paid in securities rather than cash.

Ticker The instrument that prints prices and volume of security transactions in cities and towns throughout the United States within minutes after each trade on the floor.

TOP 10 BIGGEST U.S. EMPLOYERS, 1996
(by number of employees)

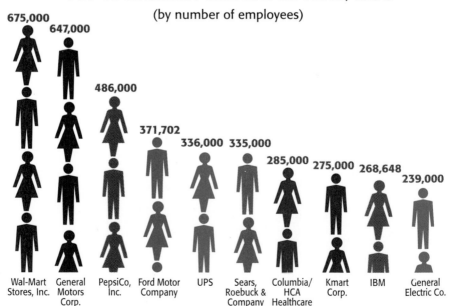

675,000 — Wal-Mart Stores, Inc.
647,000 — General Motors Corp.
486,000 — PepsiCo, Inc.
371,702 — Ford Motor Company
336,000 — UPS
335,000 — Sears, Roebuck & Company
285,000 — Columbia/HCA Healthcare Corp.
275,000 — Kmart Corp.
268,648 — IBM
239,000 — General Electric Co.

Source: Based on data from www.fortune.com/*Fortune* magazine.

WHO IS ON OUR BILLS?

Bill		Portrait
$1		George Washington
$2		Thomas Jefferson
$5		Abraham Lincoln
$10		Alexander Hamilton
$20		Andrew Jackson
$50		Ulysses S. Grant
$100		Benjamin Franklin
$500		William McKinley
$1,000		Grover Cleveland
$5,000		James Madison
$10,000		Salmon P. Chase
$100,000		Woodrow Wilson

ANATOMY OF A PERSONAL CHECK

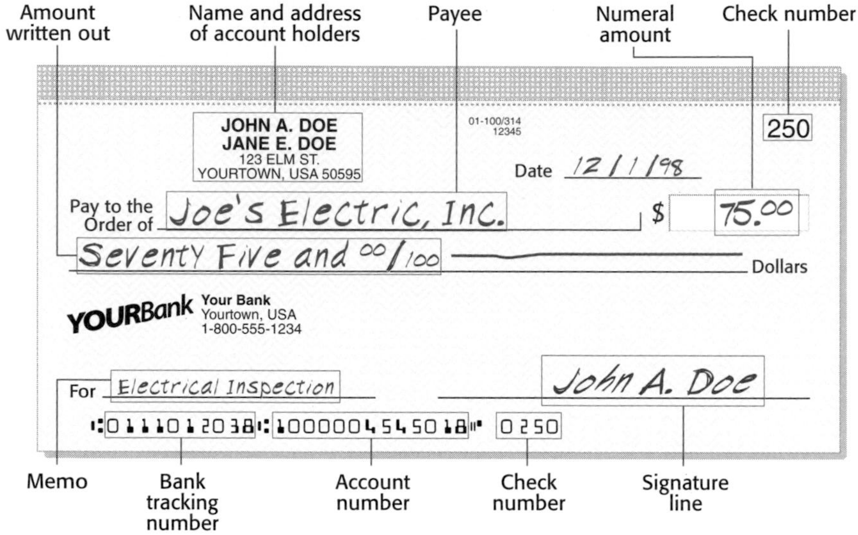
Amount written out
Name and address of account holders
Payee
Numeral amount
Check number
JOHN A. DOE
JANE E. DOE
123 ELM ST.
YOURTOWN, USA 50595
01-100/314
12345
250
Date 12/1/98
Pay to the Order of Joe's Electric, Inc.
$ 75.00
Seventy Five and 00/100
Dollars
YOURBank
Your Bank
Yourtown, USA
1-800-555-1234
For Electrical Inspection
John A. Doe
⑆011101203⑆100000454501⑈ 0250
Memo
Bank tracking number
Account number
Check number
Signature line

ANATOMY OF A PERSONAL CHECK REGISTER

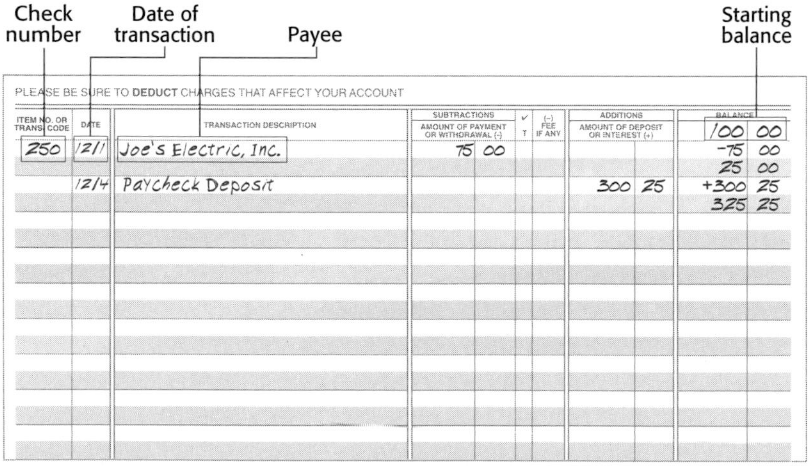
Check number
Date of transaction
Payee
Starting balance
PLEASE BE SURE TO DEDUCT CHARGES THAT AFFECT YOUR ACCOUNT
ITEM NO. OR TRANS. CODE
DATE
TRANSACTION DESCRIPTION
SUBTRACTIONS
AMOUNT OF PAYMENT OR WITHDRAWAL (-)
✓ T
(-) FEE IF ANY
ADDITIONS
AMOUNT OF DEPOSIT OR INTEREST (+)
BALANCE
100 00
250
12/1
Joe's Electric, Inc.
75 00
-75 00
25 00
12/4
Paycheck Deposit
300 25
+300 25
325 25

WHO IS ON OUR COINS?

Coin		Portrait
Cent		Abraham Lincoln
Nickel		Thomas Jefferson
Dime		Franklin D. Roosevelt
Quarter		George Washington
Half Dollar		John F. Kennedy
Dollar		Dwight D. Eisenhower
Dollar		Susan B. Anthony

EXCHANGE RATES FOR SELECTED CURRENCIES, 1998

(how many per $1 U.S.?)

	Country	Currency	Exchange
	Canada	dollar	1.52 = $1
	Germany	deutsche mark	1.72 = $1
	Greece	drachma	294.40 = $1
	Italy	lira	1,699.00 = $1
	Japan	yen	137.00 = $1
	Singapore	dollar	1.74 = $1
	Spain	peseta	146.11 = $1
	United Kingdom	pound	.5998 = $1

Source: *Statistical Abstract of the United States, 1996,* based on data from the Board of Governors of the Federal Reserve System, *Federal Reserve Bulletin,* monthly; *New York Times,* September 1998.

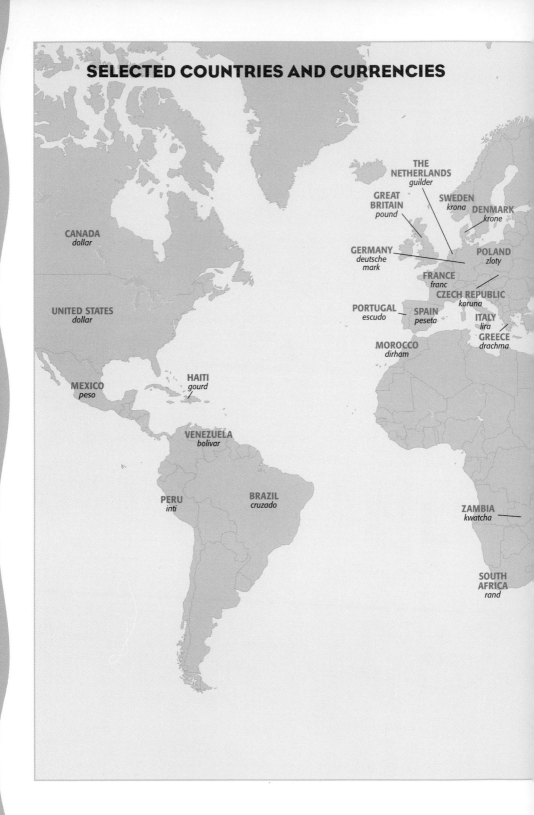

SELECTED COUNTRIES AND CURRENCIES

THE NETHERLANDS
guilder

GREAT BRITAIN
pound

SWEDEN
krona

DENMARK
krone

CANADA
dollar

GERMANY
deutsche mark

POLAND
zloty

FRANCE
franc

CZECH REPUBLIC
koruna

UNITED STATES
dollar

PORTUGAL
escudo

SPAIN
peseta

ITALY
lira

GREECE
drachma

MOROCCO
dirham

MEXICO
peso

HAITI
gourd

VENEZUELA
bolivar

PERU
inti

BRAZIL
cruzado

ZAMBIA
kwatcha

SOUTH AFRICA
rand

RUSSIA
ruble

MONGOLIA
tugrik

JORDAN
dinar

ISRAEL
shekel

CHINA
yuan

SOUTH
KOREA
wan

JAPAN
yen

SAUDI
ARABIA
riyal

INDIA
rupee

LAOS
kip

THAILAND
baht

MALAYSIA
ringgit

AUSTRALIA
dollar

Source: *CIA World Factbook*

CALENDARS AND HOLIDAYS

JUNE

Calendars help people keep track of passing time, note special days, and plan events. They can also show what phase the moon is in or what birthstone is associated with a particular month.

Calendars are based mainly on the movements of Earth and the moon. In the calendar used by most of the world today, a day is the time it takes Earth to spin once on its axis. A year is the time it takes Earth to orbit the sun, or nearly so. There are 365 days in a calendar year, but a full orbit takes a bit longer. To make up the difference, an extra day is added to February every fourth year. Those years are leap years. Holidays and celebrations around the world use this yearly cycle to mark important events and seasons.

Originally, a month was one lunar cycle—the time from one new moon to the next. But the moon runs through its phases in 29 1/2 days. Twelve lunar months would add up to just 354 days, well short of a year. So each calendar month is 28 to 31 days long, bringing the total days in the year to 365.

Our calendar developed from one used by the ancient Romans. The seven-day week came from the ancient Hebrews. Our years are traditionally numbered from the birth of Jesus.

Calendars also mark holidays in certain religions. The Hebrew, Islamic, and Chinese lunar calendars are the most widely used.

Yearbook

2773 B.C. (or earlier) The Egyptians have introduced a 365-day calendar.

circa 1400 B.C. Egyptians begin using a water clock, made from a kind of stone called "alabaster."

46 B.C. Caesar introduces a calendar with three 365-day years, followed by one 366-day year (leap year).

1280 The first mechanical clocks appear in Europe.

1582 Pope Gregory XIII introduces the Gregorian calendar.

1920s and 1930s The quartz crystal clock replaces the pendulum clock.

• Notables •

Julius Caesar (100 B.C.–44 B.C.) Roman general; introduced the idea of leap year.

Christoph Clavius (1537–1612) German astronomer and mathematician; made major changes in the Julian (Julius Caesar's) calendar so religious holidays would always occur during the same season each year.

Denys le Petit (?–540) French; proposed dating each year according to the number of years it came before or after the birth of Jesus.

Hipparchus (flourished 146–127 B.C.) Greek astronomer; first to observe that the solar year is 365 1/4 days long.

St. Nicholas (?–A.D. 342) Turkish bishop; his generous spirit and love for children made him a symbol of Christmas.

Eli Terry (1772–1852) American manufacturer; perfected clocks with wooden moving parts.

KEY IDEAS

B.C. Before the birth of Christ. The year 300 B.C. occurred 300 years before the birth of Jesus.

A.D. *Anno Domini*, Latin for "in the year of Lord." It refers to the year Jesus was born. A.D. 100 is 100 years after Jesus's birth.

equinox The first day of spring and the first day of fall, when the sun is directly above Earth's equator.

Gregorian calendar The secular calendar in use throughout the world.

leap year A year that has 366 days instead of 365. Every four years, February has 29 days.

lunar calendar The earliest calendar, based on the time between one new moon and the next.

solar calendar A calendar based on the time it takes Earth to orbit around the sun.

solstice The first day of summer and the first day of winter.

CHINESE YEARS, 1900–2007

Rat	Ox	Tiger	Hare (Rabbit)	Dragon	Snake
1900	1901	1902	1903	1904	1905
1912	1913	1914	1915	1916	1917
1924	1925	1926	1927	1928	1929
1936	1937	1938	1939	1940	1941
1948	1949	1950	1951	1952	1953
1960	1961	1962	1963	1964	1965
1972	1973	1974	1975	1976	1977
1984	1985	1986	1987	1988	1989
1996	1997	1998	1999	2000	2001

Horse	Sheep (Goat)	Monkey	Rooster	Dog	Pig
1906	1907	1908	1909	1910	1911
1918	1919	1920	1921	1922	1923
1930	1931	1932	1933	1934	1935
1942	1943	1944	1945	1946	1947
1954	1955	1956	1957	1958	1959
1966	1967	1968	1969	1970	1971
1978	1979	1980	1981	1982	1983
1990	1991	1992	1993	1994	1995
2002	2003	2004	2005	2006	2007

MONTHS OF THE YEAR

Gregorian	Hebrew	Hindu	Muslim
January	Shebat	Magha	Muharram
February	Adar	Phalguna	Safar
March	Nisan	Caitra	Rabi I
April	Iyar	Vaisakha	Rabi II
May	Sivan	Jyaistha	Jumada I
June	Tammuz	Asadha	Jumada II
July	Ab	Sravana	Rajab
August	Elul	Bhadrapada	Sha'ban
September	Tishri	Asvina	Ramadan
October	Heshvan	Karttika	Shawwal
November	Kislev	Margasiva	Dhu'l-Qa'dah
December	Tebet	Pansa	Dhu'l-Hijja

BIRTHSTONES

Month	Stone	Color
January	garnet	*deep red*
February	amethyst	*light purple*
March	aquamarine	*light blue*
April	diamond	*colorless*
May	emerald	*green*
June	pearl	*white*
July	ruby	*red*
August	peridot	*light greenish-yellow*
September	sapphire	*dark blue*
October	opal	*iridescent*
November	topaz	*brownish-yellow*
December	turquoise	*blue-green*

PERIODS OF TIME

annual	yearly
biannual	twice a year (at unequally spaced intervals)
bicentennial	marking a period of 200 years
biennial	marking a period of two years
bimonthly	every two months; twice a month
biweekly	every two weeks; twice a week
centennial	marking a period of 100 years
decennial	marking a period 10 years
diurnal	daily; of a day
duodecennial	marking a period of 12 years
millennial	marking a period of 1,000 years
novennial	marking a period of nine years
octennial	marking a period of eight years
perennial	occurring year after year
quadrennial	marking a period of four years
quadricentennial	marking a period of 400 years
quincentennial	marking a period of 500 years
quindecennial	marking a period of 15 years
quinquennial	marking a period of five years
semiannual	every six months (at equally spaced intervals)
semicentennial	marking a period of 50 years
semidiurnal	twice a day
semiweekly	twice a week
septennial	marking a period of seven years
sesquicentennial	marking a period of 150 years
sexennial	marking a period of six years
thrice weekly	three times a week
tricennial	marking a period of 30 years
triennial	marking a period of three years
trimonthly	every three months
triweekly	every three weeks; three times a week
undecennial	marking a period of 11 years
vicennial	marking a period of 20 years

WEDDING ANNIVERSARY GIFT CHART

	1st	paper, clocks		13th	lace, textiles, furs
	2nd	cotton, china		14th	ivory, gold jewelry
	3rd	leather, crystal, glass		15th	crystal, watches
	4th	linen (silk), appliances		20th	china, platinum
	5th	wood, silverware		25th	silver, sterling silver
	6th	iron, wood objects		30th	pearl, diamond
	7th	wool (copper), desk sets		35th	coral (jade)
	8th	bronze, linens, lace		40th	ruby
	9th	pottery (china), leather goods		45th	sapphire
	10th	tin, aluminum, diamond		50th	gold
	11th	steel, fashion jewelry		55th	emerald
	12th	silk, pearls, colored gems		60th	diamond

ECLIPSE CALENDAR FOR THE 21ST CENTURY

During the 21st century, Halley's Comet will return (2061–2062), and there will be eight solar eclipses visible in the continental U.S. The first comes after a long gap; the last one to be seen was on Feb. 26, 1979, in the northwestern U.S.

Date	Path of Totality/Full View
Aug. 21, 2017	Oregon to South Carolina
April 8, 2024	Mexico to Texas and up through Maine
Aug. 23, 2044	Montana to North Dakota
Aug. 12, 2045	N. California to Florida
Mar. 30, 2052	Florida to Georgia
May 11, 2078	Louisiana to North Carolina
May 1, 2079	New Jersey to the lower edge of New England
Sept. 14, 2099	North Dakota to Virginia

KIDS' CALENDAR

	American Camp Week	February 1
	Read to Your Child Day	February 14
	Once Upon a Time Day	February 24
	Youth Art Month	March 1
	Absolutely Incredible Kids Day	March 19
	International Children's Book Day	April 2
	YMCA Healthy Kids Day	April 11
	Week of the Young Child	April 19
	National Playground Safety Week	April 27
	Spank Out Day USA	April 30
	National Baby Day	May 2
	National Pet Week	May 3
	National Safe Kids Week	May 3
	Read To Me Week	May 4
	National Families Month	May 10
	Girls Incorporated Week	May 10
	National Missing Children's Day	May 25
	Love the Children Day	May 29
	Stepparent's Week	June 1
	National Families Day	June 6
	National Little League Baseball Week	June 8
	Children's Good Manners Month	September 1
	Video Games Day	September 12
	National Kids Day	September 19
	National Communicate With Your Kids Month	October 1
	Universal Children's Week	October 1
	Children's Day	October 5
	National School Celebration	October 9
	National School Lunch Week	October 12
	International Creative Child & Adult Month	November 1
	Children's Goal-Setting Day	November 14
	National Young Readers Day	November 11
	National Children's Book Week	November 16
	Universal Children's Day	November 20

MILLENNIUM CALENDAR OF EVENTS

1999

With the scheduled launch of the space shuttle *Atlantis*, Jan. 14, construction work continues on the International Space Station for the next century. Another 16 space shuttle missions are planned through Nov. 30, 2000.

Mayflower 2000, a full-size reconstruction of the vessel that carried the Pilgrims from England to Plymouth, MA, in 1620, sails from its berth on the Thames River in the spring for a 66-day voyage, with port calls at Southampton, England; New York City; and Provincetown, MA, on Cape Cod.

The Saturn-bound *Cassini* spacecraft makes its planned Earth flyby in Aug. 1999, gaining a speed boost from Earth's gravity. It is scheduled to pass Jupiter in Dec. 2000.

After 150 years under Portuguese sovereignty, Macau becomes a special administrative region of China toward the end of the millennium, on Dec. 20.

The U.S. transfers control over the Panama Canal to Panama, Dec. 31. Worldwide, tens of millions of people gather in thousands of cities to celebrate what, for most people, is the dawn of the new millennium.

2000

Some four million pilgrims are expected to visit Bethlehem, Nazareth, Jerusalem, and other sacred places in Israel and the West Bank for Holy Land 2000, Jan. 1–Dec. 31. Odyssey 2000, a round-the-world bicycle trek, has enlisted about 250 participants to cycle some 20,000 miles across some 54 countries during the same period.

New Zealand hosts the America's Cup 2000 championship yacht races, Feb. 26–Mar. 16. (Challenger eliminations start in 1999.)

The first centennial leap year since 1600 adds a day to the calendar, Feb. 29.

Organizers hope to enlist more than 300 million people to participate in the largest Earth Day ever.

Up to 40 million people are expected to visit Hannover, Germany, June 1–Oct. 31, for the Expo 2000 world's fair.

Participation by more than 30 million people is the goal for the global March for Jesus, June 10, with prayer and worship processions in more than 2,000 cities.

The XXVII Olympiad is held in Sydney, Australia, Sept. 15–Oct. 1. Sydney also hosts "Harbour of Life," an Olympic arts festival.

The U.S. elects its first president of the third millennium, Nov. 7.

New Millennium's Eve, Dec. 31. Most authorities say the third millennium technically begins Jan. 1, 2001.

IMPORTANT DATES IN THE U.S. AND CANADA, 1999-2002

Event	1999	2000	2001	2002
New Year's Day[1]	Jan. 1	Jan. 1	Jan. 1	Jan. 1
Martin Luther King, Jr., Day[1]	Jan. 18	Jan. 16	Jan. 15	Jan. 14
Groundhog Day	Feb. 2	Feb. 2	Feb. 2	Feb. 2
St. Valentine's Day	Feb. 14	Feb. 14	Feb. 14	Feb. 14
Susan B. Anthony Day	Feb. 15	Feb. 15	Feb. 15	Feb. 15
Presidents' Day[1]	Feb. 15	Feb. 20	Feb. 19	Feb. 18
Mardi Gras	Feb. 16	Mar. 7	Feb. 27	Feb. 12
St. Patrick's Day	Mar. 17	Mar. 17	Mar. 17	Mar. 17
April Fool's Day	Apr. 1	Apr. 1	Apr. 1	Apr. 1
Daylight saving time begins	Apr. 4	Apr. 2	Apr. 1	Apr. 7
Arbor Day	Apr. 30	Apr. 28	Apr. 27	Apr. 26
National Teacher Day	May 4	May 9	May 8	May 7
Mother's Day	May 9	May 14	May 13	May 12
Armed Forces Day	May 15	May 20	May 19	May 18
Victoria Day[2]	May 24	May 22	May 21	May 20
National Maritime Day	May 22	May 22	May 22	May 22
Memorial Day[1]	May 31	May 29	May 28	May 27
Flag Day	June 14	June 14	June 14	June 14
Father's Day	June 20	June 18	June 17	June 16
Canada Day[2]	July 1	July 1	July 1	July 1
Independence Day[1]	July 4	July 4	July 4	July 4
Labor Day[1,2]	Sept. 6	Sept. 4	Sept. 3	Sept. 2
Citizenship Day	Sept. 17	Sept. 17	Sept. 17	Sept. 17
Columbus Day[1]	Oct. 11	Oct. 9	Oct. 8	Oct. 14
Thanksgiving Day (Canada)[2]	Oct. 11	Oct. 9	Oct. 8	Oct. 14
United Nations Day	Oct. 24	Oct. 24	Oct. 24	Oct. 24
Daylight saving time ends	Oct. 31	Oct. 29	Oct. 28	Oct. 27
Halloween	Oct. 31	Oct. 31	Oct. 31	Oct. 31
Election Day (U.S.)	Nov. 2	Nov. 7	Nov. 6	Nov. 5
Veterans' Day[1,3]	Nov. 11	Nov. 11	Nov. 11	Nov. 11
Remembrance Day[2]	Nov. 11	Nov. 11	Nov. 11	Nov. 11
Thanksgiving Day (U.S.)[1]	Nov. 25	Nov. 23	Nov. 29	Nov. 28
Christmas Day[1,2]	Dec. 25	Dec. 25	Dec. 25	Dec. 25
Boxing Day[2]	Dec. 26	Dec. 26	Dec. 26	Dec. 26
New Year's Eve	Dec. 31	Dec. 31	Dec. 31	Dec. 31

1. Federal holiday in U.S.   2. Federal holiday in Canada.
3. Also known as Armistice Day.

CALENDAR OF COMETS, 1999–2092

Every 1–10 years
Every 11–20 years
More than 21 years

Name	Discovered	Last Appearance	Next Appearance	Period (in years)
Arend	1951	1991	1999	7.99
Ashbrook-Jackson	1948	1993	2001	7.49
Borrelly	1904	1994	2001	6.88
Brooks 2	1889	1994	2001	6.89
Bus	1981	1994	2000	6.52
Clark	1973	1995	2000	5.50
Comas Solá	1926	1996	2005	8.83
Daniel	1909	1992	2000	7.06
d'Arrest	1851	1995	2002	6.39
du Toit	1944	1974	2004	15.00
Faye	1843	1991	1999	7.34
Finlay	1886	1995	2002	6.95
Forbes	1929	1993	1999	6.13
Gehrels 1	1972	1987	2002	15.10
Gehrels 3	1975	1993	2001	8.11
Giclas	1978	1992	1999	6.96
Gunn	1970	1989	1996	6.83
Halley	240 B.C.	1986	2061	76.00
Harrington	1953	1994	2001	6.78
Harrington-Abell	1955	1991	1999	7.59
Herschel-Rigollet	1788	1939	2092	155.00
Holmes	1892	1993	2000	7.09
Honda-Mrkós-Pajdusáková	1948	1995	2001	5.30
Jackson-Neujmin	1936	1995	2004	8.24
Kearns-Kwee	1963	1990	1999	8.96
Kohoutek	1975	1994	2001	6.65
Kopff	1906	1996	2002	6.45
Kowal 1	1977	1992	2007	15.02
Machholz 1	1986	1996	2001	5.24
Neujmin 1	1913	1984	2002	18.21
Neujmin 3	1929	1993	2004	10.63
Olbers	1815	1956	2024	69.56
Pons-Brooks	1812	1954	2024	70.92
Reinmuth 1	1928	1995	2002	7.31
Reinmuth 2	1947	1994	2001	6.64
Russell 2	1980	1994	2002	7.38
Sanguin	1977	1990	2002	12.50
Schaumasse	1911	1993	2001	8.22
Schwassmann-Wachmann 1	1927	1989	2004	14.85
Schwassmann-Wachmann 2	1929	1994	2002	6.39
Schwassmann-Wachmann 3	1930	1995	2001	5.34
Shajn-Schaldach	1949	1993	2001	7.49
Slaughter-Burnham	1958	1993	2005	11.59
Smirnova-Chernukh	1975	1992	2001	8.57
Swift-Gehrels	1889	1991	2000	9.21
Tempel 1	1867	1994	2000	5.50
Tempel 2	1873	1994	1999	5.48
Tsuchinshan 2	1965	1992	1999	6.82
Tuttle	1790	1994	2008	13.51
Tuttle-Giacobini-Kresák	1858	1995	2001	5.46
Väisälä 1	1939	1993	2004	10.80
West-Kohoutek-Ikemura	1975	1993	2000	6.41
Whipple	1933	1994	2003	8.53
Wild 1	1960	1973	1999	13.30
Wild 3	1980	1994	2001	6.91
Wolf	1884	1992	2000	8.25

MAJOR WORLD HOLIDAYS

January 1 New Year's Day throughout the Western world and in India, Indonesia, Japan, Korea, the Philippines, Singapore, Taiwan, and Thailand; founding of Republic of China (Taiwan)

January 2 Berchtoldstag in Switzerland

January 3 Genshi-Sai (First Beginning) in Japan

January 5 Twelfth Night (Wassail Eve or Eve of Epiphany) in England

January 6 Epiphany, observed by Catholics throughout Europe and Latin America

mid-January Martin Luther King, Jr.'s, Birthday on the third Monday in the Virgin Islands

January 15 Adults' Day in Japan

January 20 St. Agnes Eve in Great Britain

January 24 Australia Day in Australia

January 26 Republic Day in India

January–February Chinese New Year and Vietnamese New Year (Tet)

February Hamstrom on the first Sunday in Switzerland

February 3 Setsubun (Bean-throwing Festival) in Japan

February 5 Promulgation of the Constitution Day in Mexico

February 11 National Foundation Day in Japan

February 27 Independence Day in the Dominican Republic

March 1 Independence Movement Day in Korea; Constitution Day in Panama

March 8 Women's Day in many socialist countries

March 17 St. Patrick's Day in Ireland and Northern Ireland

March 19 St. Joseph's Day in Colombia, Costa Rica, Italy, and Spain

March 21 Benito Juarez's Birthday in Mexico

March 22 Arab League Day in Arab League countries

March 23 Pakistan Day in Pakistan

March 25 Independence Day in Greece; Lady Day (Quarter Day) in Great Britain

March 26 Fiesta del Arbol (Arbor Day) in Spain

March 29 Youth and Martyr's Day in Taiwan

March 30 Muslim New Year in Indonesia

March–April Carnival/Lent/Easter; The pre-Lenten celebration of Carnival (Mardi Gras) and the post-Lenten celebration of Easter are moveable feasts widely observed in Christian countries

April 1 Victory Day in Spain; April Fools' Day (All Fools' Day) in Great Britain

April 5 Arbor Day in Korea

April 6 Van Riebeeck Day in South Africa

April 7 World Health Day in UN member nations

April 8 Buddha's Birthday in Korea and Japan; Hana Matsuri (Flower Festival) in Japan

April 14 Pan American Day in the Americas

April 19 Declaration of Independence Day in Venezuela

April 22 Queen Isabella Day in Spain

April 23 St. George's Day in England

April 25 Liberation Day in Italy; ANZAC Day in Australia and New Zealand

April 29 Emperor's Day in Japan

April 30 Queen's Birthday in the Netherlands; Walpurgis Night in Germany and Scandinavia

May Constitution Day on first Monday in Japan

May 1 May Day–Labor Day in Russia and most of Europe and Latin America

May 5 Children's Day in Japan and Korea; Victory of General Zaragoza Day in Mexico; Liberation Day in the Netherlands

May 8 V-E Day in Europe

May 9 Victory over Fascism Day in Russia

May 19 Victory Day in Canada

May 31 Republic Day in South Africa

June 2 Founding of the Republic Day in Italy

June 5 Constitution Day in Denmark

June 6 Memorial Day in Korea; Flag Day in Sweden

June 8 Muhammad's Birthday in Indonesia

June 10 Portugal Day in Portugal

June 12 Independence Day in the Philippines

mid-June Queen's Official Birthday on second Saturday in Great Britain

June 16 Soweto Day in UN member nations

June 17 German Unity Day in Germany

June 20 Flag Day in Argentina

June 22 Midsummer's Day in Finland

June 24 Midsummer's Day in Great Britain

June 29 Feasts of Saints Peter and Paul in Chile, Colombia, Italy, Peru, Spain, and Venezuela

July 1 Canada Day in Canada; Half-year Holiday in Hong Kong; Bank Holiday in Taiwan

July 5 Independence Day in Venezuela

July 9 Independence Day in Argentina

July 10 Bon (Feast of Fortune) in Japan

July 12 Orangemen's Day in Northern Ireland

July 14 Bastille Day in France

mid-July Feria de San Fermin during second week in Spain

July 17   Constitution Day in Korea
July 18   National Day in Spain
July 20   Independence Day in Colombia
July 21–22   National Holiday in Belgium
July 22   National Liberation Day in Poland
July 24   Simón Bolívar's Birthday in Ecuador and Venezuela
July 25   St. James Day in Spain
July 28–29   Independence Day in Peru

August 1   Lammas Day in England; National Day in Switzerland
August 5   Discovery Day in Trinidad and Tobago
August   Holiday on first Monday in Fuji, Grenada, Guyana, Hong Kong, Ireland, and Malawi; Independence Day on first Tuesday in Jamaica
August 9   National Day in Singapore
August 10   Independence Day in Ecuador
August 12   Queen's Birthday in Thailand
August 14   Independence Day in Pakistan
August 15   Independence Day in India and Korea; Assumption Day in Catholic countries
August 16   National Restoration Day in the Dominican Republic
August 17   Independence Day in Indonesia
August 31   Independence Day in Trinidad and Tobago

September   Rose of Tralee Festival in Ireland
September 7   Independence Day in Brazil
September 9   Choxo-no-Sekku (Chrysanthemum Day) in Japan
September 14   Battle of San Jacinto Day in Nicaragua
mid-September   Sherry Wine Harvest in Spain
September 15   Independence Day in Costa Rica, Guatemala, and Nicaragua; Respect for the Aged Day in Japan
September 16   Independence Day in Mexico and Papua New Guinea
September 18–19   Independence Day in Chile; St. Gennaro Day in Italy
September 28   Confucius's Birthday in Taiwan

October 1   National Day in People's Republic of China; Armed Forces Day in Korea; National Holiday in Nigeria
October 2   National Day in People's Republic of China; Mahatma Ghandi's Birthday in India
October 3   National Foundation Day in Korea
October 5   Proclamation of the Portuguese Republic Day in Portugal

October 7   Foundation in the German Democratic Republic
October 9   Korean Alphabet Day in Korea

October 10   Kruger Day in South Africa; Founding of the Republic of China in Taiwan
October 12   Columbus Day in Spain and widely throughout Latin America
October 19   Ascension of Muhammad Day in Indonesia
October 20   Revolution Day in Guatemala; Kenyatta Day in Kenya
October 24   United Nations Day in UN member nations
October 26   National Holiday in Austria
October 28   Greek National Day in Greece

November 1   All Saints' Day, observed by Catholics in most countries
November 2   All Souls' Day in Ecuador, El Salvador, Luxembourg, Macao, Mexico (Day of the Dead), San Marino, Uruguay, and Vatican City
November 4   National Unity Day in Italy
November 5   Guy Fawkes Day in Great Britain
November 7–8   October Revolution Day in Russia
November 11   Armistice Day in Belgium, France, French Guiana, and Tahiti; Remembrance Day in Canada
November 12   Sun Yat-sen's Birthday in Taiwan
November 15   Proclamation of the Republic Day in Brazil
November 17   Day of Penance in Federal Republic of Germany
November 19   National Holiday in Monaco
November 20   Anniversary of the Revolution in Mexico
November 23   Kinro-Kansha-No-Hi (Labor Thanksgiving Day) in Japan
November 30   National Heroes' Day in the Philippines

December 5   Discovery by Columbus Day in Haiti; Constitution Day in Russia
December 6   Independence Day in Finland
December 8   Feast of the Immaculate Conception, widely observed in Catholic countries
December 10   Constitution Day in Thailand; Human Rights Day in UN member nations
December 12   Janhuri Day in Kenya; Guadalupe Day in Mexico
mid-December   Nine Days of Posada during third week in Mexico

December 25   Christmas Day, widely observed in all Christian countries
December 26   St. Stephen's Day in Austria, Ireland, Italy, Lichtenstein, San Marino, Switzerland, and Barcelona (Spain); Boxing Day in Canada, Australia, Great Britain, and Northern Ireland
December 26–January 1   Kwanzaa in the United States
December 28   National Day in Nepal

December 31   New Year's Eve throughout the world; Omisoka (Grand Last Day) in Japan; Hogmanay Day in Scotland

MAJOR HOLIDAYS ON THE AMERICAN CALENDAR

JANUARY

New Year's Day (January 1): This holiday has its origins in Roman times, when sacrifices were offered to the god Janus in the wintertime. Janus was a two-faced god who looked back on the past and forward to the future at the same time.

Epiphany (January 6): Celebrated on the twelfth day after Christmas. This holiday is in observance of the manifestation of Jesus as the Son of God. Epiphany originally marked the beginning of the carnival season that preceded Lent.

Martin Luther King, Jr.'s, Birthday (observed on the third Monday in January): Honors the slain civil rights leader who preached nonviolence and led the March on Washington in 1963. Dr. King's most famous speech is entitled "I Have a Dream."

FEBRUARY

Groundhog Day (February 2): According to legend, if a groundhog in Punxatawnie, Pennsylvania, peeks his head out of his burrow and sees his shadow, he'll return to his hole and there will be six more weeks of winter.

Abraham Lincoln's Birthday (February 12): Honors the sixteenth president of the United States, who led the nation through the Civil War (1861–1865) and was then assassinated. This holiday was first formally observed in Washington, D.C., in 1866, when both houses of Congress gathered to pay tribute to the slain president.

Valentine's Day (February 14): This holiday of love originated as a festival for two martyrs from the third century, both named St. Valentine. The holiday's association with romance may have come from an ancient belief that birds mate on this day.

Presidents' Day (second Monday in February): This official government holiday was created in observance of both Washington's and Lincoln's birthdays.

Washington's Birthday (February 22): Honors the first president of the United States, known as the Father of Our Country. This holiday was first observed in America in 1796, a year before Washington left office.

Shrove Tuesday (February 20): Observed on the day before Ash Wednesday. This holiday marks the end of carnival season.

Ash Wednesday (February 21): This is the first day of the Lenten season, which lasts a total of 40 days. This day of penance has been observed by Roman Catholics since before A.D. 1000.

MARCH AND APRIL

St. Patrick's Day (March 17): Honors the patron saint of Ireland. Most often celebrated in the United States with parties and special dinners, the most famous event is the annual St. Patrick's Day parade on Fifth Avenue in New York City.

Palm Sunday (Sunday before Easter): Commemorates the entry of Jesus into Jerusalem.

Good Friday (Friday before Easter): Commemorates the Crucifixion, which is retold during the services.

Passover (March or April): Also called the Feast of Unleavened Bread, this holiday is observed by Jews all over the world. The focus of the holiday is a special feast called a seder, which incorporates foods that commemorate the escape of the Jews from Ancient Egypt.

Easter Sunday (March or April): Commemorates the Resurrection of Jesus Christ; celebrated on the first Sunday after the full moon that occurs on or after March 21. (Easter is usually between March 22 and April 25.)

MAY

Mother's Day (second Sunday in May): First proposed by Anna Jarvis of Philadelphia in 1907, this holiday has become a national time for gathering family and showing appreciation to mothers.

Memorial Day (last Monday in May): Also known as Decoration Day, this legal holiday was created in 1868 by order of General John A. Logan as a day on which the graves of Civil War soldiers would be decorated. Since that time, the day has been set aside to honor all American soldiers who have given their lives for their country.

JUNE

Flag Day (June 14): Set aside to commemorate the adoption of the Stars and Stripes by the Continental Congress on June 14, 1777. It is a legal holiday only in Pennsylvania but is generally acknowleged and observed in many states each year.

Father's Day (third Sunday in June): Honors the role of the father in the American family, as Mother's Day honors the role of the mother.

JULY

Independence Day (July 4): Anniversary of the signing of the Declaration of Independence, July 4, 1776. The holiday has been celebrated nationwide since 1777, the first anniversary of the signing.

SEPTEMBER

Labor Day (first Monday in September): First proposed by Peter J. McGuire in New York, 1882, this holiday was created to honor the labor unions and workers who built the nation.

Rosh Hashanah (September): On the Hebrew calendar, this marks the Jewish New Year. It also begins a 10-day period of penitence that leads to Yom Kippur.

Yom Kippur (September): Also known as the Day of Atonement, this is the most solemn of all Jewish holidays.

OCTOBER

Columbus Day (October 12): Commemorates the "discovery" of the "New World" by Italian explorer Christopher Columbus in 1492. Even though the land was already populated by Native Americans when Columbus arrived, this "discovery" marks the beginning of European influence in America.

United Nations Day (October 24): Marks the founding of the United Nations, which began in its present capacity in 1945 but had already been in operation as the League of Nations.

Halloween (October 31): Also known as All Hallows Eve, this holiday has its origins in ancient Celtic rituals that marked the beginning of winter with bonfires, masquerades, and the telling of ghost stories.

NOVEMBER

Election Day (first Tuesday after the first Monday in November): Since it was declared an official holiday by Congress in 1845, presidential elections have been taking place on this day every four years. Most statewide elections are also held on this day, but election years vary according to state.

Veterans Day (November 11): Originally called Armistice Day, this holiday was created to celebrate the end of World War I in 1918. In June 1954, Congress changed the name of the holiday to Veterans Day and declared that the day would honor all men and women who have served in America's armed forces.

Thanksgiving (fourth Thursday in November): President Lincoln was the first president to proclaim Thanksgiving a national holiday in 1863. Most people believe the tradition of reserving a day of thanks began with an order given by Governor Bradford of Plymouth Colony in New England 1621.

DECEMBER

Hanukkah (usually December): Also known as the Festival of Lights, this Jewish holiday commemorates the repurification of the Temple of Jerusalem in 162. Purification involved the burning of holy oil, and a one-day supply miraculously burned for eight days. Today, on each of the eight nights, an additional candle is added to the menorah, or candelabra.

Christmas (December 25): This day, which celebrates the birth of Jesus, is the most widely celebrated holiday of the Christian year. Customs associated with Christmas are centuries old. The use of mistletoe, for example, comes from the Druids.

Kwanzaa (December 26): This is a spiritual festival for African Americans that celebrates the goodness of life.

CHEMISTRY

A researcher closes in on a cure for a deadly disease. An oil company announces a new fuel that will produce less pollution. You bake a batch of cookies. All these activities have chemistry in common. Chemistry is the science of substances—their composition and properties, and how they interact and change. It underlies almost every other branch of science, and it is part of everyday life.

Ancient Greeks believed that all things were made up of tiny particles called atoms and that substances changed if their atoms were rearranged. But for centuries, people carried these ideas in the wrong direction. Alchemy, which reached a peak in the Middle Ages, was based on the belief that common metals, such as lead, could change into gold—if only the right formula were found.

Alchemists failed to turn lead into gold. But alchemy gave rise to the science of chemistry. In the 1500s and 1600s, scientists focused on the study of materials. In the 1700s, Antoine Lavoisier of France set standards for experiments and helped devise a system for naming chemicals. And in the 1800s, British chemist John Dalton developed a new atomic theory. Elements such as lead and gold, he said, are the most basic substances. Each is formed of unique atoms. The atoms don't change. But they can combine to form compounds.

Today chemistry has many branches within it. These specialties help fight disease, control pollution, increase the supply of food, and improve modern life in countless other ways.

Yearbook

1661 Robert Boyle introduces the modern definition of an element—a chemical that cannot be broken down into another substance. He also explains acids and alkali.

1808–1810 John Dalton sums up his atomic theory in his published work *New System of Chemical Philosophy*.

1869 Dmitry Mendeleyev publishes the first periodic table of elements.

1930s Linus Pauling develops a theory of chemical bonding—the strong electrical force that holds atoms together in molecules and crystals.

• Notables •

Robert Boyle (1627–1691) English; helped establish the science of chemistry.

Paul Crutzen (1933–   ) Dutch chemist; cowinner, 1995 Nobel Prize in Chemistry for research on the ozone layer.

John Dalton (1766–1844) English chemist and physicist; offered the first clear explanation of an atomic theory.

Sir Humphry Davy (1778–1829) English chemist; discovered sodium, potassium, calcium, and other elements.

Michael Faraday (1791–1867) English chemist; discovered the laws of electrolysis.

Antoine Lavoisier (1743–1794) French; regarded as the founder of modern chemistry.

Linus Pauling (1901–1994) American chemist; explained role of electrons in the formation of molecules.

Joseph Priestley (1733–1804) Discovered the gas we now call oxygen.

KEY IDEAS

acid A substance with a sour taste that will react with another substance, called a "base," to form a salt.

alkali A type of base.

atom The smallest particle of an element that can exist by itself or in combination with other atoms.

compound A substance formed by the combination of two or more elements.

electrolyte Any chemical that conducts an electrical current when the chemical is dissolved in water or melted.

electron A small particle that moves around the center, or nucleus, of an atom.

molecule The smallest part of a substance that has all of its qualities. It is made up of one or more atoms.

periodic table A display of all of the chemical elements, which are arranged according to the structure of their atoms.

table A display of all of the chemical elements, which are arranged according to the structure of their atoms.

TIME LINE OF NOTABLE DISCOVERIES IN CHEMISTRY

1627–1691	Robert Boyle, an English chemist, helps found the modern science of chemistry. He studies calcination of metals and develops the standard definition of *element*.
1669	Phosphorus, discovered by Hennig Brand (died c. 1692).
1735	Cobalt, discovered by Georg Brandt (1694–1768).
1735	Platinum, discovered by Antonio de Ulloa (1716–1795).
1751	Nickel, discovered by Baron Axel F. Cronstedt (1722–1765).
1766	English chemist and physicist Henry Cavendish (1731–1810) discovers hydrogen.
1772	Nitrogen, discovered by Daniel Rutherford (1749–1819).
1774	Oxygen is discovered by Joseph Priestley (1733–1804). He calls it "dephlogisticated air." Previous discovery by Karl W. Schleele (1742–1786) is not published until 1777.
1774	Chlorine and manganese, discovered by Karl W. Schleele (1742–1786).
1789	Uranium and zirconium, discovered by Martin H. Klaproth (1743–1817).
1791	Titanium, discovered by William Gregor (1761–1817).
1800	Italian physicist Alessandro Volta (1745–1827) invents first battery, proving that electricity can be generated by chemical action. His "voltaic pile" uses disks of silver and zinc.
1807	Sodium and potassium, discovered by Sir Humphry Davy (1778–1829).
1808	Barium, calcium, strontium, and magnesium, discovered by Sir Humphry Davy.
1808–1810	English chemist John Dalton (1766–1844) publishes his revolutionary atomic theory of matter in his *New System of Chemical Philosophy*. He holds that all elements are made of tiny atoms, each of same weight. His work further confirms Joseph Louis Proust's theory of constant proportions.
1811	Iodine, discovered by Bernard Courtois (1777–1838).
1817	Cadmium, discovered by Friedrich Stromeyer (1776–1835).
1817	Lithium, discovered by Johan A. Arfwedson (1792–1841).
1818	Selenium, discovered by Jöns Jakob Berzelius (1779–1848).
c. 1824	Silicon, discovered by Jöns Jakob Berzelius.
1825	Aluminum, discovered by Hans C. Oersted (1777–1851).
1826	Bromine, discovered by Antoine J. Balard (1802–1876).
1833	British chemist and physicist Michael Faraday (1791–1867) formulates his law of electrolysis.
1868	Helium, discovered by Pierre Janssen (1824–1907) and Joseph N. Lockyer (1836–1920).
1869	Dmitry Mendeleyev (1834–1907) first publishes his periodic table of elements.
1886	Fluorine, discovered by Henri Moissan (1852–1907).
1894	Argon, discovered by John Strutt, Baron Rayleigh (1842–1919), and Sir William Ramsay (1852–1916).
1898	Krypton, neon, and xenon, discovered by Sir William Ramsay (1852–1916) and Morris W. Travers (1872–1961).
1898	Radium and polonium (first element discovered by radiochemical analysis), discovered by Pierre Curie (1859–1906) and Marie Curie (1867–1934).
1900	Radon, discovered by Friedrich E. Dorn (1848–1916).
1931	U.S. chemist Linus Pauling (1901–1994) introduces chemical theory of resonance to explain bonding of atoms in certain molecules, notably benzene.
1940	Plutonium, discovered by Glenn T. Seaborg (b. 1912) et al.
1957	Polypropylene, lightweight plastic, is created.
c. 1964	Simplified technique for synthesizing proteins is introduced by American researcher Bruce Merrifield (b. 1921). It soon is adapted to automatic machines and becomes important in gene synthesis in 1980s.
1970	Human growth hormone is synthesized.
1983	American Chemical Society reports the number of chemicals it has recorded to date has reached six million. Millions of others are believed known but not formally recorded.

THE PERIODIC TABLE OF ELEMENTS

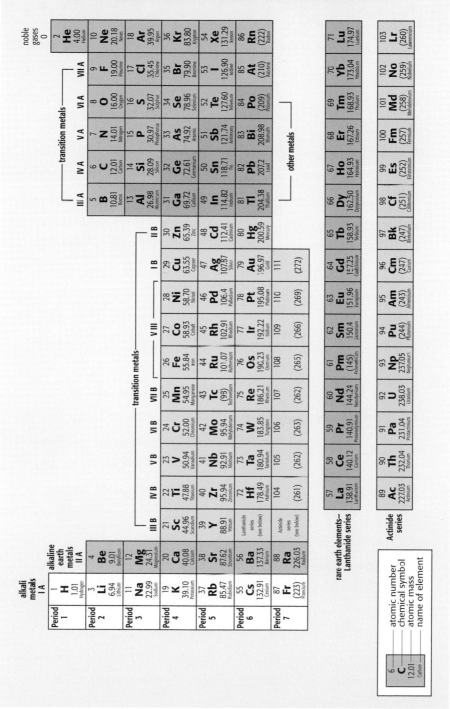

COMMUNICATION

Send a birthday card to your aunt in Kalamazoo. It will be one of more than 170 billion pieces of mail the U.S. Postal Service handles in a year. Call your friend across town. Almost 94 percent of American households have phone service. Today's communication systems make it easy to reach almost anyone, in almost any part of the world, in almost no time.

People have always looked for better ways to send information over long distances. In ancient times, they sent signals with drums, bells, smoke, beacon fires, and sunlight reflected from mirrors. Runners, riders, and pigeons carried messages.

Postal service for ordinary citizens began in England in the 1500s, and the idea came to America with British colonists. In the 1760s, when Benjamin Franklin was postmaster for the colonies, post riders carried mail between New York and Philadelphia—once a week. Mail service expanded with the country. Then, beginning in the mid-1870s, a series of inventions changed communication forever. People could telegraph messages over vast distances in an instant. They could speak to people far away by telephone.

Today communications satellites orbit Earth, relaying information around the world. People use facsimile (fax) machines to send copies of documents over phone lines. They also link computers over those lines. And cellular telephones allow people to call from, or be called at, any location, even their cars. This advanced technology has made communicating with someone in another country as fast and easy as talking to your next-door neighbor!

Yearbook

2900 B.C. Egyptians develop a form of writing now called "hieroglyphic."

A.D. 1250s Communication in Egypt is helped by carrier pigeons.

1440s Gutenberg and Koster invent modern printing with movable type.

1784 The first mail coach in England leaves Bristol for London.

1895 The first motion picture ("movie") is shown in a Paris café.

1960 *Echo*, the first communications satellite, is launched.

1983 The first U.S. cellular telephone system goes into operation.

• Notables •

Alexander Graham Bell (1847–1922) American; credited with inventing the telephone. He established the Bell Telephone Company and the journal *Science*.

Claude Chappe (1763–1805) French engineer; in 1793, introduced a system for transmitting messages by moving signs on the tops of towers, now called semaphores.

Arthur Korn (1870–1945) German physicist; in 1902 developed the first facsimile machine, which was capable of transmitting photographs.

August (1862–1954) and Louis (1864–1948) Lumière French brothers; patented a method for movie projection.

Guglielmo Marconi (1874–1937) Italian; invented radio communication.

Samuel Morse (1791–1872) American; developed a system for transmitting messages through an electric telegraph.

KEY IDEAS

broadcast To transmit sound or images through radio or television.

electromagnet A magnet that appears when an electric current is on and disappears when the current is off.

frequency The number of cycles per second of a radio wave.

microwave An electromagnetic wave that can pass through solid objects. Microwaves are well suited to long-distance communication and are used, for example, to transmit television, telephone, and telegraph signals.

multiplexing The transmission of several telephone conversations over one wire.

radio A way of communicating using electromagnetic waves that are broadcast from a central antenna.

semaphore An apparatus or a system for sending visual signals, such as movable arms or hand-held flags.

POSTAL ABBREVIATIONS FOR STATES AND TERRITORIES

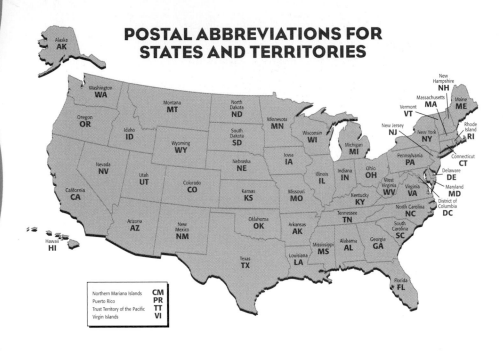

Northern Mariana Islands	**CM**
Puerto Rico	**PR**
Trust Territory of the Pacific	**TT**
Virgin Islands	**VI**

INTERNET DEFINITIONS AND TERMS

Browser — Short for Web browser, it is a program that allows you to search the Internet for information.

Download 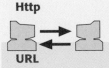 — The transfer of information from the Internet to your computer.

E-mail — Electronic mail that allows you to send and receive messages though the Internet.

Http — Hypertext Transfer Protocol. A set of rules that tells computers how to communicate with one another.

URL — Uniform Resource Locator. The address of each Internet site.

WWW — World Wide Web. The multimedia database of information on the Internet.

TOP 5 MOST LINKED-TO SITES ON THE WORLD WIDE WEB

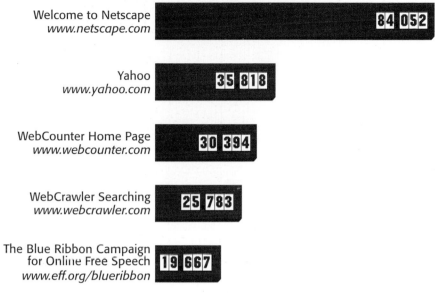

Welcome to Netscape
www.netscape.com
84 052

Yahoo
www.yahoo.com
35 818

WebCounter Home Page
www.webcounter.com
30 394

WebCrawler Searching
www.webcrawler.com
25 783

The Blue Ribbon Campaign
for Online Free Speech
www.eff.org/blueribbon
19 667

Source: WebCrawler (www.webcrawler.com), June 1997

TOP 5 INTERNET SITES BY TYPE

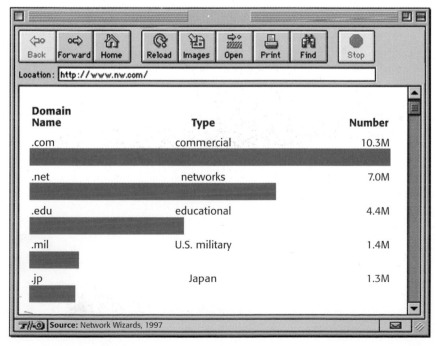

Location: http://www.nw.com/

Domain Name	Type	Number
.com	commercial	10.3M
.net	networks	7.0M
.edu	educational	4.4M
.mil	U.S. military	1.4M
.jp	Japan	1.3M

Source: Network Wizards, 1997

TOP 5 COUNTRIES WITH THE MOST POST OFFICES

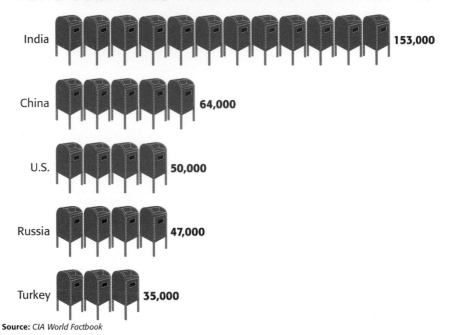

India   153,000

China   64,000

U.S.   50,000

Russia   47,000

Turkey   35,000

Source: *CIA World Factbook*

TOP 5 COUNTRIES WITH THE MOST FAX MACHINES

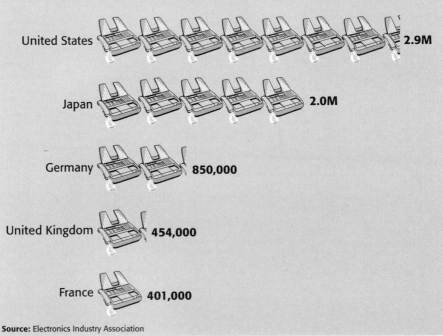

United States   2.9M

Japan   2.0M

Germany   850,000

United Kingdom   454,000

France   401,000

Source: Electronics Industry Association

TOP 5 COUNTRIES WITH THE MOST TELEPHONES

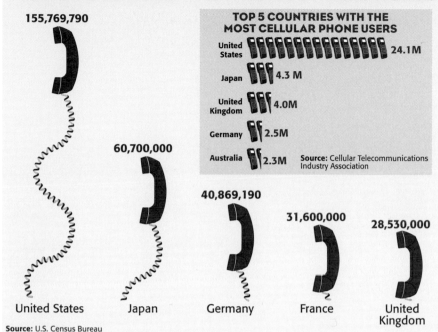

155,769,790

TOP 5 COUNTRIES WITH THE MOST CELLULAR PHONE USERS

United States	24.1M
Japan	4.3 M
United Kingdom	4.0M
Germany	2.5M
Australia	2.3M

Source: Cellular Telecommunications Industry Association

60,700,000

40,869,190

31,600,000

28,530,000

| United States | Japan | Germany | France | United Kingdom |

Source: U.S. Census Bureau

TOP 5 DAILY U.S. NEWSPAPERS
(by circulation)

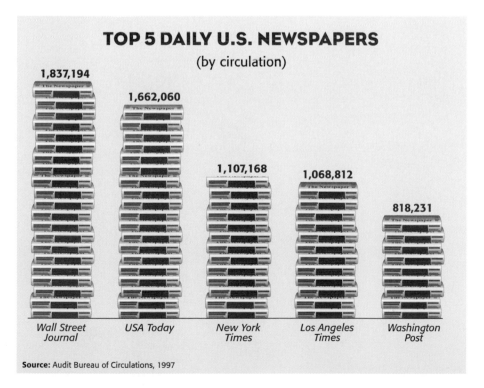

1,837,194

1,662,060

1,107,168

1,068,812

818,231

| Wall Street Journal | USA Today | New York Times | Los Angeles Times | Washington Post |

Source: Audit Bureau of Circulations, 1997

THE TOP-SELLING U.S. KIDS' MAGAZINES, 1996

(based on total paid circulation)

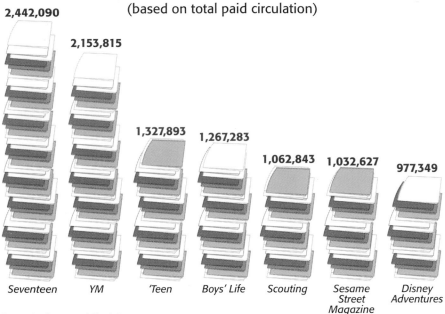

2,442,090

2,153,815

1,327,893

1,267,283

1,062,843

1,032,627

977,349

Seventeen YM 'Teen Boys' Life Scouting Sesame Street Magazine Disney Adventures

Source: Audit Bureau of Circulations, 1997

RADIO FORMATS OF THE WORLD

(as percentage of all listening)

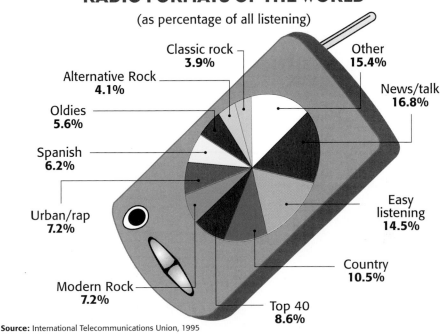

Classic rock
3.9%

Alternative Rock
4.1%

Oldies
5.6%

Spanish
6.2%

Urban/rap
7.2%

Modern Rock
7.2%

Other
15.4%

News/talk
16.8%

Easy listening
14.5%

Country
10.5%

Top 40
8.6%

Source: International Telecommunications Union, 1995

SELECTED HOT LINES AND INFORMATION SERVICES

AIDS hot line	800-342-AIDS
Auto safety hot line	800-424-9393 202-426-0123 in Washington, D.C.
Child abuse hot line	800-4-A-CHILD
College money hot line	800-638-6700 800-492-6602 in Maryland
Drug hot line	800-662-HELP
National Center for Missing and Exploited Children	800-843-5678
Parents Anonymous/Abuse prevention hot line	800-421-0353
Parents who have kidnapped their children hot line	800-A-WAY-OUT
Poison hot line	800-343-2722
Product safety hot line—Consumer Product Safety Commission	800-638-2772
Runaway hot line	800-621-4000 800-972-6004 in Illinois
Shriner's Hospital free children's hospital care referral line	800-237-5055

HOW TO GET IN TOUCH WITH
SELECTED GOVERNMENT AGENCIES

SENATE

Senator's name
United States Senate
Washington, DC 20510

HOUSE OF REPRESENTATIVES

Representative's name
United States Senate
Washington, DC 20510

DEPARTMENT OF AGRICULTURE

14th Street and Independence Avenue SW
Washington, DC 20250
Main number: (202) 720-2791
Web site: http://www.usda.gov/

For information on: **animal and plant health; consumer affairs; family nutrition; food safety and inspection; human nutrition; veterinary medicine.**

DEPARTMENT OF COMMERCE

14th Street and Constitution Avenue NW
Washington, DC 20230
Main number: (202) 482-2000
Reference: (202) 377-2161
Web site: http://www.doc.gov/

For information on: **business outlook analyses; economic and demographic statistics; engineering; imports and exports; minority-owned business; patents and trademarks; technology; travel; weather and atmosphere.**

DEPARTMENT OF DEFENSE

The Pentagon
Washington, DC 20301-1400
Main number: (703) 545-6700
Web site: http://www.dtic.dla.mil/

For information on: **atomic energy; foreign country security; mapping; military history; nuclear operations and technology; tactical warfare.**

DEPARTMENT OF EDUCATION

400 Maryland Avenue SW
Washington, DC 20202
Main office: (202) 401-2000
Web site: http://www.ed.gov/

For information on: **adult education; bilingual education; civil rights; educational statistics; elementary and secondary education; handicapped; higher education; libraries; special education.**

DEPARTMENT OF ENERGY

Forrestal Building
1000 Independence Avenue SW
Washington, DC 20585
Main number: (202) 586-5000
Public affairs: (202) 586-6827
Web site: http://www.doe.gov/

For information on: **coal liquids, gas, shale, oil; conservation; energy emergencies; fusion energy; inventions; nuclear energy; nuclear physics.**

DEPARTMENT OF HEALTH AND HUMAN SERVICES

200 Independence Avenue SW
Washington, DC 20201
Main number: (202) 619-0257
Web site: http://www.os.dhhs.gov/

For information on: **AIDS; alcohol abuse; diseases; drug abuse; drug research, family planning; food safety; minority health; occupational safety; smoking; statistical data; toxic substances; veterinary medicine.**

DEPARTMENT OF THE INTERIOR

18th and C Street NW
Washington, DC 20240
Main number: (202) 208-3100
Web site: http://www.info.usgs.gov/doi

For information on: **archaeology; fish and wildlife; geology; mapping; minerals; Native Americans; natural resources; water.**

DEPARTMENT OF JUSTICE

10th Street and Constitution Avenue NW
Washington, DC 20530
Main number: (202) 633-2000
Public affairs: (202) 633-2007
Web site: http://www.usdoj.gov/

For information on: **civil rights; drug enforcement; immigration; justice statistics; juvenile justice; prisons.**

DEPARTMENT OF TRANSPORTATION

400 7th Street SW
Washington, DC 20590
Main number: (202) 366-4000
Public affairs: (202) 366-4570
Web site: http://www.dot.gov/

For information on: **automobile safety; aviation safety; aviation standards; boating; hazardous materials transportation; highway safety; mass transit; railroad safety; shipbuilding; vehicle accident statistics; vehicle crashworthiness.**

DEPARTMENT OF THE TREASURY

15th Street and Pennsylvania Avenue NW
Washington, DC 20220
Main number: (202) 622-2000
Web site: http://www.ustreas.gov/

For information on: **coin and medal production; currency production; currency research and development; customs; savings bonds; secret service protection; taxpayer assistance; tax return investigation.**

ENVIRONMENTAL PROTECTION AGENCY

401 M Street SW
Washington, DC 20460
Main number: (202) 260-2090
Web site: http://www.epa.gov/

For information on: **air and radiation; pesticides and toxic substances; acid deposition; environmental monitoring and quality assurance; solid waste and emergency response; water; noise control.**

FEDERAL COMMUNICATIONS COMMISSION

1919 M Street NW
Washington, DC 20554
Main number: (202) 418-0200
Web site: http://www.fcc.gov/

For information on: **cable television; broadcast stations; radio regulation.**

NATIONAL AERONAUTICS AND SPACE ADMINISTRATION

600 Independence Avenue SW
Washington, DC 20546
Main number: (202) 358-0000
Web site: http://www.nasa.gov/

For information on: **aeronautics and space technology; life sciences; astrophysics; earth sciences; solar system exploration; space shuttle payload; Mars observer program; microgravity science; upper atmosphere research; solar flares.**

NATIONAL ENDOWMENT FOR THE ARTS

1100 Pennsylvania Avenue NW
Washington, DC 20506
Main number: (202) 682-5400
Web site: http://www.arts.endow.gov/

For information on: **literature; museums; folk arts; visual arts; dance arts; theater; opera; history; language.**

NATIONAL ENDOWMENT FOR THE HUMANITIES

1100 Pennsylvania Avenue NW, Room 406
Washington, DC 20506
Main number: (202) 606-8400
Web site: http://www.neh.fed.us/

For information on: **literature; museums; folk arts; visual arts; dance arts; music arts; theater arts and musical theater; opera; media arts (film, radio, TV); history; language.**

NATIONAL SCIENCE FOUNDATION

1800 G Street NW, Room 527
Washington, DC 20550
Main number: (703) 306-1234
Web site: http://www.nsf.gov/

For information on: **atmospheric/astronomical and earth-ocean sciences; mathematical and physical sciences; arctic and antarctic research; anthropology; engineering; biology; genetic biology; chemistry; computer science; earthquakes; economics; ethics and science; meteorology; galactic and extragalactic astronomy; geography; geology; history and philosophy of science; nutrition; linguistics; marine chemistry; minority research; science and technology to aid the handicapped.**

COMPUTERS

Fifty years ago, computers were huge—big enough to fill a room. Today most computers are small enough to sit on a desk. And they can do much more than early models. They help people find information, compose letters and reports, and keep track of business profits. They track statistics and forecast the weather. They let people visualize things that are too small to see, like molecules, or too distant, like the surface of Mars.

A computer's "brain" is its central processing unit (CPU). The CPU follows a program—a set of coded instructions—to process information in an electronic code. Millions of electronic pulses pass through its circuits, which are etched onto tiny chips of silicon. The computer stores information on magnetic disks and other memory devices. It receives information through input devices (such as a keyboard) and displays it through output devices (such as a monitor).

More than a third of American households have at least one personal computer, more than any other country. With CD-ROM drives, computers can tap into huge amounts of information—even sound and video clips—stored on compact discs. With modems, they can link up via telephone lines, or go "on-line."

Worldwide, some 30 million computers have access to the Internet. Most people use commercial on-line services to reach a section of the Net called the World Wide Web, where information is stored in easily viewed form. They can send messages, research distant libraries, shop, and more in the electronic world called cyberspace.

Yearbook

1623 Wilhelm Schickard, a German professor, builds the first known mechanical calculator.

1943 The American mathematician Howard Aiken builds a 50-foot (15 m) digital computer, which for the first time expresses numbers as digits.

1971 The Intel 4004 chip is completed; the first microprocessor.

1975 The first desktop microcomputer becomes available.

1980 The Microsoft Corporation adapts an operating system for personal computers.

• Notables •

Charles Babbage (1792–1871) English mathematician; regarded as the father of modern computers. Planned an "analytical engine" that was never built. On paper, the engine had in mechanical form most of the basic components found in electronic computers.

George Boole (1815–1864) English mathematician; developed a form of algebra that later provided the basis for planning electric circuits in computers.

William (Bill) Gates III (1955–   ) American; cofounder of the Microsoft Corporation. (See also Business Notables.)

Marcian E. Hoff (1937–   ) American engineer; invented the Intel 4004 chip, introduced in 1971.

Steven Jobs (1955–   ) American computer engineer and cofounder, with Stephen Wozniak, of Apple Computer, Inc., which manufactures the Macintosh computer.

KEY IDEAS

ASCII (American Standard Code for Information Interchange) A system that converts keyboard characters into binary numbers.

binary A numbering system that uses only two digits, 0 and 1.

bit Binary digit, the smallest piece of computer information.

byte A combination of eight bits that represent one character of data.

CD-ROM (Compact disc read-only memory) Uses laser discs and readers connected to a computer.

chip A wafer of silicon containing electric circuits that can store information.

hypertext A system for retrieving and referencing related documents.

RAM (Random access memory) Basic type of memory that can be added to, retrieved from, or altered.

server A computer that shares its resources and information with other computers in a network.

World Wide Web A network of servers that use hypertext-linked databases and files.

COMPUTERS IN USE: U.S. vs. THE WORLD

All others
27%

U.S.
43%

Japan
7%

Europe
23%

Source: Based on data from *Computer Industry Almanac*, 1994

COMPUTERS PER CAPITA: U.S. vs. THE WORLD

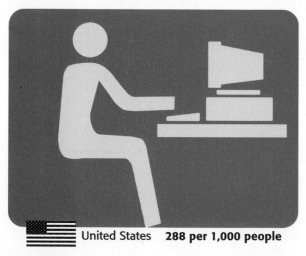

 United States   **288 per 1,000 people**

 Worldwide average   **31 per 1,000 people**

Source: Based on data from *Computer Industry Almanac*, 1994

INTERNET TIME LINE

1969 ARPA (Advanced Research Projects Agency) goes on-line in December. It connects four major U.S. universities. Designed for research, education, and government organizations, it provides a communications network linking the country in the event that a military attack destroys conventional communications systems.

1972 Electronic mail is introduced. Queen Elizabeth sends her first e-mail in 1976.

1973 Transmission Control Protocol/Internet Protocol (TCP/IP) is designed. In 1983 it becomes the standard for communicating between computers over the Internet. One of these protocols, FTP (file transfer protocol), allows users to log onto a remote computer, list the files on that computer, and download files from that computer.

1989 Peter Deutsch at McGill University in Montreal creates the first effort to index the Internet. He devises archie, an archive of FTP sites. Tim Berners-Lee of CERN (European Laboratory for Particle Physics) develops a new technique for distributing information on the Internet, which is eventually called the World Wide Web. The Web is based on hypertext, which permits the user to connect from one document to another at different sites on the Internet via hyperlinks (specially programmed words, phrases, buttons, or graphics). Unlike other Internet protocols, such as FTP and e-mail, the Web is accessible through a graphical user interface.

1991 Gopher, the first user-friendly interface, is created at the University of Miami and named after the school mascot. Gopher becomes the most popular interface for several years.

1993 Mosaic is developed by Marc Andreeson at the National Center for Supercomputing Applications (NCSA). It becomes the dominant navigating system for the World Wide Web, which at this time accounts for merely 1% of all Internet traffic.

1994 U.S. White House launches its own Web page. Initial commerce sites are established and mass marketing campaigns are launched via e-mail, introducing the term "spamming" to the Internet vocabulary.

1996 The number of Internet users grows to approximately 45 million, with roughly 30 million of those in North America (United States and Canada), 9 million in Europe, and 6 million in Asia/Pacific (Australia, Japan, etc.). 43.2 million (44%) of U.S. households own a personal computer, and 14 million of them are on-line.

1997 Approximately 66% of North American computer-owners— 15% of Europe, and 14% of Asia/Pacific—are online.

Sources: International Data Corporation, the W3C Consortium, and the Internet Society

WHO'S ON THE WORLD WIDE WEB, 1996

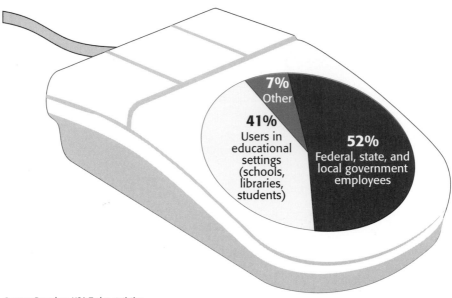

7% Other

41% Users in educational settings (schools, libraries, students)

52% Federal, state, and local government employees

Source: Based on *USA Today* statistics

INTERNET USE GROWS AT THE LIBRARY, 1994–1997

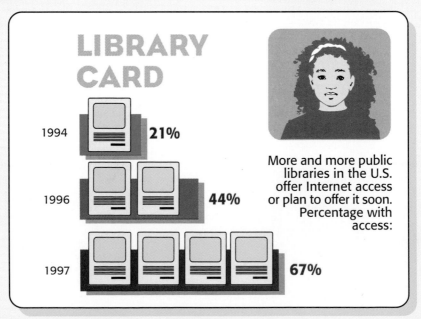

LIBRARY CARD

1994   **21%**

1996   **44%**

1997   **67%**

More and more public libraries in the U.S. offer Internet access or plan to offer it soon. Percentage with access:

Source: American Library Association

U.S. ON-LINE USERS PROFILE

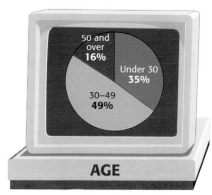

50 and over **16%**

Under 30 **35%**

30–49 **49%**

AGE

How many people over 16 are on-line?

Estimate: **35 million**

How many use PCs?

Estimate: **About 100 million**

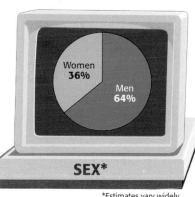

Women **36%**

Men **64%**

SEX*

*Estimates vary widely.

Hispanic **10%**

Asian **2%**

Black **15%**

White **71%**

ETHNICITY

What Users Do

Use Internet **90%**

Use World Wide Web **68%**

Use e-mail **75%**

Use online service **67%**

Average Time Spent On-line per Week

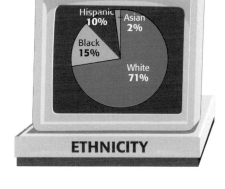

20+ hours **8%**

1 hour or less **20%**

10–19 hours **12%**

2 hours **19%**

5–9 hours **22%**

3–4 hours **19%**

Source: Based on information from the U.S. Census Bureau and *USA Today*, 1997

U.S. NET USERS UNDER 18, 1995 vs. 2000
(projected usage)

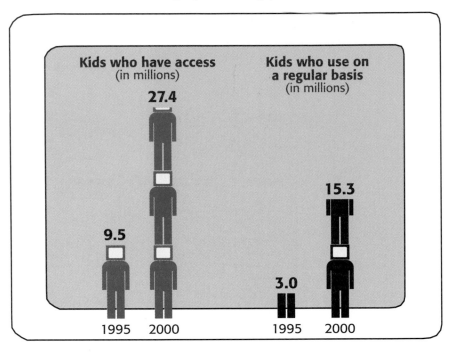

Kids who have access
(in millions)

27.4

9.5

1995   2000

Kids who use on a regular basis
(in millions)

15.3

3.0

1995   2000

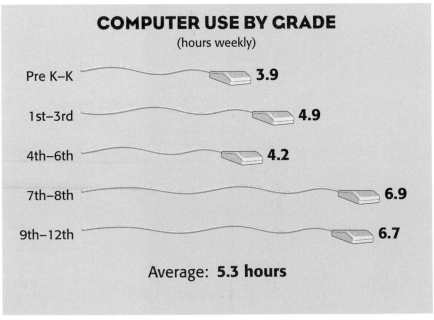

COMPUTER USE BY GRADE
(hours weekly)

Pre K–K	3.9
1st–3rd	4.9
4th–6th	4.2
7th–8th	6.9
9th–12th	6.7

Average: **5.3 hours**

Source: U.S. Census Bureau; Jupiter Communications; Find/SVP American Learning Households Survey

U.S. HOUSEHOLDS WITH COMPUTERS, BY INCOME LEVEL

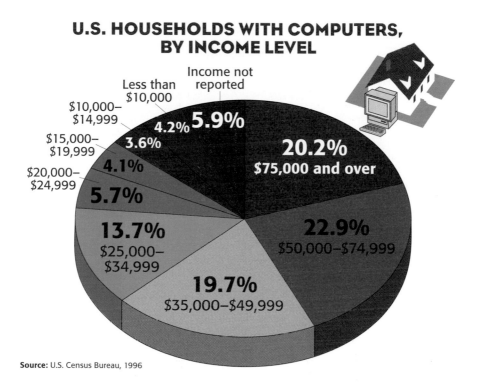

Income not reported **5.9%**

Less than $10,000 **4.2%**

$10,000–$14,999 **3.6%**

$15,000–$19,999 **4.1%**

$20,000–$24,999 **5.7%**

13.7%
$25,000–$34,999

19.7%
$35,000–$49,999

20.2%
$75,000 and over

22.9%
$50,000–$74,999

Source: U.S. Census Bureau, 1996

COMPUTERS IN U.S. HOMES, 1996

Percentage of households with:

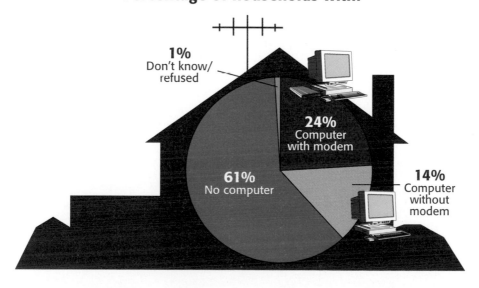

1%
Don't know/ refused

24%
Computer with modem

61%
No computer

14%
Computer without modem

Source: Based on *Statistical Abstract of the United States; USA Today* statistics

TVs, PHONES, AND COMPUTERS IN U.S.

(number in use per 1,000 people)

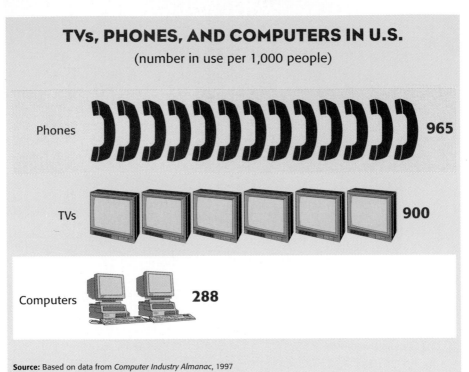

Phones — 965

TVs — 900

Computers — 288

Source: Based on data from *Computer Industry Almanac*, 1997

U.S. COMPUTER USERS, AGES 3 TO 17, BY RACE

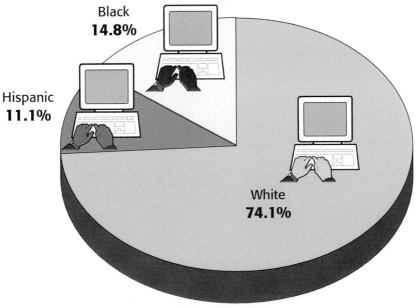

Black
14.8%

Hispanic
11.1%

White
74.1%

Source: U.S. Census Bureau, 1997

PERCENTAGE OF KIDS IN U.S....
(ages 3 to 17)

... With Access to Computers

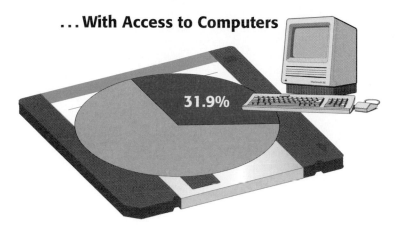

31.9%

... Who Use Computers at Home

74.7%

... Who Use Computers at School

60.6%

Source: U.S. Census Bureau, 1996

U.S. COMPUTER MARKETS AND EXPECTED GROWTH, 1996–2000

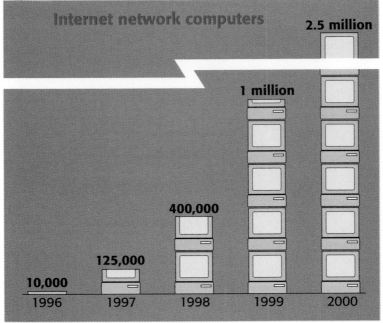

Internet network computers

2.5 million

1 million

400,000

125,000

10,000

| 1996 | 1997 | 1998 | 1999 | 2000 |

Note: Break indicates large jump; part of bar has been omitted.

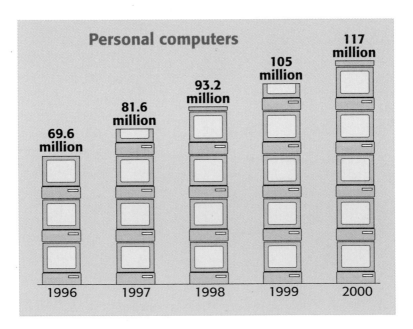

Personal computers

117 million

105 million

93.2 million

81.6 million

69.6 million

| 1996 | 1997 | 1998 | 1999 | 2000 |

Source: Based on statistics from International Data; *USA Today*

CD-ROM MARKET: PROFILE

(average percentage of total units sold annually)

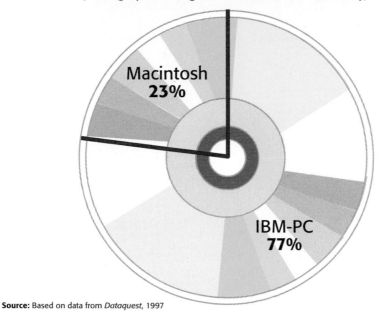

Macintosh
23%

IBM-PC
77%

Source: Based on data from *Dataquest*, 1997

TOP 5 COUNTRIES PROJECTED TO HAVE THE MOST COMPUTERS BY 2000

United States — 160.5M

Japan — 46.8M

Germany — 29.8M

United Kingdom — 26.0M

France — 21.0M

Source: Based on data from the Computer Industry Almanac Inc.

Note: M=million

EARTH SCIENCE

Earth science is the study of the planet Earth—and the ways in which it has changed since it formed more than 4.5 billion years ago. Earth science is actually many separate sciences, including, among others, oceanography (the study of oceans), meteorology (the study of weather and the atmosphere), and volcanology (the study of volcanoes). Two of the largest branches of Earth science are geology and paleontology.

Geology is concerned with how Earth's features formed and changed over time. Earth's interior is so hot that the rock in its outer core is liquid. This intense heat creates powerful forces that move continents, push up mountain ranges, create volcanoes, and cause earthquakes. At the surface, wind and water erode (wear away) land. Fine particles of rock are washed away and deposited as sediment in other areas. By studying layers of sediment, types of rock, and their locations, geologists can "read" the history of a place.

Paleontology examines the history of life on Earth, especially as that history is recorded in fossils and other geologic evidence. Fossils are traces of ancient living things that have been preserved in rock. Each fossil can potentially tell paleontologists a story about how life evolved on Earth. Paleontologists are a lot like detectives, reading fossil clues. Through fossils, these scientists have charted the development of life from tiny one-celled organisms to giant dinosaurs and the ancestors of modern humans.

See Environment, Geography, Life Science, and Weather for information on related subjects.

Yearbook

circa 300 B.C. The Greek philosopher Theophrastus makes the first written study of rocks and minerals.

1895 The development of X rays enables scientists to study the internal structures of minerals for the first time.

1968 American earth scientists develop the theory of plate tectonics, the theory that Earth's outer shell is made up of rigid plates that are in constant motion.

1980 A thin layer of clay is discovered around the world dating from the age of the dinosaurs. In 1997, scientists find evidence that an asteroid crashed on Earth around the time of the last dinosaurs.

• Notables •

Louis Agassiz (1807–1873) American naturalist; developed the theory that glaciers once covered much of Europe and changed the surface of the land.

Eratosthenes (circa 276–194 B.C.) Greek mathematician; calculated the tilt of Earth's axis and the size of its circumference.

Matthew Maury (1806–1873) American naval officer; first person to make a systematic study of the ocean floor.

Pytheas (dates unknown) Greek explorer; about 330 B.C., identified the moon as the cause of tides in the oceans.

Charles Richter (1900–1985) American seismologist; developed the Richter scale to measure the strength of earthquakes.

Nicolaus Steno (1638–1686) Danish physician; showed that different layers of rock have been deposited according to their age, with the oldest rock layers on the bottom.

KEY IDEAS

continental drift The formation of Earth's continents from one large landmass that gradually broke apart.

era In geology, a span of time composed of shorter periods. For example, the Paleozoic Era includes six periods of geologic time.

mineral A substance found in nature that is neither animal nor plant. Examples are gold, salt, and sulfur.

sea vent A place that is deep below the surface of the ocean, where very hot water and minerals shoot out of Earth's crust, attracting unusual forms of sea life, such as one-foot-wide clams.

sediment In geology, rocks, sand, or dirt that has been deposited by water, wind, or a glacier.

sedimentary rock Rock that has been formed by layers of sediment in the ground that were pressed together.

seismologist A scientist who studies earthquakes.

tsunami A large, destructive wave caused by an underwater earthquake or volcano.

LAYERS OF THE EARTH

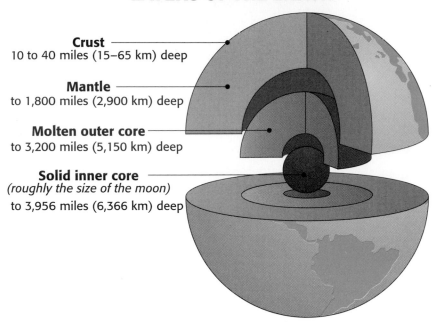

Crust
10 to 40 miles (15–65 km) deep

Mantle
to 1,800 miles (2,900 km) deep

Molten outer core
to 3,200 miles (5,150 km) deep

Solid inner core
(roughly the size of the moon)
to 3,956 miles (6,366 km) deep

WHAT'S IN THE EARTH'S CRUST?

The earth's crust is the outermost solid layer of the planet. Under the continents, the crust varies from 19 to 37 miles (30 to 60 km) in thickness. Under the oceans it is generally much thinner, only 3 to 5 miles (5 to 8 km) thick. Continental crust is made up of granite and other relatively light rocks, while oceanic crust is made up chiefly of basalt. The crust that is accessible to accurate scientific measurements contains the following principal elements:

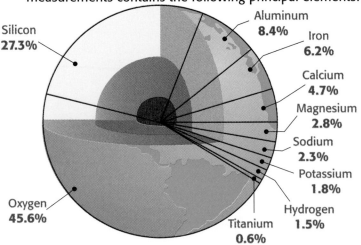

Silicon
27.3%

Aluminum
8.4%

Iron
6.2%

Calcium
4.7%

Magnesium
2.8%

Sodium
2.3%

Potassium
1.8%

Hydrogen **1.5%**

Titanium
0.6%

Oxygen
45.6%

THE GEOLOGIC TIME SCALE

BYA = Billion years ago   MYA = Million years ago

PRECAMBRIAN ERA 4.6 BYA–545 MYA		Few life-forms, limited to oceans; bacteria and algae; possibly sponges, corals, jellyfish
PALEOZOIC ERA 545–251 MYA	Cambrian Period 545–505 MYA	First shell-bearing marine invertebrates; plant life is algae; no known land life
	Ordovician Period 505–440 MYA	Many sea invertebrates; microscopic animals, mollusks, urchinlike creatures; first known vertebrates (armored jawless fish)
	Silurian Period 440–410 MYA	Most animal forms still invertebrates; large, scorpion-like arthropods, coral reefs; primitive fish in streams; first true land plants; first true land animals resembling scorpions and millipedes
	Devonian Period 410–360 MYA	Many fish, including sharks, lungfish, and bony fish; appearance of first true land vertebrates (amphibians); rise of trees similar to present-day ferns, horsetails, and club mosses; first seed plants
	Mississippian Period 360–320 MYA	Amphibians and possibly first reptiles; large sharks; swamps with forests on land, spore-producing trees
	Pennsylvanian Period 320–290 MYA	First true reptiles; many amphibians; appearance of first true insects (huge cockroaches and dragonflies); land covered by swamps and dense forests of mosses, ferns, rushes, horsetails, and early cone-bearing trees
	Permian Period 290–251 MYA	Many land animals, freshwater fish; mammal-like reptiles; insects; spread of cone-bearing trees
MESOZOIC ERA 251–65 MYA	Triassic Period 251–205 MYA	Age of reptiles begins; early dinosaurs, large amphibians
	Jurassic Period 205–145 MYA	Many kinds of dinosaurs; flying "dragons," "sea serpents," and giant lizards; first true mammals; first birds; appearance of frogs and toads; first flowering plants
	Cretaceous Period 145–65 MYA	Dominance of dinosaurs and reptiles on land; first snakes; large marine invertebrates; by end, total extinction of most typical mesozoic life-forms, including dinosaurs
CENOZOIC ERA 65 MYA–Present	Tertiary Period 65 MYA–1.6 MYA	Rise and dominance of advanced mammals; rise of primates and human ancestors; giant toothless birds resembling ostriches and emus
	Quaternary Period 1.6 MYA–present	Appearance of modern life-forms; extinction of many earlier life forms (mammoths, wooly rhinoceroses, and mastodons); rise of humans

THE STRUCTURE OF THE ATMOSPHERE

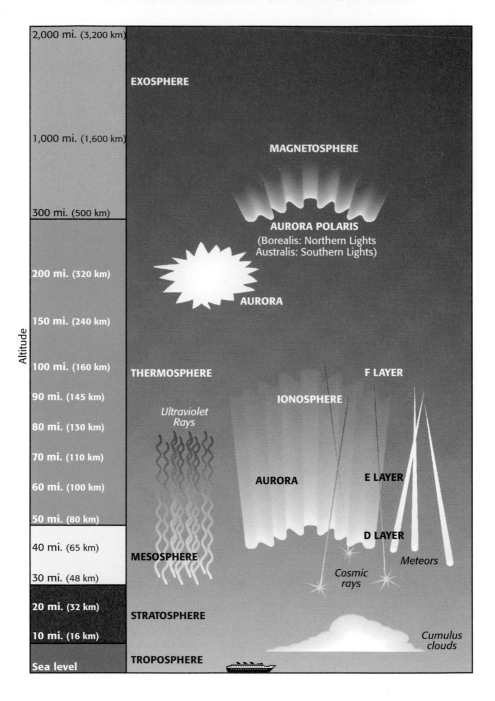

Altitude

2,000 mi. (3,200 km)

EXOSPHERE

1,000 mi. (1,600 km)

MAGNETOSPHERE

300 mi. (500 km)

AURORA POLARIS
(Borealis: Northern Lights
Australis: Southern Lights)

200 mi. (320 km)

AURORA

150 mi. (240 km)

100 mi. (160 km)

THERMOSPHERE

F LAYER

90 mi. (145 km)

IONOSPHERE

80 mi. (130 km)

Ultraviolet
Rays

70 mi. (110 km)

60 mi. (100 km)

AURORA

E LAYER

50 mi. (80 km)

40 mi. (65 km)

MESOSPHERE

D LAYER

Meteors

30 mi. (48 km)

Cosmic
rays

20 mi. (32 km)

STRATOSPHERE

10 mi. (16 km)

Cumulus
clouds

Sea level

TROPOSPHERE

TOP 10 MOST DEADLY EARTHQUAKES, 526–1999
(by number of resulting deaths)

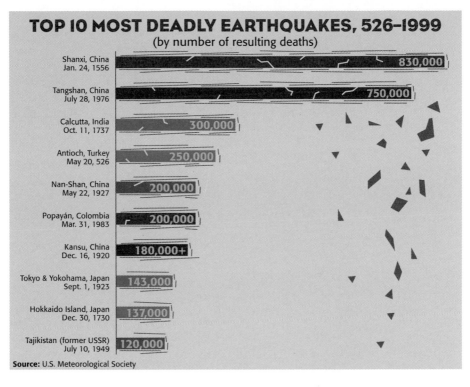

Location	Date	Deaths
Shanxi, China	Jan. 24, 1556	830,000
Tangshan, China	July 28, 1976	750,000
Calcutta, India	Oct. 11, 1737	300,000
Antioch, Turkey	May 20, 526	250,000
Nan-Shan, China	May 22, 1927	200,000
Popayán, Colombia	Mar. 31, 1983	200,000
Kansu, China	Dec. 16, 1920	180,000+
Tokyo & Yokohama, Japan	Sept. 1, 1923	143,000
Hokkaido Island, Japan	Dec. 30, 1730	137,000
Tajikistan (former USSR)	July 10, 1949	120,000

Source: U.S. Meteorological Society

TOP 10 MOST DEADLY VOLCANOES
(by number of resulting deaths)

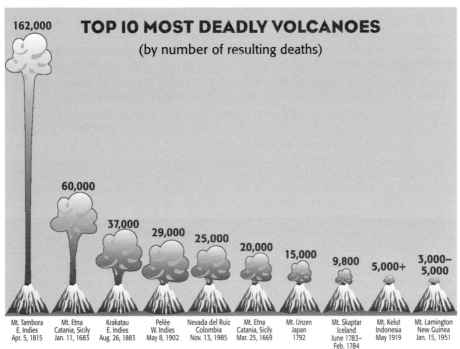

Volcano	Location	Date	Deaths
Mt. Tambora	E. Indies	Apr. 5, 1815	162,000
Mt. Etna	Catania, Sicily	Jan. 11, 1683	60,000
Krakatau	E. Indies	Aug. 26, 1883	37,000
Pelée	W. Indies	May 8, 1902	29,000
Nevada del Ruiz	Colombia	Nov. 13, 1985	25,000
Mt. Etna	Catania, Sicily	Mar. 25, 1669	20,000
Mt. Unzen	Japan	1792	15,000
Mt. Skaptar	Iceland	June 1783–Feb. 1784	9,800
Mt. Kelut	Indonesia	May 1919	5,000+
Mt. Lamington	New Guinea	Jan. 15, 1951	3,000–5,000

Source: U.S. Meteorological Society

EDUCATION

If you're like most young people, school is a major part of your life. Your goals for the future probably depend on getting the best education you can. But in another time and place, you might never have had a chance to go to school.

For much of history, formal education was for the upper classes. Children of average families often had only a few years of schooling. The idea of education for everyone didn't take hold until the 1700s.

Today most American children start school with preschool or kindergarten. They move up a sort of educational ladder, through elementary school, middle school, and high school. Four out of five finish high school, and many continue with vocational or college studies. Some go on from college to graduate school. Education is lifelong for many adults, who continue to take evening courses.

The great majority of U.S. schools are public schools. They are funded by taxes, and students attend them for free.

About 10 percent of U.S. students go to private elementary or secondary schools. They pay tuition to attend. Although their programs differ, public and private schools teach the same core subjects—language arts, mathematics, social studies, science. School sports, clubs, and activities give students a chance for other kinds of learning, and some fun.

A third option is home schooling, with parents or tutors as teachers. Home schooling is growing in popularity. But home school students are still a small fraction of the more than 50 million elementary and secondary students in the United States.

Yearbook

circa 100 B.C. Romans develop a large educational system for children.

1500 Primary schools open in Europe.

1647 A Massachusetts law requires that every town of 50 families or more must hire a schoolteacher.

1745 Pennsylvania Quakers found the first elementary school for African-American children.

1837 Mount Holyoke, the first permanent college for women in the United States, is established.

1954 The U.S. Supreme Court declares it illegal to have separate schools based on race.

• Notables •

John Dewey (1859–1952) American educator; leader of the progressive education movement in the United States at the turn of the century.

Thomas Jefferson (1743–1826) Third U.S. president; proposed the first modern state school system with free tuition; all children could attend except for slaves.

Horace Mann (1796–1859) American teacher; considered the father of American public education; encouraged the growth of local public elementary schools.

Maria Montessori (1870–1952) Italian physician and educator; opened first Montessori school in Rome, 1907.

Jean Piaget (1896–1980) Swiss psychologist; investigated the way children think and learn; published groundbreaking studies on child development.

KEY IDEAS

curriculum The learning opportunities provided by a school.

desegregation The elimination of racial segregation, or separation, in schools.

elementary school A school that includes at least the first four, and sometimes eight grades, and often kindergarten.

multiculturalism In education, the inclusion of many cultures in a school's curriculum.

SAT (Scholastic Aptitude Test) A standardized test that is given to high school students who intend to go to college. The test scores, which measure reading and mathematical abilities, help college admissions officers decide whom to admit.

secondary school A school that includes ninth through twelfth grades and sometimes fifth through eighth grades (or a similar range) as well.

PROFILE: U.S. SCHOOL ENROLLMENT BY GRADE, 1999*

(public and private)

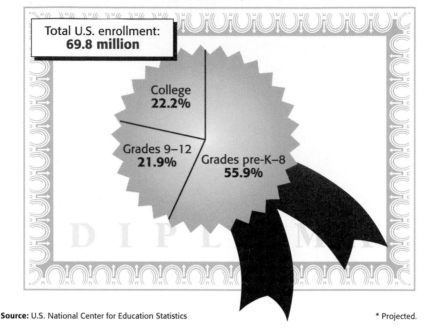

Total U.S. enrollment:
69.8 million

College
22.2%

Grades 9–12
21.9%

Grades pre-K–8
55.9%

Source: U.S. National Center for Education Statistics   * Projected.

U.S. POPULATION PROFILE:
HIGHEST EDUCATION DEGREE EARNED

(of people with some education)

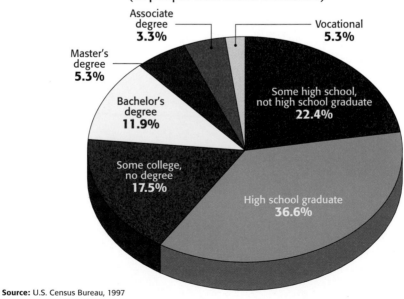

Associate
degree
3.3%

Vocational
5.3%

Master's
degree
5.3%

Some high school,
not high school graduate
22.4%

Bachelor's
degree
11.9%

Some college,
no degree
17.5%

High school graduate
36.6%

Source: U.S. Census Bureau, 1997

U.S. POPULATION PROFILE:
LEVEL OF EDUCATION, AGES 25 AND OVER, 1996

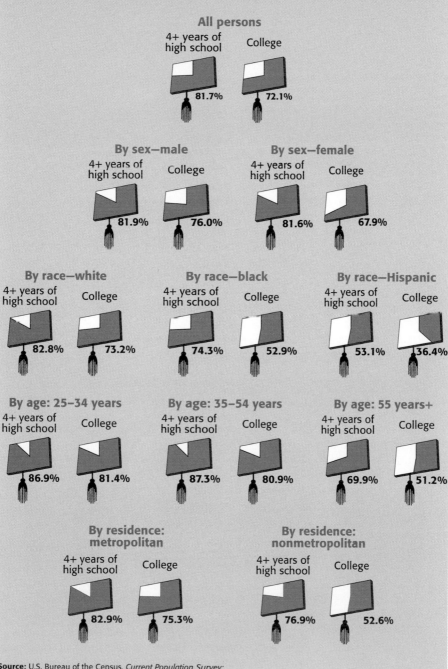

All persons
4+ years of high school — **81.7%**
College — **72.1%**

By sex—male
4+ years of high school — **81.9%**
College — **76.0%**

By sex—female
4+ years of high school — **81.6%**
College — **67.9%**

By race—white
4+ years of high school — **82.8%**
College — **73.2%**

By race—black
4+ years of high school — **74.3%**
College — **52.9%**

By race—Hispanic
4+ years of high school — **53.1%**
College — **36.4%**

By age: 25–34 years
4+ years of high school — **86.9%**
College — **81.4%**

By age: 35–54 years
4+ years of high school — **87.3%**
College — **80.9%**

By age: 55 years+
4+ years of high school — **69.9%**
College — **51.2%**

By residence: metropolitan
4+ years of high school — **82.9%**
College — **75.3%**

By residence: nonmetropolitan
4+ years of high school — **76.9%**
College — **52.6%**

Source: U.S. Bureau of the Census, *Current Population Survey: Educational Attainment in the United States, March 1996,* 1997

SCHOOL ENROLLMENT, 1966–2006 (PROJECTED)

(in millions)

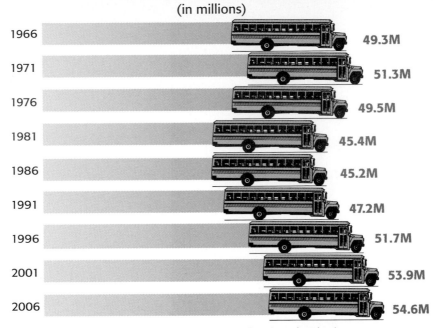

Year	Enrollment
1966	49.3M
1971	51.3M
1976	49.5M
1981	45.4M
1986	45.2M
1991	47.2M
1996	51.7M
2001	53.9M
2006	54.6M

Source: National Education Association survey; American Association of Colleges for Teacher Education

ETHNIC MAKEUP OF U.S. TEACHERS

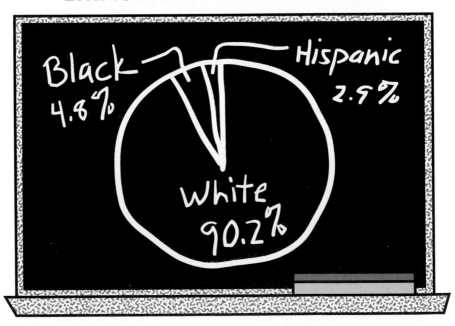

Black 4.8%

Hispanic 2.9%

White 90.2%

Source: National Education Association survey; American Association of Colleges for Teacher Education, 1996

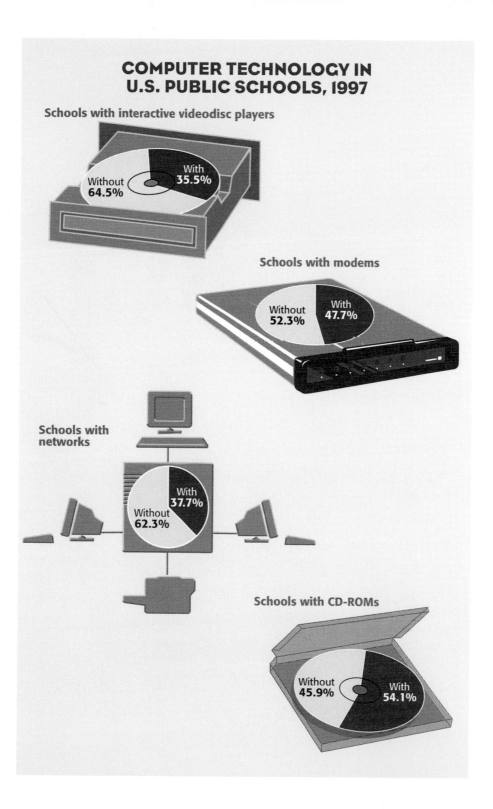

COMPUTER TECHNOLOGY IN U.S. PUBLIC SCHOOLS, 1997

Schools with interactive videodisc players

With
35.5%

Without
64.5%

Schools with modems

Without
52.3%

With
47.7%

Schools with networks

With
37.7%

Without
62.3%

Schools with CD-ROMs

Without
45.9%

With
54.1%

MEAN SAT SCORES, MATH AND ENGLISH COMBINED, 1980–1997

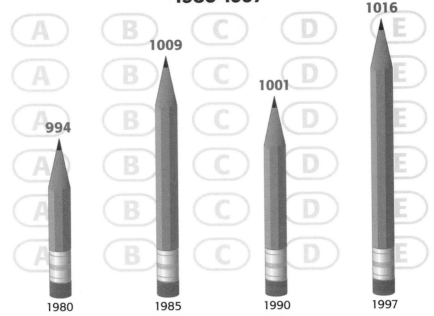

1980 — 994
1985 — 1009
1990 — 1001
1997 — 1016

Source: The College Board

TOP 10 MOST POPULAR MAJORS AMONG INCOMING COLLEGE FRESHMEN, 1996

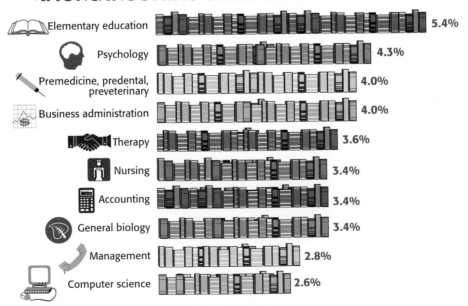

Elementary education — 5.4%
Psychology — 4.3%
Premedicine, predental, preveterinary — 4.0%
Business administration — 4.0%
Therapy — 3.6%
Nursing — 3.4%
Accounting — 3.4%
General biology — 3.4%
Management — 2.8%
Computer science — 2.6%

Source: Higher Education Research Institute, University of California, Los Angeles, *The American Freshman: National Norms for the Fall, 1996*

SELECTED DEGREES AND THEIR ABBREVIATIONS

Abbreviation	Degree
A.B. or B.A.	Bachelor of Arts
B.F.A.	Bachelor of Fine Arts
B.S.	Bachelor of Science
D.D.S.	Doctor of Dental Surgery or Doctor of Dental Science
D.V.M.	Doctor of Veterinary Medicine
Ed.D.	Doctor of Education
LL.B.	Bachelor of Laws
M.A.	Master of Arts
M.B.A.	Master of Business Administration
M.D.	Doctor of Medicine
M.Div.	Master of Divinity
M.E.	Master of Engineering
M.Ed.	Master of Education
M.F.A.	Master of Fine Arts
M.L.S.	Master of Library Science
M.S.	Master of Science
M.S.W.	Master of Social Work
Ph.D.	Doctor of Philosophy
S.B.	Bachelor of Science

AVERAGE COST OF 4-YEAR COLLEGES, 1978–1996

(tuition and fees, per year)

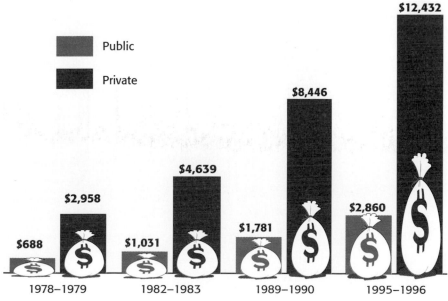

Public

Private

$688 $2,958

$1,031 $4,639

$1,781 $8,446

$2,860 $12,432

1978–1979   1982–1983   1989–1990   1995–1996

Source: The College Board

ENERGY

The world runs on energy. Energy lights and heats homes and businesses. It powers computers, factories, and farm equipment. It runs cars, trucks, trains, ships, and planes. As the world's population grows and as nations develop industry, the demand for energy increases. Demand is highest of all in the United States, which uses more energy than any other country.

Most of the energy Americans use comes from fossil fuels—coal, natural gas, oil, gasoline. These fuels are burned to produce energy directly. Cars run on gasoline, and many people cook or heat their homes with natural gas. Power plants also burn fossil fuels, especially coal, to produce electricity. Some electricity is also produced by nuclear power plants, which unlock the energy inside atoms. Hydroelectric plants harness the energy of fast-moving water.

There are problems with each of these energy sources. Supplies of fossil fuels are limited. They will eventually run out. In addition, fossil fuels create pollution and other environmental problems. Nuclear power carries risks. So far, scientists haven't found a safe way to dispose of the dangerous radioactive wastes it produces. Hydroelectric power is clean, but rivers must be dammed to produce it.

Solar energy and wind power show promise as alternative energy sources. But so far, people haven't found ways to obtain enough low-cost energy from them. Until people come up with safe, clean, and abundant sources, the best solution to the energy problem is conservation—using less.

Yearbook

circa **1200** Windmills are built in Europe; Scotland operates coal mines.

1712 The first steam engine is put to work in England.

1859 The first commercial oil well is established in Titusville, Pennsylvania; the internal combustion engine is developed in Europe.

1942 The first nuclear reactor begins operation at the University of Chicago.

1954 The first photovoltaic cell produces electric power from sunlight.

1955 Initial use of electricity powered by a nuclear reactor in the United States.

• Notables •

Rudolf Diesel (1858–1913) German mechanical engineer; built the first successful diesel engine, powered by gas.

Thomas Alva Edison (1847–1931) American inventor and businessman; patented more than 1,000 inventions, including the incandescent electric lightbulb.

Enrico Fermi (1901–1954) American (Italian-born) physicist; made important discoveries about nuclear reactions; worked on the first atomic bombs at Los Alamos, New Mexico.

Etienne Lenoir (1822–1900) French inventor; developed the first important internal combustion engine in 1859, using coal gas as fuel.

Wernher von Braun (1912–1977) American (German-born) engineer; pioneered the development of rocket engines in Germany and in the United States.

KEY IDEAS

British thermal unit (Btu) A unit of heat energy. It is the amount of heat required to raise the temperature of 1 pound of water from 60 to 61 degrees Fahrenheit.

combustion A chemical process that produces heat.

crude oil Oil in its natural state, before it has been refined.

horsepower A unit of power equal in the United States to 746 watts.

hydroelectric power Electricity produced with waterpower.

internal combustion engine A heat-producing engine in which combustion takes place inside the engine.

nuclear power Energy that is produced from a nuclear reaction, usually by splitting atoms.

turbine Water, steam, or gas passes through the wheel blades of an engine, forcing it to turn.

watt A unit for measuring electrical power.

115

PROFILE: LEADING ENERGY PRODUCERS OF THE WORLD
(by percentage of total produced)

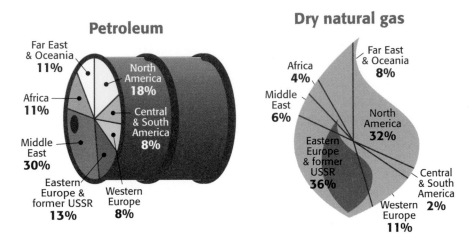

Petroleum

Far East & Oceania **11%**
North America **18%**
Africa **11%**
Central & South America **8%**
Middle East **30%**
Eastern Europe & former USSR **13%**
Western Europe **8%**

Dry natural gas

Far East & Oceania **8%**
Africa **4%**
Middle East **6%**
North America **32%**
Eastern Europe & former USSR **36%**
Central & South America **2%**
Western Europe **11%**

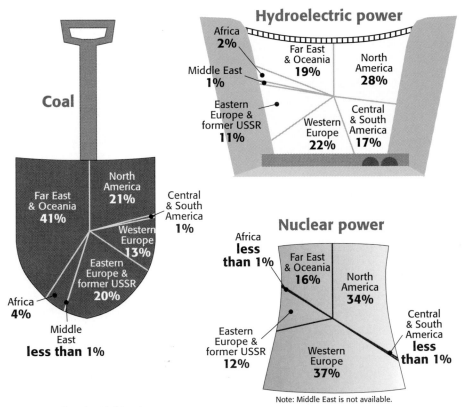

Coal

North America **21%**
Far East & Oceania **41%**
Central & South America **1%**
Western Europe **13%**
Eastern Europe & former USSR **20%**
Africa **4%**
Middle East **less than 1%**

Hydroelectric power

Africa **2%**
Far East & Oceania **19%**
North America **28%**
Middle East **1%**
Eastern Europe & former USSR **11%**
Western Europe **22%**
Central & South America **17%**

Nuclear power

Africa **less than 1%**
Far East & Oceania **16%**
North America **34%**
Eastern Europe & former USSR **12%**
Western Europe **37%**
Central & South America **less than 1%**

Note: Middle East is not available.

Source: Energy Information Administration

PROFILE: LEADING ENERGY CONSUMERS OF THE WORLD
(by percentage of total consumed)

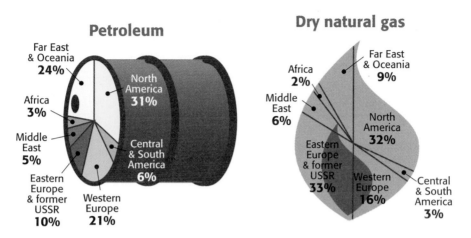

Petroleum

- Far East & Oceania **24%**
- Africa **3%**
- Middle East **5%**
- Eastern Europe & former USSR **10%**
- Western Europe **21%**
- North America **31%**
- Central & South America **6%**

Dry natural gas

- Far East & Oceania **9%**
- Africa **2%**
- Middle East **6%**
- Eastern Europe & former USSR **33%**
- North America **32%**
- Western Europe **16%**
- Central & South America **3%**

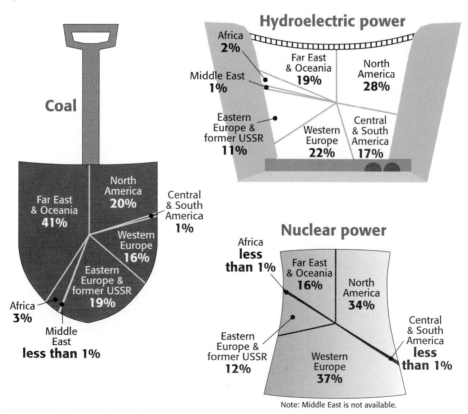

Coal

- Far East & Oceania **41%**
- North America **20%**
- Central & South America **1%**
- Western Europe **16%**
- Eastern Europe & former USSR **19%**
- Africa **3%**
- Middle East **less than 1%**

Hydroelectric power

- Africa **2%**
- Middle East **1%**
- Far East & Oceania **19%**
- North America **28%**
- Eastern Europe & former USSR **11%**
- Western Europe **22%**
- Central & South America **17%**

Nuclear power

- Africa **less than 1%**
- Far East & Oceania **16%**
- North America **34%**
- Eastern Europe & former USSR **12%**
- Western Europe **37%**
- Central & South America **less than 1%**

Note: Middle East is not available.

Source: Energy Information Administration

PROFILE: WORLD PRIMARY ENERGY PRODUCTION BY SOURCE

(as percentage of all energy produced)

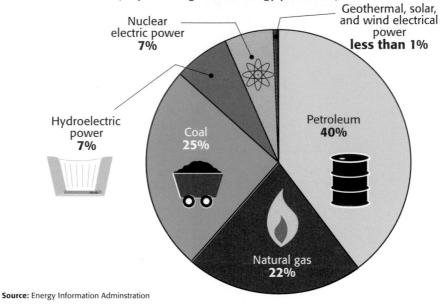

Nuclear electric power
7%

Geothermal, solar, and wind electrical power
less than 1%

Hydroelectric power
7%

Coal
25%

Petroleum
40%

Natural gas
22%

Source: Energy Information Adminstration

PROFILE: U.S. ENERGY PRODUCTION
(as percentage of all energy produced)

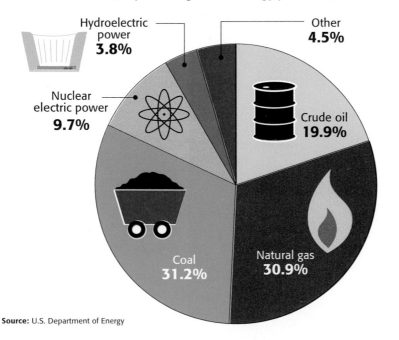

Hydroelectric power
3.8%

Other
4.5%

Nuclear electric power
9.7%

Crude oil
19.9%

Coal
31.2%

Natural gas
30.9%

Source: U.S. Department of Energy

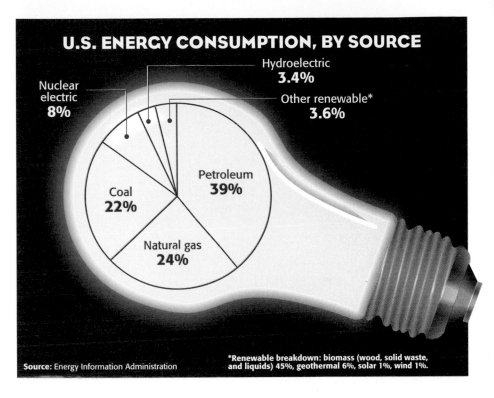

U.S. ENERGY CONSUMPTION, BY SOURCE

Hydroelectric
3.4%

Nuclear electric
8%

Other renewable*
3.6%

Petroleum
39%

Coal
22%

Natural gas
24%

Source: Energy Information Administration

*Renewable breakdown: biomass (wood, solid waste, and liquids) 45%, geothermal 6%, solar 1%, wind 1%.

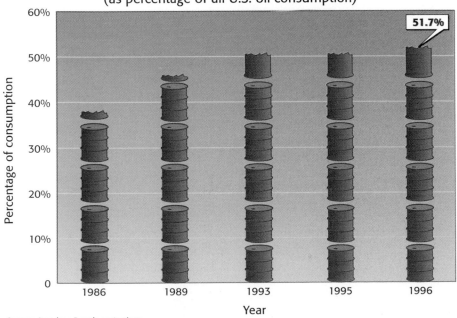

U.S. CONSUMPTION OF FOREIGN OIL, 1986–1996

(as percentage of all U.S. oil consumption)

51.7%

Percentage of consumption

60%

50%

40%

30%

20%

10%

0

1986   1989   1993   1995   1996

Year

Source: American Petroleum Institute

WHO SUPPLIES U.S. OIL?

The United States imports about half of all the oil it consumes. That means each day, nearly nine million barrels are imported. Half of that amount comes from the OPEC (Organization of Petroleum Exporting Countries) nations. The rest comes from Canada, Mexico, and other countries.

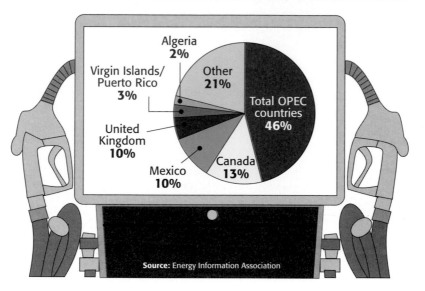

Algeria
2%

Virgin Islands/
Puerto Rico
3%

Other
21%

Total OPEC
countries
46%

United
Kingdom
10%

Mexico
10%

Canada
13%

Source: Energy Information Association

HOW U.S. HOMES ARE HEATED

(by heat source, in percentage of homes)

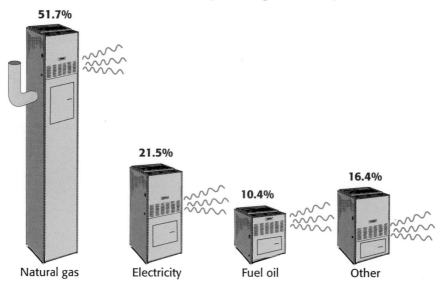

51.7%

21.5%

10.4%

16.4%

Natural gas

Electricity

Fuel oil

Other

Source: U.S. Energy Information Administration

U.S. ENERGY USE, BY HOUSEHOLD

(how energy is used in U.S. households, by percentage)

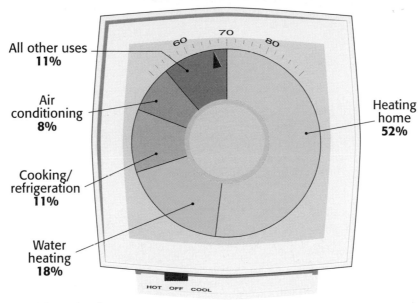

All other uses
11%

Air
conditioning
8%

Cooking/
refrigeration
11%

Water
heating
18%

Heating
home
52%

Source: U.S. Energy Information Center

COMMERCIAL NUCLEAR PLANTS
IN OPERATION, BY STATE, 1997

As of January 1, 1997, there were 109
operable nuclear reactors in 32 states.

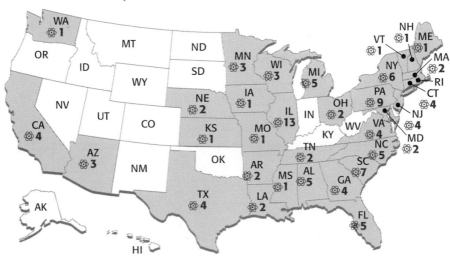

Source: U.S. Department of Energy, *World Nuclear Outlook 1994*, 1994

PROFILE: APPLIANCE OWNERSHIP
(as percentage of all U.S. households)

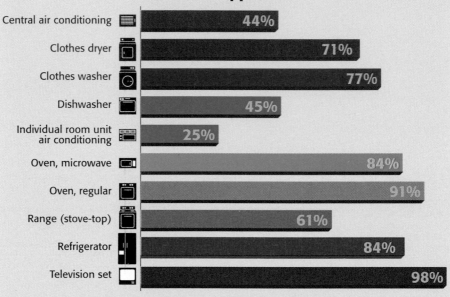

Electrical appliances

Appliance	Percentage
Central air conditioning	44%
Clothes dryer	71%
Clothes washer	77%
Dishwasher	45%
Individual room unit air conditioning	25%
Oven, microwave	84%
Oven, regular	91%
Range (stove-top)	61%
Refrigerator	84%
Television set	98%

Gas appliances

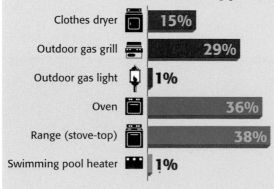

Appliance	Percentage
Clothes dryer	15%
Outdoor gas grill	29%
Outdoor gas light	1%
Oven	36%
Range (stove-top)	38%
Swimming pool heater	1%

Source: Energy Information Administration, U.S. Department of Energy, *Annual Energy Review 1995*

FUEL EFFICIENCY OF MOTOR VEHICLES IN U.S., 1980–1996

Average passenger cars, miles per gallon of gas

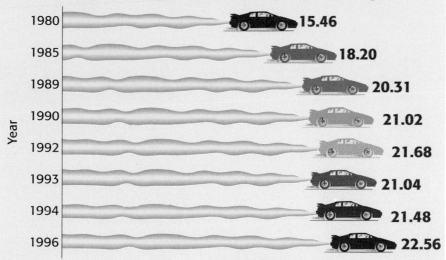

Year	
1980	15.46
1985	18.20
1989	20.31
1990	21.02
1992	21.68
1993	21.04
1994	21.48
1996	22.56

All motor vehicles, miles per gallon of gas

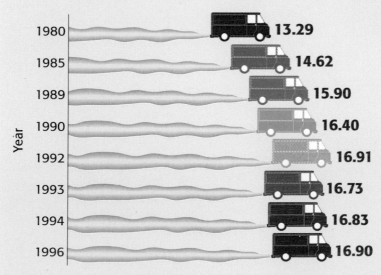

Year	
1980	13.29
1985	14.62
1989	15.90
1990	16.40
1992	16.91
1993	16.73
1994	16.83
1996	16.90

Source: U.S. Department of Transportation, Federal Highway Administration

ENVIRONMENT

How should people take care of the environment? That has become one of today's most important questions. The answers will help decide the future of Earth's community of life.

"Environment" is a broad term for the natural world—the air, water, and land, and everything that helps support living things. For thousands of years, people have been taking actions that change the natural world. Even in ancient times, people cut forests to get wood for fires and for building. They plowed land to plant crops and changed the course of streams to bring water where they needed it.

Today human actions are having a far bigger effect on the natural world than ever before. The world's population is growing fast. People need food, water, clothing, and shelter. They use energy for everything from heat to transportation. They also use a wide range of goods, from automobiles to zippers. Industries fill those needs. It also increases pollution.

People have often been wasteful and careless in the way they have treated the natural world. But today many people are concerned about environmental issues. Among the most serious problems are air and water pollution, from the burning of fossil fuels like oil and coal and from other causes. The destruction of natural areas, such as forests and wetlands, is another concern. So is the disposal of wastes, from everyday garbage to toxic materials. To one degree or another, these problems exist all over the world. They affect the survival of all living things.

Yearbook

1681 William Penn requires settlers to leave one out of five acres as undisturbed forest land.

1872 The U.S. government creates Yellowstone National Park, first in the National Park System.

1966 The first of several U.S. Endangered Species Acts is passed.

1979 Three Mile Island (nuclear power plant) has a partial meltdown.

1985 Scientists discover a hole that develops periodically in the ozone layer.

1992 A U.N.–sponsored Earth Summit is held in Rio de Janeiro.

• Notables •

Helen Caldicott (1938–   ) Australian pediatrician; founded Physicians for Social Responsibility, an American organization of doctors committed to warning colleagues about the dangers of nuclear power and nuclear weapons.

Rachel Carson (1907–1964) American marine biologist; wrote *Silent Spring*, a book that warned about the damage to the environment caused by pesticides.

John Muir (1838–1914) American naturalist; successfully campaigned for the establishment of Yosemite National Park. Among Muir's books are *Yosemite* and *Travels in Alaska*.

Theodore Roosevelt (1859–1919) 26th president of the United States; in 1908, held a conference to discuss the conservation of wildlife and natural resources.

KEY IDEAS

acid rain Rain that is polluted by acid in the atmosphere, produced mainly by the burning of fossil fuels.

conservation The protection of wildlife, natural resources, forests, and wetlands.

deforestation Large-scale clearing of forested land.

endangered species A type of plant or animal that is in danger of dying out completely.

erosion The wearing away of surface soil or rock.

fossil fuel A fuel such as coal, oil, or natural gas formed by the fossil remains of ancient life.

global warming The warming of the atmosphere as a result of heat from the sun that is trapped in the atmosphere by gases such as carbon dioxide.

meltdown The accidental melting of a nuclear reactor core.

ozone layer A layer of ozone, which is a form of oxygen, that blocks out some of the sun's harmful rays.

WHICH MATERIALS GET RECYCLED MOST?

(percent of total waste recovered; averages)

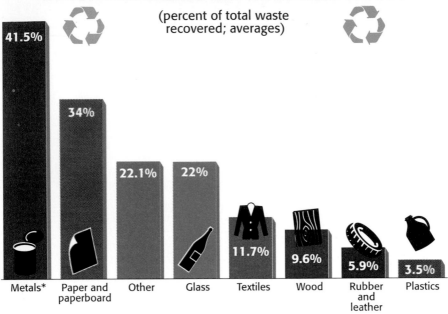

- **41.5%** — Metals*
- **34%** — Paper and paperboard
- **22.1%** — Other
- **22%** — Glass
- **11.7%** — Textiles
- **9.6%** — Wood
- **5.9%** — Rubber and leather
- **3.5%** — Plastics

Source: Environmental Protection Agency, 1996

*Includes ferrous (containing iron) and nonferrous metals.

TOP 5 RECYCLING STATES

(highest recycling rate of recyclable materials)

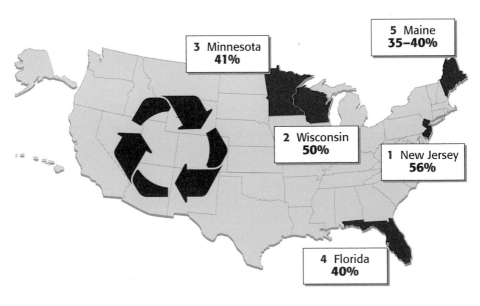

- 3 Minnesota **41%**
- 5 Maine **35–40%**
- 2 Wisconsin **50%**
- 1 New Jersey **56%**
- 4 Florida **40%**

Source: National Solid Waste Management Association, 1996

RISING CARBON DIOXIDE LEVELS, RISING TEMPERATURES, 1865–1995

The concentration of carbon dioxide in the atmosphere, shown in the chart below, has been rising for the past century and a half, largely as a result of people burning fuel. But has the earth's temperature risen as a result? After studying global temperature charts, such as the one at the bottom of the page, most experts have concluded that it has.

Rise in CO_2 Concentration in the Atmosphere

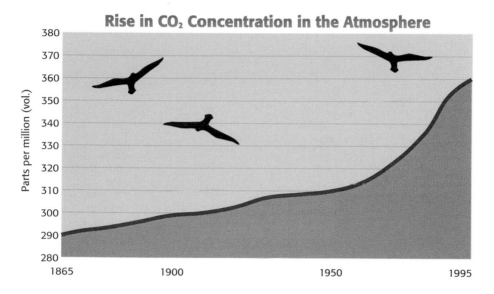

Rise in Global Annual Temperature

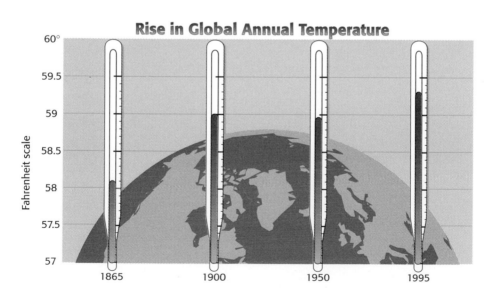

Source: IPCC, NASA

THE WORLD'S TOP 10 WORST CARBON DIOXIDE PRODUCING COUNTRIES

(by average CO_2 production, per person, per year)

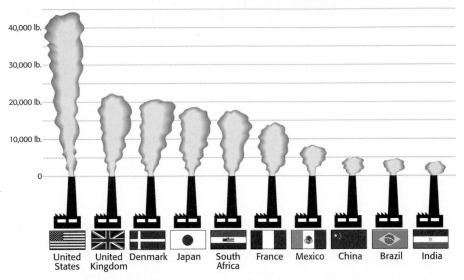

Source: Oak Ridge National Laboratory, 1992

TOP 5 WORST U.S. METROPOLITAN AREAS IN CARBON MONOXIDE, 1994

(by number of days exceeding standards)

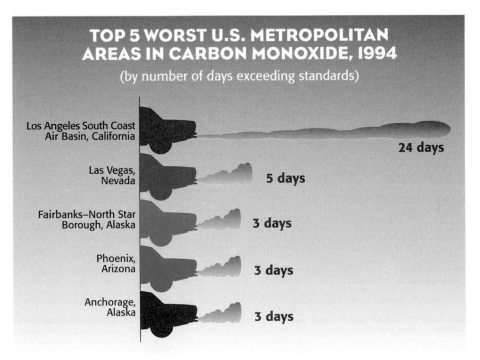

Los Angeles South Coast Air Basin, California — **24 days**

Las Vegas, Nevada — **5 days**

Fairbanks–North Star Borough, Alaska — **3 days**

Phoenix, Arizona — **3 days**

Anchorage, Alaska — **3 days**

Source: U.S. Environmental Protection Agency

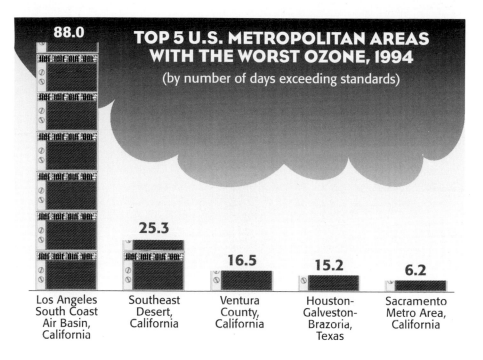

TOP 5 U.S. METROPOLITAN AREAS WITH THE WORST OZONE, 1994

(by number of days exceeding standards)

- 88.0 — Los Angeles South Coast Air Basin, California
- 25.3 — Southeast Desert, California
- 16.5 — Ventura County, California
- 15.2 — Houston-Galveston-Brazoria, Texas
- 6.2 — Sacramento Metro Area, California

Source: U.S. Environmental Protection Agency

U.S. WATERS RECEIVING THE GREATEST AMOUNTS OF TOXIC DISCHARGES, 1990–1994

(by amount of discharge, in pounds/kilograms)

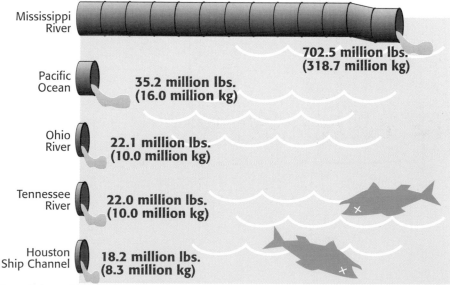

- Mississippi River — 702.5 million lbs. (318.7 million kg)
- Pacific Ocean — 35.2 million lbs. (16.0 million kg)
- Ohio River — 22.1 million lbs. (10.0 million kg)
- Tennessee River — 22.0 million lbs. (10.0 million kg)
- Houston Ship Channel — 18.2 million lbs. (8.3 million kg)

Source: Environmental Working Group, U.S. PIRG

Environment • 129

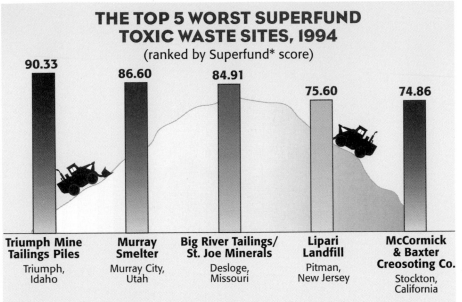

THE TOP 5 WORST SUPERFUND TOXIC WASTE SITES, 1994

(ranked by Superfund* score)

90.33	86.60	84.91	75.60	74.86
Triumph Mine Tailings Piles	Murray Smelter	Big River Tailings/ St. Joe Minerals	Lipari Landfill	McCormick & Baxter Creosoting Co.
Triumph, Idaho	Murray City, Utah	Desloge, Missouri	Pitman, New Jersey	Stockton, California

*In 1980, Congress enacted the Comprehensive Environmental Response, Compensation and Liability Act (CERCLA), better known as the Superfund, a $1.6 billion, five-year program to clean up thousands of hazardous waste sites. The fund was renewed in 1986 and again in 1991.

The Superfund uses a numerically based system that factors in toxic contaminant risks to groundwater, surface water, and air, as well as their mobility.

Source: Environmental Protection Agency

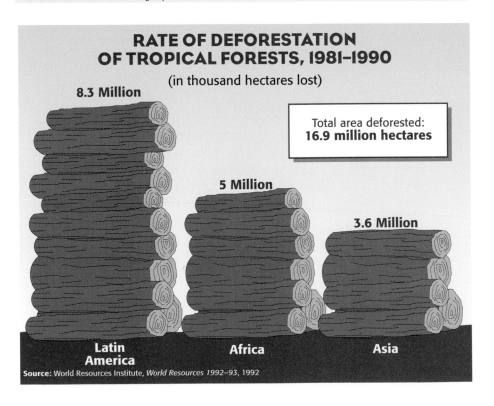

RATE OF DEFORESTATION OF TROPICAL FORESTS, 1981–1990

(in thousand hectares lost)

8.3 Million

Total area deforested:
16.9 million hectares

5 Million

3.6 Million

Latin America   **Africa**   **Asia**

Source: World Resources Institute, *World Resources 1992–93*, 1992

TOP 5 WORST OIL SPILLS
(100,000 tons or more)

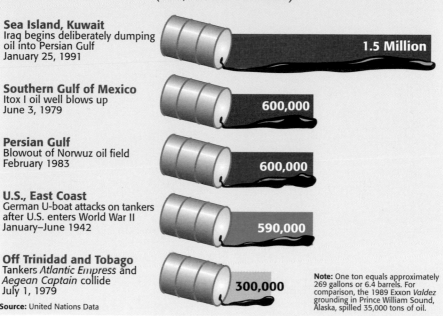

Sea Island, Kuwait
Iraq begins deliberately dumping oil into Persian Gulf
January 25, 1991
1.5 Million

Southern Gulf of Mexico
Itox I oil well blows up
June 3, 1979
600,000

Persian Gulf
Blowout of Norwuz oil field
February 1983
600,000

U.S., East Coast
German U-boat attacks on tankers after U.S. enters World War II
January–June 1942
590,000

Off Trinidad and Tobago
Tankers *Atlantic Empress* and *Aegean Captain* collide
July 1, 1979
300,000

Source: United Nations Data

Note: One ton equals approximately 269 gallons or 6.4 barrels. For comparison, the 1989 Exxon *Valdez* grounding in Prince William Sound, Alaska, spilled 35,000 tons of oil.

THE TOP 5 COSTLIEST NATURAL DISASTERS IN U.S. HISTORY
(in billions of dollars)

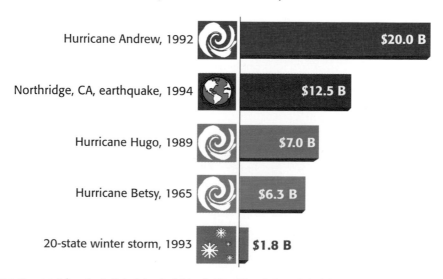

Hurricane Andrew, 1992 — **$20.0 B**

Northridge, CA, earthquake, 1994 — **$12.5 B**

Hurricane Hugo, 1989 — **$7.0 B**

Hurricane Betsy, 1965 — **$6.3 B**

20-state winter storm, 1993 — **$1.8 B**

Source: Insurance Information Institute; University of Colorado Natural Hazards Center, Federal Emergency Management Agency

GEOGRAPHY (U.S.)

Maps tell the story of the United States, its land, and its people. The United States is the fourth largest country in the world, covering 3,732,396 square miles (9,704,230 sq km). Only Russia, China, and Canada are larger.

Political maps show the country's borders and divisions. All but one of the 50 states and the District of Columbia, site of the nation's capital, are in North America. From Maine, on the Atlantic coast, to California on the Pacific, they stretch some 3,000 miles (4,800 km). Alaska, separated from the rest of the states by Canada, reaches even farther west. And the fiftieth state, Hawaii, lies far out in the Pacific Ocean, some 2,400 miles (3,840 km) from California. The U.S. Virgin Islands in the Caribbean, and Guam and American Samoa in the Pacific, are territories of the United States. Puerto Rico in the Caribbean is a commonwealth of the United States.

Topographical maps show the range of landforms within U.S. borders. In the west are the peaks of the Rocky Mountains. In the east, a coastal plain rises to the highlands of the Appalachian Mountains. In the center of the country, fertile plains stretch for miles. The largest lakes are the five Great Lakes, on the Canadian border.

Special maps and graphs tell more about the United States. Some maps show where our nation's most cherished sites are located—monuments, parks, and historic places. Population graphs show which states and cities have the most and least people—and which have the most and least per square mile. If you look at a political map while you read the data on some graphs, you'll see that more Americans live near the east and west coasts than in the middle of the country.

Yearbook

circa 600–700 Native Americans live along the Mississippi, Arkansas, and Tennessee rivers, among others.

1804–1806 Meriwether Lewis and William Clark explore the American West, from St. Louis, Missouri, to the Pacific Ocean.

1872 Yellowstone, the world's first national park, is established on the border of Wyoming, Montana, and Idaho.

1959 Hawaii becomes the nation's fiftieth state.

1982 The Vietnam Veterans Memorial is dedicated, designed by Maya Lin.

• Notables •

Frederic-Auguste Bartholdi (1834–1904) French sculptor; created Statue of Liberty.

Henry Hudson (birth date unknown; died 1611) English navigator; explored the Hudson River in present-day New York and claimed it for the Dutch.

Louis Jolliet (1645–1700) and Jacques Marquette (1637–1675) French explorers; discovered the upper Mississippi River.

Stephen Mather (1867–1930) American conservationist; organized National Park Service, became first director.

John Smith (circa 1580–1631) Englishman; helped found the colony of Jamestown in 1607.

KEY IDEAS

Continental Divide The highest points of land in the Rocky Mountains that separate the rivers flowing west from those that flow east.

landmark A structure or building that is historically important.

national forest A large forest that is protected by law and can only be logged under government supervision.

plains Large, treeless areas, either flat or rolling.

population density The ratio of population to the given size of an area; for example, number of people per square mile.

territory A part of the United States that is not included within any state but has a separate legislature (law-making body).

topography The natural features of an area; the art of representing an area's natural and human-made features on a map or chart.

U.S. STATES AND THEIR CAPITAL CITIES

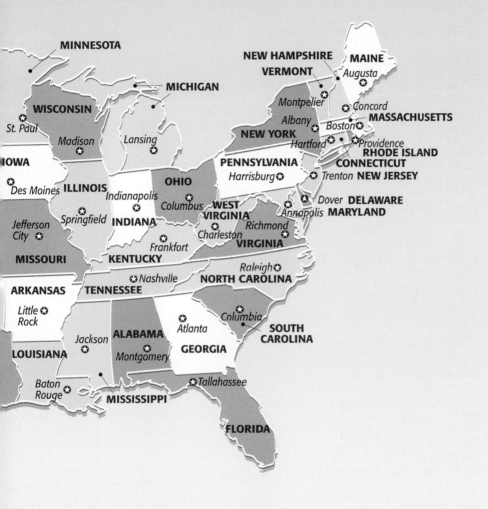

MINNESOTA

MICHIGAN

WISCONSIN

St. Paul ✪

Madison ✪

Lansing ✪

IOWA

Des Moines ✪

ILLINOIS

Indianapolis ✪

OHIO

Columbus ✪

Springfield ✪

INDIANA

Jefferson
City ✪

MISSOURI

Frankfort ✪

KENTUCKY

ARKANSAS

Little ✪
Rock

✪ Nashville

TENNESSEE

LOUISIANA

Jackson ✪

ALABAMA

Montgomery ✪

Baton ✪
Rouge

MISSISSIPPI

Atlanta ✪

GEORGIA

✪ Tallahassee

FLORIDA

NEW HAMPSHIRE

VERMONT

MAINE

Augusta ✪

Montpelier

Concord ✪

Albany ✪

Boston ✪

MASSACHUSETTS

NEW YORK

Hartford ✪

Providence ✪

RHODE ISLAND

PENNSYLVANIA

CONNECTICUT

Harrisburg ✪

Trenton ✪

NEW JERSEY

Dover ✪

DELAWARE

WEST
VIRGINIA

Annapolis ✪

MARYLAND

Charleston ✪

Richmond ✪

VIRGINIA

Raleigh ✪

NORTH CAROLINA

Columbia ✪

SOUTH
CAROLINA

THE STATES AT A GLANCE

Flag	State	Capital	Nickname	Area	Rank in area
	Alabama	Montgomery	The Heart of Dixie	51,718 sq. mi. 133,950 sq. km	29
	Alaska	Juneau	Last Frontier	587,878 sq. mi. 1,522,596 sq. km	1
	Arizona	Phoenix	Grand Canyon State	114,007 sq. mi. 295,276 sq. km	6
	Arkansas	Little Rock	Land of Opportunity	53,183 sq. mi. 137,742 sq. km	27
	California	Sacramento	Golden State	158,648 sq. mi. 410,896 sq. km	3
	Colorado	Denver	Centennial State	104,100 sq. mi. 269,618 sq. km	8
	Connecticut	Hartford	Constitution State	5,006 sq. mi. 12,966 sq. km	48
	Delaware	Dover	First State	2,026 sq. mi. 5,246 sq. km	49
	Florida	Tallahassee	Sunshine State	58,681 sq. mi. 151,982 sq. km	22
	Georgia	Atlanta	Empire State of the South	58,930 sq. mi. 152,627 sq. km	21
	Hawaii	Honolulu	Aloha State	6,459 sq. mi. 16,729 sq. km	47
	Idaho	Boise	Gem State	83,574 sq. mi. 216,456 sq. km	13
	Illinois	Springfield	Land of Lincoln	56,343 sq. mi. 145,928 sq. km	24
	Indiana	Indianapolis	Hoosier State	36,185 sq. mi. 93,720 sq. km	38
	Iowa	Des Moines	Hawkeye State	56,276 sq. mi. 145,754 sq. km	25
	Kansas	Topeka	Sunflower State	82,282 sq. mi. 213,110 sq. km	14
	Kentucky	Frankfort	Bluegrass State	40,411 sq. mi. 104,655 sq. km	37
	Louisiana	Baton Rouge	Pelican State	47,720 sq. mi. 123,593 sq. km	31
	Maine	Augusta	Pine Tree State	33,128 sq. mi. 85,801 sq. km	39
	Maryland	Annapolis	Old Line State	10,455 sq. mi. 27,077 sq. km	42
	Massachusetts	Boston	Bay State	8,262 sq. mi. 21,398 sq. km	45
	Michigan	Lansing	Wolverine State	58,513 sq. mi. 151,548 sq. km	23
	Minnesota	St. Paul	Gopher State	84,397 sq. mi. 218,587 sq. km	12
	Mississippi	Jackson	Magnolia State	47,695 sq. mi. 123,530 sq. km	32
	Missouri	Jefferson City	Show Me State	69,709 sq. mi. 180,546 sq. km	19

Flag	State	Capital	Nickname	Area	Rank in area
	Montana	Helena	Treasure State	147,047 sq. mi. 380,849 sq. km	4
	Nebraska	Lincoln	Cornhusker State	77,359 sq. mi. 200,358 sq. km	15
	Nevada	Carson City	Silver State	110,567 sq. mi. 286,367 sq. km	7
	New Hampshire	Concord	Granite State	9,283 sq. mi. 24,044 sq. km	44
	New Jersey	Trenton	Garden State	7,790 sq. mi. 20,175 sq. km	46
	New Mexico	Santa Fe	Land of Enchantment	121,599 sq. mi. 314,939 sq. km	5
	New York	Albany	Empire State	49,112 sq. mi. 127,200 sq. km	30
	North Carolina	Raleigh	Tar Heel State	52,672 sq. mi. 136,421 sq. km	28
	North Dakota	Bismarck	Flickertail State	70,704 sq. mi. 183,123 sq. km	17
	Ohio	Columbus	Buckeye State	41,328 sq. mi. 107,040 sq. km	35
	Oklahoma	Oklahoma City	Sooner State	69,903 sq. mi. 181,048 sq. km	18
	Oregon	Salem	Beaver State	97,052 sq. mi 251,365 sq. km	10
	Pennsylvania	Harrisburg	Keystone State	45,310 sq. mi. 117,351 sq. km	33
	Rhode Island	Providence	Ocean State	1,213 sq. mi. 3,142 sq. km	50
	South Carolina	Columbia	Palmetto State	31,117 sq. mi. 80,593 sq. km	40
	South Dakota	Pierre	Mount Rushmore State	77,122 sq. mi. 199,744 sq. km	16
	Tennessee	Nashville	Volunteer State	42,146 sq. mi. 109,158 sq. km	34
	Texas	Austin	Lone Star State	266,874 sq. mi. 691,201 sq. km	2
	Utah	Salt Lake City	Beehive State	84,905 sq. mi. 219,902 sq. km	11
	Vermont	Montpelier	Green Mountain State	9,615 sq. mi. 24,903 sq. km	43
	Virginia	Richmond	Old Dominion	40,598 sq. mi. 105,149 sq. km	36
	Washington	Olympia	Evergreen State	68,126 sq. mi. 176,446 sq. km	20
	West Virginia	Charleston	Mountain State	24,231 sq. mi. 62,759 sq. km	41
	Wisconsin	Madison	Badger State	56,145 sq. mi. 145,414 sq. km	26
	Wyoming	Cheyenne	Equality State	97,818 sq. mi. 253,349 sq. km	9

Source: *World Book* Encyclopedia

TOP 10 STATES IN LAND AREA
(ranked by size in square miles & square kilometers)

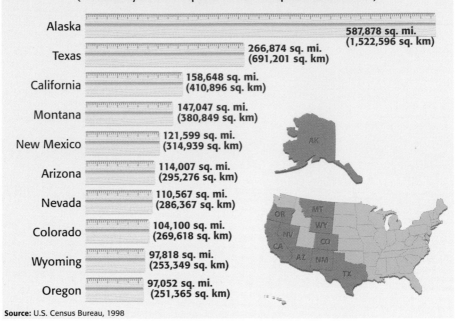

Alaska — 587,878 sq. mi. (1,522,596 sq. km)
Texas — 266,874 sq. mi. (691,201 sq. km)
California — 158,648 sq. mi. (410,896 sq. km)
Montana — 147,047 sq. mi. (380,849 sq. km)
New Mexico — 121,599 sq. mi. (314,939 sq. km)
Arizona — 114,007 sq. mi. (295,276 sq. km)
Nevada — 110,567 sq. mi. (286,367 sq. km)
Colorado — 104,100 sq. mi. (269,618 sq. km)
Wyoming — 97,818 sq. mi. (253,349 sq. km)
Oregon — 97,052 sq. mi. (251,365 sq. km)

Source: U.S. Census Bureau, 1998

TOP 10 SMALLEST U.S. STATES
(ranked by size in square miles & square kilometers)

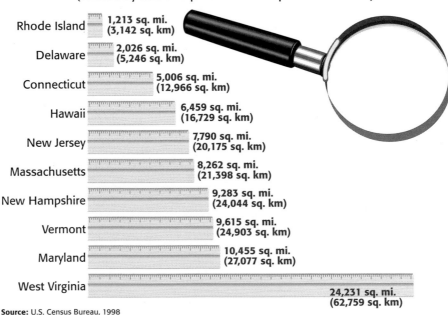

Rhode Island — 1,213 sq. mi. (3,142 sq. km)
Delaware — 2,026 sq. mi. (5,246 sq. km)
Connecticut — 5,006 sq. mi. (12,966 sq. km)
Hawaii — 6,459 sq. mi. (16,729 sq. km)
New Jersey — 7,790 sq. mi. (20,175 sq. km)
Massachusetts — 8,262 sq. mi. (21,398 sq. km)
New Hampshire — 9,283 sq. mi. (24,044 sq. km)
Vermont — 9,615 sq. mi. (24,903 sq. km)
Maryland — 10,455 sq. mi. (27,077 sq. km)
West Virginia — 24,231 sq. mi. (62,759 sq. km)

Source: U.S. Census Bureau, 1998

TOPOGRAPHICAL MAP OF THE CONTINENTAL UNITED STATES

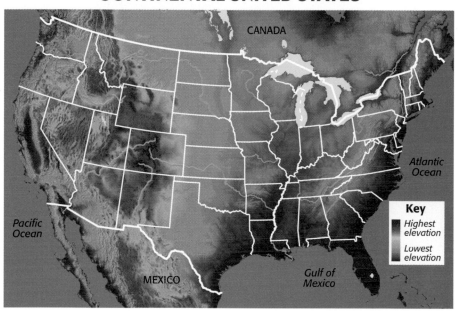

CANADA

Atlantic Ocean

Pacific Ocean

Key

Highest elevation

Lowest elevation

MEXICO

Gulf of Mexico

TOP 5 HIGHEST U.S. MOUNTAINS
(by elevation)

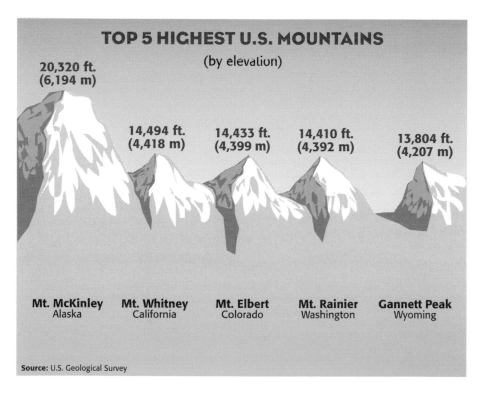

20,320 ft. (6,194 m)

14,494 ft. (4,418 m)

14,433 ft. (4,399 m)

14,410 ft. (4,392 m)

13,804 ft. (4,207 m)

Mt. McKinley Alaska

Mt. Whitney California

Mt. Elbert Colorado

Mt. Rainier Washington

Gannett Peak Wyoming

Source: U.S. Geological Survey

THE GREAT LAKES—FACTS AND FIGURES

NAME	AREA		BORDERS	MAJOR PORTS
	Square miles	Square kilometers		
Lake Superior	31,820	82,414	Minnesota, Wisconsin, Michigan (United States); Ontario (Canada)	Duluth, Superior, Sault Sainte Marie (United States); Sault Sainte Marie, Thunder Bay (Canada)
Lake Huron	23,010	59,596	Michigan (United States); Ontario (Canada)	Port Huron (United States); Sarnia (Canada)
Lake Michigan	22,400	58,016	Illinois, Indiana, Michigan, Wisconsin (United States)	Milwaukee, Racine, Kenosha, Chicago, Gary, Muskegon (United States)
Lake Erie	9,940	25,745	Michigan, New York, Ohio, Pennsylvania (United States); Ontario (Canada)	Toledo, Sandusky, Lorain, Cleveland, Erie, Buffalo (United States)
Lake Ontario	7,540	19,529	New York (United States); Ontario (Canada)	Rochester, Oswego (United States); Toronto, Hamilton (Canada)
Total Area	97,710	245,300		

TOP 10 U.S. RIVERS, BY LENGTH
(in miles and kilometers)

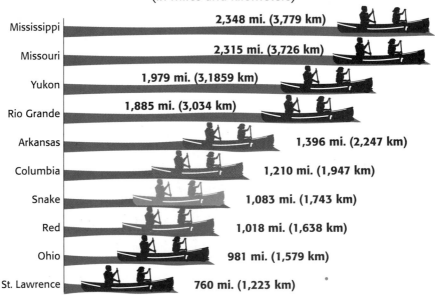

Mississippi	2,348 mi. (3,779 km)
Missouri	2,315 mi. (3,726 km)
Yukon	1,979 mi. (3,1859 km)
Rio Grande	1,885 mi. (3,034 km)
Arkansas	1,396 mi. (2,247 km)
Columbia	1,210 mi. (1,947 km)
Snake	1,083 mi. (1,743 km)
Red	1,018 mi. (1,638 km)
Ohio	981 mi. (1,579 km)
St. Lawrence	760 mi. (1,223 km)

Source: National Oceanic and Atmospheric Administration, *Distances between United States Ports*, 1987

TOP 10 MOST POPULOUS STATES

(ranked by estimated census data, 1998)

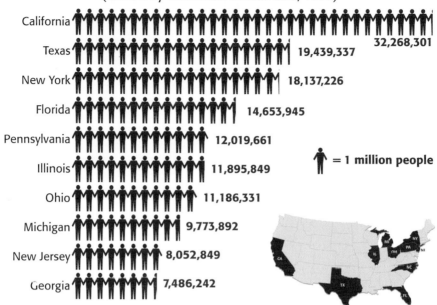

California — 32,268,301
Texas — 19,439,337
New York — 18,137,226
Florida — 14,653,945
Pennsylvania — 12,019,661
Illinois — 11,895,849
Ohio — 11,186,331
Michigan — 9,773,892
New Jersey — 8,052,849
Georgia — 7,486,242

= 1 million people

Source: U.S. Census Bureau, population estimate as of 10/30/98

TOP 10 LEAST POPULOUS STATES

(ranked by estimated census data, 1998)

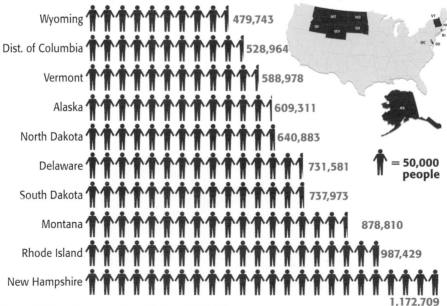

Wyoming — 479,743
Dist. of Columbia — 528,964
Vermont — 588,978
Alaska — 609,311
North Dakota — 640,883
Delaware — 731,581
South Dakota — 737,973
Montana — 878,810
Rhode Island — 987,429
New Hampshire — 1,172,709

= 50,000 people

Source: U.S. Census Bureau, population estimate as of 10/30/98

WHICH STATES HAVE THE MOST LAND FOR RECREATION AND CONSERVATION?

(by total acreage [hectares] of state parks and recreation areas)

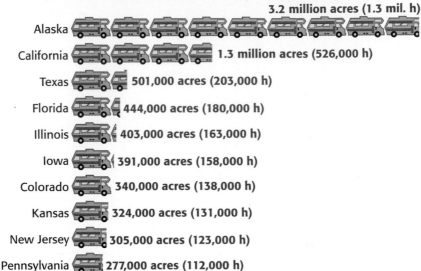

3.2 million acres (1.3 mil. h)

Alaska

California — **1.3 million acres (526,000 h)**

Texas — **501,000 acres (203,000 h)**

Florida — **444,000 acres (180,000 h)**

Illinois — **403,000 acres (163,000 h)**

Iowa — **391,000 acres (158,000 h)**

Colorado — **340,000 acres (138,000 h)**

Kansas — **324,000 acres (131,000 h)**

New Jersey — **305,000 acres (123,000 h)**

Pennsylvania — **277,000 acres (112,000 h)**

Source: National Association of State Park Directors

TOP 10 LARGEST NATIONAL HISTORICAL PARKS

(by total acreage [hectares])

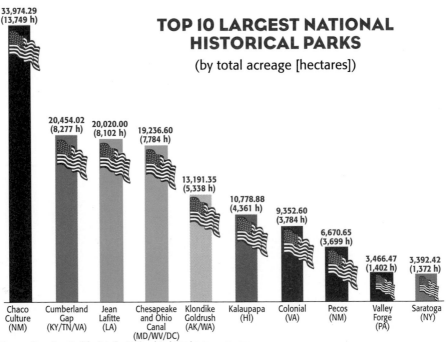

Park	Acreage (hectares)
Chaco Culture (NM)	33,974.29 (13,749 h)
Cumberland Gap (KY/TN/VA)	20,454.02 (8,277 h)
Jean Lafitte (LA)	20,020.00 (8,102 h)
Chesapeake and Ohio Canal (MD/WV/DC)	19,236.60 (7,784 h)
Klondike Goldrush (AK/WA)	13,191.35 (5,338 h)
Kalaupapa (HI)	10,778.88 (4,361 h)
Colonial (VA)	9,352.60 (3,784 h)
Pecos (NM)	6,670.65 (3,699 h)
Valley Forge (PA)	3,466.47 (1,402 h)
Saratoga (NY)	3,392.42 (1,372 h)

Source: Department of the Interior, National Park Service. www.nps.gov

TOP 5 MOST-VISITED NATIONAL PARKS IN THE U.S.
(average yearly visits)

9,265,667 — Great Smoky Mountains National Park, North Carolina/Tennessee

4,537,703 — Grand Canyon National Park, Arizona

4,046,207 — Yosemite National Park, California

3,348,723 — Olympic National Park, Washington

3,012,171 — Yellowstone National Park, Wyoming

Source: National Park Service, 1998

TOP 10 MOST-VISITED SITES IN THE NATIONAL PARK SYSTEM, 1996
(by number of visitors)

Site	Visitors
Blue Ridge Parkway (NC, VA)	17,169,062
Golden Gate National Recreation Area (CA)	14,043,984
Lake Mead National Recreation Area (AZ, NV)	9,350,847
Great Smoky Mountains National Park (TN, NC)	9,265,667
Gateway National Recreation Area (NY, NJ)	6,381,502
George Washington Memorial National Parkway (VA, MD, DC)	6,126,490
National Capital Parks (DC)	6,094,875
Natchez Trace National Parkway (MS, AL, TN)	6,088,610
Cape Cod National Seashore (MA)	4,901,782
Delaware Water Gap National Recreation Area (PA, NJ)	4,657,735

Source: National Park Service, Department of the Interior

Geography (U.S.) • 143

LOCATIONS OF U.S. NATIONAL MEMORIALS

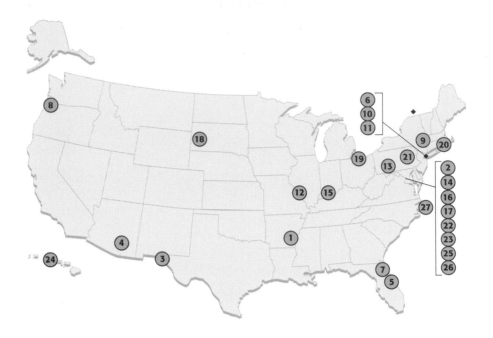

1. **Arkansas Post** Arkansas–First permanent French settlement in the lower Mississippi River valley.

2. **Arlington House, the Robert E. Lee Memorial** Virginia–Lee's home overlooking the Potomac.

3. **Chamizal** El Paso, Texas–Commemorates 1963 settlement of 99-year border dispute with Mexico.

4. **Coronado** Arizona–Commemorates first European exploration of the Southwest.

5. **DeSoto** Florida–Commemorates 16th-century Spanish explorations.

6. **Federal Hall** New York–First seat of U.S. government under the Constitution.

7. **Fort Caroline** Florida–On St. Johns River, overlooks site of a French Huguenot colony.

8. **Fort Clatsop** Oregon–Lewis and Clark encampment, 1805–1806.

9. **Franklin Delano Roosevelt** New York–Statues of Pres. Roosevelt and Eleanor Roosevelt, as well as waterfalls and gardens. Dedicated May 2, 1997.

10. **General Grant** New York–Grant's tomb.

11. **Hamilton Grange** New York–Home of Alexander Hamilton.

12. **Jefferson National Expansion Memorial** St. Louis, Missouri–Commemorates westward expansion.

13. **Johnstown Flood** Pennsylvania–Commemorates tragic flood of 1889.

14. **Korean War Veterans** Washington, D.C.–Dedicated in 1995, honors those who served in the Korean War.

15. **Lincoln Boyhood** Indiana–Abraham Lincoln grew up here.

16. **Lincoln Memorial** Washington, D.C.–Marble statue of the 16th U.S. president.

17. **Lyndon B. Johnson Grove on the Potomac** Washington, D.C.–Overlooks the Potomac River vista of the capital.

18. **Mount Rushmore** South Dakota–World-famous sculpture of four presidents.

19. **Perry's Victory and International Peace Memorial** Put-in-Bay, Ohio–The world's most massive Doric column, constructed 1912–1915, promotes pursuit of international peace through arbitration and disarmament.

20. **Roger Williams** Providence, Rhode Island–Memorial to founder of Rhode Island.

21. **Thaddeus Kosciuszko** Pennsylvania–Memorial to Polish hero of American Revolution.

22. **Theodore Roosevelt Island** Washington, D.C.–Statue of Roosevelt in wooded island sanctuary.

23. **Thomas Jefferson Memorial** Washington, D.C.–Statue of Jefferson in an inscribed circular, colonnaded structure.

24. **USS *Arizona*** Hawaii–Memorializes American losses at Pearl Harbor.

25. **Vietnam Veterans** Washington, D.C.–Black granite wall inscribed with names of those missing or killed in action in the Vietnam War.

26. **Washington Monument** Washington, D.C.–Obelisk honoring the first U.S. president.

27. **Wright Brothers** North Carolina–Site of first powered flight.

Note: These are the 27 National Memorials designated by the National Park Service.

Source: National Park Service

LOCATIONS OF U.S. NATIONAL BATTLEFIELDS

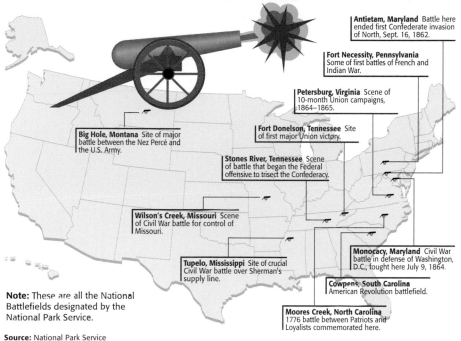

Antietam, Maryland Battle here ended first Confederate invasion of North, Sept. 16, 1862.

Fort Necessity, Pennsylvania Some of first battles of French and Indian War.

Petersburg, Virginia Scene of 10-month Union campaigns, 1864–1865.

Big Hole, Montana Site of major battle between the Nez Percé and the U.S. Army.

Fort Donelson, Tennessee Site of first major Union victory.

Stones River, Tennessee Scene of battle that began the Federal offensive to trisect the Confederacy.

Wilson's Creek, Missouri Scene of Civil War battle for control of Missouri.

Monocacy, Maryland Civil War battle in defense of Washington, D.C., fought here July 9, 1864.

Tupelo, Mississippi Site of crucial Civil War battle over Sherman's supply line.

Cowpens, South Carolina American Revolution battlefield.

Moores Creek, North Carolina 1776 battle between Patriots and Loyalists commemorated here.

Note: These are all the National Battlefields designated by the National Park Service.

Source: National Park Service

LOCATIONS OF SELECTED U.S. NATIONAL MONUMENTS
(with year first designated and total acreage)

❶ Cabrillo (California, 1913) 137 acres.

❷ Devil's Tower (Wyoming, 1906) 1,347 acres.

❸ Dinosaur (Colorado-Utah, 1915) 210,844 acres.

❹ Effigy Mounds (Iowa, 1949) 1,481 acres.

❺ El Malpais (New Mexico, 1987) 114,277 acres.

❻ El Morro (New Mexico, 1906) 1,279 acres.

❼ Fort McHenry National Monument & Historic Shrine (Maryland, 1925) 43 acres.

❽ Fort Sumter (South Carolina, 1948) 195 acres.

❾ George Washington Carver (Missouri, 1943) 210 acres.

❿ Little Bighorn Battlefield (Montana, 1879) 765 acres.

⓫ Muir Woods (California, 1908) 554 acres.

⓬ Statue of Liberty (New York, 1924) 58 acres.

⓭ White Sands (New Mexico, 1933) 143,733 acres.

Source: National Park Service

SELECTED NATIONAL SITES OF WASHINGTON, D.C.

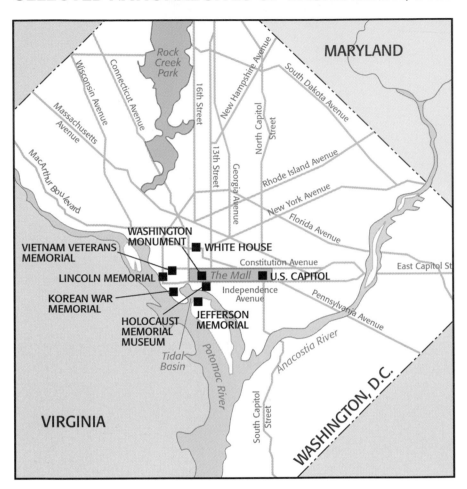

Capitol

To observe the debate in the House or Senate while Congress is in session, individuals living in the U.S. may obtain tickets to the visitors' galleries from their congressperson or senator. Between Constitution and Independence Aves., at Pennsylvania Ave.
Phone 202-225-6827.

Holocaust Memorial Museum

The museum is open daily, 10 A.M.–5:30 P.M., except Yom Kippur and Dec. 25. 100 Raoul Wallenburg Pl., SW (formerly 15th St., SW), near Independence Ave.
Phone 202-488-0400.

Jefferson Memorial

The memorial, which is located on the south edge of the Tidal Basin, is open daily, 8 A.M.–midnight. An elevator and curb ramps for the handicapped are in service.
Phone 202-426-6841.

Korean War Memorial

The $18 million military memorial, which was funded by private donations, is open 24 hours daily.
Phone 202-426-6841.

Lincoln Memorial

The memorial, which is located on the south edge of the Tidal Basin, is open daily, 8 A.M.–midnight. An elevator and curb ramps for the handicapped are in service.
Phone 202-426-6841.

Vietnam Veterans Memorial

The memorial is open 24 hours daily. Phone 202-426-6841.

Washington Monument

Open daily except Dec. 25, 9 A.M.–4:30 P.M.; 8 A.M.–midnight, April–Labor Day.
Phone 202-426-6841.

White House

Free reserved tickets for guided tours can be obtained 8–10 weeks in advance from your local congressperson or senator. 1600 Pennsylvania Ave.
Phone 202-4546-7041.

Source: Washington Convention and Visitor's Bureau

STATS ON THE STATUE OF LIBERTY

Dimensions	Ft.	In.
Height from base to torch (45.3 m)	151	1
Foundation from pedestal to torch (91.5 m)	305	1
Heel to top of head (33.8 m)	111	1
Length of hand (5 m)	16	5
Index finger (2.4 m)	8	0
Circumference at second joint (1 m)	3	6
Size of fingernail (33 cm x 25 cm)		13x10
Head from chin to cranium (5 m)	17	3
Head thickness from ear to ear (3 m)	10	0
Distance across the eye (.76 m)	2	6
Length of nose (1.4 m)	4	6
Right arm, length (12.8 m)	42	0
Right arm, greatest thickness (3.7 m)	12	0
Thickness of waist (10.7 m)	35	0
Width of mouth (1 m)	3	0
Tablet, length (7.2 m)	23	7
Tablet, width (4.1 m)	13	7
Tablet, thickness (.60 m)	2	0

Source: U.S. National Park Service

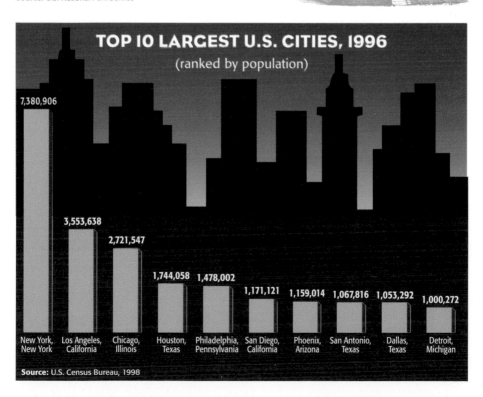

TOP 10 LARGEST U.S. CITIES, 1996
(ranked by population)

- New York, New York — 7,380,906
- Los Angeles, California — 3,553,638
- Chicago, Illinois — 2,721,547
- Houston, Texas — 1,744,058
- Philadelphia, Pennsylvania — 1,478,002
- San Diego, California — 1,171,121
- Phoenix, Arizona — 1,159,014
- San Antonio, Texas — 1,067,816
- Dallas, Texas — 1,053,292
- Detroit, Michigan — 1,000,272

Source: U.S. Census Bureau, 1998

TOP 10 MOST DENSELY POPULATED U.S. CITIES, 1997

(population per square mile)

| New York, New York **24,287** | Paterson, New Jersey **16,693** | San Francisco, California **15,603** | Jersey City, New Jersey **15,337** | Chicago, Illinois **12,204** |

| Boston, Massachusetts **12,167** | Inglewood, California **11,952** | Philadelphia, Pennsylvania **11,659** | Newark, New Jersey **11,554** | El Monte, California **11,175** |

Source: U.S. Census Bureau, 1998   = 1,000 people

TOP 10 FASTEST-GROWING MAJOR U.S. CITIES, 1990–1996

(ranked by percent change)

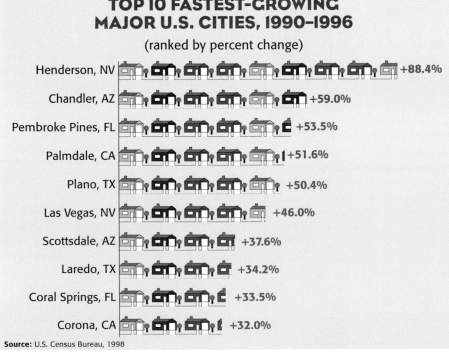

Henderson, NV	+88.4%
Chandler, AZ	+59.0%
Pembroke Pines, FL	+53.5%
Palmdale, CA	+51.6%
Plano, TX	+50.4%
Las Vegas, NV	+46.0%
Scottsdale, AZ	+37.6%
Laredo, TX	+34.2%
Coral Springs, FL	+33.5%
Corona, CA	+32.0%

Source: U.S. Census Bureau, 1998

TOP 10 LARGEST U.S. CITIES BY RACE

(percentage of population)

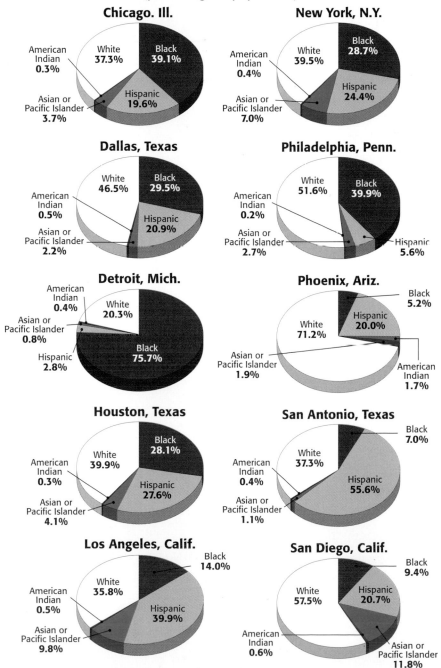

Chicago. Ill.
American Indian 0.3%
White 37.3%
Black 39.1%
Asian or Pacific Islander 3.7%
Hispanic 19.6%

New York, N.Y.
American Indian 0.4%
White 39.5%
Black 28.7%
Asian or Pacific Islander 7.0%
Hispanic 24.4%

Dallas, Texas
White 46.5%
Black 29.5%
American Indian 0.5%
Asian or Pacific Islander 2.2%
Hispanic 20.9%

Philadelphia, Penn.
White 51.6%
Black 39.9%
American Indian 0.2%
Asian or Pacific Islander 2.7%
Hispanic 5.6%

Detroit, Mich.
American Indian 0.4%
White 20.3%
Asian or Pacific Islander 0.8%
Black 75.7%
Hispanic 2.8%

Phoenix, Ariz.
Black 5.2%
Hispanic 20.0%
White 71.2%
Asian or Pacific Islander 1.9%
American Indian 1.7%

Houston, Texas
American Indian 0.3%
White 39.9%
Black 28.1%
Asian or Pacific Islander 4.1%
Hispanic 27.6%

San Antonio, Texas
Black 7.0%
White 37.3%
American Indian 0.4%
Hispanic 55.6%
Asian or Pacific Islander 1.1%

Los Angeles, Calif.
Black 14.0%
White 35.8%
American Indian 0.5%
Hispanic 39.9%
Asian or Pacific Islander 9.8%

San Diego, Calif.
Black 9.4%
White 57.5%
Hispanic 20.7%
American Indian 0.6%
Asian or Pacific Islander 11.8%

Source: U.S. Census Bureau, Based on 1998 data

GEOGRAPHY (WORLD)

In ancient times people knew little about what lay beyond the horizon. Travelers who ventured outside familiar territory might meet terrible monsters or even fall off the edge of the world, they thought. But as methods of transportation and navigation improved, people began to learn about the true shape of the world. By the 1500s European navigators and explorers had sighted all the continents except Australia and Antarctica. They wrote detailed descriptions and drew maps to guide others.

Geography deals with Earth's surface features—its mountains and plains, rivers and seas, deserts and forests, and climates. Geographers explore, measure, map, and report about these features. To do this, today's geographers are helped by such tools as computers and satellite photography.

Photographs taken from space confirm what early geographers discovered: The world is a globe, and two thirds of its surface is covered by water. Ice caps cover the North and South poles year-round. From space, great mountain chains stand out.

Learning about Earth's surface is only part of geography. Geographers are especially concerned with the ways in which people affect, and are affected by, the world. There are nearly 200 independent nations in the world, daily life varies widely among them, and each nation has a unique story to tell.

Yearbook

circa 100 The Greek geographer Ptolemy writes his *Geography*; he estimates the size of Earth, describes its surface, and locates places according to their latitude and longitude.

1492 Christopher Columbus discovers the New World.

1909 American explorers Robert Peary and Matthew Henson are the first to reach the North Pole.

1960 The Swiss oceanographer Jacques Piccard and Lieutenant Don Walsh take a submersible 35,800 feet (10,912 m) below the Pacific and explore the Mariana Trench.

• Notables •

Christopher Columbus (1451–1506) Italian-born Spanish explorer; left Europe on August 3, 1492 with three sailing ships, hoping to reach Asia. Instead, he discovered the New World.

Vasco da Gama (circa 1469–1524) Portuguese navigator; the first European to travel to India by boat; established an important trade route to Asia.

Samuel de Champlain (1567–1635) French explorer; founded the city of Quebec in 1608.

Ferdinand Magellan (c. 1480–1521) Portuguese navigator; searched for a westward route from Europe, past the Americas, to Asia. Reached the Phillipine Islands; some crew continued, sailing completely around the world for the first time.

KEY IDEAS

altitude The height of a place or thing, as measured from sea level or from the surface of the land.

continental shelf The edge of a continent that is covered by shallow water.

hemisphere Half of Earth's surface. The northern hemisphere is north of the equator; the southern hemisphere is south of it.

latitude The distance of a place from the equator; the distance is measured in imaginary parallel lines that run north and south of the equator. When the latitude and longitude of a place is known, it can easily be found on a world map.

longitude The distance of a place from Greenwich, England; the distance is measured in imaginary, vertical lines running between the North and South Poles.

tundra A treeless plain near the Arctic Circle. The soil beneath the top layer of the tundra is permanently frozen.

COUNTRIES OF THE WORLD

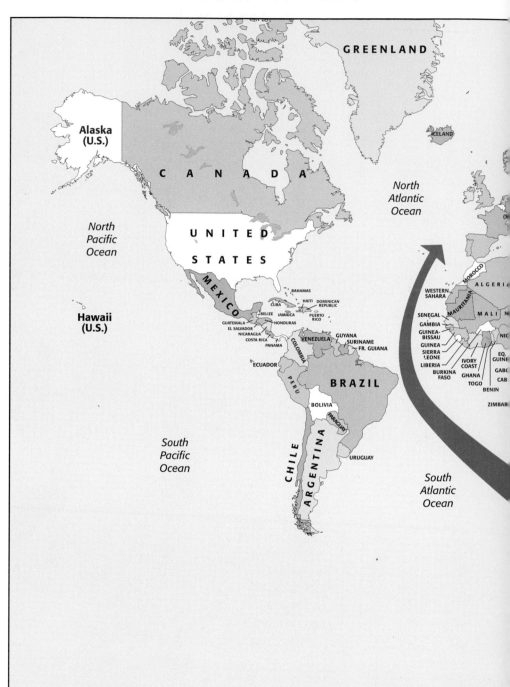

GREENLAND

ICELAND

Alaska (U.S.)

C A N A D A

North Atlantic Ocean

North Pacific Ocean

U N I T E D   S T A T E S

Hawaii (U.S.)

M E X I C O

BAHAMAS

CUBA

HAITI   DOMINICAN REPUBLIC

BELIZE   JAMAICA   PUERTO RICO

GUATEMALA
EL SALVADOR   HONDURAS
NICARAGUA
COSTA RICA
PANAMA

VENEZUELA   GUYANA   SURINAME   FR. GUIANA

COLOMBIA

ECUADOR

P E R U

BRAZIL

BOLIVIA

PARAGUAY

CHILE

ARGENTINA

URUGUAY

South Pacific Ocean

South Atlantic Ocean

MOROCCO   ALGERIA

WESTERN SAHARA

SENEGAL   MAURITANIA   MALI   N
GAMBIA
GUINEA-BISSAU
GUINEA
SIERRA LEONE   NIC
LIBERIA   IVORY COAST   EQ. GUINE
BURKINA FASO   GHANA   GABO
TOGO   CAB
BENIN
ZIMBAB

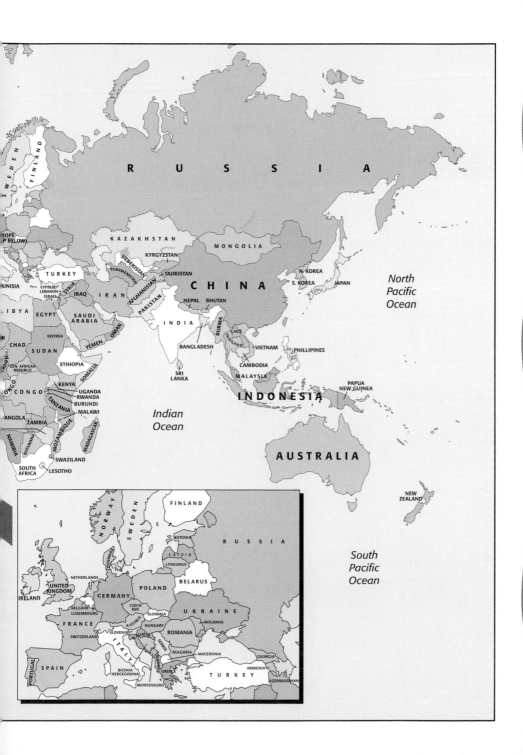

COUNTRIES OF THE WORLD

AFGHANISTAN

cap: Kabul
pop: 18,400,000
area (sq. mi.): 251,773
lang: Dari Persian, Pashtu,
Uzbek
money: afghani
gov: In transition

ALBANIA

cap: Tiranë
pop: 3,500,000
area (sq. mi.): 11,100
lang: Albanian, Greek
money: lek
gov: Republic

ALGERIA

cap: Algiers
pop: 28,400,000
area (sq. mi.): 918,497
lang: Arabic, Berber,
French
money: dinar
gov: Republic

ANDORRA

cap: Andorra la Vella
pop: 162,000
area (sq. mi.): 185
lang: Catalan, French,
Spanish
money: franc, peseta
gov: Parliamentary
co-principality

ANGOLA

cap: Luanda
pop: 11,500,000
area (sq. mi.): 481,353
lang: Portuguese, Bantu
money: kwanza
gov: Republic

ANTIGUA AND BARBUDA

cap: St. John's
pop: 100,000
area (sq. mi.): 171
lang: English
money: dollar
gov: Constitutional
monarchy with British-
style parliament

ARGENTINA

cap: Buenos Aires
pop: 34,600,000
area (sq. mi.): 1,065,189
lang: Spanish, Italian
money: peso
gov: Republic

ARMENIA

cap: Yerevan
pop: 3,700,000
area (sq. mi.): 11,306
lang: Armenian
money: dram
gov: Republic

AUSTRALIA

cap: Canberra
pop: 18,400,000
area (sq. mi.): 2,966,420
lang: English, aboriginal
languages
money: dollar
gov: Democratic, federal
state system

AUSTRIA

cap: Vienna
pop: 8,100,000
area (sq. mi.): 32,377
lang: German
money: schilling
gov: Parliamentary
democracy

AZERBAIJAN

cap: Baku
pop: 7,300,000
area (sq. mi.): 33,400
lang: Azeri, Russian,
Armenian
money: manat
gov: Republic

BAHAMAS

cap: Nassau
pop: 300,000
area (sq. mi.): 5,380
lang: English, Creole
money: dollar
gov: Independent
commonwealth

BAHRAIN

cap: Manama
pop: 4,600,000
area (sq. mi.): 268
lang: Arabic, English,
Farsi, Urdu
money: dinar
gov: Traditional
monarchy

BANGLADESH

cap: Dhaka
pop: 119,200,000
area (sq. mi.): 55,813
lang: Bengali, Chakma,
Bagh
money: taka
gov: Parliamentary
democracy

BARBADOS

cap: Bridgetown
pop: 300,000
area (sq. mi.): 166
lang: English
money: dollar
gov: Parliamentary
democracy

BELARUS

cap: Minsk
pop: 10,373,000
area (sq. mi.): 80,134
lang: Byelorussian,
Russian
money: ruble
gov: Republic

COUNTRIES OF THE WORLD (cont.)

BELGIUM

cap: Brussels
pop: 10,200,000
area (sq. mi.): 11,799
lang: Flemish, French,
German
money: franc
gov: Parliamentary
democracy

BELIZE

cap: Belmopan
pop: 200,000
area (sq. mi.): 8,867
lang: English, Spanish,
Creole
money: dollar
gov: Parliamentary
democracy

BENIN

cap: Porto-Novo
pop: 5,400,000
area (sq. mi.): 43,483
lang: French, Fon,
Yoruba
money: CFA franc
gov: Republic

BHUTAN

cap: Thimphu
pop: 800,000
area (sq. mi.): 18,147
lang: Dzongkha, Nepali,
Tibetan
money: ngultrum
gov: Monarchy

BOLIVIA

cap: Sucre
pop: 7,400,000
area (sq. mi.): 421,165
lang: Spanish, Quecha,
Aymara
money: boliviano
gov: Republic

BOSNIA & HERZEGOVINA

cap: Sarajevo
pop: 3,500,000
area (sq. mi.): 19,741
lang: Serbo-Croatian
money: dinar
gov: Republic

BOTSWANA

cap: Gabarone
pop: 1,500,000
area (sq. mi.): 231,804
lang: English, Setswana
money: pula
gov: Parliamentary
republic

BRAZIL

cap: Brasília
pop: 157,800,000
area (sq. mi.): 3,286,470
lang: Portuguese,
Spanish, others
money: real
gov: Federal republic

BRUNEI DARUSSALAM

cap: Bandar Seri Begawan
pop: 300,000
area (sq. mi.): 2,226
lang: Malay, English,
Chinese
money: dollar
gov: Independent
sultanate

BULGARIA

cap: Sofia
pop: 8,500,000
area (sq. mi.): 44,365
lang: Bulgarian, Turkish
money: leva
gov: Republic

BURKINA FASO

cap: Ouagadougou
pop: 10,100,00
area (sq. mi.): 105,869
lang: French, Sudanic
languages
money: CFA franc
gov: Republic

BURUNDI

cap: Bujumbura
pop: 6,400,000
area (sq. mi.): 10,759
lang: French, Kirundi,
Swahili
money: franc
gov: In transition

CAMBODIA

cap: Phnom Penh
pop: 10,600,000
area (sq. mi.): 70,238
lang: Kmer, French
money: rie
gov: Constitutional
monarchy

CAMEROON

cap: Yaoundé
pop: 13,500,000
area (sq. mi.): 179,714
lang: English, French,
others
money: CFA franc
gov: Republic

CANADA

cap: Ottawa
pop: 29,600,000
area (sq. mi.): 3,849,672
lang: English, French
money: dollar
gov: Confederation
with parliamentary
democracy

CAPE VERDE

cap: Praia
pop: 400,000
area (sq. mi.): 1,557
lang: Portuguese, Crioulo
money: escudo
gov: Republic

COUNTRIES OF THE WORLD (cont.)

CENTRAL AFRICAN REPUBLIC

cap: Bangui
pop: 3,200,000
area (sq. mi.): 240,534
lang: French, Sangho, others
money: CFA franc
gov: Republic

CHAD

cap: N'Djamena
pop: 6,400,000
area (sq. mi.): 495,755
lang: French, Arabic, others
money: CFA franc
gov: Republic

CHILE

cap: Santiago
pop: 14,300,000
area (sq. mi.): 302,779
lang: Spanish
money: peso
gov: Republic

CHINA, People's Rep. of

cap: Beijing
pop: 1,218,800,00
area (sq. mi.): 3,696,100
lang: Mandarin, Yue, others
money: yuan
gov: Communist Party–led state

CHINA, Rep. of (Taiwan)

cap: Taipai
pop: 21,200,000
area (sq. mi.): 13,885
lang: Mandarin, Malay, others
money: dollar
gov: Communist

COLOMBIA

cap: Bogotá
pop: 37,700,000
area (sq. mi.): 439,735
lang: Spanish
money: peso
gov: Republic

COMOROS

cap: Moroni
pop: 500,000
area (sq. mi.): 838
lang: Arabic, French, Comoran
money: CFA franc
gov: In transition

CONGO (formerly Zaire)

cap: Kinshasa
pop: 44,100,000
area (sq. mi.): 905,563
lang: French, Kongo, others
money: zaire
gov: In transition

CONGO REPUBLIC

cap: Brazzaville
pop: 2,500,000
area (sq. mi.): 132,046
lang: French, Kongo, Teke
money: CFA franc
gov: Republic

COSTA RICA

cap: San José
pop: 3,300,000
area (sq. mi.): 19,652
lang: Spanish, English
money: colones
gov: Republic

CÔTE D'IVOIRE (Ivory Coast)

cap: Yamoussoukro
pop: 14,300,000
area (sq. mi.): 124,503
lang: French, Dioula, others
money: CFA franc
gov: Republic

CROATIA

cap: Zagreb
pop: 450,000
area (sq. mi.): 21,829
lang: Serbo-Croatian
money: kuna
gov: Parliamentary democracy

CUBA

cap: Havana
pop: 11,200,000
area (sq. mi.): 44,218
lang: Spanish
money: peso
gov: Communist state

CYPRUS

cap: Nicosia
pop: 700,000
area (sq. mi.): 44,218
lang: Greek, Turkish, English
money: pound
gov: Republic

CZECH REPUBLIC

cap: Prague
pop: 10,400,000
area (sq. mi.): 30,449
lang: Czech, Slovak
money: koruna
gov: Republic

DENMARK

cap: Copenhagen
pop: 5,200,000
area (sq. mi.): 16,633
lang: Danish
money: krone
gov: Constitutional monarchy

COUNTRIES OF THE WORLD (cont.)

DJIBOUTI

cap: Djibouti
pop: 600,000
area (sq. mi.): 8,950
lang: French, Arabic, Afar, Somali
money: franc
gov: Republic

DOMINICA

cap: Roseau
pop: 100,000
area (sq. mi.): 290
lang: English, Creole
money: dollar
gov: Parliamentary democracy

DOMINICAN REPUBLIC

cap: Santo Domingo
pop: 7,800,000
area (sq. mi.): 18,704
lang: Spanish
money: peso
gov: Republic

ECUADOR

cap: Quito
pop: 11,500,000
area (sq. mi.): 109,483
lang: Spanish, Quechua, Jivaroan
money: sucre
gov: Republic

EGYPT

cap: Cairo
pop: 61,900,000
area (sq. mi.): 386,650
lang: Arabic, English, French
money: pound
gov: Republic

EL SALVADOR

cap: San Salvador
pop: 5,900,000
area (sq. mi.): 8,124
lang: Spanish, Nahuatl
money: colon
gov: Republic

EQUATORIAL GUINEA

cap: Malabo
pop: 40,000
area (sq. mi.): 10,832
lang: Spanish, Fang, Bubi
money: CFA franc
gov: Republic

ERITREA

cap: Asmara
pop: 3,500,000
area (sq. mi.): 36,170
lang: Tigre, Kunama, others
money: birr
gov: In transition

ESTONIA

cap: Tallinn
pop: 1,500,000
area (sq. mi.): 17,413
lang: Estonian, Russian, Latvian
money: kroon
gov: Republic

ETHIOPIA

cap: Addis Ababa
pop: 56,200,000
area (sq. mi.): 435,606
lang: Amharic, Tigre, Galla
money: birr
gov: Federal republic

FIJI

cap: Suva
pop: 800,000
area (sq. mi.): 7,056
lang: English, Fijian, Hindi
money: dollar
gov: Republic

FINLAND

cap: Helsinki
pop: 510,000
area (sq. mi.): 130,119
lang: Finnish, Swedish
money: markka
gov: Constitutional republic

FRANCE

cap: Paris
pop: 58,100,000
area (sq. mi.): 220,668
lang: French
money: franc
gov: Republic

GABON

cap: Libreville
pop: 1,300,000
area (sq. mi.): 103,346
lang: French, Fang, others
money: CFA franc
gov: Republic

GAMBIA

cap: Banjul
pop: 1,100,000
area (sq. mi.): 4,127
lang: English, Mandinka, Wolof
money: dalasi
gov: Republic

GEORGIA

cap: Tbilisi
pop: 5,570,000
area (sq. mi.): 26,911
lang: Georgian, Russian, Armenian
money: tetri
gov: Republic

COUNTRIES OF THE WORLD (cont.)

GERMANY

cap: Berlin
pop: 81,700,000
area (sq. mi.): 137,838
lang: German
money: mark
gov: Federal republic

GHANA

cap: Accra
pop: 17,500,000
area (sq. mi.): 92,098
lang: English, Akan,
   others
money: cedi
gov: Republic

GREECE

cap: Athens
pop: 10,500,000
area (sq. mi.): 51,146
lang: Greek, English,
   French
money: drachma
gov: Parliamentary
   republic

GRENADA

cap: St. George's
pop: 100,000
area (sq. mi.): 133
lang: English,
   French patois
money: dollar
gov: Parliamentary
   democracy

GUATEMALA

cap: Guatemala City
pop: 10,600,000
area (sq. mi.): 42,042
lang: Spanish, Mayan
money: quetzal
gov: Republic

GUINEA

cap: Conakry
pop: 6,500,000
area (sq. mi.): 94,964
lang: French, Peul, Mande
money: franc
gov: Republic

GUINEA-BISSAU

cap: Bissau
pop: 1,100,000
area (sq. mi.): 13,948
lang: Portuguese,
   Crioulo, others
money: peso
gov: Republic

GUYANA

cap: Georgetown
pop: 800,000
area (sq. mi.): 83,000
lang: English, Indian
   languages
money: dollar
gov: Republic

HAITI

cap: Port-au-Prince
pop: 7,200,000
area (sq. mi.): 10,579
lang: French, Creole
money: gourde
gov: Republic

HONDURAS

cap: Tegucigalpa
pop: 5,500,000
area (sq. mi.): 43,277
lang: Spanish, Indian
   languages
money: lempira
gov: Republic

HUNGARY

cap: Budapest
pop: 10,200,000
area (sq. mi.): 35,919
lang: Hungarian
money: forint
gov: Parliamentary
   democracy

ICELAND

cap: Reykjavik
pop: 300,000
area (sq. mi.): 39,769
lang: Icelandic
money: kronur
gov: Constitutional
   republic

INDIA

cap: New Dehli
pop: 930,600,000
area (sq. mi.): 1,266,595
lang: Hindi, English, others
money: rupee
gov: Federal republic

INDONESIA

cap: Jakarta
pop: 198,040,000
area (sq. mi.): 735,268
lang: Bahasa Indonesian,
   Javanese, others
money: rupiah
gov: Republic

IRAN

cap: Tehran
pop: 61,300,000
area (sq. mi.): 636,293
lang: Farsi, Turkic, Kurdish
money: rial
gov: Islamic republic

IRAQ

cap: Baghdad
pop: 20,600,000
area (sq. mi.): 167,924
lang: Arabic, Kurdish
money: dinar
gov: Republic

COUNTRIES OF THE WORLD (cont.)

IRELAND

cap: Dublin
pop: 3,600,000
area (sq. mi.): 27,137
lang: English, Gaelic
money: punt
gov: Parliamentary
republic

ISRAEL

cap: Jerusalem
pop: 5,500,000
area (sq. mi.): 7,847
lang: Hebrew, Arabic,
English
money: new sheqalim
gov: Republic

ITALY

cap: Rome
pop: 57,700,000
area (sq. mi.): 116,303
lang: Italian
money: lira
gov: Republic

JAMAICA

cap: Kingston
pop: 2,400,000
area (sq. mi.): 4,232
lang: English, Jamaican
Creole
money: dollar
gov: Parliamentary
democracy

JAPAN

cap: Tokyo
pop: 125,200,000
area (sq. mi.): 145,856
lang: Japanese
money: yen
gov: Parliamentary
democracy

JORDAN

cap: Amman
pop: 4,100,000
area (sq. mi.): 37,737
lang: Arabic, English
money: dinar
gov: Constitutional
monarchy

KAZAKHSTAN

cap: Almaty
pop: 16,900,000
area (sq. mi.): 1,049,200
lang: Kazakh, Russian,
German
money: tenge
gov: Republic

KENYA

cap: Nairobi
pop: 28,300,000
area (sq. mi.): 224,960
lang: Swahili, English,
others
money: shilling
gov: Republic

KIRIBATI

cap: Tarawa
pop: 76,320
area (sq. mi.): 266
lang: English, Gilbertese
money: dollar
gov: Republic

KOREA, Dem. People's Rep. of (North Korea)

cap: Pyongyang
pop: 25,500,000
area (sq. mi.): 46,540
lang: Korean
money: won
gov: Communist
state

KOREA, Rep. of (South Korea)

cap: Seoul
pop: 44,900,000
area (sq. mi.): 38,025
lang: Korean
money: won
gov: Republic, with power
centralized in a strong
executive

KUWAIT
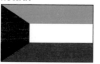
cap: Kuwait
pop: 1,500,000
area (sq. mi.): 6,880
lang: Arabic, English
money: dinar
gov: Constitutional
monarchy

KYRGYZSTAN

cap: Bishkek
pop: 4,400,000
area (sq. mi.): 76,642
lang: Kyrgyz, Russian,
Turkic
money: som
gov: Republic

LAOS
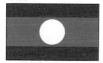
cap: Vientiane
pop: 4,800,000
area (sq. mi.): 91,428
lang: Lao, French, Sino-
Tibetan languages
money: new kip
gov: Communist state

LATVIA

cap: Riga
pop: 2,500,000
area (sq. mi.): 24,900
lang: Latvian, Lithuanian,
Russian
money: lat
gov: Republic

LEBANON

cap: Beirut
pop: 3,700,000
area (sq. mi.): 4,015
lang: Arabic, French,
others
money: pound
gov: Republic

COUNTRIES OF THE WORLD (cont.)

LESOTHO

cap: Maseru
pop: 2,100,000
area (sq. mi.): 11,716
lang: English, Sesotho, others
money: malati
gov: Modified constitutional monarchy

LIBERIA

cap: Monrovia
pop: 3,000,000
area (sq. mi.): 38,250
lang: English, Niger-Congo languages
money: dollar
gov: Republic

LIBYA

cap: Tripoli
pop: 5,200,000
area (sq. mi.): 679,359
lang: Arabic, Italian, English
money: dinar
gov: Islamic Arabic Socialist "mass-state"

LIECHTENSTEIN

cap: Vaduz
pop: 30,000
area (sq. mi.): 62
lang: German, Alemannic dialect
money: Swiss franc
gov: Hereditary constitutional monarchy

LITHUANIA

cap: Vilnius
pop: 3,788,000
area (sq. mi.): 25,170
lang: Lithuanian, Polish, Russian
money: litas
gov: Republic

LUXEMBOURG

cap: Luxembourg
pop: 400,000
area (sq. mi.): 998
lang: French, German, Luxembourgisch
money: franc
gov: Constitutional monarchy

MACEDONIA

cap: Skopje
pop: 2,100,000
area (sq. mi.): 9,928
lang: Macedonian, Albanian, others
money: dinar
gov: Republic

MADAGASCAR

cap: Antananarivo
pop: 14,800,000
area (sq. mi.): 226,657
lang: French, Malagasy
money: franc
gov: Republic

MALAWI

cap: Lilongwe
pop: 9,700,000
area (sq. mi.): 45,747
lang: English, Chichewa, Bantu languages
money: kwacha
gov: Multiparty democracy

MALAYSIA

cap: Kuala Lumpur
pop: 19,900,000
area (sq. mi.): 127,316
lang: Malay, English, others
money: ringgit
gov: Federal parliamentary democracy with a constitutional monarchy

MALDIVES

cap: Male
pop: 300,000
area (sq. mi.): 115
lang: Divehi, English
money: rufiyaa
gov: Republic

MALI

cap: Bamako
pop: 9,400,000
area (sq. mi.): 478,764
lang: French, Bambara, Senufo
money: franc
gov: Republic

MALTA

cap: Valletta
pop: 400,000
area (sq. mi.): 122
lang: Maltese, English
money: lirs
gov: Parliamentary democracy

MARSHALL ISLANDS

cap: Majuro
pop: 100,000
area (sq. mi.): 70
lang: English, Marshallese, Japananese
money: U.S. dollar
gov: Republic

MAURITANIA

cap: Nouakchott
pop: 2,300,000
area (sq. mi.): 419,212
lang: Hassanya Arabic, Wolof, others
money: ouguiya
gov: Islamic republic

MAURITIUS

cap: Port Louis
pop: 1,100,000
area (sq. mi.): 720
lang: English, Creole, others
money: rupee
gov: Republic

COUNTRIES OF THE WORLD (cont.)

MEXICO

cap: Mexico City
pop: 93,700,000
area (sq. mi.): 761,604
lang: Spanish, Mayan, others
money: peso
gov: Federal republic

MICRONESIA

cap: Palikir
pop: 111,000
area (sq. mi.): 270
lang: English, Trukese, others
money: dollar
gov: Republic

MOLDOVA

cap: Chisinau
pop: 4,300,000
area (sq. mi.): 13,012
lang: Moldovan, Russian
money: ruble
gov: Republic

MONACO

cap: Monaco
pop: 31,000
area (sq. mi.): 0.6
lang: French, English, Monegasque
money: franc
gov: Constitutional monarchy

MONGOLIA

cap: Ulan Bator
pop: 2,300,000
area (sq. mi.): 604,247
lang: Mongolian, Turkic, Russian
money: tugrik
gov: Republic

MOROCCO

cap: Rabat
pop: 29,200,000
area (sq. mi.): 172,413
lang: Arabic, Berber languages, French
money: dirham
gov: Constitutional monarchy

MOZAMBIQUE

cap: Maputo
pop: 17,400,000
area (sq. mi.): 303,769
lang: Portuguese, African languages
money: metica
gov: Republic

MYANMAR

cap: Yangon
pop: 44,800,000
area (sq. mi.): 261,789
lang: Burmese, Karen, Shan
money: kyat
gov: Military

NAMIBIA

cap: Windhoek
pop: 17,400,000
area (sq. mi.): 317,818
lang: Afrikaans, English, others
money: dollar
gov: Republic

NAURU

cap: Yaren
pop: 9,880
area (sq. mi.): 8
lang: Nauruan, English
money: dollar
gov: Republic

NEPAL

cap: Kathmandu
pop: 22,600,000
area (sq. mi.): 56,136
lang: Nepali, others
money: rupee
gov: Constitutional monarchy

NETHERLANDS

cap: Amsterdam
pop: 15,500,000
area (sq. mi.): 15,770
lang: Dutch
money: guilder
gov: Parliamentary democracy under a constitutional monarch

NEW ZEALAND

cap: Wellington
pop: 3,500,000
area (sq. mi.): 103,736
lang: English, Maori
money: dollar
gov: Parliamentary democracy

NICARAGUA

cap: Managua
pop: 4,400,000
area (sq. mi.): 50,193
lang: Spanish, Indian languages
money: cordoba oro
gov: Republic

NIGER

cap: Niamey
pop: 9,200,000
area (sq. mi.): 489,189
lang: French, Hausa, Djema
money: CFA franc
gov: Republic

NIGERIA

cap: Abuja
pop: 101,200,000
area (sq. mi.): 356,667
lang: English, Hausa, others
money: naira
gov: In transition

COUNTRIES OF THE WORLD (cont.)

NORWAY

cap: Oslo
pop: 4,300,000
area (sq. mi.): 125,181
lang: Norwegian, Lapp, Finnish
money: kroner
gov: Hereditary constitutional monarchy

OMAN

cap: Muscat
pop: 2,200,000
area (sq. mi.): 82,030
lang: Arabic, Balachi, others
money: rial omani
gov: Absolute monarchy

PAKISTAN

cap: Islamabad
pop: 129,700,000
area (sq. mi.): 310,403
lang: Urdu, English, others
money: rupee
gov: Republic

PALAU

cap: Koror
pop: 15,000
area (sq. mi.): 179
lang: English
money: dollar
gov: Republic

PANAMA

cap: Panama City
pop: 2,600,000
area (sq. mi.): 29,762
lang: Spanish, English
money: balboa
gov: Constitutional republic

PAPUA NEW GUINEA

cap: Port Moresby
pop: 4,100,000
area (sq. mi.): 178,260
lang: English, Melanesian, Papuan
money: kina
gov: Parliamentary democracy

PARAGUAY

cap: Asunción
pop: 5,000,000
area (sq. mi.): 157,047
lang: Spanish, Guarani
money: guarani
gov: Republic

PERU

cap: Lima
pop: 24,000,000
area (sq. mi.): 496,222
lang: Spanish, Quecha, Aymara
money: nuevo sol
gov: Republic

PHILIPPINES

cap: Manila
pop: 68,400,000
area (sq. mi.): 115,831
lang: Filipino, English, others
money: peso
gov: Republic

POLAND

cap: Warsaw
pop: 38,600,000
area (sq. mi.): 120,727
lang: Polish
money: zloty
gov: Republic

PORTUGAL

cap: Lisbon
pop: 9,900,000
area (sq. mi.): 36,390
lang: Portuguese
money: escudo
gov: Republic

QATAR

cap: Doha
pop: 500,000
area (sq. mi.): 4,247
lang: Arabic, English
money: riyal
gov: Traditional monarchy

ROMANIA

cap: Bucharest
pop: 22,700,000
area (sq. mi.): 91,699
lang: Romanian, Hungarian, German
money: leu
gov: Republic

RUSSIA

cap: Moscow
pop: 147,500,000
area (sq. mi.): 6,592,800
lang: Russian, Ukrainian, others
money: ruble
gov: Federation

RWANDA

cap: Kigali
pop: 7,800,000
area (sq. mi.): 10,169
lang: French, Kinyarwanda, Bantu
money: franc
gov: Republic

ST. KITTS AND NEVIS

cap: Basseterre
pop: 40,000
area (sq. mi.): 101
lang: English
money: dollar
gov: Constitutional monarchy

COUNTRIES OF THE WORLD (cont.)

ST. LUCIA

cap: Castries
pop: 151,000
area (sq. mi.): 238
lang: English, French patois
money: dollar
gov: Parliamentary democracy

ST. VINCENT AND THE GRENADINES

cap: Kingstown
pop: 114,000
area (sq. mi.): 150
lang: English, French patois
money: dollar
gov: Constitutional monarchy

SAMOA

cap: Apia
pop: 200,000
area (sq. mi.): 1,133
lang: Samoan, English
money: tala
gov: Constitutional monarchy

SAN MARINO

cap: San Marino
pop: 30,000
area (sq. mi.): 24
lang: Italian
money: lira
gov: Republic

SÃO TOMÉ AND PRINCIPE

cap: São Tomé
pop: 100,000
area (sq. mi.): 372
lang: Portuguese
money: dobra
gov: Republic

SAUDI ARABIA

cap: Riyadh
pop: 18,500,000
area (sq. mi.): 839,996
lang: Arabic
money: riyal
gov: Monarch with council of ministers

SENEGAL

cap: Dakar
pop: 8,300,000
area (sq. mi.): 75,750
lang: French, Wolof, others
money: CFA franc
gov: Republic

SEYCHELLES

cap: Victoria
pop: 100,000
area (sq. mi.): 171
lang: English, French, Creole
money: rupee
gov: Republic

SIERRE LEONE

cap: Freetown
pop: 4,500,000
area (sq. mi.): 27,925
lang: English, Kiro, others
money: leone
gov: In transition

SINGAPORE

cap: Singapore
pop: 3,000,000
area (sq. mi.): 224
lang: Malay, Tamil, Chinese, English
money: dollar
gov: Republic

SLOVAKIA

cap: Bratislava
pop: 5,400,000
area (sq. mi.): 18,932
lang: Slovak, Hungarian, others
money: koruna
gov: Republic

SLOVENIA

cap: Ljubljana
pop: 2,000,000
area (sq. mi.): 7,819
lang: Slovenian, Serbo-Croatian, others
money: tolar
gov: Republic

SOLOMON ISLANDS

cap: Honiara
pop: 400,000
area (sq. mi.): 10,640
lang: English, Papuan, others
money: dollar
gov: Parliamentary democracy with the Commonwealth of Nations

SOMALIA

cap: Mogadishu
pop: 9,300,000
area (sq. mi.): 246,300
lang: Somali, Arabic, others
money: shilling
gov: In transition

SOUTH AFRICA

cap: Pretoria, Cape Town, and Bloemfontein
pop: 43,500,000
area (sq. mi.): 472,359
lang: Afrikaans, English, Nguni, others
money: rand
gov: Federal republic with bicameral parliament and universal suffrage

SPAIN

cap: Madrid
pop: 39,100,000
area (sq. mi.): 194,896
lang: Spanish, Catalan, others
money: peseta
gov: Constitutional monarchy

COUNTRIES OF THE WORLD (cont.)

SRI LANKA

cap: Colombo
pop: 18,200,000
area (sq. mi.): 25,332
lang: Sinhalese, Tamil, English
money: rupee
gov: Republic

SUDAN

cap: Khartoum
pop: 28,100,000
area (sq. mi.): 966,757
lang: Arabic, Dinka, others
money: dinar
gov: Military

SURINAME

cap: Paramaribo
pop: 410,000
area (sq. mi.): 63,037
lang: Dutch, Sranan Tongo, English
money: guilder
gov: Republic

SWAZILAND

cap: Mlabane
pop: 1,000,000
area (sq. mi.): 6,704
lang: Siswati, English
money: lilageni
gov: Constitutional monarchy

SWEDEN

cap: Stockholm
pop: 8,900,000
area (sq. mi.): 173,731
lang: Swedish, Lapp, Finnish
money: krona
gov: Constitutional monarchy

SWITZERLAND

cap: Bern
pop: 7,000,000
area (sq. mi.): 15,941
lang: French, German, Italian, Romansch
money: franc
gov: Federal republic

SYRIA

cap: Damascus
pop: 14,700,000
area (sq. mi.): 71,498
lang: Arabic, Kurdish, Armenian
money: pound
gov: Republic (under military regime)

TAJIKISTAN

cap: Dushanbe
pop: 5,800,000
area (sq. mi.): 54,019
lang: Tadzhik, Russian
money: ruble
gov: Republic

TANZANIA

cap: Dar-es-Salaam
pop: 28,500,000
area (sq. mi.): 364,886
lang: Swahili, English, others
money: shilling
gov: Republic

THAILAND

cap: Bangkok
pop: 60,200,000
area (sq. mi.): 198,456
lang: Thai, Chinese, others
money: baht
gov: Constitutional monarchy

TOGO

cap: Lomé
pop: 4,400,000
area (sq. mi.): 21,622
lang: French, Ewe, others
money: CFA franc
gov: Republic

TONGA

cap: Nuku'alofa
pop: 104,000
area (sq. mi.): 270
lang: Tongan, English
money: pa'anga
gov: Constitutional monarchy

TRINIDAD AND TOBAGO

cap: Port of Spain
pop: 1,300,000
area (sq. mi.): 1,980
lang: English, Hindi, others
money: dollar
gov: Parliamentary democracy

TUNISIA

cap: Tunis
pop: 8,900,000
area (sq. mi.): 63,170
lang: Arabic, French
money: dinar
gov: Republic

TURKEY

cap: Ankara
pop: 61,400,000
area (sq. mi.): 301,381
lang: Turkish, Kurdish, Arabic
money: lira
gov: Republic

TURKMENISTAN

cap: Ashgabad
pop: 14,500,000
area (sq. mi.): 188,417
lang: Turkmen, Russian, others
money: manat
gov: Republic

COUNTRIES OF THE WORLD (cont.)

TUVALU

cap: Funafuti
pop: 9,670
area (sq. mi.): 10
lang: Tuvaluan, English
money: dollar
gov: Constitutional
monarchy

UGANDA

cap: Kampala
pop: 21,300,000
area (sq. mi.): 93,354
lang: English, Luganda,
Swahili
money: shilling
gov: Republic

UKRAINE

cap: Kyiv
pop: 52,000,000
area (sq. mi.): 23,100
lang: Ukrainian, Russian,
others
money: karbovanet
gov: Constitutional
republic

UNITED ARAB EMIRATES

cap: Abu Dhabi
pop: 1,900,000
area (sq. mi.): 32,000
lang: Arabic, Persian,
others
money: dirham
gov: Federation of
emirates

UNITED KINGDOM

cap: London
pop: 56,600,800
area (sq. mi.): 94,226
lang: English, Welsh,
Scottish, Gaelic
money: pound
gov: Constitutional
monarchy

UNITED STATES

cap: Washington, DC
pop: 263,200,000
area (sq. mi.): 3,618,770
lang: English, Spanish,
others
money: dollar
gov: Federal republic, strong
democratic tradition

URUGUAY

cap: Montevideo
pop: 3,200,000
area (sq. mi.): 68,037
lang: Spanish
money: new peso
gov: Republic

UZBEKISTAN

cap: Tashkent
pop: 22,700,000
area (sq. mi.): 172,700
lang: Uzbek, Russian,
others
money: som
gov: Republic

VANUATU

cap: Port-Vila
pop: 200,000
area (sq. mi.): 5,700
lang: Bislama, English,
French
money: vatu
gov: Republic

VATICAN CITY

cap: Vatican City
pop: 800
area (sq. mi.): 0.17
lang: Italian, Latin
money: lira

VENEZUELA

cap: Caracas
pop: 21,800,000
area (sq. mi.): 352,143
lang: Spanish, Indian
languages
money: bolivar
gov: Federal republic

VIETNAM

cap: Hanoi
pop: 75,000,000
area (sq. mi.): 127,330
lang: Vietnamese,
Chinese, others
money: dong
gov: Communist

YEMEN

cap: Sanaa
pop: 13,200,000
area (sq. mi.): 203,796
lang: Arabic
money: rial
gov: Republic

YUGOSLAVIA, Fed. Rep. of (Serbia and Montenegro)

cap: Belgrade
pop: 10,500,000
area (sq. mi.): 26,940
lang: Serbo-Croatian,
Albanian
money: dinar
gov: Republic

ZAMBIA

cap: Lusaka
pop: 9,100,000
area (sq. mi.): 290,586
lang: English, Bantu
languages
money: kwacha
gov: Republic

ZIMBABWE

cap: Harare
pop: 11,300,000
area (sq. mi.): 150,803
lang: English, Shona,
others
money: dollar
gov: Republic

Source: *CIA World Factbook*

WORLD POPULATION AND LAND AREAS

Estimated Population, 1997

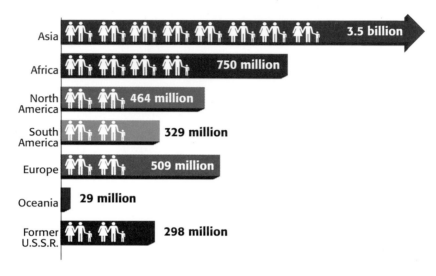

Asia	3.5 billion
Africa	750 million
North America	464 million
South America	329 million
Europe	509 million
Oceania	29 million
Former U.S.S.R.	298 million

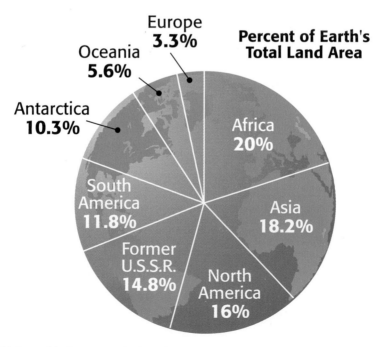

Percent of Earth's Total Land Area

Europe 3.3%
Oceania 5.6%
Antarctica 10.3%
South America 11.8%
Former U.S.S.R. 14.8%
Africa 20%
Asia 18.2%
North America 16%

Source: U.S. Bureau of the Census, International Data Base

TOP 5 HIGHEST MOUNTAINS IN THE WORLD

(height of principal peak; lower peaks of same mountain excluded)

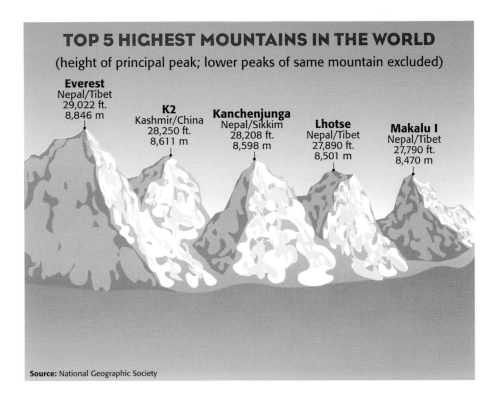

Everest
Nepal/Tibet
29,022 ft.
8,846 m

K2
Kashmir/China
28,250 ft.
8,611 m

Kanchenjunga
Nepal/Sikkim
28,208 ft.
8,598 m

Lhotse
Nepal/Tibet
27,890 ft.
8,501 m

Makalu I
Nepal/Tibet
27,790 ft.
8,470 m

Source: National Geographic Society

TOP 5 HIGHEST WATERFALLS IN THE WORLD

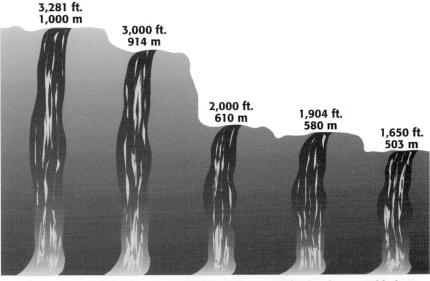

3,281 ft.
1,000 m

3,000 ft.
914 m

2,000 ft.
610 m

1,904 ft.
580 m

1,650 ft.
503 m

Angel
Venezuela
*Tributary of
Caroní River*

Tugela
Natal, South Africa
Tugela River

Cuquenán
Venezuela
Cuquenán River

Sutherland
South Island, N.Z.
Arthur River

Takkakaw
British Columbia
*Tributary of
Yoho River*

Source: Geological Survey, U.S. Department of the Interior

WORLD'S TOP 5 LARGEST OCEANS AND SEAS

(by area in square miles and millions of square kilometers [msk])

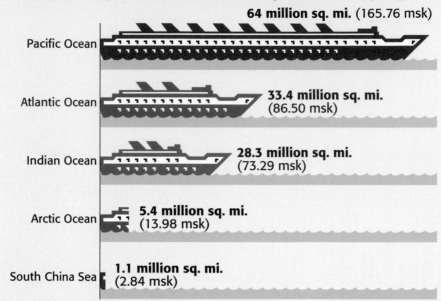

64 million sq. mi. (165.76 msk)

Pacific Ocean

Atlantic Ocean — **33.4 million sq. mi.** (86.50 msk)

Indian Ocean — **28.3 million sq. mi.** (73.29 msk)

Arctic Ocean — **5.4 million sq. mi.** (13.98 msk)

South China Sea — **1.1 million sq. mi.** (2.84 msk)

Source: Geological Survey, U.S. Department of the Interior

TOP 5 DEEPEST OCEANS AND SEAS IN THE WORLD

(ranked by average depth)

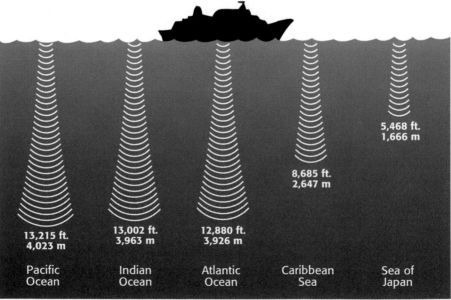

13,215 ft.
4,023 m
Pacific
Ocean

13,002 ft.
3,963 m
Indian
Ocean

12,880 ft.
3,926 m
Atlantic
Ocean

8,685 ft.
2,647 m
Caribbean
Sea

5,468 ft.
1,666 m
Sea of
Japan

Source: U.S. Department of Defense; National Geographic Society

TOP 5 LARGEST LAKES IN THE WORLD

(ranked by approximate area in square miles/square kilometers)

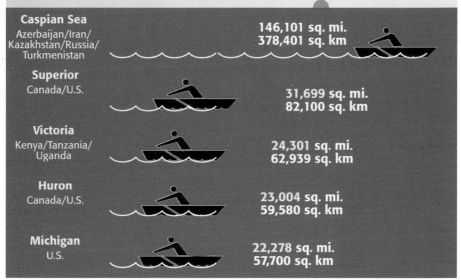

Caspian Sea Azerbaijan/Iran/ Kazakhstan/Russia/ Turkmenistan	146,101 sq. mi. 378,401 sq. km
Superior Canada/U.S.	31,699 sq. mi. 82,100 sq. km
Victoria Kenya/Tanzania/ Uganda	24,301 sq. mi. 62,939 sq. km
Huron Canada/U.S.	23,004 sq. mi. 59,580 sq. km
Michigan U.S.	22,278 sq. mi. 57,700 sq. km

Source: Geological Survey, U.S. Department of the Interior

TOP 5 LONGEST RIVERS IN THE WORLD

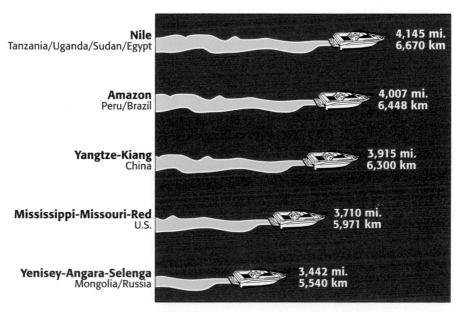

Nile Tanzania/Uganda/Sudan/Egypt	4,145 mi. 6,670 km
Amazon Peru/Brazil	4,007 mi. 6,448 km
Yangtze-Kiang China	3,915 mi. 6,300 km
Mississippi-Missouri-Red U.S.	3,710 mi. 5,971 km
Yenisey-Angara-Selenga Mongolia/Russia	3,442 mi. 5,540 km

Source: Geological Survey, U.S. Department of the Interior

GOVERNMENT (U.S.)

The United States is a democratic republic, with a federal system of government. In a democratic republic, the people vote regularly to elect government leaders. In a federal system, the central (or national) government shares power with state and local governments. The U.S. national government is often called the federal government.

The U.S. Constitution outlines the structure and powers of the federal government. In 1787, when the Constitution was written, Americans worried that a strong central government might restrict their rights. One way in which the authors of the Constitution guarded against this was by setting up three branches of government and dividing powers among them. The U.S. Congress, the legislative branch, creates laws. The president (and the government departments that report to the president) represents the executive branch, which enforces laws. The Supreme Court and other federal courts form the judicial branch. They can overturn laws that violate the provisions of the Constitution. This system of "checks and balances" prevents any of the three branches from gaining too much power.

Individual freedom is protected by the Bill of Rights, the first 10 amendments to the Constitution. Amendments have ended slavery, extended citizenship and voting rights, and set rules for presidential elections. Today the federal government employs millions of people. But the Constitution still controls its actions and preserves individual rights.

Yearbook

1789 The Constitution is ratified by 11 of 13 states. George Washington becomes the first U.S. president.

1803 For the first time, the Supreme Court finds that a law passed by Congress is unconstitutional. The case—*Marbury* v. *Madison*—greatly expands the power of the court.

1860 South Carolina secedes from the union and is followed by six more southern states; together they form the Confederate States of America.

1920 The Nineteenth Amendment is ratified, giving women the right to vote.

• Notables •

Madeleine Albright (1937–   )
First woman secretary of state.

Louis Brandeis (1856–1941) Supreme Court justice; known for his devotion to the First ("Free Speech") Amendment.

Thomas Jefferson (1743–1826)
Author of the Declaration of Independence; third U.S. president; noted statesman.

Abraham Lincoln (1802–1865)
Sixteenth U.S. president; provided strong leadership during Civil War; freed slaves.

Franklin D. Roosevelt (1882–1945)
U.S. president from 1933 to 1945; only president elected for a fourth term; known for social welfare legislation ("New Deal") developed during the Depression.

Elizabeth Cady Stanton (1815–1902) Leader of woman suffrage movement that led to passage of the Nineteenth Amendment.

KEY IDEAS

amendment A change or addition to a proposed law or to the U.S. Constitution. Constitutional amendments must be approved by Congress and then ratified (formally approved) by the states.

cabinet The heads of the U.S. government's 14 major departments: Agriculture, Attorney General, Commerce, Defense, Education, Energy, Health and Human Services, Housing and Urban Development, Interior, Labor, State, Transportation, Treasury, and Veteran Affairs.

constitution The basic laws and principles that determine the powers and duties of government and the rights of its people.

democracy A government in which the highest power is given to the people through a system of representation.

veto A U.S. president's refusal to sign a bill (proposed law). Congress can override the veto if two thirds of the Senate and House of Representatives approves the bill. In that case, it becomes a law.

THE BRANCHES OF GOVERNMENT

EXECUTIVE

The President

- Symbol of our nation and head of state
- Shapes and conducts foreign policy and acts as chief diplomat
- Chief administrator of the federal government
- Commander in chief of armed forces
- Has authority to pass or veto congressional bills, plans, and programs
- Appoints and removes nonelected officials
- Leader of his or her political party

LEGISLATIVE

The Congress:
The Senate
The House of Representatives

- Chief lawmaking body
- Conducts investigations into matters of national importance
- Has power to impeach or remove any civil officer from office, including the president
- Can amend the Constitution
- The Senate is made up of 100 senators—2 from each state
- The House of Representatives is made up of 435 congressional representatives, apportioned to each state according to population

JUDICIAL

The Supreme Court

- Protects the Constitution
- Enforces commands of the executive and legislative branches
- Protects the rights of individuals and shields citizens from unfair laws
- Can declare laws unconstitutional
- Defines the laws of our nation

FEDERAL EMPLOYMENT BY BRANCH, 1996

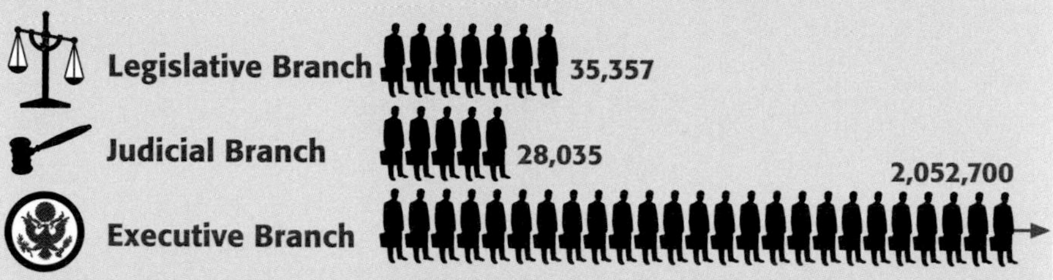

Legislative Branch 35,357

Judicial Branch 28,035

Executive Branch 2,052,700

Department of Defense	868,300
Department of Veterans Affairs	227,700
Department of the Treasury	157,300
Department of Labor	117,500
Department of Agriculture	109,800
Department of Justice	95,300
Department of the Interior	76,300
Department of Transportation	66,400
Social Security Administration	64,500
Department of Health and Human Services	62,900
Department of Commerce	36,000
Department of State	25,200
National Aeronautics and Space Administration (NASA)	23,900
Department of Energy	19,800
General Services Administration	19,500
Environmental Protection Agency	17,600
Department of Housing and Urban Development	13,100
Small Business Administration	6,300
Office of Personnel Management	5,300
Department of Education	4,800
Other independent agencies	98,592
Totals	**2,116,092**

Source: Office of Management and Budget, *Budget of the United States Government, FY1996,* 1995

PROFILE: WHERE THE U.S. GOVERNMENT GETS ITS MONEY

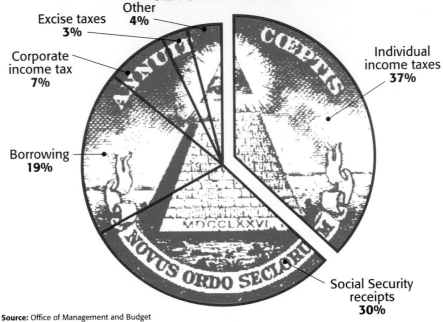

Other 4%

Excise taxes 3%

Corporate income tax 7%

Borrowing 19%

Individual income taxes 37%

Social Security receipts 30%

Source: Office of Management and Budget

HOW THE GOVERNMENT SPENDS ITS MONEY

(in billions, based on the 1995 budget)

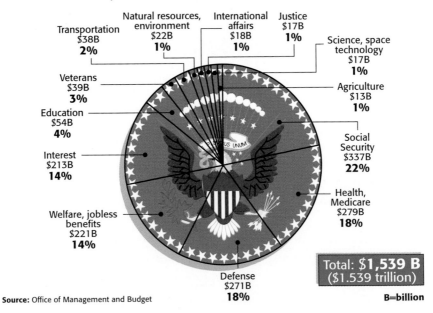

Transportation $38B 2%

Natural resources, environment $22B 1%

International affairs $18B 1%

Justice $17B 1%

Science, space technology $17B 1%

Veterans $39B 3%

Education $54B 4%

Agriculture $13B 1%

Interest $213B 14%

Social Security $337B 22%

Welfare, jobless benefits $221B 14%

Health, Medicare $279B 18%

Defense $271B 18%

Total: **$1,539 B** ($1.539 trillion)

B=billion

Source: Office of Management and Budget

174 • Government (U.S.)

HOW A BILL INTRODUCED IN THE HOUSE OF REPRESENTATIVES BECOMES A LAW

(a similar procedure is followed for bills introduced in the Senate)

HOW BILLS ORIGINATE

The executive branch inspires much legislation. The president usually outlines broad objectives in the yearly State of the Union address.

Members of the president's staff may draft bills and ask Congresspersons who are friendly to the legislation to introduce them.

Other bills originate independently of the administration, perhaps to fulfill a campaign pledge made by a Congressperson.

HOW BILLS ARE INTRODUCED

Each bill must be introduced by a member of the House. The speaker then assigns the bill to the appropriate committee.

The committee conducts hearings during which members of the administration and others may testify for or against the bill.

If the committee votes to proceed, the bill goes to the Rules Committee, which decides whether to place it before the House.

THE HOUSE VOTES

A bill submitted to the House is voted on, with or without a debate. If a majority approves it, the bill is sent to the Senate.

SENATE PROCEDURE

The Senate assigns a bill to a Senate committee, which holds hearings and then approves, rejects, rewrites, or shelves the bill.

If the committee votes to proceed, it is submitted to the Senate for a vote, which may be taken with or without a debate.

RESULTS

If the Senate does not change the House version of the bill and a majority approves it, the bill goes to the president for signing.

If the bill the Senate approves differs from the House version, the bill is sent to a House-Senate conference for a compromise solution.

If the conference produces a compromise bill and it is approved by both the House and Senate, the bill goes to the president for signing.

WHEN A BILL BECOMES LAW

The bill becomes law if the president signs it. If the president vetoes it, two thirds of both the House and Senate must approve it again before it can become law. If the bill comes to the president soon before Congress adjourns, the president may not do anything at all. If the bill is not signed before Congress adjourns, the bill dies. This is called the president's "pocket veto."

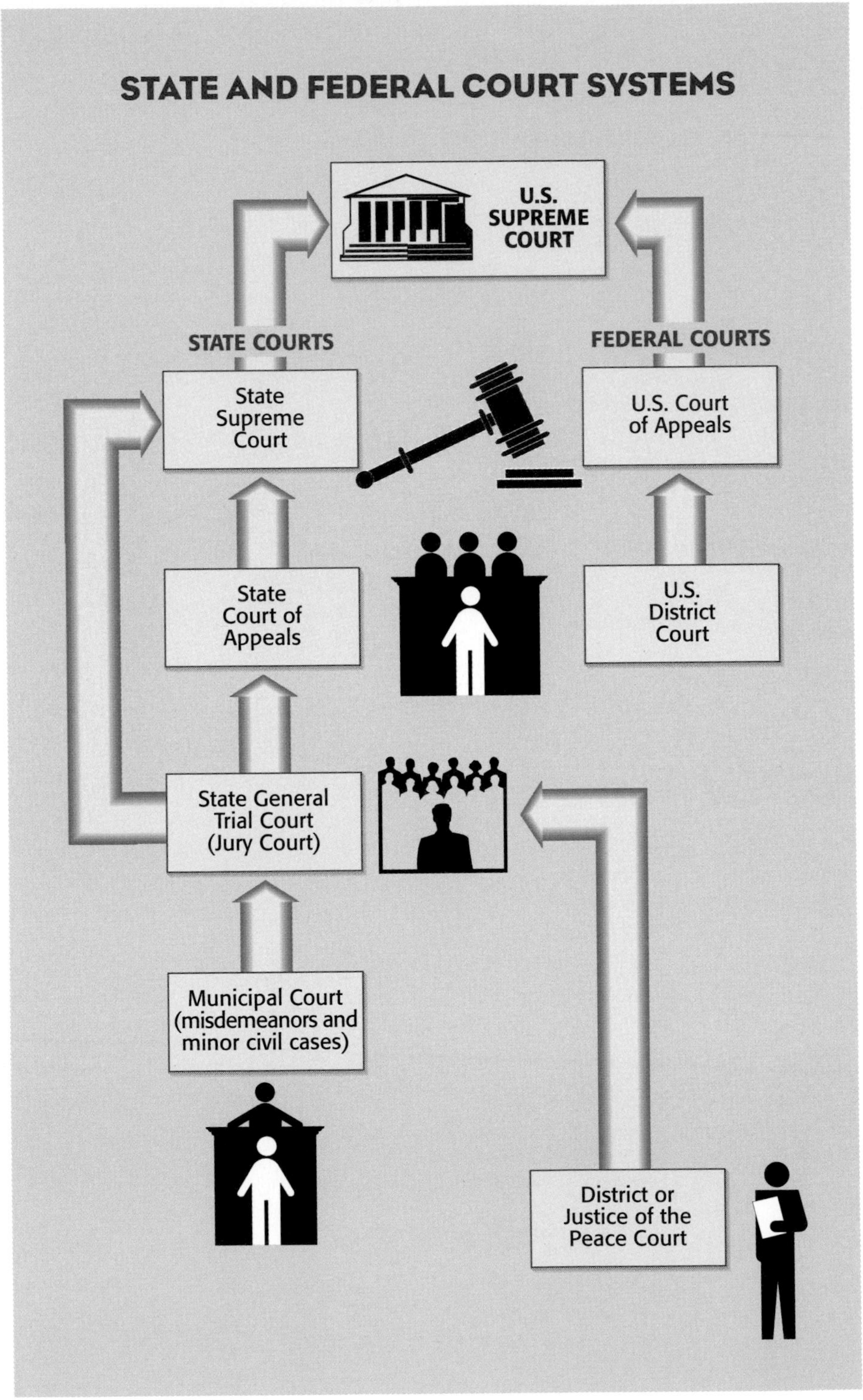

STATE AND FEDERAL COURT SYSTEMS

U.S. SUPREME COURT

STATE COURTS

FEDERAL COURTS

State Supreme Court

U.S. Court of Appeals

State Court of Appeals

U.S. District Court

State General Trial Court (Jury Court)

Municipal Court (misdemeanors and minor civil cases)

District or Justice of the Peace Court

THE SEQUENCE OF PRESIDENTIAL SUCCESSION

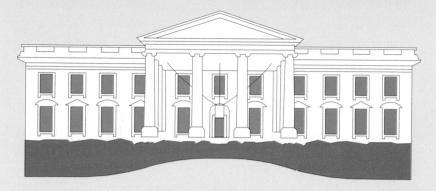

1. Vice President
2. Speaker of the House
3. President Pro Tempore of the Senate
4. Secretary of State
5. Secretary of Treasury
6. Secretary of Defense
7. Attorney General
8. Secretary of the Interior
9. Secretary of Agriculture
10. Secretary of Commerce
11. Secretary of Labor
12. Secretary of Health and Human Services
13. Secretary of Housing and Urban Development
14. Secretary of Transportation
15. Secretary of Energy
16. Secretary of Education

VOTING

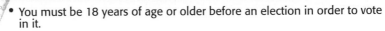

Basic Laws and Requirements

- You must be 18 years of age or older before an election in order to vote in it.
- You must be an American citizen to vote.
- You must register before voting.
- You must show proof of residence in order to register.

How to Register

- Registering often only requires filling out a simple form.
- It does not cost anything to register.
- You need not be a member of any party to register.
- To find out where to register, you can call your town hall or city board of elections.
- You can find out more information on voting and registering at:

   http://members.tripod.com/~voterinfo/voterguide.html

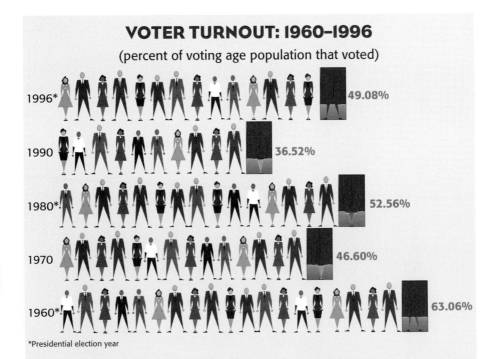

VOTER TURNOUT: 1960–1996
(percent of voting age population that voted)

1996*   49.08%

1990   36.52%

1980*   52.56%

1970   46.60%

1960*   63.06%

*Presidential election year

Source: Congressional Research Service reports; Election Data Services, Inc.; State Election Offices

VOTER PROFILE, BY SELECTED CHARACTERISTICS, 1996 ELECTION

(percent of eligible population that voted)

By Sex

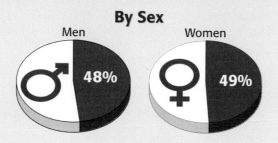

Men — 48%

Women — 49%

By Age

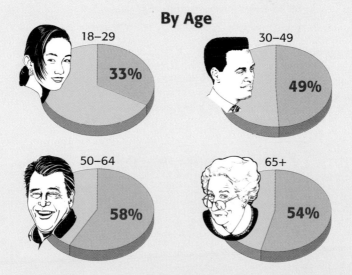

18–29 — 33%

30–49 — 49%

50–64 — 58%

65+ — 54%

By Race

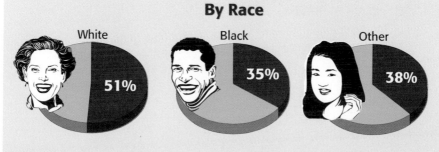

White — 51%

Black — 35%

Other — 38%

Source: Based on data from *Vital Statistics on American Politics; Statistical Abstract of the United States, 1997*

THE ELECTORAL COLLEGE

Although people go out on Election Day and cast their votes for president, the president and vice president are only indirectly elected by the American people. In fact, the president and vice president are the only elected federal officials not chosen by direct vote of the people. These two people are elected by the Electoral College, which was created by the Framers of the Constitution.

Here is a simple outline of how the Electoral College works:

- There are a total of 538 electoral votes.
- The votes are divided by the states and the District of Columbia. The number of votes that each state has is equal to the number of senators and representatives for that state. (California has 52 representatives and 2 senators; it has a total of 54 electoral votes.)
- During an election, the candidate who wins the majority of popular votes in a given state wins all the electoral votes from that state.
- A presidential candidate needs 270 electoral votes to win.

You may have heard that it is possible for a presidential candidate who has not won the most popular votes to win an election. This can happen. If a candidate wins the popular vote in large states (ones with lots of electoral votes) by only a slim margin and loses the popular votes in smaller states by a wide margin, it is possible that the popular vote winner will actually lose the election.

Electoral Votes for President
(based on 1990 Census)

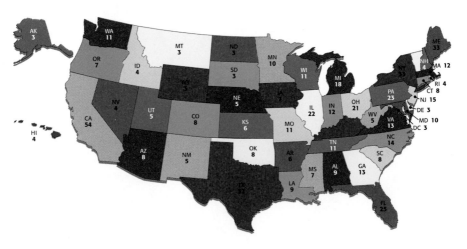

Source: Voter News Service; Federal Election Committee

U.S. PRESIDENTS WITH THE MOST ELECTORAL VOTES

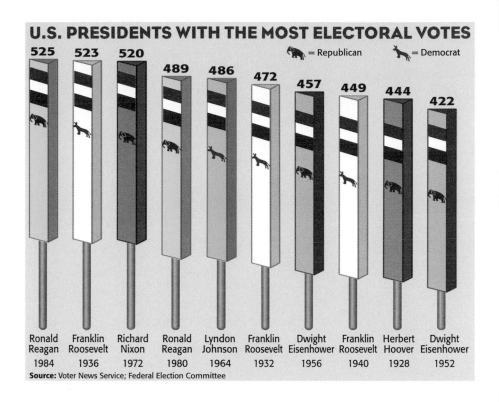

= Republican   = Democrat

Votes	President	Year
525	Ronald Reagan	1984
523	Franklin Roosevelt	1936
520	Richard Nixon	1972
489	Ronald Reagan	1980
486	Lyndon Johnson	1964
472	Franklin Roosevelt	1932
457	Dwight Eisenhower	1956
449	Franklin Roosevelt	1940
444	Herbert Hoover	1928
422	Dwight Eisenhower	1952

Source: Voter News Service; Federal Election Committee

TOP 5 U.S. PRESIDENTS WITH
THE GREATEST NUMBER OF POPULAR VOTES

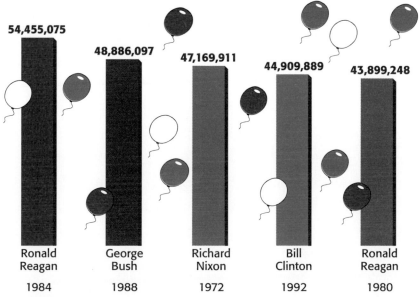

Votes	President	Year
54,455,075	Ronald Reagan	1984
48,886,097	George Bush	1988
47,169,911	Richard Nixon	1972
44,909,889	Bill Clinton	1992
43,899,248	Ronald Reagan	1980

Source: Federal Election Commission

HEALTH

Good health gives you a sense of well-being that carries you through the day. It takes a combination of many things to produce that feeling. Most are simple things that you can easily do on your own. Regular exercise keeps your muscles, bones, heart, and lungs in top shape. Sleep gives your body a chance to rest; most young people need at least eight hours of sleep a night. Food gives your body the energy and nutrients it needs. A good diet has lots of fruits, vegetables, and whole grains but few high-fat foods or sweet desserts.

It's also important to protect good health with regular medical checkups and immunization against disease. People who want to stay well need to avoid tobacco, immoderate use of alcohol, and illegal drugs, all of which can do serious harm. Government plays a role in controlling these substances and other health hazards, such as pollution and improperly processed food.

Since the 1970s, a health and fitness craze has swept America. Today people exercise and watch what they eat more than they did 25 years ago. Still, Americans tend to be overweight and to exercise too little. Those factors contribute to heart disease and other serious health problems. Fortunately, Americans have an excellent health-care system, including some of the world's most advanced medical facilities, to treat diseases. But health care in the United States is expensive. One of the country's most important tasks is to find ways to make sure that all people have access to good care.

Yearbook

circa 2500 B.C. The Chinese begin the therapeutic practice of acupuncture.

1928 Penicillin is discovered in molds; by the 1940s it is used to cure bacterial infections such as pneumonia.

1981 The U.S. Centers for Disease Control recognizes acquired immune deficiency syndrome (AIDS) for the first time.

1992 The U.S. Department of Agriculture publishes *The Food Guide Pyramid* to help Americans understand the basics of good nutrition and the ingredients of a healthy diet.

• Notables •

Christiaan Barnard (1922–) South African surgeon; performed the first heart transplant in 1967.

Hippocrates (circa 460 to 377 B.C.) Considered the father of medicine; writings later provided scientific and ethical foundation for Western medicine.

Edward Jenner (1749–1823) English physician; introduced vaccine against smallpox, a deadly disease.

Jonas E. Salk (1914–1995) American; developed vaccine against polio, a crippling and highly contagious disease.

Benjamin Spock (1903–1998) American pediatrician; authored *Baby and Child Care*, the most popular and influential guide in the United States to raising a child for over 50 years.

KEY IDEAS

acupuncture Puncturing the body with needles at particular points in order to improve health.

aerobics An exercise program that is strenuous enough to cause a temporary increase in a person's heartbeat and rate of breathing.

bacteria Any of a group of microscopic forms of life that live in the bodies of plants and animals, among other places. Many are harmless, but some can cause disease.

carbohydrates Foods that contain the elements carbon, hydrogen, and oxygen. Starches and sugars are carbohydrates.

dietary fiber A carbohydrate that comes from plants and cannot be digested by humans, aiding in elimination of wastes.

immune system Bodily system that protects from foreign substances, such as bacteria.

vaccine Substance containing dead, weakened, or living organisms that trigger the body to produce antibodies that protect from a disease.

183

THE SIX SYSTEMS OF THE HUMAN BODY

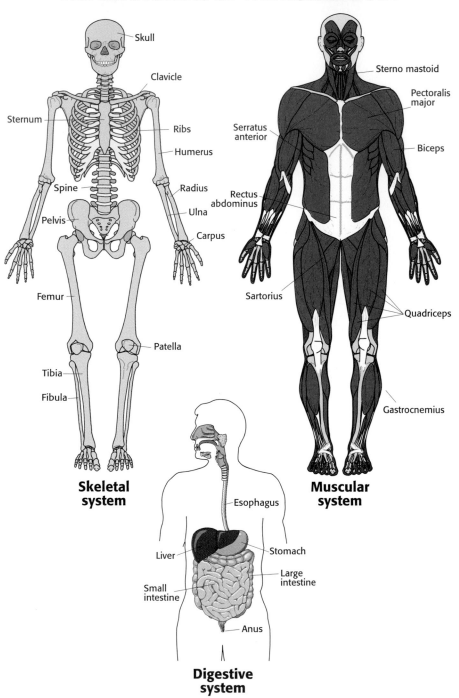

Skeletal system

- Skull
- Clavicle
- Sternum
- Ribs
- Humerus
- Spine
- Radius
- Ulna
- Pelvis
- Carpus
- Femur
- Patella
- Tibia
- Fibula

Muscular system

- Sterno mastoid
- Pectoralis major
- Serratus anterior
- Biceps
- Rectus abdominus
- Sartorius
- Quadriceps
- Gastrocnemius

Digestive system

- Esophagus
- Liver
- Stomach
- Small intestine
- Large intestine
- Anus

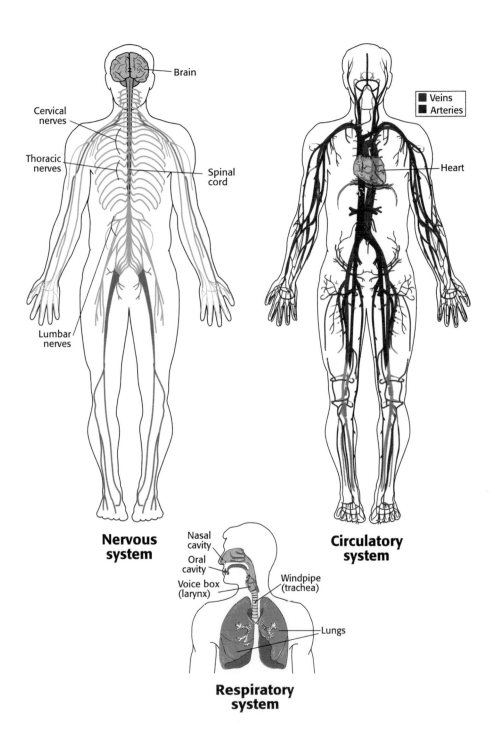

Brain

Cervical
nerves

Thoracic
nerves

Spinal
cord

Lumbar
nerves

**Nervous
system**

Veins
Arteries

Heart

**Circulatory
system**

Nasal
cavity

Oral
cavity

Voice box
(larynx)

Windpipe
(trachea)

Lungs

**Respiratory
system**

THE FOOD PYRAMID

The U.S. Department of Agriculture (USDA) has created this recommended balance of food groups for good nutrition.

Fats, oils, & sweets
USE SPARINGLY

Meats, poultry, fish,
dry beans, eggs,
& nuts group
2–3 SERVINGS
DAILY

Milk, yogurt,
& cheese group
2–3 SERVINGS
DAILY

Vegetable group
3–5 SERVINGS
DAILY

Fruit group
2–4 SERVINGS
DAILY

Bread, cereal, rice, & pasta group 6–11 SERVINGS DAILY

Source: U.S. Department of Agriculture

DIET KIDS

Nearly one in five U.S. kids ages 9–13 say
they've already been on a weight-loss diet.

Boys

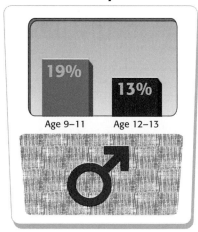

19%
13%
Age 9–11   Age 12–13

Girls

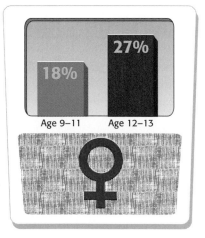

27%
18%
Age 9–11   Age 12–13

Source: Data based on *Sports Illustrated for KIDS Omnibus Study,* 1996

AVERAGE HEIGHT AND WEIGHT FOR CHILDREN

Boys

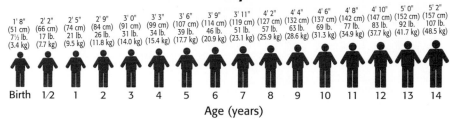

	Birth	½	1	2	3	4	5	6	7	8	9	10	11	12	13	14

1' 8" (51 cm) 7½ lb. (3.4 kg) — 2' 2" (66 cm) 17 lb. (7.7 kg) — 2' 5" (74 cm) 21 lb. (9.5 kg) — 2' 9" (84 cm) 26 lb. (11.8 kg) — 3' 0" (91 cm) 31 lb. (14.0 kg) — 3' 3" (99 cm) 34 lb. (15.4 kg) — 3' 6" (107 cm) 39 lb. (17.7 kg) — 3' 9" (114 cm) 46 lb. (20.9 kg) — 3' 11" (119 cm) 51 lb. (23.1 kg) — 4' 2" (127 cm) 57 lb. (25.9 kg) — 4' 4" (132 cm) 63 lb. (28.6 kg) — 4' 6" (137 cm) 69 lb. (31.3 kg) — 4' 8" (142 cm) 77 lb. (34.9 kg) — 4' 10" (147 cm) 83 lb. (37.7 kg) — 5' 0" (152 cm) 92 lb. (41.7 kg) — 5' 2" (157 cm) 107 lb. (48.5 kg)

Age (years)

Girls

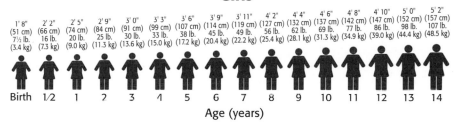

1' 8" (51 cm) 7½ lb. (3.4 kg) — 2' 2" (66 cm) 16 lb. (7.3 kg) — 2' 5" (74 cm) 20 lb. (9.0 kg) — 2' 9" (84 cm) 25 lb. (11.3 kg) — 3' 0" (91 cm) 30 lb. (13.6 kg) — 3' 3" (99 cm) 33 lb. (15.0 kg) — 3' 6" (107 cm) 38 lb. (17.2 kg) — 3' 9" (114 cm) 45 lb. (20.4 kg) — 3' 11" (119 cm) 49 lb. (22.2 kg) — 4' 2" (127 cm) 56 lb. (25.4 kg) — 4' 4" (132 cm) 62 lb. (28.1 kg) — 4' 6" (137 cm) 69 lb. (31.3 kg) — 4' 8" (142 cm) 77 lb. (34.9 kg) — 4' 10" (147 cm) 86 lb. (39.0 kg) — 5' 0" (152 cm) 98 lb. (44.4 kg) — 5' 2" (157 cm) 107 lb. (48.5 kg)

	Birth	½	1	2	3	4	5	6	7	8	9	10	11	12	13	14

Age (years)

Source: *Physicians Handbook*, 1990

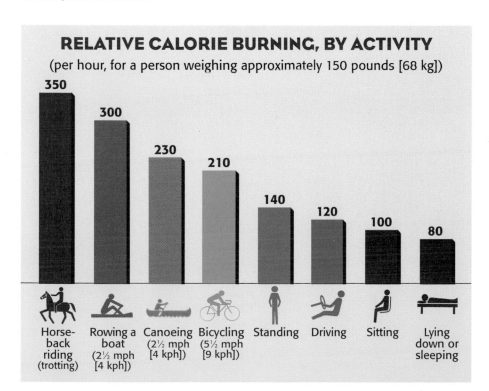

RELATIVE CALORIE BURNING, BY ACTIVITY

(per hour, for a person weighing approximately 150 pounds [68 kg])

Activity	Calories
Horseback riding (trotting)	350
Rowing a boat (2½ mph [4 kph])	300
Canoeing (2½ mph [4 kph])	230
Bicycling (5½ mph [9 kph])	210
Standing	140
Driving	120
Sitting	100
Lying down or sleeping	80

HOW AMERICANS KEEP FIT

About 54 million Americans 6 and older participated frequently (100 or more times) in fitness activities in 1995. Their top activities, in millions of participants:

Fitness walking 17.2M

Free weights 11.3M

Stationary biking 9.4M

Running/jogging 9.4M

Treadmill 7.0M

Resistance machines 6.2M

Source: The Fitness Products Council

TOP 5 REASONS FOR EMERGENCY ROOM VISITS

(as given by patients)

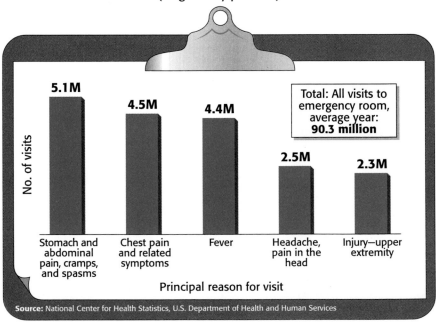

No. of visits

5.1M — Stomach and abdominal pain, cramps, and spasms

4.5M — Chest pain and related symptoms

4.4M — Fever

2.5M — Headache, pain in the head

2.3M — Injury—upper extremity

Total: All visits to emergency room, average year: **90.3 million**

Principal reason for visit

Source: National Center for Health Statistics, U.S. Department of Health and Human Services

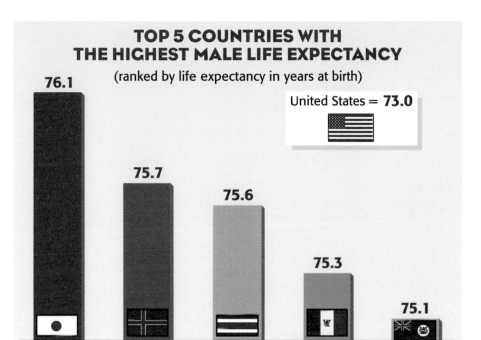

TOP 5 COUNTRIES WITH
THE HIGHEST MALE LIFE EXPECTANCY

(ranked by life expectancy in years at birth)

United States = **73.0**

76.1	75.7	75.6	75.3	75.1
Japan	Iceland	Costa Rica	Andorra	Hong Kong

Source: World Health Organization, 1996

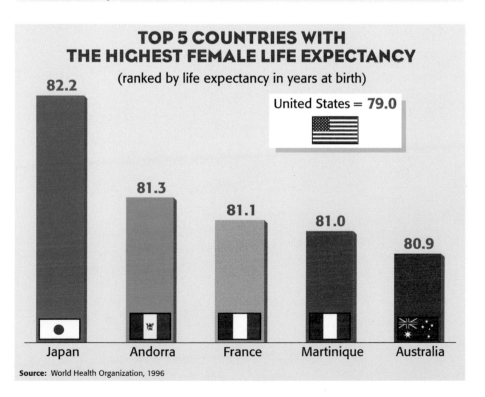

TOP 5 COUNTRIES WITH
THE HIGHEST FEMALE LIFE EXPECTANCY

(ranked by life expectancy in years at birth)

United States = **79.0**

82.2	81.3	81.1	81.0	80.9
Japan	Andorra	France	Martinique	Australia

Source: World Health Organization, 1996

TOP 10 LEADING CAUSES OF DEATH IN U.S.

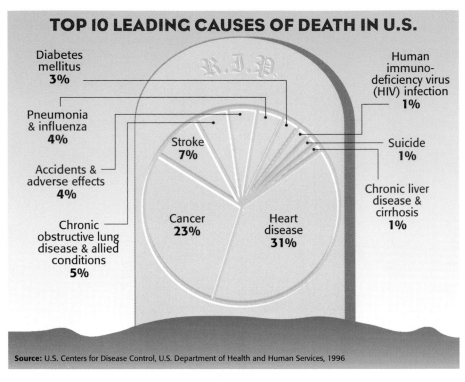

Diabetes mellitus 3%

Pneumonia & influenza 4%

Accidents & adverse effects 4%

Chronic obstructive lung disease & allied conditions 5%

Cancer 23%

Stroke 7%

Heart disease 31%

Human immuno-deficiency virus (HIV) infection 1%

Suicide 1%

Chronic liver disease & cirrhosis 1%

Source: U.S. Centers for Disease Control, U.S. Department of Health and Human Services, 1996

DEATH RATES BY NATION

(comparative death rates* for selected nations, 1994 and 2000 [projected])

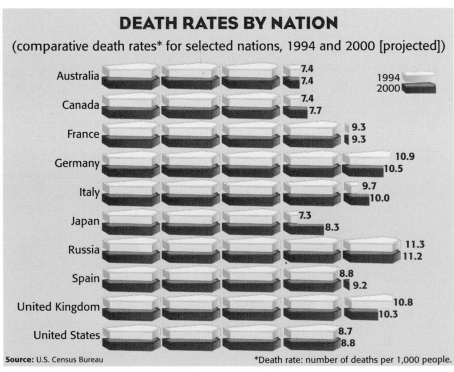

Nation	1994	2000
Australia	7.4	7.4
Canada	7.4	7.7
France	9.3	9.3
Germany	10.9	10.5
Italy	9.7	10.0
Japan	7.3	8.3
Russia	11.3	11.2
Spain	8.8	9.2
United Kingdom	10.8	10.3
United States	8.7	8.8

Source: U.S. Census Bureau

*Death rate: number of deaths per 1,000 people.

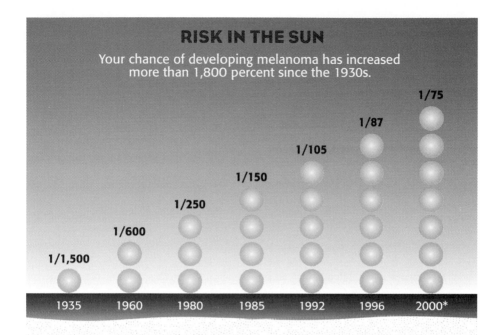

RISK IN THE SUN

Your chance of developing melanoma has increased more than 1,800 percent since the 1930s.

| 1/1,500 | 1/600 | 1/250 | 1/150 | 1/105 | 1/87 | 1/75 |
| 1935 | 1960 | 1980 | 1985 | 1992 | 1996 | 2000* |

Source: *Journal of the American Academy of Dermatology,* May 1996

* Projected.

TOP 4 FATAL CANCERS
(in expected deaths for 1998)

Lung cancer is the leading cause of cancer death among U.S. men and women.

Lung 160,100

Colorectal 56,500

Breast 43,900

Prostate 39,200

Source: American Cancer Society

ACCIDENTAL DEATHS FOR KIDS

(number of deaths, kids 5–14 years old, by types of accident per year)

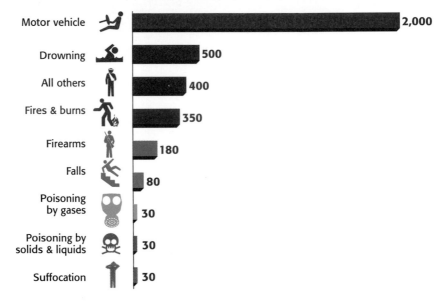

Motor vehicle	2,000
Drowning	500
All others	400
Fires & burns	350
Firearms	180
Falls	80
Poisoning by gases	30
Poisoning by solids & liquids	30
Suffocation	30

Source: National Safety Council, 1996

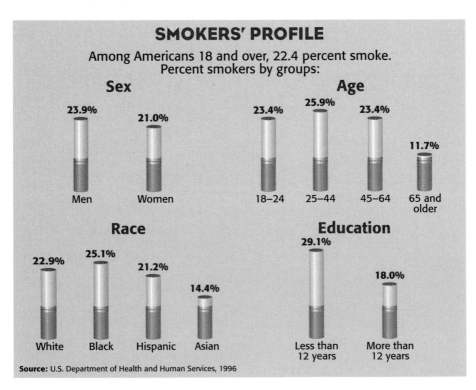

SMOKERS' PROFILE

Among Americans 18 and over, 22.4 percent smoke.
Percent smokers by groups:

Sex

Men	Women
23.9%	21.0%

Age

18–24	25–44	45–64	65 and older
23.4%	25.9%	23.4%	11.7%

Race

White	Black	Hispanic	Asian
22.9%	25.1%	21.2%	14.4%

Education

Less than 12 years	More than 12 years
29.1%	18.0%

Source: U.S. Department of Health and Human Services, 1996

PROFILE: CIGARETTES IN SCHOOL

Where high school students under age 18 get cigarettes, according to a national survey of 2,989 students:

41.3%
27.2%
32.6%

BOUGHT IN STORE

41.0%
31.3%
33.1%

BORROWED FROM SOMEONE

	White
	Black
	Hispanic

17.8%
7.3%
11.7%

GAVE MONEY TO SOMEONE ELSE TO BUY

3.7%
7.9%
5.1%

STOLEN

1.8%
6.1%
2.1%

BOUGHT IN VENDING MACHINE

15.4%
10.5%
3.9%

OBTAINED ANOTHER WAY

Cigarette use by grade level

Grade	Use
9	31.2%
10	33.1%
11	35.8%
12	38.2%
Average	**34.8%**

Teen cigarette use by race/ethnicity

Race	Male	Female
Whites	37.0%	39.8%
Blacks	27.8%	12.2%
Hispanics	34.9%	32.9%

Source: U.S. Centers for Disease Control and Prevention, 1996

WORLD AIDS CASES

(by continent or region)

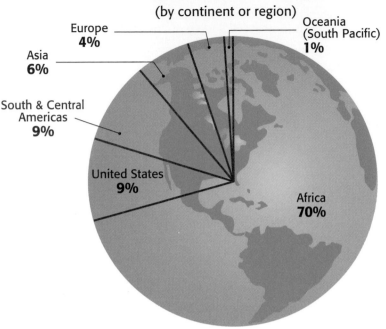

- Europe 4%
- Oceania (South Pacific) 1%
- Asia 6%
- South & Central Americas 9%
- United States 9%
- Africa 70%

Source: World Health Organization, 1996

NUMBER OF AIDS CASES DIAGNOSED THROUGH JUNE 1996

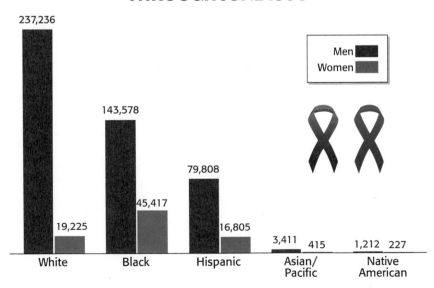

Men
Women

- White: 237,236 / 19,225
- Black: 143,578 / 45,417
- Hispanic: 79,808 / 16,805
- Asian/Pacific: 3,411 / 415
- Native American: 1,212 / 227

Source: U.S. Centers for Disease Control and Prevention

PROFILE: HOW ADULTS AND ADOLESCENTS GET AIDS

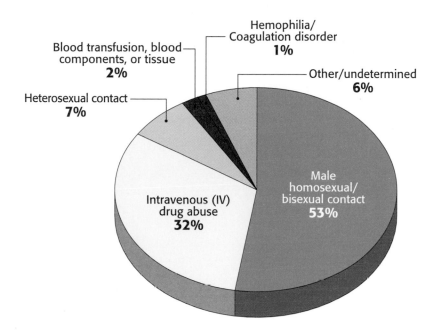

Hemophilia/
Coagulation disorder
1%

Blood transfusion, blood
components, or tissue
2%

Other/undetermined
6%

Heterosexual contact
7%

Male
homosexual/
bisexual contact
53%

Intravenous (IV)
drug abuse
32%

HOW CHILDREN GET AIDS

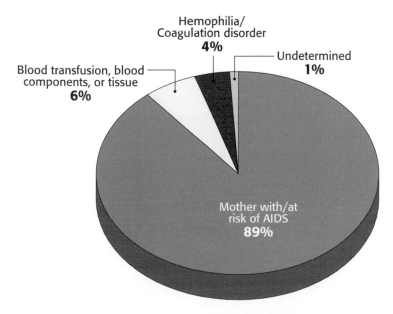

Hemophilia/
Coagulation disorder
4%

Undetermined
1%

Blood transfusion, blood
components, or tissue
6%

Mother with/at
risk of AIDS
89%

Source: U.S. Department of Health and Human Services, U.S. Centers for Disease Control and Prevention

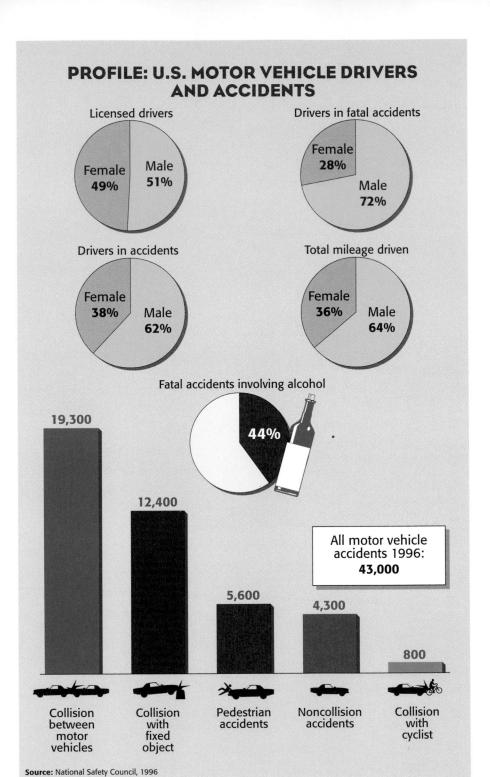

PROFILE: U.S. MOTOR VEHICLE DRIVERS AND ACCIDENTS

Licensed drivers

Female 49%
Male 51%

Drivers in fatal accidents

Female 28%
Male 72%

Drivers in accidents

Female 38%
Male 62%

Total mileage driven

Female 36%
Male 64%

Fatal accidents involving alcohol

44%

All motor vehicle accidents 1996: 43,000

19,300 — Collision between motor vehicles

12,400 — Collision with fixed object

5,600 — Pedestrian accidents

4,300 — Noncollision accidents

800 — Collision with cyclist

Source: National Safety Council, 1996

KIDS AGES 5–14 KILLED BY GUNS

Boys:	**602**
Girls:	**174**
Total firearms deaths, kids 5–14:	**776**

Homicides

Boys 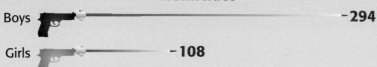 ‑**294**

Girls ‑**108**

Accidents

Boys 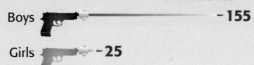 ‑**155**

Girls ‑**25**

Suicides

Boys 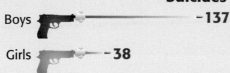 ‑**137**

Girls ‑**38**

Undetermined

Boys  ‑**16**

Girls ‑**3**

Source: National Safety Council, 1996

HISTORY (U.S.)

Although Native Americans lived throughout North America thousands of years ago, the events that led to the founding of the United States started with the arrival of the European explorers, such as Columbus in 1492.

Explorers were followed by settlers. By the mid-1600s, Britain, France, and Spain had established a chain of colonies along the East Coast. Many colonists came hoping to find religious and political freedom. Some came hoping to get rich, or at least to make a good living, farming the fertile land of the New World. And some came against their will—as slaves, imported from Africa.

The desire for freedom, the search for wealth, and the problem of slavery marked the history of the United States for many years. Desire for freedom led British colonists to rebel in 1775. On July 4, 1776, representatives of Britain's American colonies declared their independence. Once independence was won, the promise of wealth drew Americans westward in search of land, furs, gold, and other riches. Native Americans were pushed off their land to make way. The problem of slavery was one of the causes of the Civil War. Slavery ended with the Emancipation Proclamation in 1863. The cost in lives was terrible, and the divisions in the country took many years to begin healing.

On these pages, you will find information about some of the events, leaders, and issues that have shaped the country from its founding to today. They are highlights in a rich and complex story that Americans are still writing.

Yearbook

1775 The American Revolution begins at Lexington and Concord, Massachusetts.

1776 The Continental Congress accepts the Declaration of Independence.

1830s and 1840s The U.S. government forces southeastern Native American tribes to give up their land and relocate to reservations.

1861–1865 Civil War; it is the only war fought on American soil; 500,000 Americans die.

1955–1965 The civil rights movement eventually improves race relations in America. The Civil Rights Act of 1964 is passed.

• Notables •

John F. Kennedy (1917–1963) 35th president of the United States; remembered for leadership during the Cold War.

Martin Luther King, Jr. (1929–1968) American minister; widely regarded as the greatest civil rights leader; delivered the "I Have a Dream" speech.

Thomas Paine (1737–1809) American political philosopher; wrote influential pamphlet *Common Sense*, urging the colonies to declare independence from Britain.

Eleanor Roosevelt (1884–1962) First Lady during Franklin D. Roosevelt's administration; admired for support of humanitarian causes.

Chief Sitting Bull (circa 1831–1890) Leader of the Sioux; fought in the battle of Little Big Horn, where General George Custer and his men died.

KEY IDEAS

Cold War The struggle for power between the Western powers (including the United States) and the Communist bloc, which was dominated by the Soviet Union.

colony A group of people living in a new territory who have legal ties to their "parent" government.

Confederate A state or soldier that withdrew (seceded) from the union of all the United States during the Civil War era.

gold rush A rush of gold diggers to a newly discovered gold field; the most famous was the California gold rush in 1848–1849.

Manifest Destiny The nineteenth-century belief that the United States was meant to expand all the way to the Pacific coast.

Reconstruction period Post–Civil War, from 1865 to 1877, when Southern state governments were reestablished and African American citizens took their places in Southern society.

Supreme Court The highest and most powerful court in the nation; the judicial branch of the U.S. government.

HISTORY TIME LINE: 1000–1700

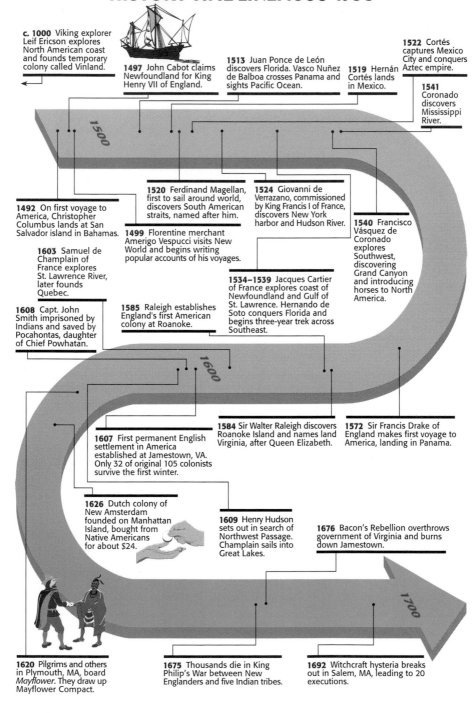

c. 1000 Viking explorer Leif Ericson explores North American coast and founds temporary colony called Vinland.

1497 John Cabot claims Newfoundland for King Henry VII of England.

1513 Juan Ponce de León discovers Florida. Vasco Nuñez de Balboa crosses Panama and sights Pacific Ocean.

1519 Hernán Cortés lands in Mexico.

1522 Cortés captures Mexico City and conquers Aztec empire.

1541 Coronado discovers Mississippi River.

1492 On first voyage to America, Christopher Columbus lands at San Salvador island in Bahamas.

1520 Ferdinand Magellan, first to sail around world, discovers South American straits, named after him.

1499 Florentine merchant Amerigo Vespucci visits New World and begins writing popular accounts of his voyages.

1524 Giovanni de Verrazano, commissioned by King Francis I of France, discovers New York harbor and Hudson River.

1540 Francisco Vásquez de Coronado explores Southwest, discovering Grand Canyon and introducing horses to North America.

1603 Samuel de Champlain of France explores St. Lawrence River, later founds Quebec.

1534–1539 Jacques Cartier of France explores coast of Newfoundland and Gulf of St. Lawrence. Hernando de Soto conquers Florida and begins three-year trek across Southeast.

1608 Capt. John Smith imprisoned by Indians and saved by Pocahontas, daughter of Chief Powhatan.

1585 Raleigh establishes England's first American colony at Roanoke.

1584 Sir Walter Raleigh discovers Roanoke Island and names land Virginia, after Queen Elizabeth.

1572 Sir Francis Drake of England makes first voyage to America, landing in Panama.

1607 First permanent English settlement in America established at Jamestown, VA. Only 32 of original 105 colonists survive the first winter.

1626 Dutch colony of New Amsterdam founded on Manhattan Island, bought from Native Americans for about $24.

1609 Henry Hudson sets out in search of Northwest Passage. Champlain sails into Great Lakes.

1676 Bacon's Rebellion overthrows government of Virginia and burns down Jamestown.

1620 Pilgrims and others in Plymouth, MA, board *Mayflower*. They draw up Mayflower Compact.

1675 Thousands die in King Philip's War between New Englanders and five Indian tribes.

1692 Witchcraft hysteria breaks out in Salem, MA, leading to 20 executions.

HISTORY TIME LINE: 1700s

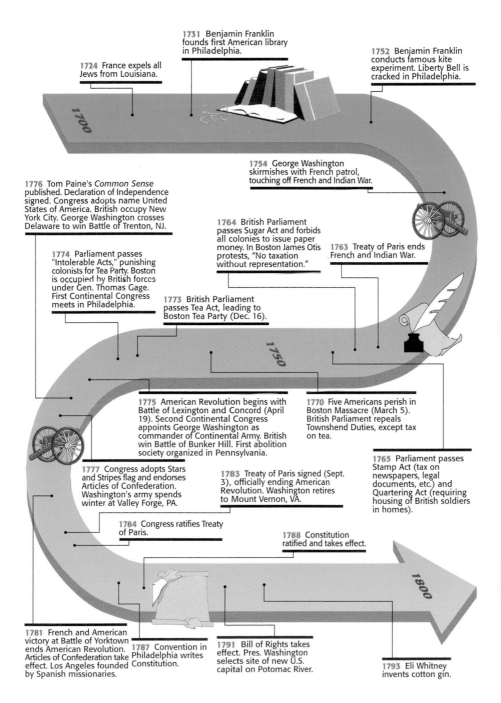

1731 Benjamin Franklin founds first American library in Philadelphia.

1724 France expels all Jews from Louisiana.

1752 Benjamin Franklin conducts famous kite experiment. Liberty Bell is cracked in Philadelphia.

1700

1754 George Washington skirmishes with French patrol, touching off French and Indian War.

1776 Tom Paine's *Common Sense* published. Declaration of Independence signed. Congress adopts name United States of America. British occupy New York City. George Washington crosses Delaware to win Battle of Trenton, NJ.

1764 British Parliament passes Sugar Act and forbids all colonies to issue paper money. In Boston James Otis protests, "No taxation without representation."

1763 Treaty of Paris ends French and Indian War.

1774 Parliament passes "Intolerable Acts," punishing colonists for Tea Party. Boston is occupied by British forces under Gen. Thomas Gage. First Continental Congress meets in Philadelphia.

1773 British Parliament passes Tea Act, leading to Boston Tea Party (Dec. 16).

1750

1775 American Revolution begins with Battle of Lexington and Concord (April 19). Second Continental Congress appoints George Washington as commander of Continental Army. British win Battle of Bunker Hill. First abolition society organized in Pennsylvania.

1770 Five Americans perish in Boston Massacre (March 5). British Parliament repeals Townshend Duties, except tax on tea.

1777 Congress adopts Stars and Stripes flag and endorses Articles of Confederation. Washington's army spends winter at Valley Forge, PA.

1783 Treaty of Paris signed (Sept. 3), officially ending American Revolution. Washington retires to Mount Vernon, VA.

1765 Parliament passes Stamp Act (tax on newspapers, legal documents, etc.) and Quartering Act (requiring housing of British soldiers in homes).

1784 Congress ratifies Treaty of Paris.

1788 Constitution ratified and takes effect.

1800

1781 French and American victory at Battle of Yorktown ends American Revolution. Articles of Confederation take effect. Los Angeles founded by Spanish missionaries.

1787 Convention in Philadelphia writes Constitution.

1791 Bill of Rights takes effect. Pres. Washington selects site of new U.S. capital on Potomac River.

1793 Eli Whitney invents cotton gin.

HISTORY TIME LINE: 1800s

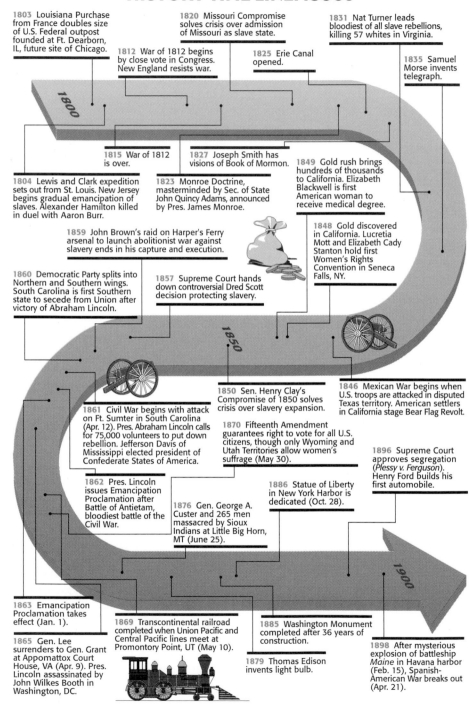

1803 Louisiana Purchase from France doubles size of U.S. Federal outpost founded at Ft. Dearborn, IL, future site of Chicago.

1812 War of 1812 begins by close vote in Congress. New England resists war.

1820 Missouri Compromise solves crisis over admission of Missouri as slave state.

1825 Erie Canal opened.

1831 Nat Turner leads bloodiest of all slave rebellions, killing 57 whites in Virginia.

1835 Samuel Morse invents telegraph.

1815 War of 1812 is over.

1827 Joseph Smith has visions of Book of Mormon.

1804 Lewis and Clark expedition sets out from St. Louis. New Jersey begins gradual emancipation of slaves. Alexander Hamilton killed in duel with Aaron Burr.

1823 Monroe Doctrine, masterminded by Sec. of State John Quincy Adams, announced by Pres. James Monroe.

1849 Gold rush brings hundreds of thousands to California. Elizabeth Blackwell is first American woman to receive medical degree.

1859 John Brown's raid on Harper's Ferry arsenal to launch abolitionist war against slavery ends in his capture and execution.

1848 Gold discovered in California. Lucretia Mott and Elizabeth Cady Stanton hold first Women's Rights Convention in Seneca Falls, NY.

1860 Democratic Party splits into Northern and Southern wings. South Carolina is first Southern state to secede from Union after victory of Abraham Lincoln.

1857 Supreme Court hands down controversial Dred Scott decision protecting slavery.

1850 Sen. Henry Clay's Compromise of 1850 solves crisis over slavery expansion.

1846 Mexican War begins when U.S. troops are attacked in disputed Texas territory. American settlers in California stage Bear Flag Revolt.

1861 Civil War begins with attack on Ft. Sumter in South Carolina (Apr. 12). Pres. Abraham Lincoln calls for 75,000 volunteers to put down rebellion. Jefferson Davis of Mississippi elected president of Confederate States of America.

1870 Fifteenth Amendment guarantees right to vote for all U.S. citizens, though only Wyoming and Utah Territories allow women's suffrage (May 30).

1896 Supreme Court approves segregation (*Plessy v. Ferguson*). Henry Ford builds his first automobile.

1862 Pres. Lincoln issues Emancipation Proclamation after Battle of Antietam, bloodiest battle of the Civil War.

1886 Statue of Liberty in New York Harbor is dedicated (Oct. 28).

1876 Gen. George A. Custer and 265 men massacred by Sioux Indians at Little Big Horn, MT (June 25).

1863 Emancipation Proclamation takes effect (Jan. 1).

1869 Transcontinental railroad completed when Union Pacific and Central Pacific lines meet at Promontory Point, UT (May 10).

1885 Washington Monument completed after 36 years of construction.

1865 Gen. Lee surrenders to Gen. Grant at Appomattox Court House, VA (Apr. 9). Pres. Lincoln assassinated by John Wilkes Booth in Washington, DC.

1879 Thomas Edison invents light bulb.

1898 After mysterious explosion of battleship *Maine* in Havana harbor (Feb. 15), Spanish-American War breaks out (Apr. 21).

THE CONFEDERATE STATES OF AMERICA, 1860–1866

State	Seceded from Union	Readmitted to Union*
1. South Carolina	Dec. 20, 1860	July 9, 1868
2. Mississippi	Jan. 9, 1861	Feb. 23, 1870
3. Florida	Jan. 10, 1861	June 25, 1868
4. Alabama	Jan. 11, 1861	July 13, 1868
5. Georgia	Jan. 19, 1861	July 15, 1870**
6. Louisiana	Jan. 26, 1861	July 9, 1868
7. Texas	March 2, 1861	March 30, 1870
8. Virginia	April 17, 1861	Jan. 26, 1870
9. Arkansas	May 6, 1861	June 22, 1868
10. North Carolina	May 20, 1861	July 4, 1868
11. Tennessee	June 8, 1861	July 24, 1866

*Date of readmission to representation in U.S. House of Representatives.
**Second readmission date. First date was July 21, 1868, but the representatives were unseated March 5, 1869.
Note: Four other slave states—Delaware, Kentucky, Maryland, and Missouri—remained in the Union.

Source: National Archives

HISTORY TIME LINE: 1900s

1903 Orville and Wilbur Wright conduct first powered flight near Kitty Hawk, NC (Dec. 17). Boston defeats Pittsburgh in first baseball World Series.

1909 Expedition team led by Robert E. Peary and Matthew Henson plants American flag at North Pole (Apr. 6). W. E. B. DuBois founds National Association for the Advancement of Colored People (NAACP).

1917 After Pres. Wilson proclaims "world must be made safe for democracy," Congress declares war on Germany (Apr. 6) and Austria-Hungary (Dec. 7), bringing U.S. into World War I.

1900

1910

1919 Versailles Treaty, including League of Nations, rejected by Senate (Nov. 19). Grand Canyon National Park created.

1918 Armistice Day ends World War I (Nov. 11); mass celebrations break out across country. Pres. Wilson goes to Europe for peace conference (Dec. 4).

1933 Banks closed for four days by presidential order (Mar. 5). During "Hundred Days" (Mar. 9–June 16), Pres. Roosevelt pushes New Deal through Congress, conducts first "fireside chat" on radio, and takes U.S. off gold standard.

1927 Charles Lindbergh completes nonstop solo flight from New York to Paris (May 20–21); returns home to huge welcoming crowds.

1929 Stock market crash on "Black Tuesday" (Oct. 29) ushers in Great Depression.

1920

1920 Nineteenth Amendment establishes women's suffrage (Aug. 26).

1930

1932 Amelia Earhart is first woman to fly solo across Atlantic.

1945 Roosevelt, Churchill, and Stalin meet for last time at Yalta in Soviet Crimea to begin postwar planning (Feb. 4–11). Germany surrenders, ending war in Europe (May 7). Pres. Harry S. Truman meets with Churchill and Stalin at Potsdam, Germany (July 17–Aug. 2). Atomic bombs dropped on Hiroshima (Aug. 6) and Nagasaki (Aug. 9); Japan surrenders (Aug. 14), ending World War II.

1941 German submarine sinks merchant ship *Robin Moor*, first U.S. casualty of war (May 21). Japanese planes attack Pearl Harbor, Hawaii, killing 2,400 U.S. servicemen and civilians (Dec. 7). U.S. declares war on Japan (Dec. 10). Germany and Italy declare war on U.S. (Dec. 11). U.S. declares war on Germany and Italy (Dec. 11).

1940

1950

1950 North Korea invades South Korea, beginning Korean War (June 27). Truman obtains U.N. support (July 7), asks Congress for a $10 billion rearmament program (July 20), and calls up reserves (Aug. 4).

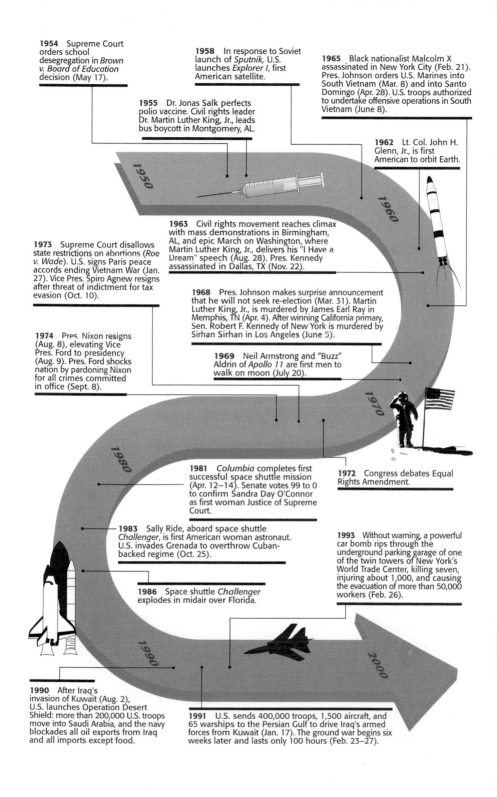

1954 Supreme Court orders school desegregation in *Brown v. Board of Education* decision (May 17).

1958 In response to Soviet launch of *Sputnik*, U.S. launches *Explorer I*, first American satellite.

1965 Black nationalist Malcolm X assassinated in New York City (Feb. 21). Pres. Johnson orders U.S. Marines into South Vietnam (Mar. 8) and into Santo Domingo (Apr. 28). U.S. troops authorized to undertake offensive operations in South Vietnam (June 8).

1955 Dr. Jonas Salk perfects polio vaccine. Civil rights leader Dr. Martin Luther King, Jr., leads bus boycott in Montgomery, AL.

1962 Lt. Col. John H. Glenn, Jr., is first American to orbit Earth.

1973 Supreme Court disallows state restrictions on abortions (*Roe v. Wade*). U.S. signs Paris peace accords ending Vietnam War (Jan. 27). Vice Pres. Spiro Agnew resigns after threat of indictment for tax evasion (Oct. 10).

1963 Civil rights movement reaches climax with mass demonstrations in Birmingham, AL, and epic March on Washington, where Martin Luther King, Jr., delivers his "I Have a Dream" speech (Aug. 28). Pres. Kennedy assassinated in Dallas, TX (Nov. 22).

1968 Pres. Johnson makes surprise announcement that he will not seek re-election (Mar. 31). Martin Luther King, Jr., is murdered by James Earl Ray in Memphis, TN (Apr. 4). After winning California primary, Sen. Robert F. Kennedy of New York is murdered by Sirhan Sirhan in Los Angeles (June 5).

1974 Pres. Nixon resigns (Aug. 8), elevating Vice Pres. Ford to presidency (Aug. 9). Pres. Ford shocks nation by pardoning Nixon for all crimes committed in office (Sept. 8).

1969 Neil Armstrong and "Buzz" Aldrin of *Apollo 11* are first men to walk on moon (July 20).

1981 *Columbia* completes first successful space shuttle mission (Apr. 12–14). Senate votes 99 to 0 to confirm Sandra Day O'Connor as first woman Justice of Supreme Court.

1972 Congress debates Equal Rights Amendment.

1983 Sally Ride, aboard space shuttle *Challenger*, is first American woman astronaut. U.S. invades Grenada to overthrow Cuban-backed regime (Oct. 25).

1993 Without warning, a powerful car bomb rips through the underground parking garage of one of the twin towers of New York's World Trade Center, killing seven, injuring about 1,000, and causing the evacuation of more than 50,000 workers (Feb. 26).

1986 Space shuttle *Challenger* explodes in midair over Florida.

1990 After Iraq's invasion of Kuwait (Aug. 2), U.S. launches Operation Desert Shield: more than 200,000 U.S. troops move into Saudi Arabia, and the navy blockades all oil exports from Iraq and all imports except food.

1991 U.S. sends 400,000 troops, 1,500 aircraft, and 65 warships to the Persian Gulf to drive Iraq's armed forces from Kuwait (Jan. 17). The ground war begins six weeks later and lasts only 100 hours (Feb. 23–27).

IMPORTANT U.S. SUPREME COURT DECISIONS

Madbury v. Madison (1803)   The Court struck down a law "repugnant to the constitution" for the first time and set the precedent for judicial review of acts of Congress. In a politically ingenious ruling on the Judiciary Act of 1789, Chief Justice John Marshall asserted the Supreme Court's power "to say what the law is," while avoiding a confrontation with Pres. Thomas Jefferson. Not until the Dred Scott case of 1857 would another federal law be ruled unconstitutional.

1800

Dred Scott v. Sanford (1857)   Dred Scott, a Missouri slave, sued for his liberty after his owner took him into free territory. The Court ruled that Congress could not bar slavery in the territories. Scott remained a slave because the Missouri Compromise of 1820, prohibiting slavery from part of the Louisiana Purchase, violated the Fifth Amendment by depriving slave owners of their right to enjoy property without due process of law. Scott himself could not even sue, for he was held to be property, not a citizen. This decision sharpened sectional conflict by sweeping away legal barriers to the expansion of slavery.

1850

Plessy v. Ferguson (1896)   The "separate but equal" doctrine supporting public segregation by law received the Court's approval in this ruling, which originated with segregated railroad cars in Louisiana. The Court held that as long as equal accommodations were provided, segregation was not discrimination and did not deprive blacks of equal protection of the laws under the Fourteenth Amendment. This decision was overturned in *Brown v. Board of Education* (1954).

1900

Brown v. Board of Education (1954)   Chief Justice Earl Warren led the Court unanimously to decide that segregated schools violated the equal protecting clause of the Fourteenth Amendment. The "separate but equal" doctrine of *Plessy v. Ferguson* (1896) was overruled after a series of cases dating back to *Missouri ex. rel. Gaines v. Canada* (1938) had already limited it. "Separate educational facilities are inherently unequal," held the Court. Efforts to desegregate Southern schools after the Brown decision met with massive resistance for many years.

1950

Miranda v Arizona (1966)   Expanding on *Gideon v. Wainwright* (1963) and *Escobedo v. Illinois* (1964), the Court set forth stringent interrogation procedures for criminal suspects, to protect their Fifth Amendment freedom from self-incrimination. Miranda's confession to kidnapping and rape was obtained without counsel and without his having been advised of his right to silence, so it was ruled inadmissible as evidence. This decision obliged police to advise suspects of their rights upon taking them into custody.

SHERIFF

Roe v. Wade (1973)   In a controversial ruling, the Court held that state laws restricting abortion were an unconstitutional invasion of a woman's right to privacy. Only in the last trimester of pregnancy, when the fetus achieved viability outside the womb, might states regulate abortion—except when the life or health of the mother was at stake. Feelings ran high on both sides in the aftermath of this decision. In *Planned Parenthood of Central Missouri v. Danforth* (1976), the Court added further that wives did not need their husbands' consent to obtain abortions.

U.S. PRESIDENTS AND THEIR PARTIES

1.	Washington[1]	1789–1797	Federalist
2.	J. Adams	1797–1801	Federalist
3.	Jefferson	1801–1809	Democratic-Republican
4.	Madison	1809–1817	Democratic-Republican
5.	Monroe	1817–1825	Democratic-Republican
6.	J. Q. Adams	1825–1829	Democratic-Republican
7.	Jackson	1829–1837	Democratic
8.	Van Buren	1837–1841	Democratic
9.	W. H. Harrison[2]	1841	Whig
10.	Tyler	1841–1845	Whig
11.	Polk	1845–1849	Democratic
12.	Taylor	1849–1850	Whig
13.	Fillmore	1850–1853	Whig
14.	Pierce	1853–1857	Democratic
15.	Buchanan	1857–1861	Democratic
16.	Lincoln[3]	1861–1865	Republican
17.	A. Johnson[4]	1865–1869	Union
18.	Grant	1869–1877	Republican
19.	Hayes	1877–1881	Republican
20.	Garfield[3]	1881	Republican
21.	Arthur	1881–1885	Republican
22.	Cleveland	1885–1889	Democratic
23.	B. Harrison	1889–1893	Republican
24.	Cleveland[5]	1893–1897	Democratic
25.	McKinley[3]	1897–1901	Republican
26.	T. Roosevelt	1901–1909	Republican
27.	Taft	1909–1913	Republican
28.	Wilson	1913–1921	Democratic
29.	Harding[2]	1921–1923	Republican
30.	Coolidge	1923–1929	Republican
31.	Hoover	1929–1933	Republican
32.	F. D. Roosevelt[2]	1933–1945	Democratic
33.	Truman	1945–1953	Democratic
34.	Eisenhower	1953–1961	Republican
35.	Kennedy[3]	1961–1963	Democratic
36.	L. B. Johnson	1963–1969	Democratic
37.	Nixon[6]	1969–1974	Republican
38.	Ford	1974–1977	Republican
39.	Carter	1977–1981	Democratic
40.	Reagan	1981–1989	Republican
41.	Bush	1989–1993	Republican
42.	Clinton	1993–	Democratic

1. No party for first election. The party system in the U.S. made its appearance during Washington's first term. 2. Died in office. 3. Assassinated in office. 4. The Republican National Convention of 1864 adopted the name Union Party. It renominated Lincoln for president; for vice president it nominated Johnson, a War Democrat. Although frequently listed as a Republican vice president and President, Johnson undoubtedly considered himself strictly a member of the Union Party. When that party broke apart after 1868, he returned to the Democratic Party. 5. Second nonconsecutive term. 6. Resigned Aug. 9, 1974.

Source: Library of Congress

THE DECLARATION OF INDEPENDENCE

In Congress, July 4, 1776

The Unanimous Declaration of the Thirteen United States of America

When in the Course of human events, it becomes necessary for one people to dissolve the political bands which have connected them with another, and to assume among the powers of the earth, the separate and equal station to which the Laws of Nature and of Nature's God entitle them, a decent respect to the opinions of mankind requires that they should declare the causes which impel them to the separation.

We hold these truths to be self-evident, that all men are created equal*, that they are endowed by their Creator with certain unalienable Rights, that among these are Life, Liberty and the pursuit of Happiness. That to secure these rights, Governments are instituted among Men, deriving their just powers from the consent of the governed, That whenever any Form of Government becomes destructive of these ends, it is the Right of the People to alter or to abolish it, and to institute new Government, laying its foundation on such principles and organizing its powers in such form, as to them shall seem most likely to effect their Safety and Happiness. Prudence, indeed, will dictate that Governments long established should not be changed for light and transient causes; and accordingly all experience hath shown, that mankind are more disposed to suffer, while evils are sufferable, than to right themselves by abolishing the forms to which they are accustomed. But when a long train of abuses and usurpations, pursuing invariably the same Object evinces a design to reduce them under absolute Despotism, it is their right, it is their duty, to throw off such Government, and to provide new Guards for their future security. Such has been the patient sufferance of these Colonies; and such is now the necessity which constrains them to alter their former Systems of Government. The history of the present King of Great Britain is a history of repeated injuries and usurpations, all having in direct object the establishment of an absolute Tyranny over these States. To prove this, let Facts be submitted to a candid world.

He has refused his Assent to Laws, the most wholesome and necessary for the public good.

He has forbidden his Governors to pass Laws of immediate and pressing importance, unless suspended in their operation till his Assent should be obtained; and when so suspended, he has utterly neglected to attend to them.

He has refused to pass other Laws for the accommodation of large districts of people, unless those people would relinquish the right of Representation in the Legislature, a right inestimable to them and formidable to tyrants only.

He has called together legislative bodies at places unusual, uncomfortable, and distant from the depository of their public Records, for the sole purpose of fatiguing them into compliance with his measures.

He has dissolved Representative Houses repeatedly, for opposing with manly firmness his invasions on the rights of the people.

He has refused for a long time, after such dissolutions, to cause others to be elected; whereby the Legislative powers, incapable of Annihilation, have returned to the People at large for their exercise; the State remaining in the mean time exposed to all the dangers of invasion from without, and convulsions within.

He has endeavored to prevent the population of these States; for that purpose obstructing the Laws for Naturalization of Foreigners; refusing to pass others to encourage their migrations hither, and raising the conditions of new Appropriations of Lands.

He has obstructed the Administration of Justice, by refusing his Assent to Laws for establishing Judiciary powers.

He has made Judges dependent on his Will alone, for the tenure of their offices, and the amount and payment of their salaries.

He has erected a multitude of New Offices, and sent hither swarms of Officers to harrass our people, and eat out their substance.

He has kept among us, in times of peace, Standing Armies without the Consent of our legislatures.

He has affected to render the Military independent of and superior to the Civil power.

Note: Phrases in red are key ideas.

He has combined with others to subject us to a jurisdiction foreign to our constitution, and unacknowledged by our laws; giving his Assent to their Acts of pretended Legislation:

For Quartering large bodies of armed troops among us:

For protecting them, by a mock Trial, from punishment for any Murders which they should commit on the Inhabitants of these States:

For cutting off our Trade with all parts of the world:

For imposing Taxes on us without our Consent:

For depriving us in many cases, of the benefits of Trial by Jury:

For transporting us beyond Seas to be tried for pretended offences:

For abolishing the free System of English Laws in a neighbouring Province, establishing therein an Arbitrary government, and enlarging its Boundaries so as to render it at once an example and fit instrument for introducing the same absolute rule into these Colonies:

For taking away our Charters, abolishing our most valuable Laws, and altering fundamentally the Forms of our Governments:

For suspending our own Legislatures, and declaring themselves invested with power to legislate for us in all cases whatsoever.

He has abdicated Government here, by declaring us out of his Protection and waging War against us.

He has plundered our seas, ravaged our Coasts, burnt our towns, and destroyed the lives of our people.

He is at this time transporting large Armies of foreign Mercenaries to compleat the works of death, desolation and tyranny, already begun with circumstances of Cruelty & perfidy scarcely paralleled in the most barbarous ages, and totally unworthy the Head of a civilized nation.

He has constrained our fellow Citizens taken Captive on the high Seas to bear Arms against their Country, to become the executioners of their friends and Brethren, or to fall themselves by their Hands.

He has excited domestic insurrections amongst us, and has endeavoured to bring on the inhabitants of our frontiers, the merciless Indian Savages, whose known rule of warfare, is an undistinguished destruction of all ages, sexes and conditions.

In every stage of these Oppressions We have Petitioned for Redress in the most humble terms: Our repeated Petitions have been answered only by repeated injury. A Prince whose character is thus marked by every act which may define a Tyrant, is unfit to be the ruler of a free people.

Nor have We been wanting in attentions to our British brethren. We have warned them from time to time of attempts by their legislature to extend an unwarrantable jurisdiction over us. We have reminded them of the circumstances of our emigration and settlement here. We have appealed to their native justice and magnanimity, and we have conjured them by the ties of our common kindred to disavow these usurpations, which, would inevitably interrupt our connections and correspondence. They too have been deaf to the voice of justice and of consanguinity. We must, therefore, acquiesce in the necessity, which denounces our Separation, and hold them, as we hold the rest of mankind, Enemies in War, in Peace Friends.

We, therefore, the Representatives of the United States of America, in General Congress, Assembled, appealing to the Supreme Judge of the world for the rectitude of our intentions, do, in the Name, and by Authority of the good People of these Colonies, solemnly publish and declare, That these United Colonies are, and of Right ought to be Free and Independent States; that they are Absolved from all Allegiance to the British Crown, and that all political connection between them and the State of Great Britain, is and ought to be totally dissolved; and that as Free and Independent States, they have full Power to levy War, conclude Peace, contract Alliances, establish Commerce, and to do all other Acts and Things which Independent States may of right do. And for the support of this Declaration, with a firm reliance on the protection of divine Providence, we mutually pledge to each other our Lives, our Fortunes and our sacred Honor.

Source: National Archives and Records Administration

THE BILL OF RIGHTS

THE FIRST 10 AMENDMENTS TO THE CONSTITUTION
[The first 10 amendments, known collectively as
the Bill of Rights, were adopted in 1791.]

Amendment I
Congress shall make no law respecting an establishment of religion, or prohibiting the free exercise thereof; or abridging the freedom of speech, or of the press; or the right of the people peaceably to assemble, and to petition the Government for a redress of grievances.

Amendment II
A well regulated Militia, being necessary to the security of a free State, the right of the people to keep and bear Arms, shall not be infringed.

Amendment III
No Soldier shall, in time of peace be quartered in any house, without the consent of the Owner, nor in time of war, but in a manner to be prescribed by law.

Amendment IV
The right of the people to be secure in their persons, houses, papers, and effects, against unreasonable searches and seizures, shall not be violated, and no Warrants shall issue, but upon probable cause, supported by Oath or affirmation, and particularly describing the place to be searched, and the persons or things to be seized.

Amendment V
No person shall be held to answer for a capital, or otherwise infamous crime, unless on a presentment or indictment of a Grand Jury, except in cases arising in the land or naval forces, or in the Militia, when in actual service in time of War or public danger; nor shall any person be subject for the same offence to be twice put in jeopardy of life or limb; nor shall be compelled in any criminal case to be a witness against himself, nor be deprived of life, liberty, or property, without due process of law; nor shall private property be taken for public use, without just compensation.

Amendment VI
In all criminal prosecutions, the accused shall enjoy the right to a speedy and public trial, by an impartial jury of the State and district wherein the crime shall have been committed, which district shall have been previously ascertained by law, and to be informed of the nature and cause of the accusation; to be confronted with the witnesses against him; to have compulsory process for obtaining witnesses in his favor, and to have the Assistance of Counsel for his defence.

Amendment VII
In suits at common law, where the value in controversy shall exceed twenty dollars, the right of trial by jury shall be preserved, and no fact tried by a jury, shall be otherwise re-examined in any Court of the United States, than according to the rules of the common law.

Amendment VIII
Excessive bail shall not be required, nor excessive fines imposed, nor cruel and unusual punishments inflicted.

Amendment IX
The enumeration in the Constitution, of certain rights, shall not be construed to deny or disparage others retained by the people.

Amendment X
The powers not delegated to the United States by the Constitution, nor prohibited by it to the States, are reserved to the States respectively, or to the people.

Source: National Archives and Records Administration   **Note:** Phrases in red are key ideas.

THE GETTYSBURG ADDRESS

 Four score and seven years ago our fathers brought forth on this continent a new nation, conceived in liberty and dedicated to the proposition that all men are created equal.

Now we are engaged in a great civil war, testing whether that nation or any nation so conceived and so dedicated can long endure. We are met on a great battlefield of that war. We have come to dedicate a portion of that field as a final resting-place for those who here gave their lives that that nation might live. It is altogether fitting and proper that we should do this.

But in a larger sense, we cannot dedicate, we cannot consecrate, we cannot hallow this ground. The brave men, living and dead who struggled here have consecrated it far above our poor power to add or detract. The world will little note nor long remember what we say here, but it can never forget what they did here. It is for us the living rather to be dedicated here to the unfinished work which they who fought here have thus far so nobly advanced. It is rather for us to be here dedicated to the great task remaining before us—that from these honored dead we take increased devotion to that cause for which they gave the last full measure of devotion—that we here highly resolve that these dead shall not have died in vain, that this nation under God shall have a new birth of freedom, and that government of the people, by the people, for the people shall not perish from the earth.

– Abraham Lincoln
Gettysburg, Pennsylvania, 1863

Source: National Archives and Records Administration

HISTORY (WORLD)

Who were the first humans, and where and how did they live? They left no written records, so no one knows for sure. But scientists have found tools, bones, and other clues. These artifacts suggest that early people walked the earth several hundred thousand years ago. They were hunters and gatherers who roamed in search of food. By 10,000 B.C., people in many parts of the world had learned to grow crops and keep domestic animals. They settled in villages and developed true societies. Villages became cities, and societies became civilizations.

About 4000 B.C., the Sumerians, who lived in the Middle East, began to keep records on clay tablets. Between then and 1500 B.C., people in many parts of the world developed systems of writing. To many people, world history begins with these early written records. The period before then is called prehistory.

Historians sift through writings and artifacts and try to make sense of them, to understand what happened in the past and why. Wars, bold voyages of discovery, powerful leaders, and new inventions and ideas are all parts of the puzzle. World history is about humankind and our own developing civilization. People see some events as important and dismiss others, based on their own experience.

Yearbook

508 B.C. A democracy is established in Athens; all free men can participate.

A.D. 618 The 300-year Tang dynasty begins in China; the arts flourish.

1519–21 Hernán Cortés conquers the Aztecs in Mexico and begins European colonization.

1917 Congress declares war on Germany, entering the U.S. in World War I.

1933–1945 The Holocaust; millions of Jews and non-Jews are murdered in Europe.

1939 Hitler's Nazi army invades Poland, setting off World War II.

• Notables •

Napoleon Bonaparte (1769–1821)
French Emperor from 1804–1814; brilliant military leader; eventually ruled much of Europe.

Julius Caesar (100–44 B.C.)
Roman general and dictator; also a great speaker and writer.

Sir Winston Churchill (1874–1965)
British statesman; prime minister of Great Britain during World War II.

Mohandas Gandhi (1869–1948)
Considered the father of India; great spiritual as well as political leader; led peaceful civil disobedience against British colonial government; assassinated by a religious fanatic.

Nelson Mandela (1918–) First black president of South Africa; helped to end apartheid in 1993.

KEY IDEAS

apartheid A policy of discriminating against non-European groups that was practiced in South Africa.

civil disobedience A group's refusal to obey a government's demands, usually by using nonviolent methods.

civil war A war between opposing groups of citizens of the same country.

dynasty A powerful group or family that keeps its position of power for a long time.

empire A country that rules over a number of territories and peoples.

fascism A system of beliefs about government that gives a government strong control over the life of the nation and its citizens.

Nazi A member of the National Socialist German Workers' Party, which, under the leadership of Adolf Hitler, eventually aimed to "purify" Europe of Jews and other groups.

TIME LINE
PREHISTORY: BEFORE COMMON ERA* (B.C.)

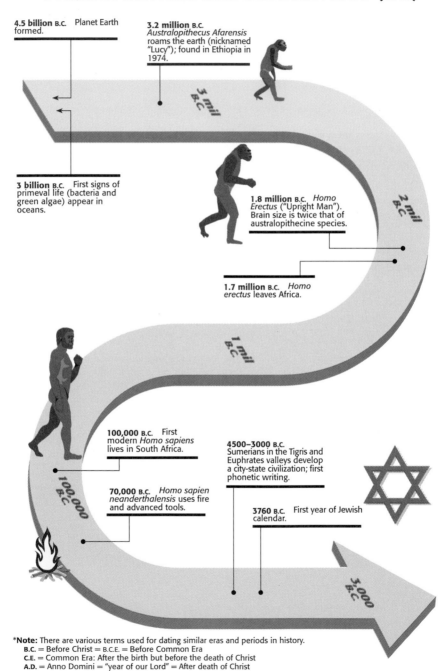

4.5 billion B.C.   Planet Earth formed.

3.2 million B.C.
Australopithecus Afarensis roams the earth (nicknamed "Lucy"); found in Ethiopia in 1974.

3 mil B.C.

3 billion B.C.   First signs of primeval life (bacteria and green algae) appear in oceans.

1.8 million B.C.   *Homo Erectus* ("Upright Man"). Brain size is twice that of australopithecine species.

2 mil B.C.

1.7 million B.C.   *Homo erectus* leaves Africa.

1 mil B.C.

100,000 B.C.   First modern *Homo sapiens* lives in South Africa.

4500–3000 B.C.
Sumerians in the Tigris and Euphrates valleys develop a city-state civilization; first phonetic writing.

100,000 B.C.

70,000 B.C.   *Homo sapien neanderthalensis* uses fire and advanced tools.

3760 B.C.   First year of Jewish calendar.

3,000 B.C.

*Note: There are various terms used for dating similar eras and periods in history.
   B.C. = Before Christ = **B.C.E.** = Before Common Era
   C.E. = Common Era: After the birth but before the death of Christ
   A.D. = Anno Domini = "year of our Lord" = After death of Christ

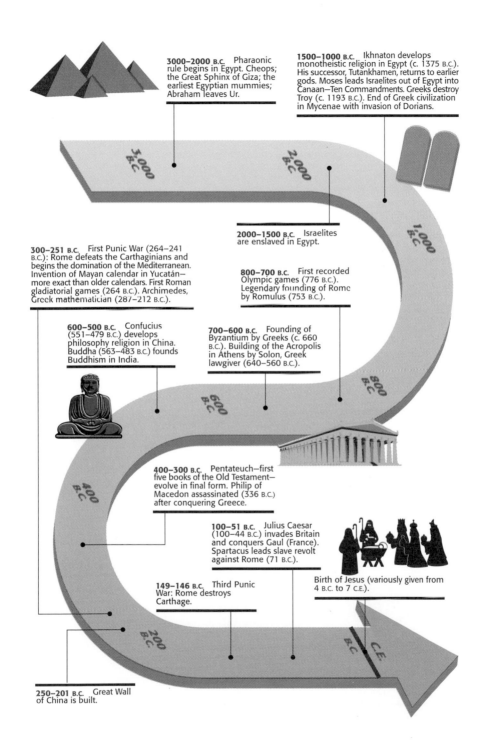

3000–2000 B.C. Pharaonic rule begins in Egypt. Cheops; the Great Sphinx of Giza; the earliest Egyptian mummies; Abraham leaves Ur.

1500–1000 B.C. Ikhnaton develops monotheistic religion in Egypt (c. 1375 B.C.). His successor, Tutankhamen, returns to earlier gods. Moses leads Israelites out of Egypt into Canaan—Ten Commandments. Greeks destroy Troy (c. 1193 B.C.). End of Greek civilization in Mycenae with invasion of Dorians.

2000–1500 B.C. Israelites are enslaved in Egypt.

300–251 B.C. First Punic War (264–241 B.C.): Rome defeats the Carthaginians and begins the domination of the Mediterranean. Invention of Mayan calendar in Yucatán—more exact than older calendars. First Roman gladiatorial games (264 B.C.). Archimedes, Greek mathematician (287–212 B.C.).

800–700 B.C. First recorded Olympic games (776 B.C.). Legendary founding of Rome by Romulus (753 B.C.).

600–500 B.C. Confucius (551–479 B.C.) develops philosophy religion in China. Buddha (563–483 B.C.) founds Buddhism in India.

700–600 B.C. Founding of Byzantium by Greeks (c. 660 B.C.). Building of the Acropolis in Athens by Solon, Greek lawgiver (640–560 B.C.).

400–300 B.C. Pentateuch—first five books of the Old Testament—evolve in final form. Philip of Macedon assassinated (336 B.C.) after conquering Greece.

100–51 B.C. Julius Caesar (100–44 B.C.) invades Britain and conquers Gaul (France). Spartacus leads slave revolt against Rome (71 B.C.).

149–146 B.C. Third Punic War: Rome destroys Carthage.

Birth of Jesus (variously given from 4 B.C. to 7 C.E.).

250–201 B.C. Great Wall of China is built.

TIME LINE
COMMON ERA: I c.e.–FIFTEENTH CENTURY

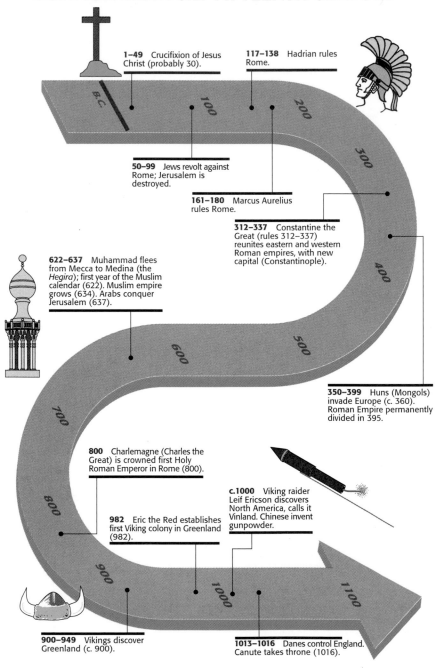

1–49 Crucifixion of Jesus Christ (probably 30).

117–138 Hadrian rules Rome.

B.C.

100

200

50–99 Jews revolt against Rome; Jerusalem is destroyed.

161–180 Marcus Aurelius rules Rome.

300

312–337 Constantine the Great (rules 312–337) reunites eastern and western Roman empires, with new capital (Constantinople).

622–637 Muhammad flees from Mecca to Medina (the *Hegira*); first year of the Muslim calendar (622). Muslim empire grows (634). Arabs conquer Jerusalem (637).

400

500

600

350–399 Huns (Mongols) invade Europe (c. 360). Roman Empire permanently divided in 395.

700

800 Charlemagne (Charles the Great) is crowned first Holy Roman Emperor in Rome (800).

c.1000 Viking raider Leif Ericson discovers North America, calls it Vinland. Chinese invent gunpowder.

800

982 Eric the Red establishes first Viking colony in Greenland (982).

900

1000

1100

900–949 Vikings discover Greenland (c. 900).

1013–1016 Danes control England. Canute takes throne (1016).

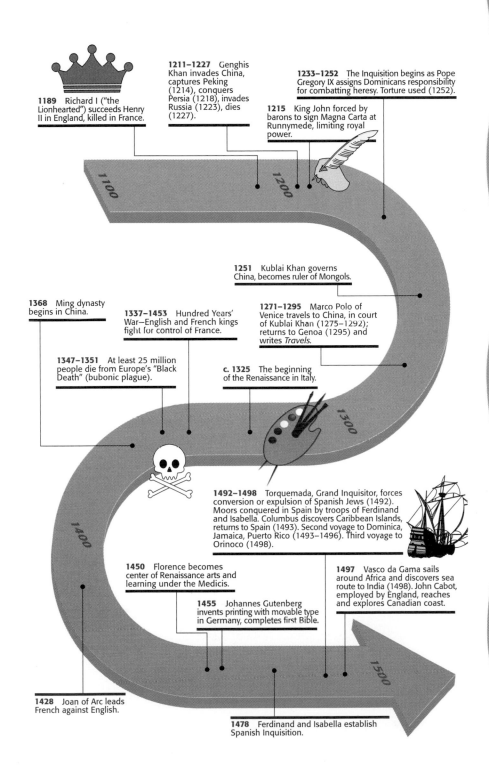

1189 Richard I ("the Lionhearted") succeeds Henry II in England, killed in France.

1211–1227 Genghis Khan invades China, captures Peking (1214), conquers Persia (1218), invades Russia (1223), dies (1227).

1215 King John forced by barons to sign Magna Carta at Runnymede, limiting royal power.

1233–1252 The Inquisition begins as Pope Gregory IX assigns Dominicans responsibility for combatting heresy. Torture used (1252).

1251 Kublai Khan governs China, becomes ruler of Mongols.

1368 Ming dynasty begins in China.

1337–1453 Hundred Years' War—English and French kings fight for control of France.

1271–1295 Marco Polo of Venice travels to China, in court of Kublai Khan (1275–1292); returns to Genoa (1295) and writes *Travels*.

1347–1351 At least 25 million people die from Europe's "Black Death" (bubonic plague).

c. 1325 The beginning of the Renaissance in Italy.

1492–1498 Torquemada, Grand Inquisitor, forces conversion or expulsion of Spanish Jews (1492). Moors conquered in Spain by troops of Ferdinand and Isabella. Columbus discovers Caribbean Islands, returns to Spain (1493). Second voyage to Dominica, Jamaica, Puerto Rico (1493–1496). Third voyage to Orinoco (1498).

1450 Florence becomes center of Renaissance arts and learning under the Medicis.

1497 Vasco da Gama sails around Africa and discovers sea route to India (1498). John Cabot, employed by England, reaches and explores Canadian coast.

1455 Johannes Gutenberg invents printing with movable type in Germany, completes first Bible.

1428 Joan of Arc leads French against English.

1478 Ferdinand and Isabella establish Spanish Inquisition.

TIME LINE
EARLY EXPLORATION: 1492–1800

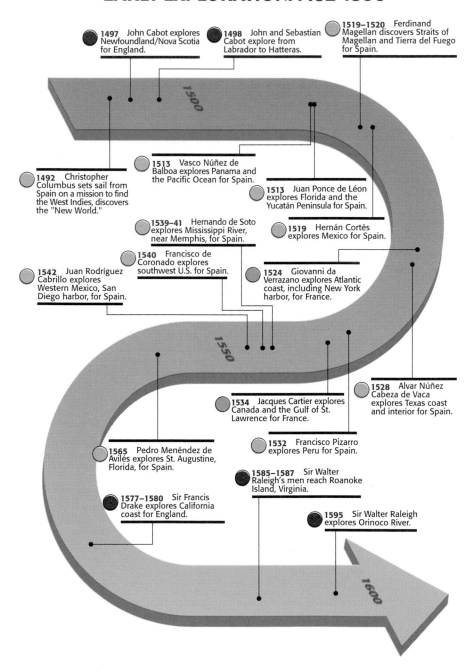

1497 John Cabot explores Newfoundland/Nova Scotia for England.

1498 John and Sebastian Cabot explore from Labrador to Hatteras.

1519–1520 Ferdinand Magellan discovers Straits of Magellan and Tierra del Fuego for Spain.

1513 Vasco Núñez de Balboa explores Panama and the Pacific Ocean for Spain.

1513 Juan Ponce de Léon explores Florida and the Yucatán Peninsula for Spain.

1492 Christopher Columbus sets sail from Spain on a mission to find the West Indies, discovers the "New World."

1539–41 Hernando de Soto explores Mississippi River, near Memphis, for Spain.

1519 Hernán Cortés explores Mexico for Spain.

1540 Francisco de Coronado explores southwest U.S. for Spain.

1542 Juan Rodríguez Cabrillo explores Western Mexico, San Diego harbor, for Spain.

1524 Giovanni da Verrazano explores Atlantic coast, including New York harbor, for France.

1534 Jacques Cartier explores Canada and the Gulf of St. Lawrence for France.

1528 Alvar Núñez Cabeza de Vaca explores Texas coast and interior for Spain.

1565 Pedro Menéndez de Avilés explores St. Augustine, Florida, for Spain.

1532 Francisco Pizarro explores Peru for Spain.

1585–1587 Sir Walter Raleigh's men reach Roanoke Island, Virginia.

1577–1580 Sir Francis Drake explores California coast for England.

1595 Sir Walter Raleigh explores Orinoco River.

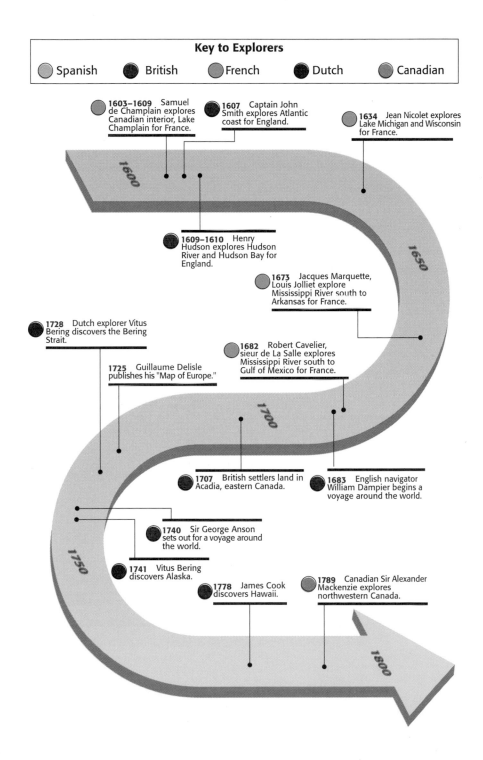

Key to Explorers

⬤ Spanish ⬤ British ⬤ French ⬤ Dutch ⬤ Canadian

1603–1609 Samuel de Champlain explores Canadian interior, Lake Champlain for France.

1607 Captain John Smith explores Atlantic coast for England.

1634 Jean Nicolet explores Lake Michigan and Wisconsin for France.

1600

1650

1609–1610 Henry Hudson explores Hudson River and Hudson Bay for England.

1673 Jacques Marquette, Louis Jolliet explore Mississippi River south to Arkansas for France.

1728 Dutch explorer Vitus Bering discovers the Bering Strait.

1682 Robert Cavelier, sieur de La Salle explores Mississippi River south to Gulf of Mexico for France.

1725 Guillaume Delisle publishes his "Map of Europe."

1700

1707 British settlers land in Acadia, eastern Canada.

1683 English navigator William Dampier begins a voyage around the world.

1740 Sir George Anson sets out for a voyage around the world.

1750

1741 Vitus Bering discovers Alaska.

1778 James Cook discovers Hawaii.

1789 Canadian Sir Alexander Mackenzie explores northwestern Canada.

1800

TIME LINE
MODERN EXPLORATION: 1800–TODAY

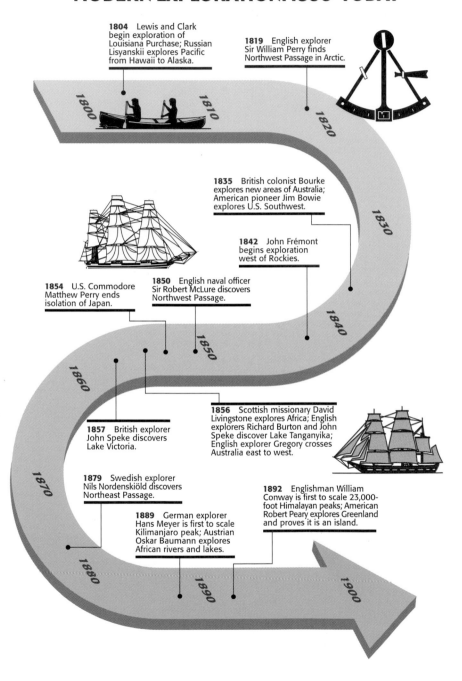

1804 Lewis and Clark begin exploration of Louisiana Purchase; Russian Lisyanskii explores Pacific from Hawaii to Alaska.

1819 English explorer Sir William Perry finds Northwest Passage in Arctic.

1800

1810

1820

1835 British colonist Bourke explores new areas of Australia; American pioneer Jim Bowie explores U.S. Southwest.

1830

1842 John Frémont begins exploration west of Rockies.

1854 U.S. Commodore Matthew Perry ends isolation of Japan.

1850 English naval officer Sir Robert McLure discovers Northwest Passage.

1840

1850

1860

1856 Scottish missionary David Livingstone explores Africa; English explorers Richard Burton and John Speke discover Lake Tanganyika; English explorer Gregory crosses Australia east to west.

1857 British explorer John Speke discovers Lake Victoria.

1879 Swedish explorer Nils Nordenskiöld discovers Northeast Passage.

1870

1892 Englishman William Conway is first to scale 23,000-foot Himalayan peaks; American Robert Peary explores Greenland and proves it is an island.

1889 German explorer Hans Meyer is first to scale Kilimanjaro peak; Austrian Oskar Baumann explores African rivers and lakes.

1880

1890

1900

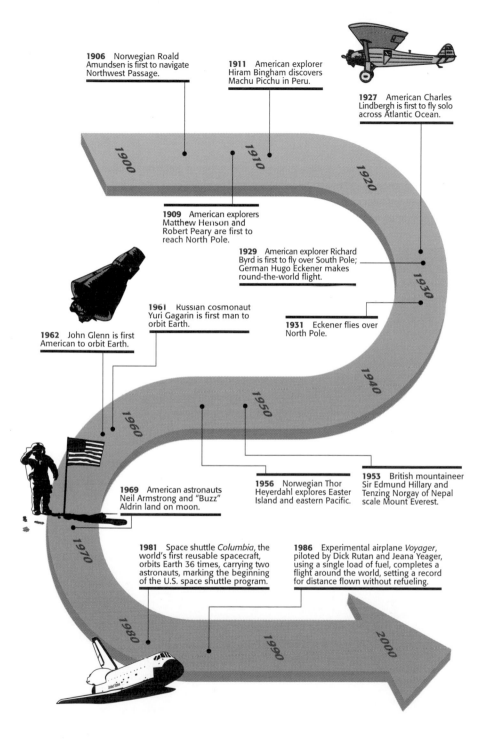

1906 Norwegian Roald Amundsen is first to navigate Northwest Passage.

1911 American explorer Hiram Bingham discovers Machu Picchu in Peru.

1927 American Charles Lindbergh is first to fly solo across Atlantic Ocean.

1909 American explorers Matthew Henson and Robert Peary are first to reach North Pole.

1929 American explorer Richard Byrd is first to fly over South Pole; German Hugo Eckener makes round-the-world flight.

1961 Russian cosmonaut Yuri Gagarin is first man to orbit Earth.

1962 John Glenn is first American to orbit Earth.

1931 Eckener flies over North Pole.

1900

1910

1920

1930

1940

1950

1960

1970

1980

1990

2000

1969 American astronauts Neil Armstrong and "Buzz" Aldrin land on moon.

1956 Norwegian Thor Heyerdahl explores Easter Island and eastern Pacific.

1953 British mountaineer Sir Edmund Hillary and Tenzing Norgay of Nepal scale Mount Everest.

1981 Space shuttle *Columbia*, the world's first reusable spacecraft, orbits Earth 36 times, carrying two astronauts, marking the beginning of the U.S. space shuttle program.

1986 Experimental airplane *Voyager*, piloted by Dick Rutan and Jeana Yeager, using a single load of fuel, completes a flight around the world, setting a record for distance flown without refueling.

LARGEST ARMED FORCES IN THE WORLD

Army

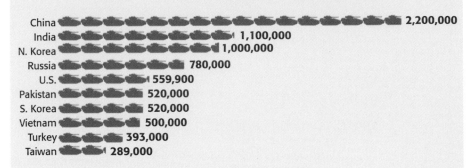

China	2,200,000
India	1,100,000
N. Korea	1,000,000
Russia	780,000
U.S.	559,900
Pakistan	520,000
S. Korea	520,000
Vietnam	500,000
Turkey	393,000
Taiwan	289,000

Navy

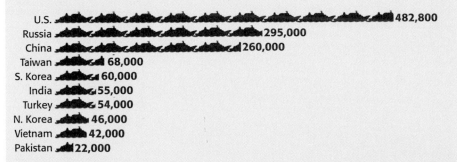

U.S.	482,800
Russia	295,000
China	260,000
Taiwan	68,000
S. Korea	60,000
India	55,000
Turkey	54,000
N. Korea	46,000
Vietnam	42,000
Pakistan	22,000

Air Force

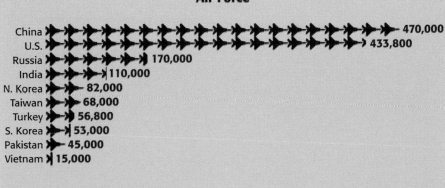

China	470,000
U.S.	433,800
Russia	170,000
India	110,000
N. Korea	82,000
Taiwan	68,000
Turkey	56,800
S. Korea	53,000
Pakistan	45,000
Vietnam	15,000

Source: U.S. Department of Defense, 1997

THE TOP 5 HIGHEST DEATH COUNTS IN WORLD WAR II

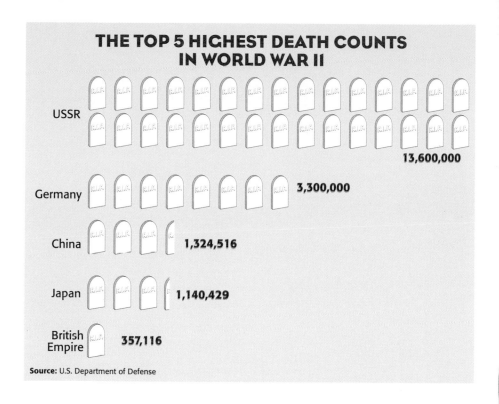

USSR — 13,600,000

Germany — 3,300,000

China — 1,324,516

Japan — 1,140,429

British Empire — 357,116

Source: U.S. Department of Defense

WORLD POPULATION GROWTH

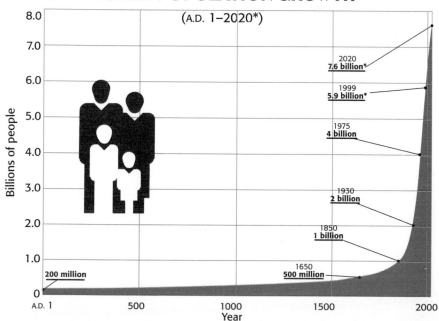

(A.D. 1–2020*)

Billions of people

2020
7.6 billion*

1999
5.9 billion*

1975
4 billion

1930
2 billion

1850
1 billion

1650
500 million

200 million

A.D. 1   500   1000   1500   2000
Year

Source: Census Bureau; U.S. Dept. of Commerce; *CIA World Factbook*

*Projected

INVENTORS AND INVENTIONS

During World War II, researchers at a secret Massachusetts laboratory tested high-frequency magnetic waves, or microwaves, for use in radar. A researcher was working near a magnetron, a device that produced the waves, and he noticed that a chocolate bar in his pocket was melting—even though the pocket felt cool. Curious, he bombarded other foods with microwaves. Popcorn popped. A raw egg exploded. The researcher, Percy Spencer, built on his discovery to develop the first microwave oven.

Ever since prehistoric people chipped out the first stone tools, inventions have changed the way people live. Many inventions start with simple observations and flashes of insight. But insight is only the beginning of a long process. An inventor must also figure out how to make that idea work.

Even then, the process of invention doesn't stop. Today's countertop microwave ovens are a far cry from the enormous and expensive early models because people worked to improve them. And one invention often leads to others.

The Wright brothers invented the first powered airplane. Other inventors include Alexander Graham Bell, who created the telephone, and Thomas Alva Edison, who developed the first practical lightbulb. Since the late 1800s, the pace of invention has exploded, especially in computers and electronic technology.

Yearbook

3600 B.C. The Sumerian people who lived in the present-day Middle East use crude wheels—wooden slabs with rounded corners.

circa 1450 The German printer Johannes Gutenberg invents a printing press with movable type; by 1500, about eight million books have been printed in Europe.

1836 John Frederic Daniell invents the Daniell cell, the first dependable source of an electric current.

1926 Robert Goddard launches the first liquid-fuel propelled rocket, which reaches a height of 184 feet (56 m) at a speed of 60 miles (97 km) per hour.

• Notables •

Howard Aiken (1900–1973) American mathematician; with three others invented the Harvard Mark I, the first electronic digital computer.

Louis Daguerre (1789–1851) French painter; invented the daguerreotype, an early photograph.

Benjamin Franklin (1706–1790) American statesman; invented lightning rods and bifocal glasses and designed wood-burning stoves, among many inventions.

Carl Gottfried von Linde (1842–1934) German; invented the first practical refrigerator.

Hans Lippershey (circa 1570–1619) Dutchman; invented the telescope.

James Watt (1736–1819) Scottish inventor; created an efficient steam engine.

KEY IDEAS

daguerreotype An early photograph produced on a silver or silver-covered copperplate.

flying shuttle loom A loom that could weave cotton much more quickly than those used before its invention in 1733; speeded up the Industrial Revolution.

Industrial Revolution A period in world history from the mid-1700s to the mid-1800s of rapid industrial growth that began in England and soon spread to many other countries, including the United States. Factories with complicated machinery became common in the cities; before this period, England was a society of farms and small businesses.

patent A document that gives an individual or a business the exclusive right to make, use, or sell something.

potter's wheel A disk that revolves on a spindle, allowing a potter to make perfectly rounded bowls and other utensils. Invented more than 4,000 years ago in China, it is still used by potters today.

TIME LINE OF MAJOR INVENTIONS

3500 B.C. to 1450

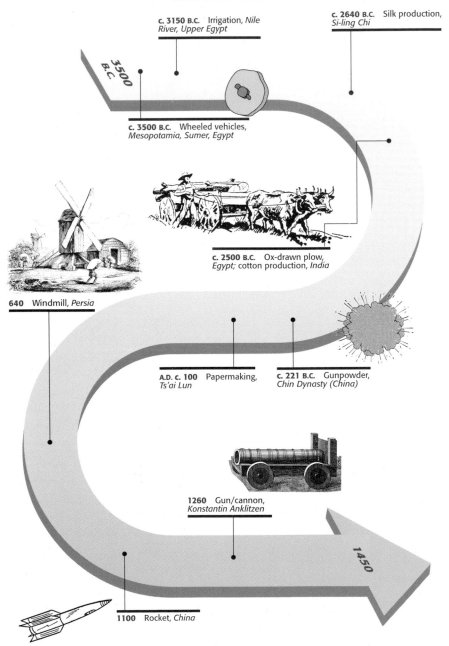

c. 3150 B.C. Irrigation, *Nile River, Upper Egypt*

c. 2640 B.C. Silk production, *Si-ling Chi*

3500 B.C.

c. 3500 B.C. Wheeled vehicles, *Mesopotamia, Sumer, Egypt*

c. 2500 B.C. Ox-drawn plow, *Egypt;* cotton production, *India*

640 Windmill, *Persia*

A.D. c. 100 Papermaking, *Ts'ai Lun*

c. 221 B.C. Gunpowder, *Chin Dynasty (China)*

1260 Gun/cannon, *Konstantin Anklitzen*

1450

1100 Rocket, *China*

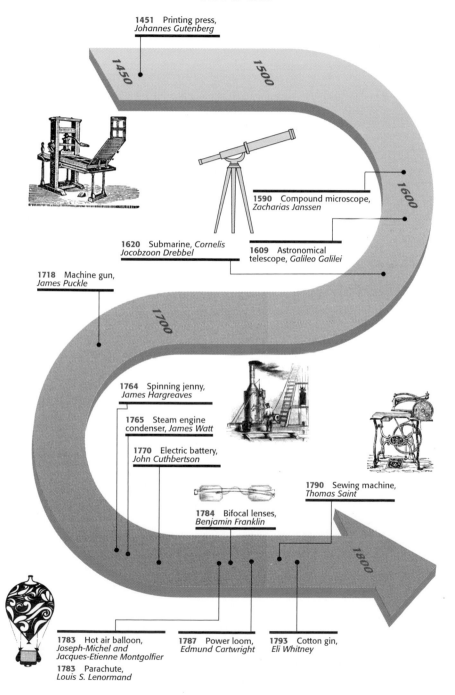

1450 to 1800

1451 Printing press, *Johannes Gutenberg*

1450

1500

1600

1590 Compound microscope, *Zacharias Janssen*

1620 Submarine, *Cornelis Jocobzoon Drebbel*

1609 Astronomical telescope, *Galileo Galilei*

1718 Machine gun, *James Puckle*

1700

1764 Spinning jenny, *James Hargreaves*

1765 Steam engine condenser, *James Watt*

1770 Electric battery, *John Cuthbertson*

1790 Sewing machine, *Thomas Saint*

1784 Bifocal lenses, *Benjamin Franklin*

1800

1783 Hot air balloon, *Joseph-Michel and Jacques-Etienne Montgolfier*

1783 Parachute, *Louis S. Lenormand*

1787 Power loom, *Edmund Cartwright*

1793 Cotton gin, *Eli Whitney*

MAJOR INVENTIONS AND THEIR INVENTORS

Air brake   George Westinghouse, U.S., 1868

Air conditioning   Willis Carrier, U.S., 1911

Airplane   Orville and Wilbur Wright, U.S., 1903

Airship   (nonrigid) Henri Giffard, France, 1852; (rigid) Ferdinand von Zeppelin, Germany, 1900

Antibiotics   Discovery of penicillin, first antibiotic, Alexander Fleming, 1928; (penicillin's infection-fighting properties) Howard Florey, Ernst Chain, England, 1940

Antiseptic   (surgery) Joseph Lister, England, 1867

Antitoxin, diptheria   Emil von Behring, Germany, 1890

Aqualung (oxygen tank)   Jacques-Yves Cousteau, Emile Gagnan, France, 1943

Aspirin   Dr. Felix Hoffman, Germany, 1899

Automobile   (first with internal combustion engine, 250 rpm) Karl Benz, Germany, 1885

Braille   Louis Braille, France, 1829

Camera   (hand-held) George Eastman, U.S., 1888; (Polaroid Land) Edwin Land, U.S., 1948

Chewing gum   (spruce based) John Curtis, U.S., 1848; (chicle based) Thomas Adams, U.S., 1870

Clock, pendulum   Christian Huygens, Netherlands, 1656

Coca-Cola   John Pemberton, U.S., 1886

Compact disc   RCA, U.S., 1972

Computer   (Mark 1, first information-processing digital computer) Howard Aiken, U.S., 1944; (ENIAC, Electronic Numerical Integrator and Calculator, first all-electronic) J. Presper Eckert, John W. Mauchly, U.S., 1946

Cotton gin   Eli Whitney, U.S., 1793

Dynamite   Alfred Nobel, Sweden, 1867

Elevator, passenger   (safety device permitting use by passengers) Elisha G. Otis, U.S., 1852; (elevator utilizing safety device) 1857

Fiber optics   Narinder Kapany, England, 1955

Gunpowder   China, c. 700

Helicopter   (double rotor) Heinrich Focke, Germany, 1936; (single rotor) Igor I. Sikorsky, U.S., 1939

Insulin   Sir Frederick C. Banting, J. J. R. MacLeod, Canada, 1922

Laser   (theoretical work on) Charles H. Townes, Arthur L. Schawlow, U.S.; N. Basov, A. Prokhorov, U.S.S.R., 1958; (first working model) T. H. Maiman, U.S., 1960

Lens, bifocal   Benjamin Franklin, U.S., c. 1784

Lightning rod   Benjamin Franklin, U.S., 1752

Locomotive   (steam powered) Richard Trevithick, England, 1804

Microphone   Charles Wheatstone, England, 1827

Microscope   (compound) Zacharias Janssen, Netherlands, 1590; (electron) Vladimir Zworykin et al., U.S., Canada, Germany, 1932–1939

Microwave oven   Percy Spencer, U.S., 1957

Motion pictures   Thomas Edison, U.S., 1893

Motor, electric   Michael Faraday, England, 1822; (alternating current) Nikola Tesla, U.S., 1892

Motorcycle   (motor tricycle) Edward Butler, England, 1884; (gasoline-engine motorcycle) Gottlieb Daimler, Germany, 1885

Paper   China, c.100 B.C.

Parachute   Louis S. Lenormand, France, 1783

Pen   (fountain) Lewis E. Waterman, U.S., 1884; (ballpoint, for marking on rough surfaces) John H. Loud, U.S., 1888; (ballpoint, for handwriting) Lazlo Biro, Argentina, 1944

Phonograph   Thomas Edison, U.S., 1877

Source: U.S. Department of Commerce; U.S. Patent and Trademark Office

Photography   (first paper negative, first photograph, on metal) Joseph Nicéphore Niepce, France, 1816–1827; (first direct positive image on silverplate, the daguerreotype) Louis Daguerre, based on work with Niepce, France, 1839; (first color images) Alexandre Becquerel, Claude Niepce de Saint-Victor, France, 1848–1850; (commercial color film with three emulsion layers, Kodachrome) U.S., 1935

Piano (Hammerklavier) Bartolommeo Cristofori, Italy, 1709; (pianoforte with sustaining and damper pedals) John Broadwood, England, 1873

Polio, vaccine against   (vaccine made from dead virus strains) Jonas E. Salk, U.S., 1954; (vaccine made from live virus strains) Albert Sabin, U.S., 1960

Printing   (block) Japan, c. 700; (movable type) Korea, c.1400; Johannes Gutenberg, Germany, 1451

Radar   (limited to one-mile range) Christian Hulsmeyer, Germany, 1904

Radio   (electromagnetism, theory of) James Clerk Maxwell, England, 1873; (first practical system of wireless telegraphy) Guglielmo Marconi, Italy, 1895; (vacuum electron tube, basis for radio telephony) Sir John Fleming, England, 1904

Refrigerator   Alexander Twining, U.S., James Harrison, Australia, 1850

Revolver   Samuel Colt, U.S., 1835

Rifle   (muzzle-loaded) Italy, Germany, c. 1475; (breech-loaded) England, France, Germany, U.S., c. 1866; (bolt-action) Paul von Mauser, Germany, 1889; (automatic) John Browning, U.S., 1918

Rocket   (liquid-fueled) Robert Goddard, U.S., 1926

Rubber   (vulcanization process) Charles Goodyear, U.S., 1839

Steam engine   (first commercial version based on principles of French physicist Denis Papin) Thomas Savery, England, 1639; (modern condensing, double acting) James Watt, England, 1765

Steamship   Claude de Jouffroy d'Abbans, France, 1783; James Rumsey, U.S., 1787; John Fitch, U.S., 1790; all preceded Robert Fulton, U.S., credited with launching first commercially successful steamship

Tank, military   Sir Ernest Swinton, England, 1914

Tape recorder   (magnetic steel tape) Valdemar Poulsen, Denmark, 1899

Telegraph   Samuel F. B. Morse, U.S., 1837

Telephone   Alexander Graham Bell, U.S., 1876

Telescope   Hans Lippershey, Netherlands, 1608; (astronomical) Galileo Galilei, Italy, 1609; (reflecting) Isaac Newton, England, 1668

Television   (mechanical disk-scanning method) successfully demonstrated by J. K. Baird, England, C. F. Jenkins, U.S., 1926; (electronic scanning method) Vladimir K. Zworykin, U.S., 1928

Thermometer   (open-column) Galileo Galilei, Italy, c. 1593; (clinical) Santorio Santorio, Padua, c.1615; (mercury, also Fahrenheit scale) Daniel G. Fahrenheit, Germany, 1714; (centigrade scale) Anders Celsius, Sweden, 1742; (absolute-temperature, or Kelvin, scale) William Thompson, Lord Kelvin, England, 1848

Tractor   Benjamin Holt, U.S., 1900

Transistor   John Bardeen, William Shockley, Walter Brittain, U.S., 1948

Video disk   Philips Co., Netherlands, 1972

Wheel   (cart, solid wood) Mesopotamia, c. 3800–3600 B.C.

Xerography   Chester Carlson, U.S., 1938

PROFILES OF MAJOR INVENTORS

Alexander Graham Bell (Scottish-American, 1874–1922) TELEGRAPHY Despite the title of this patent, the invention here was the telephone.

Emile Berliner (German-American, 1851–1929) MICROPHONE AND GRAMOPHONE Berliner's microphone made it possible to use Alexander Graham Bell's telephone over long distances. With the $50,000 patent rights payment he received from the Bell Telephone Company, Berliner developed the gramophone, the forerunner of the record player.

William Seward Burroughs (American, 1857–1898) CALCULATING MACHINE Although the calculating machine dates from the 17th century, Burroughs's was the first that could be mass produced and easily used.

Chester F. Carlson (American, 1906–1968) ELECTROPHOTOGRAPHY Carlson invented the dry copying method called xerography. Although patented in 1940, the dry copier was not marketed until 1958, by which time

Carlson had patented many improvements.

George Washington Carver (American, 1864–1943) PRODUCTS USING PEANUTS AND SWEET POTATOES A successful African American scientist in Iowa who later taught at the prestigious Tuskegee Institute, Carver developed over 300 uses for the peanut and 118 sweet potato by-products as an incentive for farmers to plant regenerative crops rather than the traditional soil-destroying cotton and tobacco.

John Deere (American, 1804–1886) PLOW Anyone who grew up near a farm knows the name John Deere. His vastly improved plow was the start of his commercial success, and the company he founded still makes farm tools.

Rudolph Diesel (German, 1858–1913) INTERNAL COMBUSTION ENGINE The pressure-ignited heat engine is still called the diesel engine.

George Eastman (American, 1854–1932) METHOD AND APPARATUS FOR COATING PLATES FOR USE IN PHOTOGRAPHY Eastman developed the dry plate negative and transparent roll film for still cameras and a motion picture film for the newly invented cinema.

Thomas Alva Edison (American, 1847–1931) ELECTRIC LAMP One of the world's greatest and most prolific inventors. In addition to the carbon-filament electric lamp, Edison patented a phonograph, the mimeograph, the fluoroscope, and motion picture cameras and projectors.

Philo Taylor Farnsworth (American, 1906–1971) TELEVISION SYSTEM Farnsworth patented many components of all-electronic television. He also worked on an electron microscope, radar, the use of ultraviolet light for seeing in the dark, and nuclear fusion.

Source: U.S. Department of Commerce; *Webster's Biographical Dictionary*

Enrico Fermi (Italian American, 1901–1954) NEUTRONIC REACTOR Fermi's nuclear reactor is the basis of nuclear power today. His many contributions to modern physics include basic theoretical work as well as experimental physics.

Henry Ford (American, 1863–1947) TRANSMISSION MECHANISM Best remembered for his innovative business practices, Ford also invented and patented numerous mechanisms used in automobiles.

Guglielmo Marconi (Italian, 1874–1937) TRANSMITTING ELECTRICAL SIGNALS Marconi's patent for using radio waves to carry coded messages is best known as wireless telegraphy.

Cyrus McCormick (American, 1809–1884) REAPER McCormick's machine for harvesting grain (patented in 1834) and his other inventions revolutionized American agriculture.

Samuel F. B. Morse (American, 1791–1872) TELEGRAPH SIGNALS Morse developed the first commercially successful telegraph. Joseph

Henry was the genius behind the electronics, but Morse and his dot-dash code made instantaneous long-distance communications possible.

Louis Pasteur (French, 1822–1895) BREWING OF BEER AND ALE Pasteur's work on beer and ale is generally considered unsuccessful, but he invented several vaccines, and he developed pasteurization, the heating process that protects beverages and food from microbe contamination.

Igor I. Sikorsky (Russian American, 1889–1972) HELICOPTER CONTROLS Sikorsky designed and built many successful airplanes, but in 1931 he made a critical breakthrough in helicopter design. His continued developments led to the helicopter of today.

An Wang (Chinese-American, 1920–1990) MAGNETIC PULSE CONTROLLING DEVICE Although best known for his state-of-the-art word processor of the 1960s and 1970s, Wang contributed many fundamental ideas to the development of

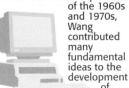

electronic computers, including the principle on which magnetic core memory is built.

George Westinghouse (American, 1846–1914) STEAM-POWERED BRAKE DEVICES In 1869 Westinghouse patented an air brake for locomotives, his most important contribution to railroad safety. His later work on signals and switches led him to form the Westinghouse Electric Co. in 1884.

Eli Whitney (American, 1765–1825) COTTON GIN By making it possible to remove seeds from cotton mechanically, the gin made large-scale cotton farming possible. Whitney also introduced interchangeable parts, the beginning of mass production.

Orville Wright (American, 1871–1948) and **Wilbur Wright** (American, 1867–1912) FLYING MACHINE The Wright Brothers not only invented the first airplane in 1903, they also popularized, manufactured, and sold the new machines.

JOBS AND UNEMPLOYMENT

In the late 1700s, most Americans worked their own land or pursued a craft or trade—baker, blacksmith, miller, tailor. By the late 1800s, that had changed. The United States was a manufacturing nation. Factories employing hundreds of workers turned out mass-produced goods.

Today the world of work has changed again. Machines have replaced people in many repetitive factory jobs. More Americans work in service industries than in manufacturing. Health care is the fastest-growing career field. More women are in the workforce than ever before. And as large corporations have "downsized" and cut jobs, more people have become self-employed, working in their own businesses—many in their own homes.

At the start of 1997, nearly 128 million Americans held jobs. About three fourths of those jobs were in services, and less than 3 percent were in farming. More than seven million people were unemployed. The official unemployment rate was 5.3 percent, a low figure. The unemployment rate rises and falls with changes in the economy. During the worst of the Great Depression of the 1930s, unemployment was nearly 25 percent. Even when unemployment is low, however, it is often worse among certain groups. In recent years African Americans have experienced unemployment at twice the national rate, and teenagers at more than three times the rate.

Yearbook

circa 1000 European merchants form associations called "guilds" in order to protect their business interests.

1802 British factory apprentices and miners win a 12-hour workday.

1935 The Social Security Act establishes unemployment compensation and other benefits for U.S. workers.

1972 Congress passes the Equal Employment Opportunity Act to encourage the promotion of women and minorities.

• Notables •

Elizabeth Blackwell (1821–1910) American; first woman doctor in the United States.

César Chávez (1927–1993) U.S. labor leader; founded the United Farm Workers Union in 1966.

Eugene Debs (1885–1926) American labor activist; organizer of the famous railroad worker strike called the Pullman strike.

Samuel Gompers (1850–1924) American social activist; founder of the Federation of Organized Trades and Labor Unions, which was later reorganized as the American Federation of Labor (AFL).

Alice Hamilton (1869–1970) American doctor; investigated the poisons to which factory workers were exposed.

KEY IDEAS

blue collar worker Someone who works at a job that requires protective clothing or work clothes, such as a factory job.

glass ceiling A figurative barrier in a company where women and minorities are not able to work in the most powerful positions. The barrier may be the attitudes of those already in power.

labor union An organization of workers that is formed in order to gain better wages and working conditions for its members.

minimum wage The lowest wage that is legally permitted to be paid in an industry.

retail Sold to the general public.

sabbatical year A year that a person spends away from his or her job, often with pay, in order to travel or do research. It is believed that this year away will help the person do a better job upon returning.

white collar worker Someone who works in an office, usually management.

PROFILE: U.S. EMPLOYMENT

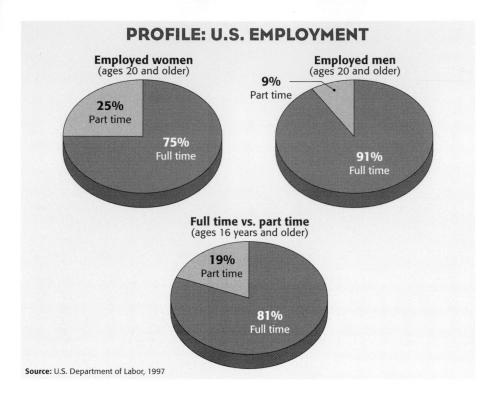

Employed women
(ages 20 and older)

25%
Part time

75%
Full time

Employed men
(ages 20 and older)

9%
Part time

91%
Full time

Full time vs. part time
(ages 16 years and older)

19%
Part time

81%
Full time

Source: U.S. Department of Labor, 1997

PROFILE: U.S. UNEMPLOYMENT

Unemployment by industry

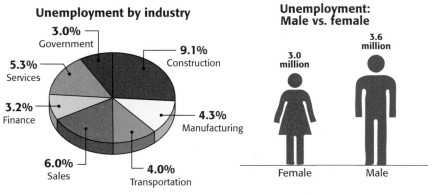

3.0%
Government

5.3%
Services

3.2%
Finance

6.0%
Sales

9.1%
Construction

4.3%
Manufacturing

4.0%
Transportation

Unemployment: Male vs. female

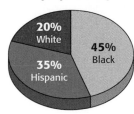

3.0 million

3.6 million

Female

Male

Unemployment by race

20%
White

45%
Black

35%
Hispanic

Note: Unemployment statistics vary from month to month. Percentages based on averages.

Source: U.S. Department of Labor, 1997

TOP 5 MOST COMMON TYPES OF JOBS IN THE U.S.

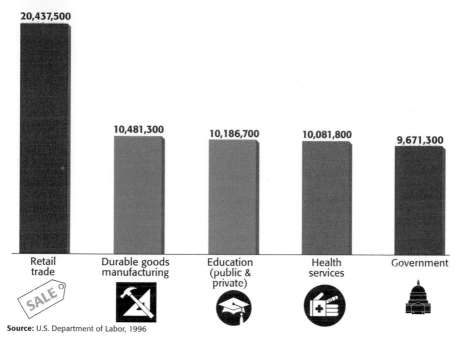

20,437,500 — Retail trade

10,481,300 — Durable goods manufacturing

10,186,700 — Education (public & private)

10,081,800 — Health services

9,671,300 — Government

Source: U.S. Department of Labor, 1996

PROFILE: AVERAGE SALARIES, BY JOB

(annual salaries, before taxes)

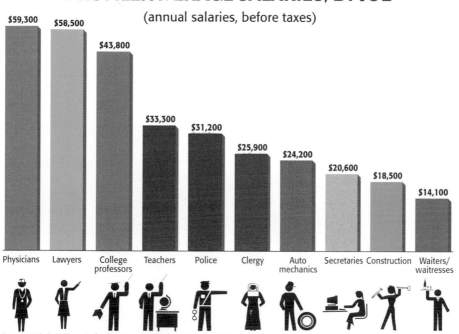

$59,300 — Physicians

$58,500 — Lawyers

$43,800 — College professors

$33,300 — Teachers

$31,200 — Police

$25,900 — Clergy

$24,200 — Auto mechanics

$20,600 — Secretaries

$18,500 — Construction

$14,100 — Waiters/waitresses

Source: U.S. Department of Labor, Bureau of Labor Statistics, 1996

LABOR FORCE BY SEX

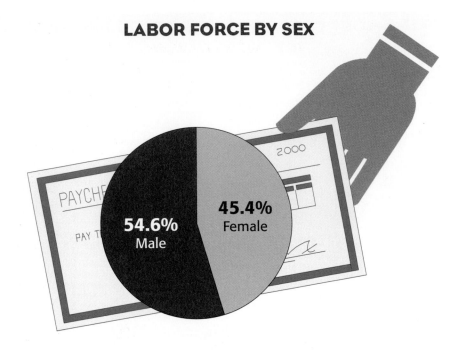

54.6%
Male

45.4%
Female

Source: U.S. Department of Labor, Bureau of Labor Statistics,1997

GROWTH OF WORKING MOTHERS IN U.S. LABOR FORCE
(percentage of all women in labor force)

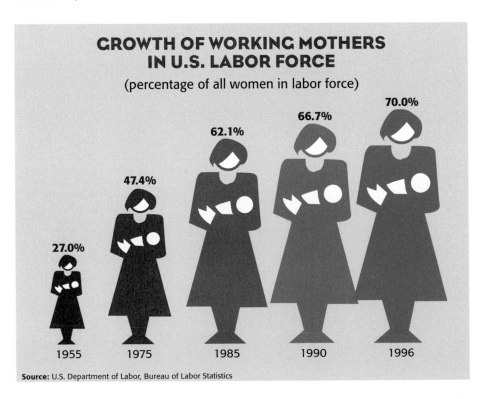

27.0% — 1955
47.4% — 1975
62.1% — 1985
66.7% — 1990
70.0% — 1996

Source: U.S. Department of Labor, Bureau of Labor Statistics

TOP 5 TOP-PAYING FIELDS FOR COLLEGE GRADS

(estimated starting salaries)

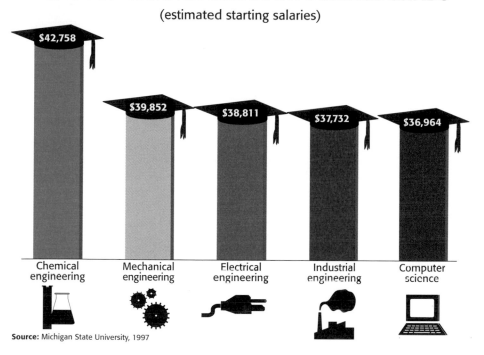

$42,758 — Chemical engineering

$39,852 — Mechanical engineering

$38,811 — Electrical engineering

$37,732 — Industrial engineering

$36,964 — Computer science

Source: Michigan State University, 1997

U.S. HOME-OFFICE OWNERS, BY TYPE

In 39 million U.S. households, at least one person has a home office.
Who has home offices (in millions):

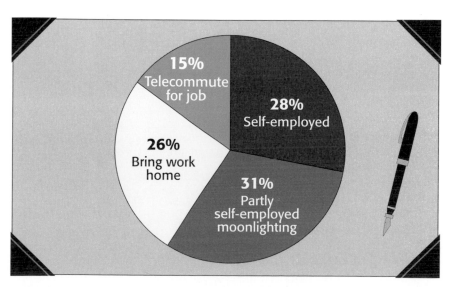

15% Telecommute for job

28% Self-employed

26% Bring work home

31% Partly self-employed moonlighting

Source: IDC/Link 1995 Home-Office Market Update

LANGUAGES

Hi Ciao Salut Hola Tag

Parla l'italiano? Italian is one of about 3,000 languages in use today. Some, such as Chinese and English, are spoken by hundreds of millions of people. Others are seldom heard. Welsh, for example, is used only in Wales.

Languages as different as Welsh, Russian, Italian, Hindi, Greek, and English probably had the same origin. People from India to Europe to the Americas speak languages that belong to the Indo-European group, one of several large language families. The first Indo-European speakers may have lived in northern Europe during prehistoric times. They spread out and settled in different areas, and their language developed differently in each place. Languages have similarities in grammar and in certain words. For example, the word for "mother" is *mater* in Latin, *Mutter* in German, *meter* in Greek, *mat'* in Russian, *mata* in Sanskrit, and *madre* in Spanish.

There are no written examples of the first Indo-European language because it died out before writing developed. About 5,500 years ago, the Sumerians developed a form of writing in which pictures represented words. Most modern languages are written with symbols that represent sounds—an alphabet. The English alphabet developed from one used by the ancient Phoenicians more than 3,000 years ago.

Languages are constantly changing. English is full of "loan" words adopted from other languages: *ballet* from French, *rodeo* from Spanish, *kindergarten* from German. People also invent new words for new things—spacecraft, television, and megabyte, for example.

Yearbook

circa 1600 B.C. An alphabet with symbols for each consonant (but none for the vowels) develops in present-day Israel.

circa 400 B.C. The Romans begin to develop a literature. A gap develops between classical, written Latin and "Vulgar Latin"—the spoken form.

circa 1500 Modern English is spoken in England. It is substantially different from Middle English, from which it evolved.

circa 1900 The field of modern linguistics develops.

• Notables •

Dante Alighieri (1265–1321) Authored *The Divine Comedy*, a literary classic in Tuscan Italian; helped to make Tuscan—which is close to modern Italian—the literary language of Italy.

Louis Braille (1809–1852) Blind Frenchman; introduced Braille—a method of writing the alphabet with a pattern of raised dots; gave blind people the ability to read.

Charles-Michel Abbé de l'Epée (1712–1789) French cleric; perfected one-handed sign language for deaf people who are unable to speak.

Sir William Jones (1746–1794) English scholar; discovered the relationship between Sanskrit and Persian and Greek and Latin.

Ferdinand de Saussure (1857–1913) Swiss scholar; a founder of modern linguistics—the study of the elements of human speech.

KEY IDEAS

consonant In English, any letter except *a, e, i, o,* and *u.* These letters are called "vowels."

dialect A variation of a language that is spoken in a particular region.

linguistics The study of the elements of human speech.

mother tongue Official or native language.

native language The first language that a person learns.

pidgin Simplified speech that a person may use when speaking to someone who does not understand his or her language.

Romance languages One of several languages developed from Latin, such as French, Italian, and Spanish.

vulgar Refers to a less formal, often spoken rather than written, form of a language.

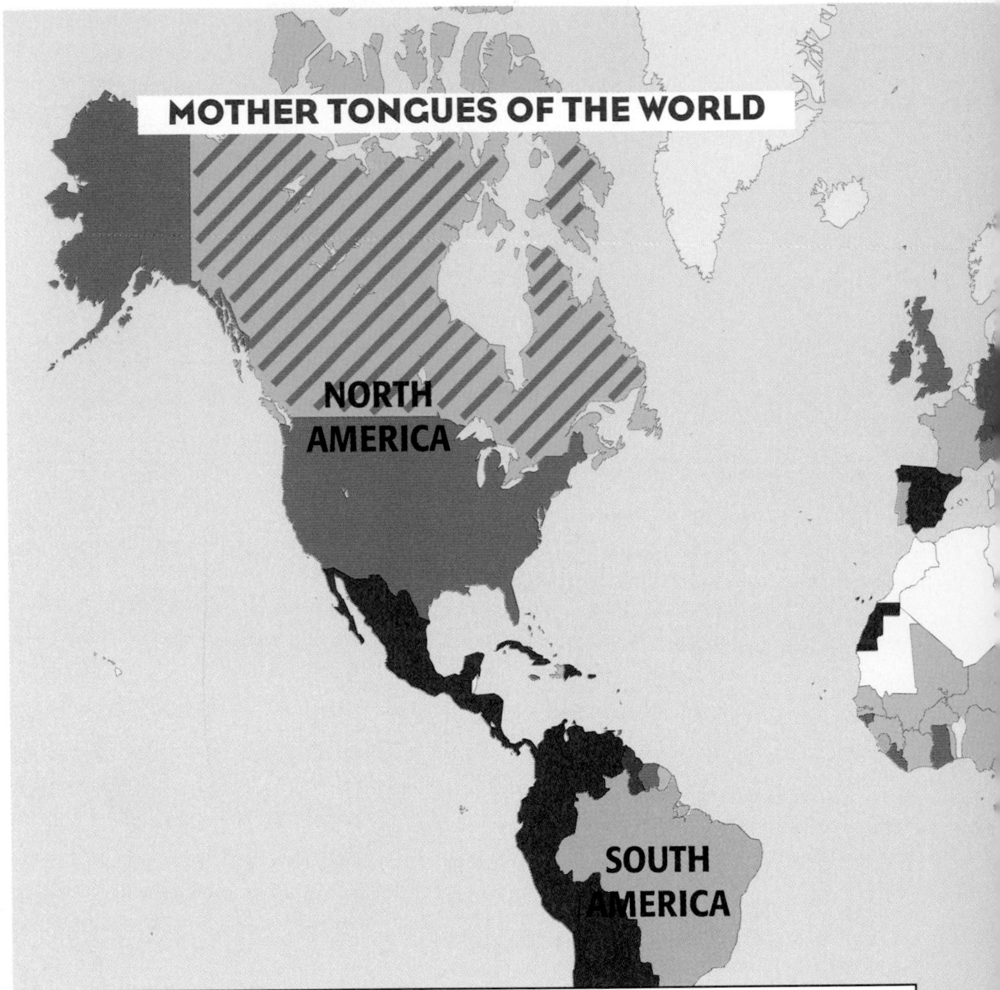

MOTHER TONGUES OF THE WORLD

NORTH
AMERICA

SOUTH
AMERICA

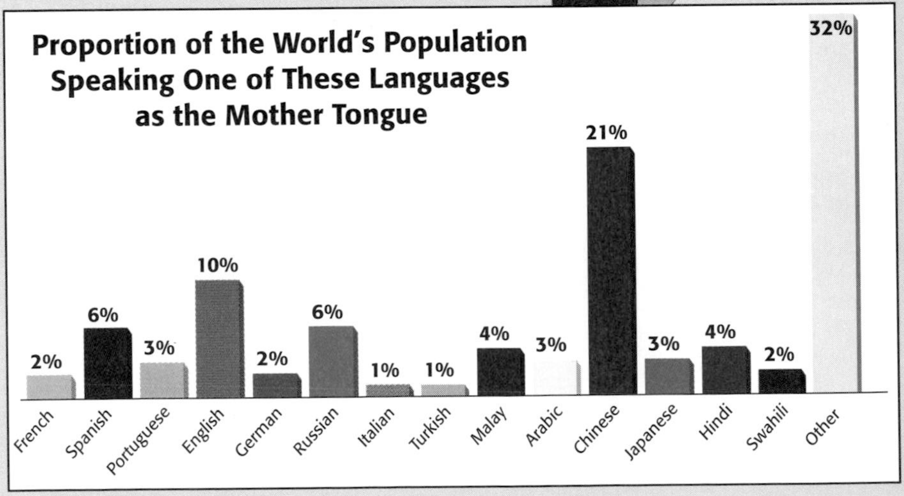

Proportion of the World's Population Speaking One of These Languages as the Mother Tongue

Language	Percentage
French	2%
Spanish	6%
Portuguese	3%
English	10%
German	2%
Russian	6%
Italian	1%
Turkish	1%
Malay	4%
Arabic	3%
Chinese	21%
Japanese	3%
Hindi	4%
Swahili	2%
Other	32%

ASIA

EUROPE

AFRICA

AUSTRALIA

Note: Other includes Nordic, Eastern European, and Persian tongues, among many.

Source: Based on data from *Peters Atlas of the World*

COMMON WORDS AND PHRASES:
SELECTED WORLD LANGUAGES

GERMAN

Hello	*Guten tag* (GOO-tn TAHK)
Good-bye	*Auf wiedersehen* (ahf VEE-dehr-zeh-hehn)
Good morning	*Guten morgen* (GOO-tn mor-gun)
Yes	*Ja* (yah)
No	*Nein* (nain)
Please	*Bitte* (BIH-teh)
Thank you	*Danke* (DAHN-keh)
One	*Ein* (ain)
Sunday	*Sonntag* (ZOHN-tahk)

ITALIAN

Hello, or so long	*Ciao* (chow)
Good-bye	*Arrivederci* (ah-ree-vay-DEHR-chee)
Good morning, good afternoon, or a general hello	*Buon giorno* (bwohn-JOOR-noh)
Good evening	*Buona sera* (BWOHN-ah SAY-rah)
Good night	*Buona notte* (BWOHN-ah NOHT-tay)
Yes	*Si* (SEE)
No	*No* (NOH)
Please	*Per favor* (purr fa-vo-ray)
Thank you	*Grazie* (GRAH-tsyay)
How are you?	*Come sta?* (KOH-may STAH)
Fine, very well	*Molto bene* (MOHL-toh BAY-nay)
Excuse me	*Scusi* (SKOO-zee)

UKRAINIAN

Hello	(prih-VEET)
Good morning	(DOH-bray RAH-nok)
Good afternoon	(DOH-bray dehn)
Good evening	(DOH-bray VEH-cheer)
Yes	(yah)
No	(nee-yet)
How are you?	(yak zhi-VESH)
Very well	(DOO-zheh DO-breh)
What's new?	(shcho no-VO-ho)

MANDARIN CHINESE

Hello	*Hao* (how)
Good-bye	*Zaijian* (zay-GEE-en)
Yes	*Shide* (SURE-duh)
No	*Bu shi* (BOO sure)
Have you eaten? (How are you?)	*Ni chiguo fan mei you?* (nee CHUR-gwaw FAHN may yo)
I've eaten (I'm fine)	*Chiguo le* (chur-gwaw-leh)
Are you hungry?	*Ni e le ma?* (nee UH leh ma)

SPANISH

Hi, Hello	*Hola* (OH-lah)
Good-bye	*Adios* (ah-dee-OS)
Good morning	*Buenos días* (BWAY-nohs DEE-ahs)
Good afternoon	*Buenas tardes* (BWAY-nahs TAHR-dehs)
Good evening	*Buenas noches* (BWAY-nahs NOH-chehs)
Yes	*Sí* (SEE)
No	*No* (NOH)
Please	*Por favor* (pour fa-vohr)
Thank you	*Gracias* (GRAH-see-us)
What's going on?	*¿Qué pasa?* (keh PAH-sah)
How are you?	*¿Cómo está Usted?* (COH-mo es-TAH oo-STEHD)
I'm well	*Estoy bien* (ehs-TOY bee-EHN)
My name is . . .	*Me llamo . . .* (may YAH-mo . . .)

EGYPTIAN ARABIC

Good-bye	*Ma salama* (MA sa-LA-ma)
Good morning	*Sabah el khair* (sa-BAH el KHAIR)
Yes	*Aiwa* (AI-wa)
No	*La* (LA)
Please	*Min fadlek* (min FAD-lek)
Thank you	*Shukran* (SHU-kran)
How are you?	*Izzayak* (iz-ZAY-ak)
My name is . . .	*Ismi . . .* (IS-mi . . .)
I speak English	*Ana bahki Ingleezi* (ana BAH-ki in-GLEEZ-i)
What is your name?	*Ismak ay?* (IS-mak AY)
No problem	*Ma feesh mushkila* (ma feesh mush-KI-la)

NIGERIAN (four of the major Nigerian language groups)

English	Fulani	Hausa	Ibo	Yoruba
I'm fine	*Jam tan* (JAM-taan)	*Kalau* (KA-lay-U)	*Adimnma* (ah-DEE-mm-NMAA)	*A dupe* (ah DEW-pay)
one	*goqo* (GO-quo)	*daya* (DA-ya)	*otu* (o-TWO)	*eni* (EE-nee)
two	*didi* (DEE-dee)	*biyu* (BEE-you)	*abua* (ah-BOO-ah)	*eji* (EE-gee)
three	*tati* (TA-tea)	*uku* (OO-coo)	*ato* (ah-TOE)	*eta* (EE-ta)
nine	*jeenayi* (gee-NA-yee)	*tara* (TAA-ra)	*iteghete* (IT-egg-HE-tea)	*esan* (EE-san)
ten	*sappo* (SAP-poe)	*goma* (GO-ma)	*iri* (EE-ree)	*ewa* (EE-wa)

LIFE SCIENCE

Biologists classify—organize and group—living things, past and present, according to their characteristics. The Greek philosopher Aristotle established the first divisions—plants and animals—in the fourth century B.C. Since then, as scientists have learned more about the fascinating variety of living things, they have established other groups and subgroups. Today, most scientists accept a five-kingdom classification system that includes animals, plants, fungi (nongreen plants), protista (algaes and protozoa), and monera (bacteria and certain algae). To further organize the living world, biologists have created standard subcategories of kingdoms, which include—among others—class, order, phylum, and species.

One of the most puzzling questions in life science is also one of the most basic: When and how did life begin? To answer this question, paleontologists (who find and interpret information from fossils) and biologists often work together. Many scientists think that life began in Earth's oceans when the planet was still young. When temperatures and other conditions were just right, certain chemicals joined to form new compounds. Over many years, more complex compounds formed. Perhaps 3.5 billion years ago, these compounds formed into one-celled organisms, like bacteria that exist today. These simple organisms had the basic characteristics of all living things. They used energy, and they were able to grow and reproduce. Much later—about 225 million years ago—the first mammals evolved. It was only about 4.5 million years ago that our relatives—the first human ancestors—appeared.

Yearbook

384–322 B.C. Aristotle's investigations lay the foundation for modern embryology. His writings include a classification for organisms (living beings).

1665 The English scientist Robert Hooke describes cells for the first time after observing them in slices of cork.

1868 French workmen building a road discover five 35,000-year-old skeletons. They are named "Cro-Magnon man" and are of the same species as modern humans.

1997 A sheep is cloned by the Scottish embryologist Jan Wilmut.

• Notables •

William Harvey (1578–1657) British physician; discovered that the heart pumps blood and blood circulates through the body.

Anton van Leeuwenhoek (1632–1723) Dutch naturalist; made microscopes; gave the first complete descriptions of bacteria, sperm, and protozoa (one-celled organisms).

Kary Mullis (1944–) Recipient of the 1993 Nobel Prize in Chemistry whose method for making trillions of copies of DNA has been used to study fossils and in criminal investigations.

Louis Pasteur (1822–1895) French scientist; discovered that fermentation is caused by very small organisms.

James Watson (1928–) and Francis Crick (1916–) American molecular biologist (Watson) and English scientist; developed a model of the DNA molecule in 1953.

KEY IDEAS

biology Life science.

classification Arranging plants or animals in groups or categories.

clone To produce an animal from a single cell of its parent. This animal, called a clone, is identical to its parent.

DNA (deoxyribonucleic acid) A molecule that occurs in living cells and stores the traits that an organism can inherit.

embryology A branch of biology that deals with the study of embryos—animals and humans in the early stages of their development, before they are born.

genetics A branch of biology that deals with heredity.

kingdom In biology, the broadest category of living things. There are five kingdoms of life.

paleontology The scientific study of fossils and prehistoric life.

THE FIVE KINGDOMS OF LIFE

Scientists classify all living things into one of five kingdoms.
Here is how they are organized.

  Includes (among others) sponges, flatworms, roundworms, mollusks, true worms, arthropods, crustaceans, vertebrates, jellyfish, corals, sea anemones, echinoderms

  Includes (among others) ferns, mosses, ginkos, horsetails, conifers, flowering plants, liverworts, hornworts

  Includes (among others) molds, mildews, blights, smuts, rusts, mushrooms, puffballs, stinkhorns, penicillia, lichens, black molds, dung fungi, yeasts, morels, truffles

  Includes (among others) yellow-green algae, golden algae, protozoa, green algae, brown algae, red algae

  Includes bacteria, blue-green algae

Source: *Our Living World*, Blackbirch Press, 1994

THE ORDER OF SCIENTIFIC CLASSIFICATION

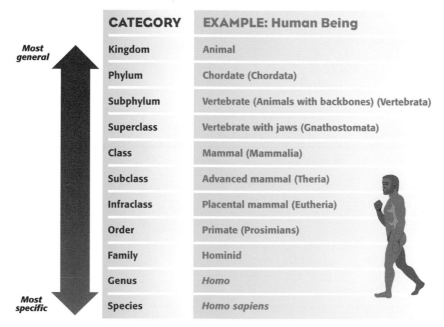

	CATEGORY	EXAMPLE: Human Being
Most general ↑	Kingdom	Animal
	Phylum	Chordate (Chordata)
	Subphylum	Vertebrate (Animals with backbones) (Vertebrata)
	Superclass	Vertebrate with jaws (Gnathostomata)
	Class	Mammal (Mammalia)
	Subclass	Advanced mammal (Theria)
	Infraclass	Placental mammal (Eutheria)
	Order	Primate (Prosimians)
	Family	Hominid
	Genus	Homo
Most specific ↓	Species	Homo sapiens

Source: *Our Living World*, Blackbirch Press, 1994

MAJOR DISCOVERIES OF HUMAN ANCESTORS

	Years Ago	Species	Major Discovery	Details
About 60 million years back to last dinosaurs	c. 4.4 million	*Ardipithecus ramidus*	1994 in Ethiopia	Oldest known human ancestor. Chimpanzee-like skull.
	c. 4.2 million	*Australopithecus anamensis*	1995, two sites at Lake Turkana, Kanapoi, and Allia Bay, Kenya	Possible ancestor of *A. afarensis* ("Lucy"). Walked upright.
	c. 3.2 million	*Australopithecus afarensis*	1974 at Hadar in the Afar triangle of eastern Ethiopia	Nicknamed "Lucy." Her skeleton is 3.5 feet (100 cm) tall. Ape-like skull. Walked fully upright. Lived in family groups throughout eastern Africa.
	c. 2.5 million	*Australopithecus africanus*	1924 at Taung, northern Cape Province, South Africa	Descendant of Lucy. Lived in social groups.
	c. 2 million	*Australopithecus robustus*	1938 in Kromdraai, South Africa	Was related to *A. africanus*.
	c. 2 million	*Homo habilis* (skillful man)	1960 in Olduvai Gorge, Tanzania	First brain expansion; is believed to have used stone tools.
	c. 1.8 million	*Homo erectus* (upright man)	1891 at Trinil, Java	Brain size twice that of australopithecine species. Regarded as ancestor of *Homo sapiens*. Invented the hand ax. Could probably make fires. Was first to migrate out of Africa.
Present	c. 100,000 (?)	*Homo sapiens* (knowing or wise man)	1868, Cro-Magnon, France	Anatomically modern humans.

PALEONTOLOGY: THE HISTORY OF LIFE

(All dates are approximate and are subject to change based on new fossil finds
or new dating techniques; but the sequence of events is generally accepted.
Dates are in billions and millions of years before the present.)

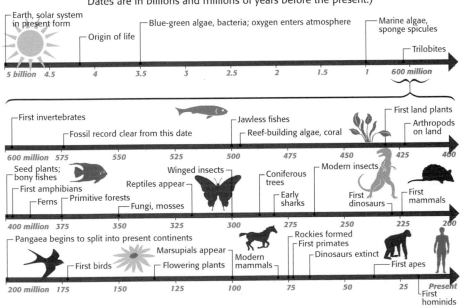

Earth, solar system in present form
Origin of life
Blue-green algae, bacteria; oxygen enters atmosphere
Marine algae, sponge spicules
Trilobites

5 billion 4.5 4 3.5 3 2.5 2 1.5 1 600 million

First invertebrates
Fossil record clear from this date
Jawless fishes
Reef-building algae, coral
First land plants
Arthropods on land

600 million 575 550 525 500 475 450 425 400

Seed plants; bony fishes
First amphibians
Ferns
Primitive forests
Reptiles appear
Fungi, mosses
Winged insects
Coniferous trees
Early sharks
Modern insects
First dinosaurs
First mammals

400 million 375 350 325 300 275 250 225 200

Pangaea begins to split into present continents
First birds
Marsupials appear
Flowering plants
Modern mammals
Rockies formed
First primates
Dinosaurs extinct
First apes
First hominids

200 million 175 150 125 100 75 50 25 Present

MAJOR DISCOVERIES IN LIFE SCIENCES

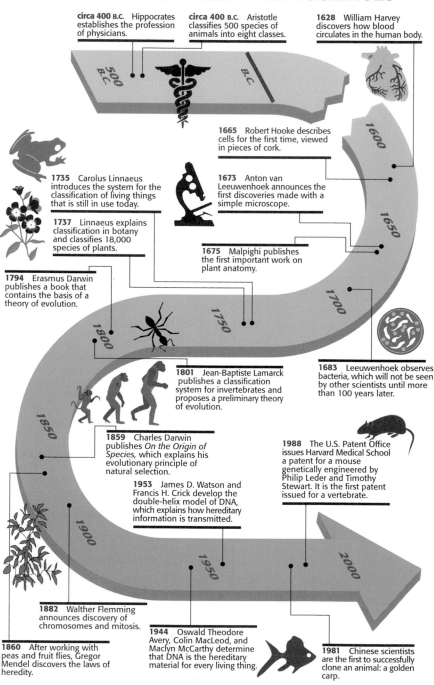

circa 400 B.C. Hippocrates establishes the profession of physicians.

circa 400 B.C. Aristotle classifies 500 species of animals into eight classes.

1628 William Harvey discovers how blood circulates in the human body.

1665 Robert Hooke describes cells for the first time, viewed in pieces of cork.

1735 Carolus Linnaeus introduces the system for the classification of living things that is still in use today.

1673 Anton van Leeuwenhoek announces the first discoveries made with a simple microscope.

1737 Linnaeus explains classification in botany and classifies 18,000 species of plants.

1675 Malpighi publishes the first important work on plant anatomy.

1794 Erasmus Darwin publishes a book that contains the basis of a theory of evolution.

1801 Jean-Baptiste Lamarck publishes a classification system for invertebrates and proposes a preliminary theory of evolution.

1683 Leeuwenhoek observes bacteria, which will not be seen by other scientists until more than 100 years later.

1859 Charles Darwin publishes *On the Origin of Species,* which explains his evolutionary principle of natural selection.

1953 James D. Watson and Francis H. Crick develop the double-helix model of DNA, which explains how hereditary information is transmitted.

1988 The U.S. Patent Office issues Harvard Medical School a patent for a mouse genetically engineered by Philip Leder and Timothy Stewart. It is the first patent issued for a vertebrate.

1882 Walther Flemming announces discovery of chromosomes and mitosis.

1944 Oswald Theodore Avery, Colin MacLeod, and Maclyn McCarthy determine that DNA is the hereditary material for every living thing.

1860 After working with peas and fruit flies, Gregor Mendel discovers the laws of heredity.

1981 Chinese scientists are the first to successfully clone an animal: a golden carp.

Source: Data from *Timetables of Science,* Touchstone, 1988

BIOLOGY: WHO STUDIES WHAT?

Scientists who study living things are called biologists. Biology however, can be broken down into many different categories. Each category is a special science unto itself. Here are some categories of biologists and what they study.

Botanists specialize in *botany*, the study of plants.

Zoologists specialize in *zoology*, the study of animals.

Microbiologists specialize in *microbiology*, the study of microscopic (super tiny) plants and animals.

Cytologists specialize in *cytology*, the study of cells.

Ecologists specialize in *ecology*, the study of the interrelationship of organisms and their environment.

Entomologists specialize in *entomology*, the study of insects.

Herpetologists specialize in *herpetology*, the study of reptiles and amphibians.

Ichthyologists specialize in *ichthyology*, the study of fish.

Mammalogists specialize in *mammalogy*, the study of mammals.

Marine biologists specialize in *marine biology*, the study of plants and animals in seas and oceans.

Ornithologists specialize in *ornithology*, the study of birds.

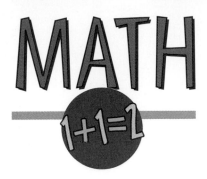

MATH

Try to get through a day without using math. Chances are you won't get far. Before you even leave for school, you'll need to figure out how many minutes you have to catch your bus and how much money to bring for lunch.

Almost everything people do, from a trip to the supermarket to a space mission, involves math. Families use math to work out their monthly budgets. Businesses use math to keep records of costs and profits. Financial firms use it to handle investments. Designers, builders, and engineers rely on mathematical calculations to plan and build everything from furniture to highways. Governments use math to predict future needs.

Math has been called "the gate and key of the sciences" because it is so essential for accurate scientific observations. Pure mathematics is the study of math for its own sake, rather than as a practical tool.

Math includes a number of separate fields. The common threads among them are quantities, numbers, and symbols. Arithmetic involves calculations through addition, subtraction, multiplication, and division. Algebra is a system of solving complicated problems through symbols and formulas. Geometry is concerned with measuring shapes and figures and with the relations between angles and measurements of figures. These three fields form the foundation for more advanced fields of mathematics, such as trigonometry, calculus, statistics, and probability.

Yearbook

circa 3500 B.C. Egyptians develop a system that can record very large numbers. There are different symbols for ones, tens, and hundreds, and larger numbers.

circa 300 B.C. Euclid's *Elements* is written. Several volumes of this 13-volume work are still the foundation of a field called "plane geometry."

1798 The German mathematician Karl Gauss writes his work on number theory.

1996 A computer programmed by American researchers offers a solution to a mathematical problem that has stumped mathematicians for 60 years.

• Notables •

Archimedes (circa 287–212 B.C.) Greek mathematician and inventor; known for work on the circle, cylinder, and other geometric shapes.

René Descartes (1596–1650) French mathematician and philosopher; invented "analytic geometry."

David Hilbert (1862–1943) German mathematician; in 1900, produced a list of 23 unsolved problems that became famous and stumped mathematicians for many years.

Blaise Pascal (1623–1662) French scientist and philosopher; with others, developed the laws of probability.

Simon Stevin (1548–1620) Dutch mathematician; invented the system of using and computing decimal fractions.

KEY IDEAS

algebra A branch of mathematics that focuses on operations (such as addition and subtraction) with sets of numbers. These numbers are represented by symbols.

calculus A branch of mathematics that studies changing quantities.

geometry A branch of mathematics that deals with measurements and also relationships between points, lines, angles, and surfaces.

imperial A system of measurement that uses gallons, miles, inches, and feet, among other terms.

metric A system of measurement.

probability In this discussion, the mathematical study of whether an event is likely to occur in a certain situation.

trigonometry The study of triangles.

MULTIPLICATION TABLE

X	1	2	3	4	5	6	7	8	9	10	11	12
1	1	2	3	4	5	6	7	8	9	10	11	12
2	2	4	6	8	10	12	14	16	18	20	22	24
3	3	6	9	12	15	18	21	24	27	30	33	36
4	4	8	12	16	20	24	28	32	36	40	44	48
5	5	10	15	20	25	30	35	40	45	50	55	60
6	6	12	18	24	30	36	42	48	54	60	66	72
7	7	14	21	28	35	42	49	56	63	70	77	84
8	8	16	24	32	40	48	56	64	72	80	88	96
9	9	18	27	36	45	54	63	72	81	90	99	108
10	10	20	30	40	50	60	70	80	90	100	110	120
11	11	22	33	44	55	66	77	88	99	110	121	132
12	12	24	36	48	60	72	84	96	108	120	132	144

SQUARES AND SQUARE ROOTS

Raising a number to a second power is also called squaring it; 3 squared (3^2), for example, is 9. By the same token, the square root of 9 is 3.

The symbol for square root is called a *radical sign* $\sqrt{}$.

Examples of squaring

2 squared: $2^2 = 2 \times 2 = 4$

3 squared: $3^2 = 3 \times 3 = 9$

4 squared: $4^2 = 4 \times 4 = 16$

Examples of square roots

Square root of 16: $\sqrt{16} = 4$

Square root of 9: $\sqrt{9} = 3$

Square root of 4: $\sqrt{4} = 2$

Square Roots to 40

$\sqrt{1}$	1	$\sqrt{121}$	11	$\sqrt{441}$	21	$\sqrt{961}$	31
$\sqrt{4}$	2	$\sqrt{144}$	12	$\sqrt{484}$	22	$\sqrt{1,024}$	32
$\sqrt{9}$	3	$\sqrt{169}$	13	$\sqrt{529}$	23	$\sqrt{1,089}$	33
$\sqrt{16}$	4	$\sqrt{196}$	14	$\sqrt{576}$	24	$\sqrt{1,156}$	34
$\sqrt{25}$	5	$\sqrt{225}$	15	$\sqrt{625}$	25	$\sqrt{1,225}$	35
$\sqrt{36}$	6	$\sqrt{256}$	16	$\sqrt{676}$	26	$\sqrt{1,296}$	36
$\sqrt{49}$	7	$\sqrt{289}$	17	$\sqrt{729}$	27	$\sqrt{1,369}$	37
$\sqrt{64}$	8	$\sqrt{324}$	18	$\sqrt{784}$	28	$\sqrt{1,444}$	38
$\sqrt{81}$	9	$\sqrt{361}$	19	$\sqrt{841}$	29	$\sqrt{1,521}$	39
$\sqrt{100}$	10	$\sqrt{400}$	20	$\sqrt{900}$	30	$\sqrt{1,600}$	40

NUMBERS GLOSSARY

COMPOSITE NUMBERS

Composite numbers are all counting numbers that are not prime numbers. In other words, composite numbers are numbers that have more than two *factors*. The number *1*, because it has only one factor (itself), is *not* a composite number.

Examples of composite numbers 4 to 100
4, 6, 8, 9, 10, 12, 14, 15, 16, 18, 20, 21, 22, 24, 25, 26, 27, 28, 30, 32, 33, 34, 35, 36, 38, 39, 40, 42, 44, 45, 46, 48, 49, 50, 51, 52, 54, 55, 56, 57, 58, 60, 62, 63, 64, 65, 66, 68, 69, 70, 72, 74, 75, 76, 77, 78, 80, 81, 82, 84, 85, 86, 87, 88, 90, 91, 92, 93, 94, 95, 96, 98, 99, 100

COUNTING NUMBERS

Counting numbers, or *natural numbers*, begin with the number *1* and continue into infinity.

$$\{1, 2, 3, 4, 5, 6, 7, 8, 9, 10 \dots\}$$

INTEGERS

Integers include *0*, all counting numbers (called *positive* whole numbers), and all whole numbers less than *0* (called *negative* whole numbers).

PRIME NUMBERS

Prime numbers are counting numbers that can be divided by only two numbers: *1* and themselves.

Prime numbers between 1 and 1,000									
	2	3	5	7	11	13	17	19	23
29	31	37	41	43	47	53	59	61	67
71	73	79	83	89	97	101	103	107	109
113	127	131	137	139	149	151	157	163	167
173	179	181	191	193	197	199	211	223	227
229	233	239	241	251	257	263	269	271	277
281	283	293	307	311	313	317	331	337	347
349	353	359	367	373	379	383	389	397	401
409	419	421	431	433	439	443	449	457	461
463	467	479	487	491	499	503	509	521	523
541	547	557	563	569	571	577	587	593	599
601	607	613	617	619	631	641	643	647	653
659	661	673	677	683	691	701	709	719	727
733	739	743	751	757	761	769	773	787	797
809	811	821	823	827	829	839	853	857	859
863	877	881	883	887	907	911	919	929	937
941	947	953	967	971	977	983	991	997	(1009)

RATIONAL NUMBERS

Rational numbers include any number that can be written in the form of a *fraction* (or a *ratio*), as long as the *denominator* (the bottom number of the fraction) is not equal to *0*.

All counting numbers and whole numbers can be written as fractions with a denominator equal to *1*. That means all counting numbers and whole numbers are also rational numbers.

WHOLE NUMBERS

Whole numbers are the same as counting numbers, except that the set of whole numbers begins with *0*.

$$\{0, 1, 2, 3, 4, 5, 6, 7, 8, 9, 10 \dots\}$$

A SELECTION OF MATHEMATICAL FORMULAS

To find the CIRCUMFERENCE of a:

Circle—Multiply the diameter by 3.1416

To find the AREA of a:

Circle—Multiply the square of the diameter by 0.7854

Rectangle—Multiply the length of the base by the height

Sphere (surface)—Multiply the square of the radius by 3.1416 and multiply by 4

Square—Square the length of one side

Trapezoid—Add the two parallel sides, multiply by the height, and divide by 2

Triangle—Multiply the base by the height and divide by 2

To find the VOLUME of a:

Cone—Multiply the square of the radius of the base by 3.1416, multiply by the height, and divide by 3

Cube—Cube (raise to the third power) the length of one edge

Cylinder—Multiply the square of the radius of the base by 3.1416 and multiply by the height

Pyramid—Multiply the area of the base by the height and divide by 3

Rectangular prism—Multiply the length by the width by the height

Sphere—Multiply the cube of the radius by 3.1416, multiply by 4, and divide by 3

LARGE NUMBERS AND HOW MANY ZEROS

million	6	1,000,000
billion	9	1,000,000,000
trillion	12	1,000,000,000,000
quadrillion	15	1,000,000,000,000,000
quintillion	18	1,000,000,000,000,000,000
sextillion	21	1,000,000,000,000,000,000,000
septillion	24	1,000,000,000,000,000,000,000,000
octillion	27	1,000,000,000,000,000,000,000,000,000
nonillion	30	1,000,000,000,000,000,000,000,000,000,000
decillion	33	1,000,000,000,000,000,000,000,000,000,000,000

ROMAN NUMERALS

I	1	XI	11	CD	400
II	2	XIX	19	D	500
III	3	XX	20	CM	900
IV	4	XXX	30	M	1,000
V	5	XL	40	$\bar{V}$	5,000
VI	6	L	50	$\bar{X}$	10,000
VII	7	LX	60	$\bar{L}$	50,000
VIII	8	XC	90	$\bar{C}$	100,000
IX	9	C	100	$\bar{D}$	500,000
X	10	CC	200	$\bar{M}$	1,000,000

FRACTIONS, DECIMALS, AND PERCENTS

To find the equivalent of a fraction in decimal form, divide the numerator (top number) by the denominator (bottom number). To change from a decimal to a percent, multiply by 100. To change from a percent to a decimal, divide by 100.

Fraction	Decimal	Percent
1/16 (= 2/32)	0.0625	6.25 %
1/8 (= 2/16)	0.125	12.5
3/16 (= 6/32)	0.1875	18.75
1/4 (= 2/8; = 4/16)	0.25	25.0
5/16 (= 10/32)	0.3125	31.25
1/3 (= 2/6, = 4/12)	0.3 . . .	33.3 . . .
3/8 (= 6/16)	0.375	37.5
7/16 (= 14/32)	0.4375	43.75
1/2 (= 2/4; = 4/8; = 8/16)	0.5	50.0
9/16 (= 18/32)	0.5625	56.25
5/8 (= 10/16)	0.625	62.5
2/3 (= 4/6, = 8/12)	0.6	66.6
11/16 (= 22/32)	0.6875	68.75
3/4 (= 6/8; = 12/16)	0.75	75.0
13/16 (= 26/32)	0.8125	81.25
7/8 (= 14/16)	0.875	87.5
15/16 (= 30/32)	0.9375	93.75
1 (= 2/2; = 4/4; = 8/8; = 16/16)	1.0	100.0

GEOMETRY GLOSSARY

Acute angle   any angle that measures less than 90°

Angle   two rays that have the same endpoint form an angle

Area   the amount of surface inside a structure

Chord   a line segment whose endpoints are on a circle

Circumference   the distance around a circle

Congruent figures   geometric figures that are the same size and shape

Degree (angle)   a unit for measuring angles

Diameter   a chord that passes through the center of a circle

Endpoint   the end of a line segment

Line of symmetry   a line that divides a figure into two parts that match if the figure is folded along the line

Obtuse angle   any angle that measures greater than 90°

Perimeter   the distance around the outside of a plane figure

Pi (π)   the ratio of the circumference of a circle to its diameter. When rounded to the nearest hundredth, pi equals 3.14

Polygon   a simple closed figure whose sides are straight lines

Protractor   an instrument used to measure angles

Quadrilateral   polygon with four sides

Radius   a straight line that connects the center of a circle to any point on the outside of the circle

Ray   a straight line with one endpoint

Rectangle   a four-sided figure with four right angles

Right angle   an angle that measures 90°

Square   a rectangle with congruent sides and 90° angles in all four corners

Surface area   the total outside area of an object

Symmetrical figure   a figure that, when folded along a line of symmetry, has two halves that superimpose exactly on each other

Triangle   a three-sided figure in one plane

Vertex   the common endpoint of two or more rays to form angles

GEOMETRIC SHAPES AND NAMES

POLYGONS

Polygons are two-dimensional or flat shapes, formed from three or more line segments that lie within one plane.

 Examples

TRIANGLES

Triangles are polygons that have three sides and three vertexes, the common endpoints of two or more rays to form angles.

Right triangles are formed when two of three line segments meet in 90 degree angles. In a right triangle, the longest side has a special name: the *hypotenuse*.

Isosceles triangles have two sides of equal length.

Scalene triangles have no sides of equal length.

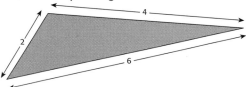

Equilateral triangles have three sides of equal length.

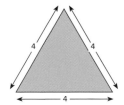

QUADRILATERALS

Quadrilaterals are polygons that have four sides and four vertices.

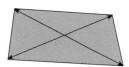

Parallelograms are quadrilaterals that have parallel line segments in both pairs of opposite sides.

Trapezoids are quadrilaterals that have parallel sides.

Squares are rectangles that have sides of equal length.

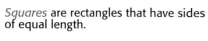

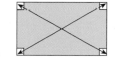

Rectangles are parallelograms formed by line segments that meet at right angles. A rectangle always has four right angles.

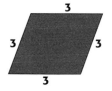

Rhombuses are parallelograms that have sides of equal length but don't meet at right angles.

CIRCLES

A *circle* is a set of points within a plane. Each point on the circle is at an equal distance from a common point inside the circle called the *center*.

The distance from the center of the circle to any point on the circle is called the *radius*. **r = radius**.

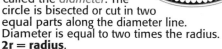

A line segment drawn through the center of the circle to points on either side of the circle is called the *diameter*. The circle is bisected or cut in two equal parts along the diameter line. Diameter is equal to two times the radius. **2r = radius**.

The distance around the circle is called the *circumference*. **πxd or x2r = circumference**.

PHYSICS

Why is steel harder than lead? What happens when water freezes or boils? What causes an electrical current to flow? A fire to burn? A star to explode? These questions fall in the realm of physics, the science of matter and energy.

Physicists study properties and forms of matter and energy—heat, light, electricity and magnetism, nuclear energy. They try to understand the forces that govern the universe. And they try to discover the natural laws these forces obey. For example, one of the basic ideas of physics is that matter and energy can't be created or destroyed. Matter and energy can only change from one form to another.

People have always wondered what makes up the world. The philosopher Democritus was near the truth when he proposed that everything was made up of tiny particles, which he called atoms.

In the 1600s, Isaac Newton and other scientists experimented with materials, light, and heat and developed many basic laws of physics. By the early 1800s, the theory of the atom had been revived. By the 1900s, scientists had discovered that atoms are made up of even smaller particles. Physicists began to study the nucleus (center) of the atom, and in the 1930s, they discovered that splitting the nucleus releases huge amounts of energy.

Several branches focus on the close links between physics and other sciences, such as astronomy (astrophysics), geology (geophysics), and biology (biophysics). Physicists have helped develop spacecraft, lasers, superconductors, and many other devices.

Yearbook

1687 The English mathematician and physicist Sir Isaac Newton publishes *Principia*, which introduces his laws of motion (movement) and his theory of gravity.

1886 The German physicist Heinrich R. Hertz produces and identifies electromagnetic waves. His discovery leads to the development of radio and television.

1942 At the University of Chicago, the physicist Enrico Fermi and colleagues create the first nuclear chain reaction. Three years later, in 1945, two atomic bombs are exploded over Japan.

• Notables •

Marie Curie (1867–1934) Polish-born French physicist; won Nobel Prize with husband Pierre for work on radiation.

Albert Einstein (1879–1955) German-born American physicist; known for his theory of relativity; explained the connection between mass and energy in his famous equation, $E=mc^2$.

Stephen Hawking (1942–) British astronomer and physicist; one of the leaders in the study of black holes in the universe.

Hans Christian Oersted (1777–1851) Danish physicist; showed the relationship between electricity and magnetism, beginning a new field of study called "electromagnetism."

Max Planck (1858–1947) German physicist; developed quantum theory, which has to do with the way matter creates and absorbs energy.

KEY IDEAS

black hole An invisible region in space with a very strong force of gravitation. Astronomers believe that black holes are created by the collapse of large stars.

electromagnetic wave A wave of energy that results from the motion of an electric charge.

gravitation The force that attracts any two particles (tiny amounts) of matter. It is experienced by all matter in the universe, from large galaxies to tiny particles.

hydrodynamics A branch of physics that deals with the movement of fluids and the forces that affect solid objects that are in fluids.

mass In physics, the quantity of matter in an object.

matter Anything that has mass, takes up space, and can be observed.

TIME LINE: MAJOR DISCOVERIES IN PHYSICS

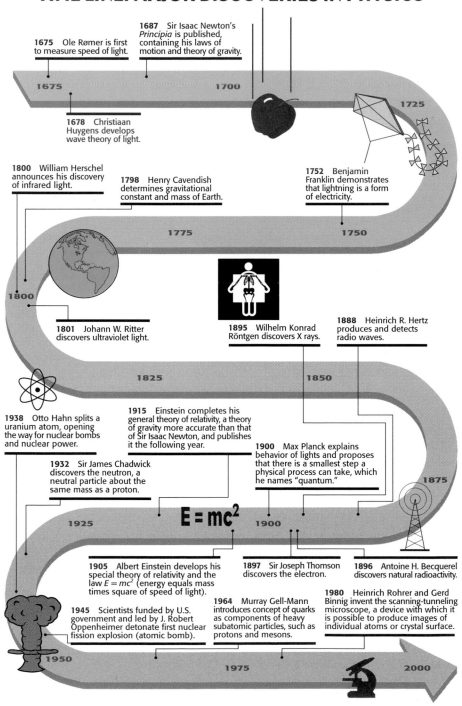

1675   Ole Rømer is first to measure speed of light.

1687   Sir Isaac Newton's *Principia* is published, containing his laws of motion and theory of gravity.

1675

1700

1725

1678   Christiaan Huygens develops wave theory of light.

1800   William Herschel announces his discovery of infrared light.

1798   Henry Cavendish determines gravitational constant and mass of Earth.

1752   Benjamin Franklin demonstrates that lightning is a form of electricity.

1775

1750

1800

1801   Johann W. Ritter discovers ultraviolet light.

1895   Wilhelm Konrad Röntgen discovers X rays.

1888   Heinrich R. Hertz produces and detects radio waves.

1825

1850

1938   Otto Hahn splits a uranium atom, opening the way for nuclear bombs and nuclear power.

1915   Einstein completes his general theory of relativity, a theory of gravity more accurate than that of Sir Isaac Newton, and publishes it the following year.

1900   Max Planck explains behavior of lights and proposes that there is a smallest step a physical process can take, which he names "quantum."

1932   Sir James Chadwick discovers the neutron, a neutral particle about the same mass as a proton.

1875

$$E = mc^2$$

1925

1900

1905   Albert Einstein develops his special theory of relativity and the law $E = mc^2$ (energy equals mass times square of speed of light).

1897   Sir Joseph Thomson discovers the electron.

1896   Antoine H. Becquerel discovers natural radioactivity.

1945   Scientists funded by U.S. government and led by J. Robert Oppenheimer detonate first nuclear fission explosion (atomic bomb).

1964   Murray Gell-Mann introduces concept of quarks as components of heavy subatomic particles, such as protons and mesons.

1980   Heinrich Rohrer and Gerd Binnig invent the scanning-tunneling microscope, a device with which it is possible to produce images of individual atoms or crystal surface.

1950

1975

2000

THE BASIC LAWS OF PHYSICS

LAW OF GRAVITY

The gravitational force between any two objects is proportional to the product of their masses and inversely proportional to the square of the distance between them.

NEWTON'S LAWS OF MOTION

1. Any object at rest tends to stay at rest. A body in motion moves at the same velocity in a straight line unless acted upon by a force.

2. The acceleration of an object is directly proportional to the force acting on it and inversely proportional to the mass of the object.

3. For every action there is an equal and opposite reaction.

CONSERVATION LAWS

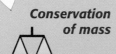

Conservation of momentum
- In a closed system, momentum stays the same. This is equivalent to Newton's third law.

Conservation of angular momentum
- An object moving in a circle has a special kind of momentum, called angular momentum. In a closed system, angular momentum is conserved.

Conservation of mass
- In a closed system, the total amount of mass appears to be conserved in all but nuclear reactions and other extreme conditions.

Conservation of energy
- In a closed system, energy appears to be conserved in all but nuclear reactions and other extreme conditions.

Conservation of mass-energy
- The total amount of energy must be conserved. $E = mc^2$. In this equation, E is the amount of energy, m is the mass, and c is the speed of light in a vacuum.

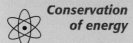

$$E = mc^2$$

THE BASIC SYMBOLS OF PHYSICS

α	alpha particle		e	electronic charge of electron
Å	angstrom unit		E	electric field
β	beta ray		G	conductance; weight
γ	gamma radiation		h	Planck's constant
ε	electromotive force		H	enthalpy
h	efficiency		L	inductance
L	equivalent conductivity; permeance		n	index of refraction
l	wavelength		P	momentum of a particle
m	magnetic moment		R	universal gas constant
u	frequency		S	entropy
r	density; specific resistance		T	absolute temperature; period
s	conductivity; cross section; surface tension		V	electrical potential; frequency
f	luminous flux; magnetic flux		W	energy
j	fluidity		X	magnification; reactance
W	ohm		Y	admittance
B	magnetic induction; magnetic field		Z	impedance
c	speed of light			

TIME LINE: NOTABLE NOBEL PRIZE WINNERS IN PHYSICS

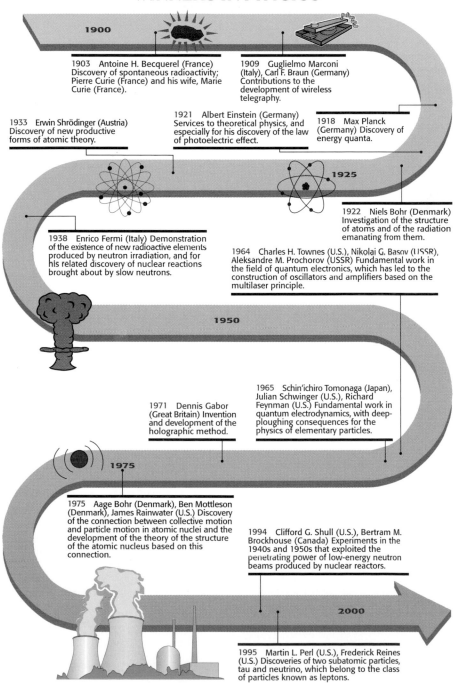

1900

1903 Antoine H. Becquerel (France) Discovery of spontaneous radioactivity; Pierre Curie (France) and his wife, Marie Curie (France).

1909 Guglielmo Marconi (Italy), Carl F. Braun (Germany) Contributions to the development of wireless telegraphy.

1933 Erwin Shrödinger (Austria) Discovery of new productive forms of atomic theory.

1921 Albert Einstein (Germany) Services to theoretical physics, and especially for his discovery of the law of photoelectric effect.

1918 Max Planck (Germany) Discovery of energy quanta.

1925

1922 Niels Bohr (Denmark) Investigation of the structure of atoms and of the radiation emanating from them.

1938 Enrico Fermi (Italy) Demonstration of the existence of new radioactive elements produced by neutron irradiation, and for his related discovery of nuclear reactions brought about by slow neutrons.

1964 Charles H. Townes (U.S.), Nikolai G. Basov (USSR), Aleksandre M. Prochorov (USSR) Fundamental work in the field of quantum electronics, which has led to the construction of oscillators and amplifiers based on the multilaser principle.

1950

1965 Schin'ichiro Tomonaga (Japan), Julian Schwinger (U.S.), Richard Feynman (U.S.) Fundamental work in quantum electrodynamics, with deep-ploughing consequences for the physics of elementary particles.

1971 Dennis Gabor (Great Britain) Invention and development of the holographic method.

1975

1975 Aage Bohr (Denmark), Ben Mottleson (Denmark), James Rainwater (U.S.) Discovery of the connection between collective motion and particle motion in atomic nuclei and the development of the theory of the structure of the atomic nucleus based on this connection.

1994 Clifford G. Shull (U.S.), Bertram M. Brockhouse (Canada) Experiments in the 1940s and 1950s that exploited the penetrating power of low-energy neutron beams produced by nuclear reactors.

2000

1995 Martin L. Perl (U.S.), Frederick Reines (U.S.) Discoveries of two subatomic particles, tau and neutrino, which belong to the class of particles known as leptons.

PLANTS

If plants disappeared from the world, life would stop. Plants are the first link in the food chain that supports life. Unlike other living things, plants produce their own food. They use the sun's energy to turn water and minerals from the soil and carbon dioxide from the air into sugar. Plants store food in leaves, fruit, roots, and seeds, which animals eat. Even predators depend on plants for food—because they eat animals that eat plants.

There are hundreds of thousands of kinds of plants. Scientists divide them into two broad groups: plants that produce flowers and fruits, and those that don't. Nonflowering plants include mosses, ferns, and conifers, which carry their seeds in cones. Flowering plants include showy garden flowers, grasses, and oak trees.

Despite their variety, most plants have the same basic parts. Roots draw water and nutrients from the soil. Stems provide support and carry the water and nutrients throughout the plant. In most plants, leaves are the food factories. A green pigment, called chlorophyll, is the agent that starts the process. Chlorophyll absorbs energy from sunlight. In a series of chemical reactions, this energy changes water and carbon dioxide into glucose, a sugar. The process is called photosynthesis. The plant can use the glucose to form starches, fats, and proteins. Plants also produce oxygen as a by-product of photosynthesis. This helps keep the atmosphere in balance.

People have been developing new plant varieties and growing methods for thousands of years. Plants provide medicines, dyes, fibers, timbers, and much more.

Yearbook

circa 9000 B.C. An agricultural revolution begins. In present-day Israel, wheat is cultivated. Pumpkins and squash are grown in Mexico and Central America.

1735 Carolus Linnaeus introduces his method for classifying (sorting) plants as well as animals.

1865 Gregor Mendel publishes his theories about heredity.

1990 Two American scientists are able to remove DNA and a gene for photosynthesis from a fossilized, 17-million-year-old magnolia leaf.

• Notables •

Leopold (?–1895) and Rudolph (1857–1939) Blaschka Father and son who created lifelike models of more than 780 species of flowers out of hand-blown glass.

Nehemiah Grew (1641–1712) English botanist; described the role of flower parts in the reproduction of flowering plants.

Jan Ingenhousz (1730–1799) Dutch physician; discovered that plants give off oxygen and take in carbon dioxide.

Mathias Schleiden (1804–1881) German botanist; with Theodor Schwann, suggested that cells are the basic unit of life in all plants and animals.

Theophrastus (circa 372–287 B.C.) Greek naturalist; described more than 550 plants in his work, *Natural History of Plants*.

KEY IDEAS

biome A major community of plants and animals, such as a rain forest or desert.

botanical garden A garden for growing, studying, and showing a variety of plants.

botany A branch of biological science that deals with the study of plants.

DNA (deoxyribonucleic acid) A molecule (tiny particle) that occurs in cells and stores the traits that a form of life can inherit.

heredity The process by which a form of life passes along certain characteristics to its descendants (the generations that come after it).

hybrid In botany, a plant that was produced from two different types of plants.

pollen Tiny, powderlike grains that are produced by a male part of a plant called a stamen. When pollen is transferred to the pistil (the female part of a plant), the process is called pollination. It is an important step in the reproduction of plants.

BIOLOGICAL CLASSIFICATION OF PLANTS

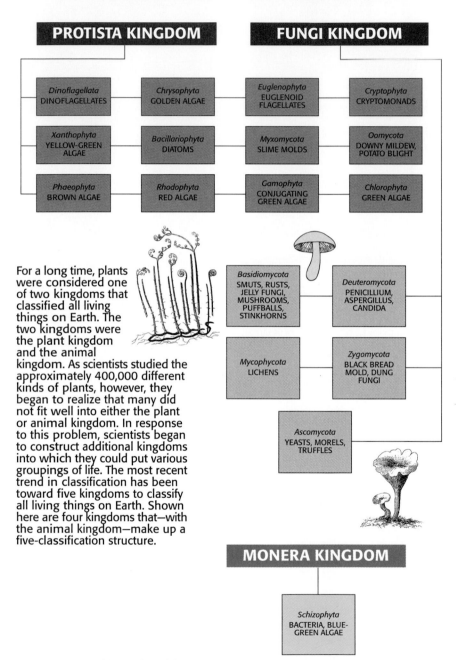

PROTISTA KINGDOM

Dinoflagellata DINOFLAGELLATES	*Chrysophyta* GOLDEN ALGAE
Xanthophyta YELLOW-GREEN ALGAE	*Bacillariophyta* DIATOMS
Phaeophyta BROWN ALGAE	*Rhodophyta* RED ALGAE

FUNGI KINGDOM

Euglenophyta EUGLENOID FLAGELLATES	*Cryptophyta* CRYPTOMONADS
Myxomycota SLIME MOLDS	*Oomycota* DOWNY MILDEW, POTATO BLIGHT
Gamophyta CONJUGATING GREEN ALGAE	*Chlorophyta* GREEN ALGAE

For a long time, plants were considered one of two kingdoms that classified all living things on Earth. The two kingdoms were the plant kingdom and the animal kingdom. As scientists studied the approximately 400,000 different kinds of plants, however, they began to realize that many did not fit well into either the plant or animal kingdom. In response to this problem, scientists began to construct additional kingdoms into which they could put various groupings of life. The most recent trend in classification has been toward five kingdoms to classify all living things on Earth. Shown here are four kingdoms that—with the animal kingdom—make up a five-classification structure.

Basidiomycota SMUTS, RUSTS, JELLY FUNGI, MUSHROOMS, PUFFBALLS, STINKHORNS

Deuteromycota PENICILLIUM, ASPERGILLUS, CANDIDA

Mycophycota LICHENS

Zygomycota BLACK BREAD MOLD, DUNG FUNGI

Ascomycota YEASTS, MORELS, TRUFFLES

MONERA KINGDOM

Schizophyta BACTERIA, BLUE-GREEN ALGAE

Source: *Our Living World, Green Plants*, Blackbirch Press, 1993

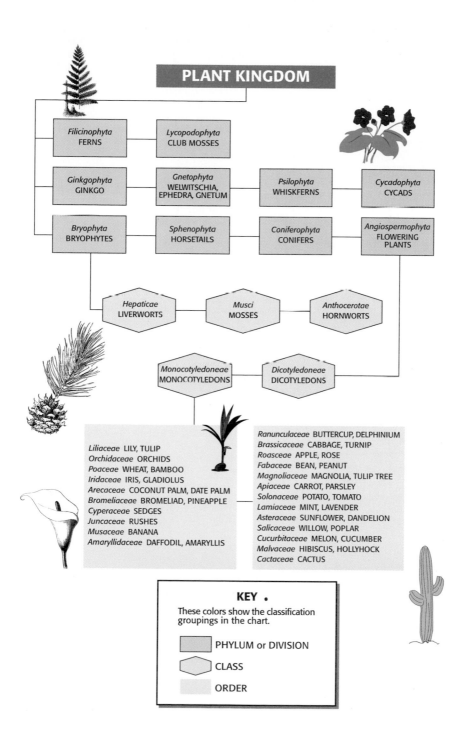

PLANT KINGDOM

Filicinophyta FERNS	*Lycopodophyta* CLUB MOSSES
Ginkgophyta GINKGO	*Gnetophyta* WELWITSCHIA, EPHEDRA, GNETUM
Bryophyta BRYOPHYTES	*Sphenophyta* HORSETAILS

Psilophyta WHISKFERNS

Cycadophyta CYCADS

Coniferophyta CONIFERS

Angiospermophyta FLOWERING PLANTS

Hepaticae LIVERWORTS

Musci MOSSES

Anthocerotae HORNWORTS

Monocotyledoneae MONOCOTYLEDONS

Dicotyledoneae DICOTYLEDONS

Liliaceae LILY, TULIP
Orchidaceae ORCHIDS
Poaceae WHEAT, BAMBOO
Iridaceae IRIS, GLADIOLUS
Arecaceae COCONUT PALM, DATE PALM
Bromeliaceae BROMELIAD, PINEAPPLE
Cyperaceae SEDGES
Juncaceae RUSHES
Musaceae BANANA
Amaryllidaceae DAFFODIL, AMARYLLIS

Ranunculaceae BUTTERCUP, DELPHINIUM
Brassicaceae CABBAGE, TURNIP
Roasceae APPLE, ROSE
Fabaceae BEAN, PEANUT
Magnoliaceae MAGNOLIA, TULIP TREE
Apiaceae CARROT, PARSLEY
Solonaceae POTATO, TOMATO
Lamiaceae MINT, LAVENDER
Asteraceae SUNFLOWER, DANDELION
Salicaceae WILLOW, POPLAR
Cucurbitaceae MELON, CUCUMBER
Malvaceae HIBISCUS, HOLLYHOCK
Cactaceae CACTUS

KEY •

These colors show the classification groupings in the chart.

PHYLUM or DIVISION

CLASS

ORDER

THE PLANT KINGDOM

There are more than 400,000 different plant species that have been identified by science. Some grow on land, others grow in the sea. Most life on the earth would not exist without plants. They are a food for many animals, and they give off the oxygen that both humans and animals need to breathe.

	Plant	Description	Examples
Seed plants	**Angiosperms (Flowering plants)** Monocot	Plants produce seeds with one food part (cotelydon), leaves have parallel veins	Grasses, palms, lilies, and orchids
	Dicot	Plants produce seeds with two food parts (cotelydon), leaves have branching veins	Oak trees, roses, broccoli, tomatoes, and many others
	Gymnosperms (Naked seed plants) Conifers and others	Plants produce exposed seeds, usually on cones, and have no flowers. Most have needlelike leaves and are evergreen	Pines, spruces, junipers, firs, and other conifers, yews, and ginkos
Some plants that don't make seeds	Moss	Produces spores, tiny green plants, no true roots, stems, or leaves, needs moist place to live	
	Liverwort	Produces spores, tiny green plants, no true roots, stems, or leaves, needs moist place to live	
	Horsetail	Produces spores, no true roots, stems, or leaves, needs moist place to live	
	Fern	Produces spores, green leafed, needs moist place to live	

Source: *Our Living World, Green Plants*, Blackbirch Press, 1993

BIOMES OF THE WORLD

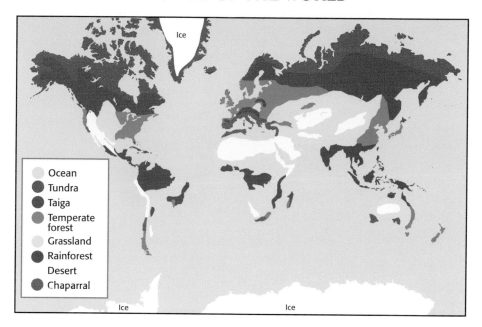

TUNDRA   Found in far northern climates, too cold for trees to grow. Tundra lies on top of a layer of ice that never melts, called permafrost.

TAIGA   Found mostly in far northern regions where summer is short and winter is long; pines, spruce, hemlock, and fir trees thrive here.

TEMPERATE FOREST   Grows in mild climates, usually along coastlines and a bit inland. The giant sequoias of the Pacific Northwest grow here.

GRASSLAND   Farming and grazing biomes; also known as prairies, savannahs, steppes, and pampas. Primarily grows thick grasses and, where cultivated, produces wheat, barley, oats, rye, and other grains.

RAIN FOREST   Warm, wet biomes near or at the equator; lush vegetation of many kinds, often broken into three levels by scientists: the floor, the understory (10 to 50 feet [3 to 15 m] up), and the canopy (75 to 100 feet [23 to 30 m] above the floor).

DESERT   This growing area usually receives less than 10 inches (25 cm) of rain a year; is only home to succulents, which are plants such as cacti that store water inside their thick, waxy leaves.

CHAPARRAL   Also known as scrubland; a coastal biome that supports hearty evergreen shrubs.

PLANTS THAT CAN KILL

The following chart lists a selection
of deadly plants and describes symptoms
of the illnesses they cause in humans.

Plants	Toxic portions	Symptoms of illness; degree of toxicity
Azalea	All parts	Nausea, vomiting, depression, breathing difficulty, prostration, coma; fatal
Belladonna	Young plants, seeds	Nausea, twitching muscles, paralysis; fatal
Castor bean	Seeds, foliage	Burning in mouth, convulsions; fatal
Daphne	Berries (red or yellow)	Severe burns to digestive tract followed by coma; fatal
Delphinium	Young plants, seeds	Nausea, twitching muscles, paralysis; fatal
Larkspur	Young plants, seeds	Nausea, twitching muscles, paralysis; fatal
Laurel	All parts	Nausea, vomiting, depression, breathing difficulty, prostration, coma; fatal
Mistletoe	All parts, especially berries	Fatal
Mushrooms, wild	All parts of many varieties	Fatal
Oleander	All parts	Severe digestive upset, heart trouble, contact dermatitis; fatal
Poinsettia	All parts	Severe digestive upset; fatal
Rhododendron	All parts	Nausea, vomiting, depression, breathing difficulty, prostration, coma; fatal
Rhubarb	Leaf blade	Kidney disorder, convulsions, coma; fatal
Rosary pea	Seeds, foliage	Burning in mouth, convulsions; fatal

AMAZING PLANT FACTS

World's oldest plant
A creosote plant found growing in southern California was in 1980 estimated to be 11,700 years old.

World's fastest growing plant
Hesperoyucca whipplei, a member of the lily family, grew 12 feet in 14 days in 1978 in Great Britain.

World's slowest flowering plant
A rare Bolivian herb, *puya raimondii*, grows for 80–150 years, blooms once, then dies.

Most nutritious fruit
An avocado has 741 calories per pound and is packed with vitamins A, C, and E.

World's Records for Vegetables

Biggest pumpkin: 710 lbs. (322 kg)

Biggest cucumber: 20 lbs., 1 oz. (9.1 kg)

Biggest zucchini: 64 lbs., 8 oz. (29.26 kg)

Biggest carrot: 11 lbs., 7.5 oz (5.2 kg)

Medicines from Plants

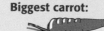

An African plant called *Strophanthus* contains a chemical that was initially used in cortisone, a medicine that helps people suffering from arthritis.

A drug called reerpine, which calms people and lowers blood pressure, was originally found in snakeroot, a plant that grows on mountainsides.

Opium, which is used to make morphine, a painkiller, comes from the poppy flower.

Bark of the cinchora tree, which grows in Peru, was used for many years as the source of quinine, the only known treatment for the dangerous fever of malaria.

Clothes from Plants

- Linen comes from the flax plant.
- Cotton provides cotton clothes, fabrics.
- Rope and twine are made from hemp and other plants.

Fuel from Plants

- Decayed plants, when mixed with soil and water and compressed for many thousands of years, form into coal, oil, and natural gas.

Wood and Paper from Trees

Millions of tons of lumber are produced every year in the United States. This wood is used in the construction of homes, offices, and countless other projects. Paper is made from the ground-up pulp of wood fibers. Paper products include everything from newspapers to magazines to your mail, and even the page you're reading right now!

POPULATION (U.S.)

When the United States government took the first census in 1790, it counted four million Americans. Today, with more than 263 million people, the United States ranks as the world's third most populous nation, behind China and India. And if current trends continue, the population will likely increase by at least 50 percent by the year 2050.

In the country's early days, immigration accounted for a large share of population growth. People came from other countries because they saw the United States as a "land of opportunity." Immigration accounts for about a third of population growth today. The rest of the growth is the result of natural increases—the difference between births and deaths.

As the U.S. population has grown, the American way of life has changed. Most Americans today live in urban and suburban areas. But many older industrial cities in the Northeast and Midwest have seen population numbers fall in recent years. Parts of the South and West have grown dramatically, putting pressure on everything from social services to water supplies.

Most Americans can trace their roots to immigrants who arrived from Europe before the middle of the twentieth century. But in recent years, minority groups have been growing rapidly. Hispanics are expected to surpass African Americans as the largest minority group by 2010. Asians and Pacific Islanders form the fastest-growing minority, increasing at four times the national rate. America's population is also growing older. People over sixty-five years of age are expected to make up a fifth of the population by 2050.

Yearbook

1665 In French Canada, the first effort is made to count people on a regular basis in an area that is larger than a city.

1790 The first census is conducted in the United States.

1882 The Chinese Exclusion Act is the first U.S. law that prevents a particular group of people from immigrating to the United States. It is repealed in 1943.

1970s The country experiences dramatic regional changes in population. Many people leave the Northeast and Midwest and move to the "sun belt"—the southern or southwestern states.

• Notables •

Emma Lazarus (1849–1887) American poet; championed the cause of Jews who were persecuted in Russia and wrote the poem that is inscribed on the base of the Statue of Liberty. It begins, "Give me your tired, your poor, your huddled masses . . . "

Thomas Malthus (1766–1834) English economist; claimed that poverty is unavoidable because the world's population increases more quickly than its food supply.

Adolphe Quetelet (1796–1874) Supervisor of statistics in Belgium; directed Belgian's important census of 1846, introducing modern methods of gathering and analyzing information about a population.

Elmo Roper (1900–1971) American public opinion analyst; pioneered modern public opinion polling techniques; founded the firm that is still considered a standard in the industry.

KEY IDEAS

census A count of a country's population by the government, usually on a regular basis.

demography The study, through numbers, of the characteristics of human population. Usually included are a population's size, rate of growth, migration (movement) patterns, and birth and death rates.

emigration The act of moving out of a country to establish a residence in a different country.

growth rate The change in a population size that results from whether there are more births than deaths, which means a rise in population, or more deaths than births, which results in a decrease in the rate of growth. The growth rate is also affected by whether more people enter a country than leave it. If more people leave, the growth rate goes down.

immigration The act of permanently moving to a country that is not the place of one's birth.

statistics Numerical information, or a branch of mathematics that deals with collecting and interpreting it.

POPULATION PROFILE

Population Growth, 1790–1997
(in millions)

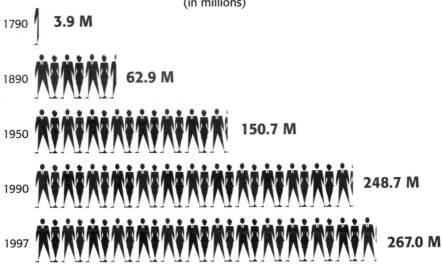

1790   3.9 M

1890   62.9 M

1950   150.7 M

1990   248.7 M

1997   267.0 M

U.S. Population by Age, 1997

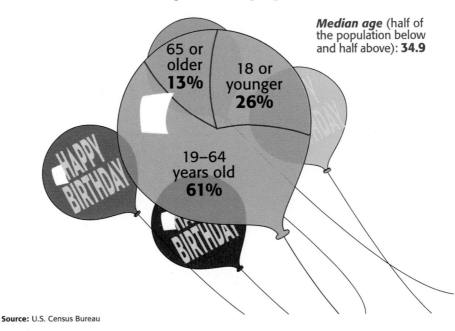

Median age (half of the population below and half above): **34.9**

65 or older **13%**

18 or younger **26%**

19–64 years old **61%**

Source: U.S. Census Bureau

U.S. POPULATION PROFILE

Racial and ethnic composition, 1997

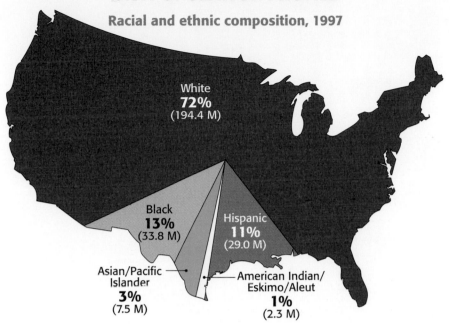

White
72%
(194.4 M)

Black
13%
(33.8 M)

Hispanic
11%
(29.0 M)

Asian/Pacific
Islander
3%
(7.5 M)

American Indian/
Eskimo/Aleut
1%
(2.3 M)

Selected Countries of Origin for Foreign-Born Population
(about 9.3% of the U.S. population is foreign-born)

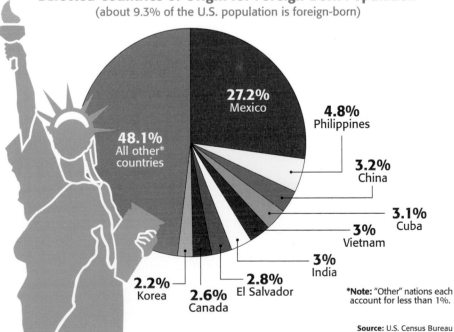

27.2%
Mexico

4.8%
Philippines

3.2%
China

3.1%
Cuba

3%
Vietnam

3%
India

48.1%
All other*
countries

2.2%
Korea

2.6%
Canada

2.8%
El Salvador

*Note: "Other" nations each
account for less than 1%.

Source: U.S. Census Bureau

U.S. POPULATION PROFILE

Population projections, 1997–2050

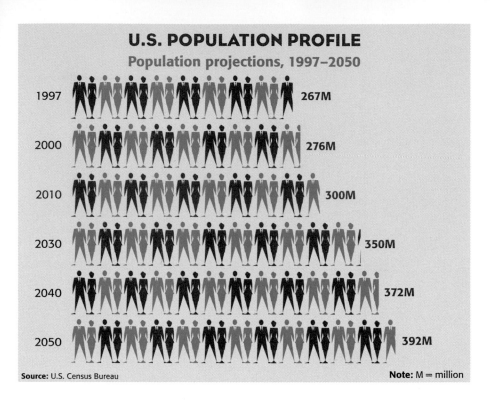

1997	267M
2000	276M
2010	300M
2030	350M
2040	372M
2050	392M

Source: U.S. Census Bureau

Note: M = million

U.S. FAMILY PROFILE

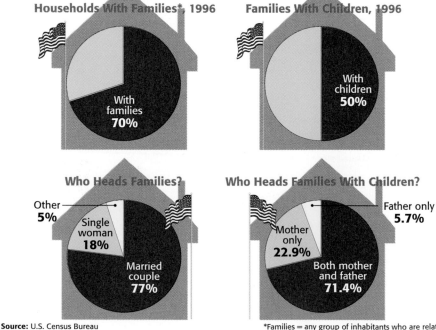

Households With Families*, 1996

With families 70%

Families With Children, 1996

With children 50%

Who Heads Families?

Other 5%
Single woman 18%
Married couple 77%

Who Heads Families With Children?

Father only 5.7%
Mother only 22.9%
Both mother and father 71.4%

Source: U.S. Census Bureau

*Families = any group of inhabitants who are related.

U.S. POPULATION PROFILE

U.S. Population by Gender, 1996

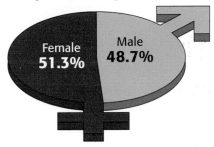

Female **51.3%** Male **48.7%**

U.S. Population by Marriage Status, 1996

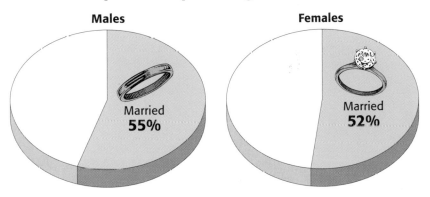

Males

Married **55%**

Females

Married **52%**

U.S. Divorce Rates, 1970–1996
(number of divorces per 1,000 people)

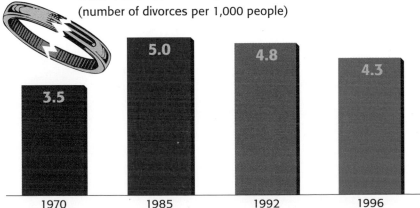

3.5	5.0	4.8	4.3
1970	1985	1992	1996

Source: U.S. Census Bureau

POPULATION PROFILE

U.S. Birth Rate, 1960–1996
(number of births per 1,000 people)

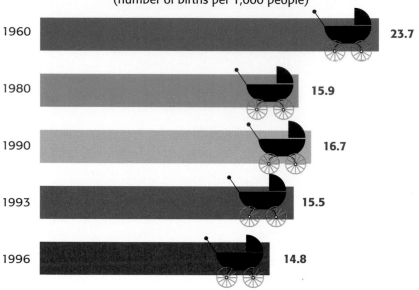

Year	Rate
1960	23.7
1980	15.9
1990	16.7
1993	15.5
1996	14.8

U.S. Death Rate, 1960–1996
(number of deaths per 1,000 people)

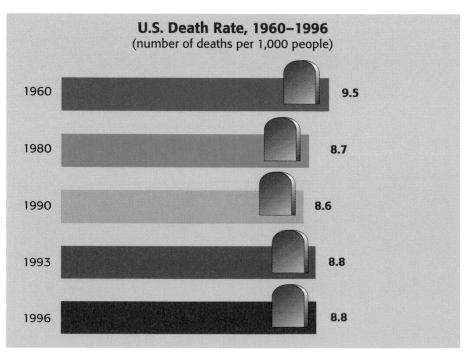

Year	Rate
1960	9.5
1980	8.7
1990	8.6
1993	8.8
1996	8.8

Source: National Center for Health Statistics, U.S. Department of Health and Human Services

U.S. POPULATION PROFILE

Christians and Non-Christians

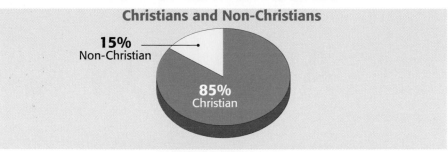

15%
Non-Christian

85%
Christian

Non-Christian Religious Followers in the U.S.
(excludes nonreligious population)

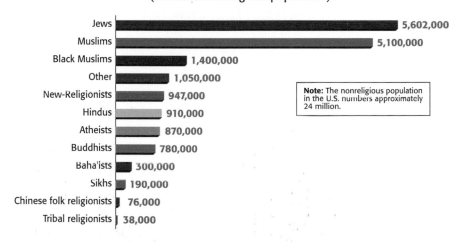

Jews	5,602,000
Muslims	5,100,000
Black Muslims	1,400,000
Other	1,050,000
New-Religionists	947,000
Hindus	910,000
Atheists	870,000
Buddhists	780,000
Baha'ists	300,000
Sikhs	190,000
Chinese folk religionists	76,000
Tribal religionists	38,000

Note: The nonreligious population in the U.S. numbers approximately 24 million.

Religious Affiliations of North America

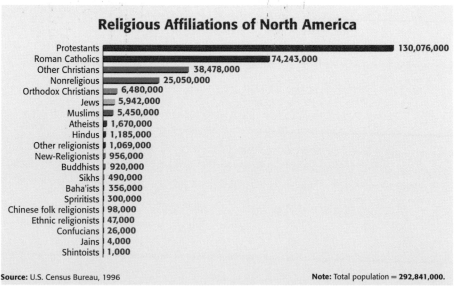

Protestants	130,076,000
Roman Catholics	74,243,000
Other Christians	38,478,000
Nonreligious	25,050,000
Orthodox Christians	6,480,000
Jews	5,942,000
Muslims	5,450,000
Atheists	1,670,000
Hindus	1,185,000
Other religionists	1,069,000
New-Religionists	956,000
Buddhists	920,000
Sikhs	490,000
Baha'ists	356,000
Spriritists	300,000
Chinese folk religionists	98,000
Ethnic religionists	47,000
Confucians	26,000
Jains	4,000
Shintoists	1,000

Source: U.S. Census Bureau, 1996

Note: Total population = **292,841,000.**

PRIZES AND AWARDS

A medical breakthrough brings doctors closer to curing a deadly disease. . . . A novelist writes a book that touches millions of readers. . . . A social worker champions the cause of the poor. . . . An actor gives the performance of a lifetime. In nearly every field, from art and entertainment to science and world diplomacy, awards and prizes recognize exceptional achievements like these.

Perhaps the most prestigious awards of all are the Nobel Prizes, given annually since 1901. Alfred Nobel, the Swedish inventor of dynamite, left $9 million to start the prizes. They honor achievements that benefit humankind in physics, chemistry, physiology or medicine, literature, peace, and (since 1969) economic science.

Newspaper publisher Joseph Pulitzer, who died in 1911, also left money to fund annual awards in his name. The Pulitzer Prizes honor American works of fiction, history, drama, biography, poetry, nonfiction, and music. Pulitzers are also given in fourteen categories of journalism. The Spingarn Medal, awarded each year since 1914, recognizes outstanding achievements by African Americans.

The entertainment industry probably awards more prizes than any other. Best known of many are the Emmy Awards, for television productions; the Tony (Antoinette Perry) Awards, for theater; the Grammy Awards, for music recording; and the Academy Awards, for motion pictures.

Yearbook

1670 The poet John Dryden becomes England's first poet laureate.

1928 First Academy Awards are given.

1963 John F. Kennedy establishes the Presidential Medal of Freedom, the nation's highest award given to someone outside the military; given every year to Americans who have made important contributions to the United States.

1994 Yassir Arafat, the Palestinian leader, and Prime Minister Yitzhak Rabin of Israel win the Nobel Peace Prize, honoring their historic peace settlement of 1993.

• Notables •

John Newbery (1713–1767) English publisher and bookseller; established children's literature as an important branch of publishing. The Newbery Medal, named in his honor, was established in the United States in 1922 to honor the American with the best children's book of the year.

Antoinette Perry (1888–1946) American actress; produced several successful plays, and was known for helping young people entering theater. The annual Antoinette Perry Awards, known as the Tony Awards, are given for outstanding performances.

Joseph Pulitzer (1847–1911) American newspaper publisher and U.S. congressman; founded Columbia University School of Journalism. Established the Pulitzer prizes to encourage excellence in journalism, history, and literature.

KEY IDEAS

Caldecott Medal An award given by the American Library Association for the best American illustrator of a picture book for children.

MTV Video Music Award An award that recognizes achievement in the field of music videos.

National Medal of Science The highest science award given by the U.S. government. It is presented annually by the president to people who have made important contributions to the fields of physical and social sciences, biology, mathematics, and engineering.

Poet laureate An honor given to a distinguished poet for his or her achievements. The word *laureate* comes from the custom, in ancient Greece and Rome, of crowning a hero with a wreath made of laurel leaves.

Pritzker Award The most prestigious award in architecture. It is awarded annually by an American committee to one of the world's most distinguished architects.

MAJOR PRIZES AND AWARDS

Prize/Award	Background	Notable facts
Academy Award (Oscar)	First given in 1928; members of the Academy of Motion Picture Arts and Sciences vote (3,000 members); members nominate in area of expertise but vote on all categories.	Films with most nominations: *Titanic* and *All About Eve* (14). Films with most awards: *Titanic* and *Ben-Hur* (11).
Emmy	First presented in 1949; members of the National Academy of Television Arts and Sciences vote in approximately 70 categories.	TV show with most nominations: *Cheers* (117). TV show with most awards: *Mary Tyler Moore Show* (29). Top Emmy-winning actor: Ed Asner (7). Top Emmy-winning actresses: Dinah Shore/ Mary Tyler Moore (8). Most consecutive wins: *Frasier* (5).
Tony	First presented in 1947; members of the American Theater Wing vote for distinguished achievement in Broadway Theater.	Multiple Tony-winning playwrights include: Arthur Miller, Tom Stoppard, Peter Shaffer, Neil Simon, Terrence McNally.
Grammy	First presented in 1959; voted by members of the National Academy of Recording Arts and Sciences.	Musicians with the most Grammys: Sir George Solti (31), Quincy Jones (26), Vladimir Horowitz (25).

Prize/Award	Background	Notable facts
Pulitzer Prizes	First awarded in 1917; Hungarian-born journalist Joseph Pulitzer endowed the Columbia School of Journalism, whose trustees award prizes.	Prizes awarded: journalism (14), literature and drama (6), and musical composition (1).
Nobel Prizes	First awarded in 1901; established by gift of $9.2 million from Alfred Nobel, a Swedish chemical engineer who invented dynamite and other explosives.	Six prizes awarded for outstanding achievement in: chemistry, physics, physiology or medicine, peace, literature, and economic sciences.
Newbery Medal	First awarded in 1922; presented by the American Library Association for outstanding children's writing; named after John Newbery, the first English publisher of children's books.	Recent winners: E. L. Konigsberg (*The View from Saturday*), Karen Hesse (*Out of the Dust*), Karen Cushman (*The Midwife's Apprentice*).
Caldecott Medal 	First awarded in 1938; presented by the American Library Association for outstanding children's picture book illustration; named in honor of English illustrator Randolph Caldecott.	Recent winners: Allen Say (*Grandfather's Journey*), David Diaz (*Smoky Night*), Paul Zelinsky (*Rapunzel*), David Wisn (*Golem*), Peggy Rathman (*Officer Buckle and Gloria*).

RELIGION

The world's major religions cut across national borders to unite people who share a common set of beliefs. Worldwide, more than 1.8 billion people follow some form of Christianity. There are more than one billion Muslims (followers of Islam) and nearly that many Hindus. Buddhism has about 750 million adherents; Judaism, more than 18 million.

Each of the major religions has followers in the United States. So do many less common faiths. Most Americans are Christians, belonging to the Roman Catholic and various Protestant churches. Judaism is the second most common faith. Islam ranks a close third, and it is growing rapidly. Smaller numbers of Hindus, Buddhists, Sikhs, Baha'is, and others also practice their faiths.

Religious freedom has been important throughout American history. The wish for freedom drew some of the first European settlers to North America, including the Puritans of Massachusetts and the Quakers of Pennsylvania. They came searching for a place where they could worship as they saw fit, without interference from the government. But the idea of religious freedom took hold, and the First Amendment to the Constitution guaranteed it. Later, as immigrants came to the United States from all over the world, they were able to keep and follow their religious beliefs.

People often feel deeply about their beliefs, and that can lead to conflict between religious groups. Today most of the major religions teach and practice tolerance toward other beliefs.

Yearbook

2000 B.C. This is the time of Abraham, the father of the Jewish people. About 1,000 years later, the earliest writings of the Jewish Bible are composed.

560 B.C. Siddhartha Gautama, later known as Buddha, is born in India. His teachings are the foundation of Buddhism, which spreads throughout Asia.

A.D. 30 Jesus of Nazareth is crucified in Jerusalem. Saint Peter begins to spread the teachings of Christianity.

630 The prophet Muhammad leads an army of 10,000 into the city of Mecca, the spiritual center of Islam.

• Notables •

K'ung-Fu-tzu (Confucius) (551–479 B.C.) Most respected person in Chinese history; taught his followers ethics and how to behave in interpersonal relationships.

Martin Luther (1483–1546) German theologian; founded the Protestant religion.

Moses ben Maimon (Maimonides) (1135–1204) Jewish philosopher; tried to adjust ancient Jewish beliefs and laws to more modern ways of thinking. His most important work was *A Guide for the Perplexed*.

Malcolm X (1925–1965) African-American Muslim leader; worked for social reform.

Mother Teresa (1910–1997) Roman Catholic nun from Albania; famous for her skill in setting up projects to help the poor; won the 1979 Nobel Peace Prize.

KEY IDEAS

Buddhism One of the great Asian religions. Among the basic ideas of Buddhism are the beliefs that living involves suffering, but that suffering ends when someone reaches a way of being called "nirvana."

ethics A system of values that explains how people should behave and what their obligations are.

Koran The holy book of Islam. It contains the beliefs and laws that, according to the Muslims, were given by God to the prophet Muhammad.

monotheism A system of beliefs based on the idea that there is only one God. Islam, Judaism, and Christianity are monotheistic religions.

scripture The holy writings of a religion.

theology The study of faith, and in particular, the study of God and of God's relation to the world. A theologian is a specialist in theology.

RELIGIONS OF THE WORLD

Key

- Roman Catholic
- Eastern Orthodox
- Protestant
- Mormon
- Mixed Christian

- Jewish
- Sunni Muslim
- Shiite Muslim
- Hindu
- Buddhist

- Buddhist and Shintoist
- Buddhist, Confucianist, Taoist
- Native
- Information unavailable

Source: Based on data from the *CIA World Factbook*, 1997

TOP 5 WORLD ORGANIZED RELIGIONS, BY MEMBERSHIP

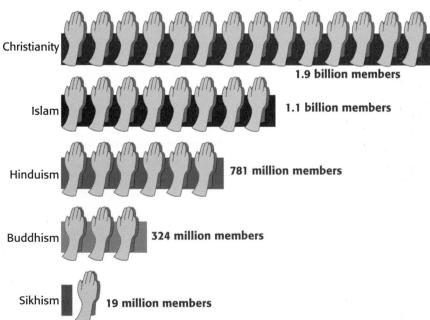

Christianity — **1.9 billion members**

Islam — **1.1 billion members**

Hinduism — **781 million members**

Buddhism — **324 million members**

Sikhism — **19 million members**

Source: *CIA World Factbook*, 1997

PROFILE OF U.S. RELIGIOUS ATTENDANCE

U.S. Religious Attendees by Marital Status

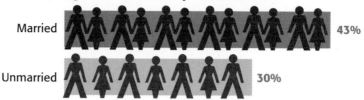

Married — 43%

Unmarried — 30%

U.S. Religious Attendees by Family Status

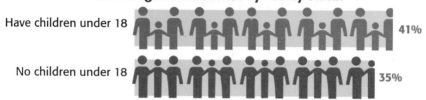

Have children under 18 — 41%

No children under 18 — 35%

Attend Religious Service on a Typical Weekend

Women — 46% Attend

Men — 28% Attend

U.S. Religious Attendees by Age

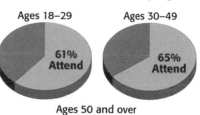

Ages 18–29 — 61% Attend

Ages 30–49 — 65% Attend

Ages 50 and over — 77% Attend

U.S. Religious Attendance by Region

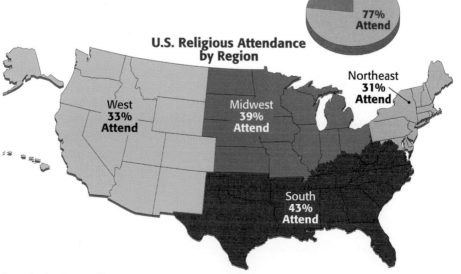

Northeast 31% Attend

West 33% Attend

Midwest 39% Attend

South 43% Attend

Source: *American Demographics,* 1997

CHRISTIAN HOLY DAYS

Sundays: The Christian Sabbath; a day of rest and a day for prayer and spiritual observance.

Easter: Most important holy day in the Christian religion; celebration of Christ's resurrection from the dead, which gives Christians the hope of salvation and eternal life. Easter is only one day, but the full observance of the holy day spans from Septuagesima Sunday (70 days before Easter Sunday), which may fall as early as January, to Pentecost, which can occur as late as June.

Lent: 40-day period of fasting and penitence beginning on Ash Wednesday and ending on Easter Sunday, is traditionally observed by fasting, performing acts of charity, and by giving up certain pleasures and amusements. (Note that the six Sundays that fall during Lent are not considered part of the 40-day period. Thus Easter occurs 46 calendar days after Ash Wednesday.)

Ash Wednesday derives its name from the rite of burning the palms carried on the Palm Sunday of the year before and using the ashes to mark worshipers' foreheads with a cross. The ashes are a symbol of atonement and are meant to remind Christians of their mortality.

Palm Sunday: Sunday before Easter, celebrates Jesus' triumphant entry into Jerusalem, where palm branches were spread before him to honor his path.

Holy (Maundy) Thursday: Anniversary of the Last Supper. Traditional services mark three events that occurred during the week before Jesus was crucified: he washed the feet of his 12 disciples; he instituted the Eucharist (the sacrament of Holy Communion); and he was arrested and imprisoned.

Good Friday marks Christ's crucifixion. Observed with fasting, mourning, and penitence.

Holy Saturday is the day that anticipates the resurrection. In the Catholic church, special vigils are held on Holy Saturday evening.

Easter Sunday marks the day of Christ's resurrection. Many worshipers celebrate the holy day with sunrise services, a custom believed to be inspired by the example of Mary Magdalene, who went to Christ's tomb "early, while it was yet dark."

Pentecost (literally, 50th day) is the end of the full ecclesiastical observance of Easter. It takes place on the seventh Sunday after Easter Sunday and commemorates the descent of the Holy Spirit upon the apostles.

All Saints' Day, celebrated on November 1, honors all of the Christian saints. In America many churches mark the nearest Sunday as a day to pay tribute to those who have died during the year. All Saints' Day is observed primarily by Roman Catholics.

Advent, a religious season that begins on the Sunday closest to November 30 and lasts until Christmas, both celebrates the birth of Jesus and anticipates his second coming. At one time Advent was a solemn season observed by fasting, but this is no longer the case.

Christmas: Celebration of the birth of Jesus. The exact date of his birth is unknown, but December 25 was probably chosen because it coincided with the ancient midwinter celebration that honored pagan deities. The 12 days of Christmas fall between Christmas and Epiphany (January 6), the day the Wise Men visited the Christ child.

JEWISH HOLY DAYS

Shabbat (Sabbath) is the first and most important Jewish holy day, occurring each week from sundown Friday to sundown Saturday. It is a day of rest and spiritual growth, given to men and women so they will remember the sweetness of freedom and keep it. Shabbat takes precedence over all other observances.

Rosh Hashanah (New Year), believed to be the birthday of the world, is also called the Day of Judgment and Remembrance and the day of the shofar—a ram's horn—which is blown to remind Jews of Abraham's willingness to sacrifice his son Isaac. The holiday takes place on the first and second days of Tishri (in September or October).

Yom Kippur (Day of Atonement) ends the 10 days of repentance that Rosh Hashanah begins and takes place from sundown on the ninth day of Tishri until sundown on the tenth. The observance begins with the recitation of the most famous passage in the Jewish liturgy—the *Kol Nidre*—which nullifies unfulfilled vows made in the past year. The entire day is spent praying and fasting.

Sukkot (Tabernacles) is a harvest festival celebrated from the fifteenth through the twenty-second of Tishri. Sukkot also commemorates the journey of the Jewish people through the wilderness to the land of Israel. Jewish families take their meals this week in a roughly constructed *sukkah* (booth)— a reminder of an agricultural society, of an exodus, and of how precarious and fragile life can be. On Simchat Torah, the twenty-third of Tishri, a congregation finishes reading the last book of the Torah and immediately starts again with the first.

Hanukkah (Feast of Dedication; Festival of Lights). The importance of the eight-day feast, which begins on the twenty-fifth day of Kislev, is its commemoration of the first war in human history fought in the cause of religious freedom. The Maccabees overcame not just the military threat to Judaism but also the internal forces for the assimilation into the culture of Israel's rulers. Jews light candles for the eight nights to mark a miracle: a day's supply of oil, found in the recaptured Temple, that burned for eight days.

Purim (Feast of Lots), set on the fourteenth day of Adar, is another celebration of survival, noting events described in the Book of Esther. At Purim Jews rejoice at Queen Esther's and her cousin Mordecai's defeat of Haman, the Persian King Ahaseurus's adviser who plotted to slaughter all the Persian Jews. Ahaseurus ruled around 400 B.C.

Pesach (Passover), begins on the fifteenth day of Nisan and lasts seven days; commemorates the exodus of the Hebrews from Egypt in about 1300 B.C. The name Passover also recalls God's sparing (passing over) the Jewish firstborn during the plagues upon the land brought by God through Moses. The holiday is marked by eating only unleavened foods and participating in a seder, or special meal.

Shavuot (Feast of Weeks) is observed on the sixth and seventh day of Sivan. Originally an agricultural festival, Shavuot is a celebration of the revelation of the Torah at Mount Sinai, by which God established his covenent with the Jewish people.

Source: *Encyclopedia Judaica*

PROFILE OF U.S. RELIGIOUS AFFILIATIONS

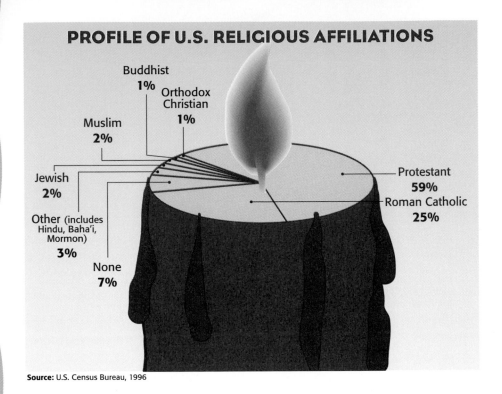

Buddhist 1%

Orthodox Christian 1%

Muslim 2%

Jewish 2%

Other (includes Hindu, Baha'i, Mormon) 3%

None 7%

Protestant 59%

Roman Catholic 25%

Source: U.S. Census Bureau, 1996

CALENDAR OF SELECTED CHRISTIAN HOLY DAYS

Year A.D.	Ash Wednesday	Good Friday	Easter Sunday	Pentecost	Trinity Sunday	Advent
1999	Feb. 17	Apr. 2	Apr. 4	May 23	May 30	Nov. 28
2000	Mar. 8	Apr. 21	Apr. 23	June 11	June 18	Dec. 3
2001	Feb. 28	Apr. 13	Apr. 15	June 3	June 10	Dec. 2

CALENDAR OF JEWISH HOLY DAYS, 5759–5762

The Jewish year is divided into the twelve months of Tishri, Heshvan, Kislev, Tebet, Shebat, Adar, Nisan, Iyar, Sivan, Tammuz, Ab, and Elul. The Jewish era begins at the creation (*anno mundi*, or A.M.), which is equal to 3761 B.C.E. (before the Christian era). By this formula, the Jewish year 5758 began in 1997 and ends in 1998 of the Gregorian calendar. (Tishri, the first month of the Jewish year, falls in either September or October of the Gregorian calendar.)

Year A.M.	Rosh Hashanah	Yom Kippur	Sukkot	Hanukkah	Purim	Pesach	Shavuot
5759	Sept. 29, 1998	Sept. 30, 1998	Oct. 5, 1998	Dec. 14, 1998	Mar. 2, 1999	Apr. 1, 1999	May 21, 1999
5760	Sept. 11, 1999	Sept. 20, 1999	Sept. 25, 1999	Dec. 4, 1999	Mar. 21, 2000	Apr. 20, 2000	June 9, 2000
5761	Sept. 30, 2000	Oct. 9, 2000	Oct. 14, 2000	Dec. 22, 2000	Mar. 9, 2001	Apr. 9, 2001	May 28, 2001
5762	Sept. 18, 2001	Sept. 27, 2001	Oct. 2, 2001	Dec. 10, 2001	Feb. 26, 2002	Apr. 3, 2002	May 17, 2002

Source: *Encyclopedia Judaica*

CALENDAR OF MUSLIM HOLY DAYS

The Islamic calendar is broken into 12 months: Muharram, Safar, Rabi I, Rabi II, Jumada I, Jumada II, Rajab, Sha'ban, Ramadan, Shawwal, Dhu'l-Qa'dah, Dhu'l-Hijja. The calendar is based on a lunar year of 12 months, each consisting of 30 and 29 days (alternating every month), and the year is equal to 354 days.

Ramadan, the ninth month of the Islamic calendar, is the Islamic faith's holiest period. To honor the month in which the Koran was revealed, all adult Muslims of sound body and mind observe fasting—going without food, water, or even a kiss—between the hours of sunrise and sunset.

Id al-Fitr This day of feasting is celebrated at the end of Ramadan. To mark the fast's break, worshipers also attend an early morning service.

Id al-Adha The Feast of Sacrifice takes place on the tenth day of Dhu'l-Hijja, the last month of the year and the season of the haj, or pilgrimage.

Fridays At noontime Muslims attend mosques or comparable gathering places to say the congregational Friday prayer that ends the week. While Friday—Jumuah—is the holy day of the weekly Muslim calendar, it is not a sabbath comparable to Christian Sundays or Jewish Saturdays, and there are no restrictions on work.

Year A.H. (A.D.)	New Year's Day, 1 Muharram	1 Ramadan	Id al-Fitr, 1 Shawwal	Id al-Adha, 10 Dhu'l-Hijja
1419 (1998–99)	Apr. 27, 1998	Dec. 20, 1998	Jan. 19, 1999	Mar. 28, 1999
1420 (1999–2000)	Apr. 17, 1999	Dec. 9, 1999	Jan. 8, 2000	Mar. 16, 2000
1421 (2000–01)	Apr. 6, 2000	Nov. 27, 2000	Dec. 27, 2000	Mar. 5, 2001

Source: Data from *Grolier Multimedia Encyclopedia*, 1996

SIGNS AND SYMBOLS

You're on your way to a friend's house, but you're lost. Should you turn around, continue straight, or turn left? It's confusing! Then, up ahead, you see the solution to your problem: a sign with no words, just a picture of a telephone receiver and an arrow. The sign points the way to a public telephone. You can call your friend and get directions.

Signs are everywhere in modern life. They direct traffic and warn of road hazards, such as bumpy pavement and sharp curves. They identify streets, homes, shops, and office buildings. They help you find classrooms, rest rooms, and other facilities. They carry advertisements.

Signs give information with words and symbols. A symbol is something that stands for something else. The eagle is a symbol of the United States, and the maple leaf is the symbol of Canada. Schools and organizations often use symbols to help people identify their facilities and services. One of the world's best-known symbols is that of the International Red Cross, the worldwide aid agency.

A picture of a telephone receiver would be recognized anywhere in the world. It's one of many international symbols meant to help people regardless of what language they speak. People who can't read can recognize these symbols and heed their warnings.

Yearbook

circa A.D. 500 The Roman philosopher Boethius gives a different letter to each of 15 musical notes.

876 The first known use of a symbol for the number zero occurs in India.

1857 Great Britain designs the International Code of Symbols as a method for people to communicate with one another on the ocean.

1935 Nazis make the swastika part of the German national flag. It continues to be a symbol of anti-Semitism (prejudice against Jews).

• Notables •

Thomas Gallaudet (1787–1851)
American educator; brought the French manual language of the deaf—a system of signs made with hands—to the United States. Today American Sign Language is widely used by hearing impaired people throughout the United States and Canada. It is the fourth most-spoken language in the United States.

Guido of Arezzo (991–1050) Italian monk; expert in music theory; perfected the musical staff, which is used in musical notation (writing down of a composition).

Ferdinand de Saussure (1857–1913)
Swiss linguist; founder of linguistics (the study of language); presented language sounds as a series of signs.

KEY IDEAS

cross A widely used symbol. For Christians, a cross is a symbol of the crucifixion of Jesus. Crosses were also used in India, Egypt, and in North America during ancient times.

Morse code A code using either dots and dashes or long and short sounds to communicate a message.

musical notation Symbols that are used to make a written record of musical sounds.

semaphore A system for sending visual signals, such as movable arms or hand-held flags. By day, it is used by ship captains and by railroad workers.

sign language A substitute for spoken language. Sign languages include the language of Trappist monks, who have a rule of silence; a language of the American Plains people; and American Sign Language, which was developed for deaf people.

BASIC SIGNS

 Fire extinguisher

 Women's room

 Men's room

 First aid

 Elevator

 Information

 Disabled parking

 Bus

 Recycle

 Fallout shelter

 No smoking

 No admittance

 No parking

 Danger

 Poison

 Stop

 Yield

 Do not enter

 No left turn

 Falling rock

 Stop ahead

 Bicycle path

 Traffic light ahead

 Railroad crossing

 Pedestrian crossing

 Intersection ahead

 Left turn

 Right turn

 Two-way traffic

 Slippery when wet

AMERICAN SIGN LANGUAGE

In the manual alphabet of the hearing impaired, the fingers of the hand are moved to positions that represent the letters of the alphabet. Whole words and ideas are also expressed in sign language.

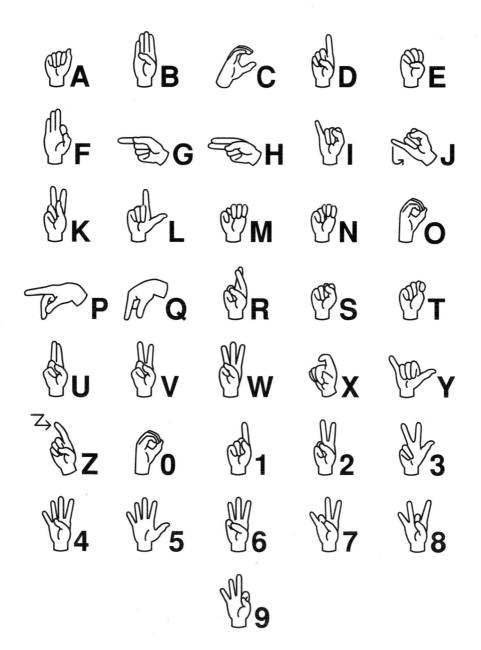

SPORTS

Whether your game is basketball, beach volleyball, or mountain biking, you're part of a sports craze that has swept America in recent years. Sports rank as favorite leisure activities for kids and grown-ups alike. People are keeping fit by swimming, walking, running, and working out. Team sports are drawing new participants to youth and amateur leagues. Traditional sports such as tennis and golf are also attracting players. And people are taking up new sports, such as in-line skating, snowboarding, and rock climbing. While men outnumber women when it comes to playing sports, more women are involved in athletics than ever before.

In addition to playing sports, Americans are great sports fans. They follow everything from local Little League baseball to Olympic figure skating. If they don't turn out to cheer their favorite professional or college teams in person, they catch the action on television or radio. That has helped fuel growth in professional sports. New teams have joined established leagues in football, basketball, baseball, and hockey. New leagues have formed for such sports as professional women's basketball and professional soccer.

Sports have become a multibillion-dollar industry. Gyms, tennis centers, ski areas, and scores of other facilities are riding sports trends. So are suppliers of everything from bicycle helmets to running shoes. Salaries of top baseball and basketball players often exceed $1 million, while product endorsements bring millions more in income. Even paying such high salaries, owners of pro teams make money.

Yearbook

circa 776 B.C. First athletic meeting takes place in ancient Greece. The games are held every four years at Olympia. The first modern Olympic games take place almost 3,000 years later, in 1896.

1500s An early form of basketball is played by the Aztec people in Mexico.

1744 The first known golf club is established in Edinburgh, Scotland.

1998 Mark McGwire and Sammy Sosa break Roger Maris's record of the most home runs batted in a season (61). McGwire hits 70 and Sosa hits 66.

• Notables •

Larissa Latynina (1934–   ) Ukrainian athlete; won the most Olympic medals to date: 18 medals in gymnastics between 1956 and 1964. Nine of them were gold.

James Naismith (1861–1939) American physical education teacher; in 1891, invented basketball for his students in Springfield, Massachusetts.

Jackie Robinson (1919–1972) First African-American baseball player in the major leagues; played for Brooklyn Dodgers from 1947 to 1956; elected to the Baseball Hall of Fame in 1962.

Margaret Court Smith (1942–   ) Australian tennis player; won a record 64 titles in major tennis tournaments.

Bill Tilden (1893–1953) American tennis player; first American to win the men's singles championship at Wimbledon.

KEY IDEAS

CART Championship Auto Racing Teams; the official organization that oversees all major racing events in the world.

coxswain The person who steers a racing shell—a long, thin canoe—and directs the rowers.

division In collegiate sports, schools are grouped by size and other factors into divisions.

grand slam The winning of all the major tournaments on a sports tour. In baseball, a grand-slam home run is made when the bases are loaded.

lacrosse A team sport played with long-handled sticks that have mesh pouches for catching and throwing the ball. Lacrosse was developed by Native Americans to train men for war.

marathon A long-distance race that is usually 26 miles long.

NCAA National Collegiate Athletic Association; the official organization that supervises college sports.

triathlon A long-distance race that has three phases, such as swimming, bicycling, and running.

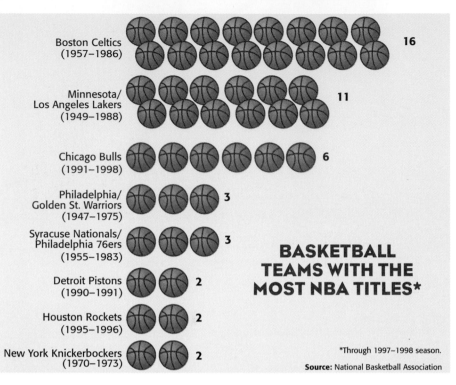

Boston Celtics
(1957–1986) — **16**

Minnesota/
Los Angeles Lakers
(1949–1988) — **11**

Chicago Bulls
(1991–1998) — **6**

Philadelphia/
Golden St. Warriors
(1947–1975) — **3**

Syracuse Nationals/
Philadelphia 76ers
(1955–1983) — **3**

Detroit Pistons
(1990–1991) — **2**

Houston Rockets
(1995–1996) — **2**

New York Knickerbockers
(1970–1973) — **2**

BASKETBALL TEAMS WITH THE MOST NBA TITLES*

*Through 1997–1998 season.
Source: National Basketball Association

BASKETBALL'S TOP 5 CAREER POINT SCORERS

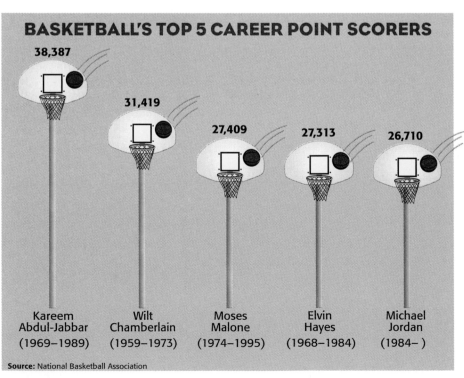

38,387	31,419	27,409	27,313	26,710
Kareem Abdul-Jabbar (1969–1989)	Wilt Chamberlain (1959–1973)	Moses Malone (1974–1995)	Elvin Hayes (1968–1984)	Michael Jordan (1984–)

Source: National Basketball Association

TOP 5 NCAA DIVISION I TEAMS IN WOMEN'S BASKETBALL*

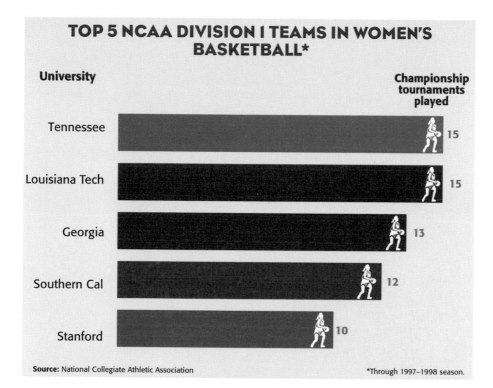

University	Championship tournaments played
Tennessee	15
Louisiana Tech	15
Georgia	13
Southern Cal	12
Stanford	10

Source: National Collegiate Athletic Association

*Through 1997–1998 season.

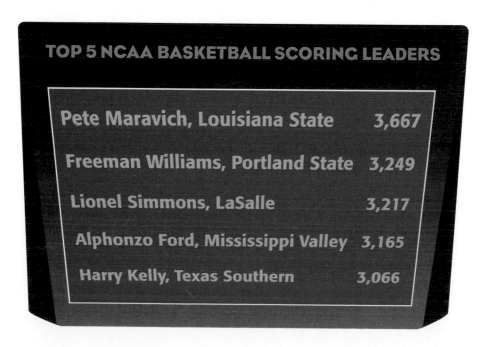

TOP 5 NCAA BASKETBALL SCORING LEADERS

Pete Maravich, Louisiana State	3,667
Freeman Williams, Portland State	3,249
Lionel Simmons, LaSalle	3,217
Alphonzo Ford, Mississippi Valley	3,165
Harry Kelly, Texas Southern	3,066

Source: National Collegiate Athletic Association

FOOTBALL'S TOP 5 CAREER PASSERS
(by total passing yards)

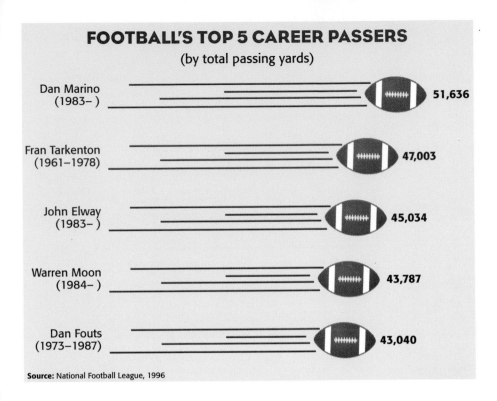

Dan Marino (1983–)	51,636
Fran Tarkenton (1961–1978)	47,003
John Elway (1983–)	45,034
Warren Moon (1984–)	43,787
Dan Fouts (1973–1987)	43,040

Source: National Football League, 1996

FOOTBALL'S TOP 5 CAREER TOUCHDOWN SCORERS

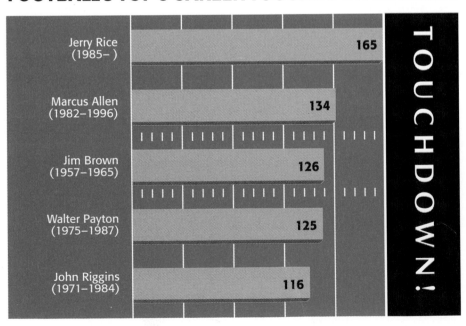

Jerry Rice (1985–)	165
Marcus Allen (1982–1996)	134
Jim Brown (1957–1965)	126
Walter Payton (1975–1987)	125
John Riggins (1971–1984)	116

TOUCHDOWN!

Source: National Football League, 1996

FOOTBALL'S TOP 5 CAREER RUSHERS

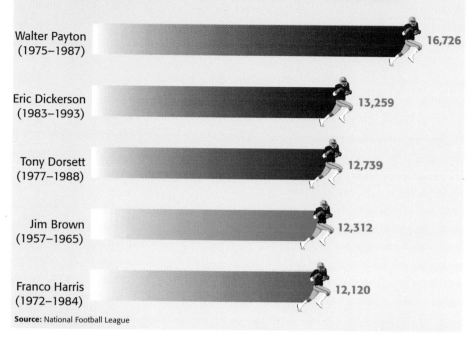

Walter Payton
(1975–1987) — 16,726

Eric Dickerson
(1983–1993) — 13,259

Tony Dorsett
(1977–1988) — 12,739

Jim Brown
(1957–1965) — 12,312

Franco Harris
(1972–1984) — 12,120

Source: National Football League

TOP 10 UNIVERSITIES WITH MOST BOWL WINS*

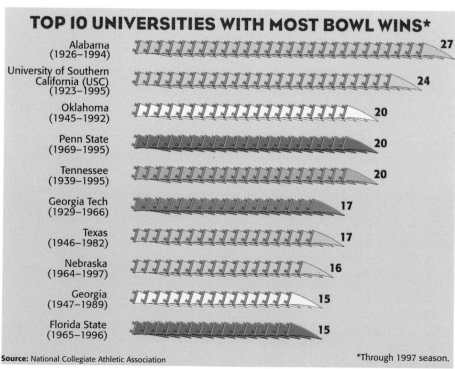

Alabama
(1926–1994) — 27

University of Southern
California (USC)
(1923–1995) — 24

Oklahoma
(1945–1992) — 20

Penn State
(1969–1995) — 20

Tennessee
(1939–1995) — 20

Georgia Tech
(1929–1966) — 17

Texas
(1946–1982) — 17

Nebraska
(1964–1997) — 16

Georgia
(1947–1989) — 15

Florida State
(1965–1996) — 15

Source: National Collegiate Athletic Association

*Through 1997 season.

BASEBALL'S TOP 5 WORLD SERIES WINNERS*

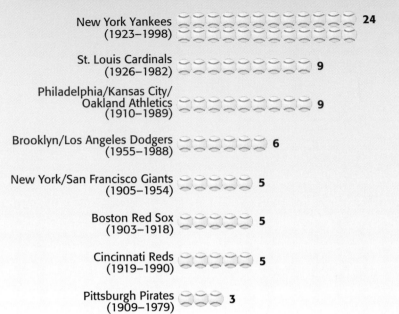

New York Yankees
(1923–1998) — 24

St. Louis Cardinals
(1926–1982) — 9

Philadelphia/Kansas City/
Oakland Athletics
(1910–1989) — 9

Brooklyn/Los Angeles Dodgers
(1955–1988) — 6

New York/San Francisco Giants
(1905–1954) — 5

Boston Red Sox
(1903–1918) — 5

Cincinnati Reds
(1919–1990) — 5

Pittsburgh Pirates
(1909–1979) — 3

Source: Major League Baseball

*Through 1998 season.

BASEBALL'S TOP 5 RUN SCORERS
(total, career)

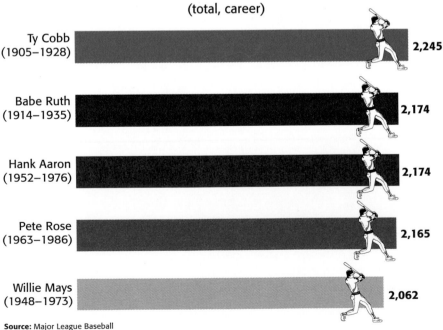

Ty Cobb
(1905–1928) — **2,245**

Babe Ruth
(1914–1935) — **2,174**

Hank Aaron
(1952–1976) — **2,174**

Pete Rose
(1963–1986) — **2,165**

Willie Mays
(1948–1973) — **2,062**

Source: Major League Baseball

HOCKEY TEAMS WITH THE MOST STANLEY CUP WINS*

Montreal Canadiens (1916–1993) — 24

Toronto Maple Leafs (1932–1967) — 14

Detroit Red Wings (1936–1998) — 9

Boston Bruins (1972–1929) — 5

Edmonton Oilers (1984–1990) — 5

New York Islanders (1980–1983) — 4

New York Rangers (1928–1994) — 4

Chicago Black Hawks (1934–1961) — 3

Philadelphia Flyers (1974–1975) — 2

Pittsburgh Penguins (1991–1992) — 2

Source: National Hockey League

*Through 1998 season.

HOCKEY'S TOP 5 CAREER GOAL SCORERS

Player	Seasons	Goals	Assists	Total points
Wayne Gretzky (1978–)	18	862	1,843	2,705
Gordie Howe (1954–1980)	26	801	1,049	1,850
Marcel Dionne (1971–1990)	18	731	1,040	1,771
Phil Esposito (1969–1980)	11	717	873	1,590
Mark Messier (1979–)	18	575	977	1,552

Source: National Hockey League

MOST-WINNING MEN IN TENNIS*

(all-time Grand Slam singles titles)

Player/Country	Australian Open	French Open	Wimbledon	U.S. Open	Total
Roy Emerson (Australia)	6	2	2	2	12 (1961–1967)
Pete Sampras (U.S.)	3	0	4	4	11 (1990–1998)
Björn Borg (Sweden)	0	6	5	0	11 (1974–1981)
Rod Laver (Australia)	3	2	4	2	11 (1960–1969)
Jimmy Connors (U.S.)	1	0	2	5	8 (1974–1983)
Ivan Lendl (Czechoslovakia)	2	3	0	3	8 (1984–1990)
Fred Perry (U.K.)	1	1	3	3	8 (1933–1936)
Ken Rosewall (Australia)	4	2	0	2	8 (1953–1972)

Source: American Tennis Professionals

* Through 1998.

MOST-WINNING WOMEN IN TENNIS*

(all-time Grand Slam singles titles)

Player/Country	Australian Open	French Open	Wimbledon	U.S. Open	Total
Margaret Smith Court (Australia)	11	5	3	5	24 (1960–1975)
Steffi Graf (Germany)	4	5	7	5	21 (1987–1996)
Helen Wills-Moody (U.S.)	0	4	8	7	19 (1923–1938)
Chris Evert-Lloyd (U.S.)	2	7	3	6	18 (1974–1986)
Martina Navratilova (Czech./U.S.)	3	2	9	4	18 (1974–1995)
Billie Jean King (U.S.)	1	1	6	4	12 (1961–1981)

Source: Women's Tennis Association

* Through 1998.

TOP 5 MOST-WINNING MALE PLAYERS IN GOLF*

(all-time wins at majors)

Player/Country		British Open	U.S. Open	Masters	PGA	Total
Jack Nicklaus (U.S.)	(1963–1986)	3	4	6	5	**18**
Walter Hagen (U.S.)	(1914–1929)	4	2	0	5	**11**
Ben Hogan (U.S.)	(1946–1953)	1	4	2	2	**9**
Gary Player (S. Africa)	(1959–1978)	3	1	3	2	**9**
Tom Watson (U.S.)	(1975–1983)	5	1	2	0	**8**

Source: Professional Golfers Association

*Through 1998.

TOP 5 MOST-WINNING WOMEN IN GOLF*

(all-time wins in majors)

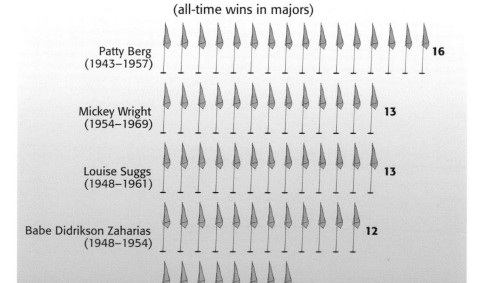

Patty Berg
(1943–1957) **16**

Mickey Wright
(1954–1969) **13**

Louise Suggs
(1948–1961) **13**

Babe Didrikson Zaharias
(1948–1954) **12**

Betsy Rawls
(1951–1975) **8**

Source: Ladies Professional Golfers Association

*Through 1998.

TOP 5 COUNTRIES IN THE WORLD CUP*

Country	Win	Runner-up	3rd	4th	Total
Germany/W. Germany (1954–1990)	3	3	2	1	**26**
Brazil (1958–1994)	4	1	3	1	**26**
Italy (1934–1982)	3	2	1	1	**21**
Argentina (1978–1986)	2	2	–	–	**14**
Uruguay (1930–1950)	2	–	–	2	**10**

*Based on 4 points for winning the tournament, 3 points for runner up, 2 points for 3rd place, and 1 point for 4th. Including 1998 World Cup.
Source: Fédération Internationale de Football Association (FIFA)

TOP 5 CHAMPIONSHIP AUTO RACING TEAM DRIVERS WITH MOST RACE WINS*

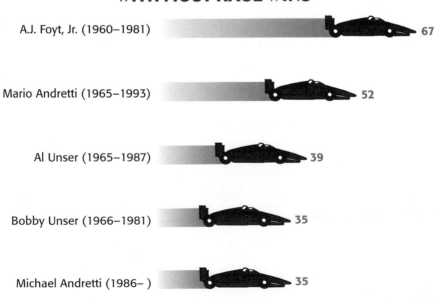

A.J. Foyt, Jr. (1960–1981) — 67

Mario Andretti (1965–1993) — 52

Al Unser (1965–1987) — 39

Bobby Unser (1966–1981) — 35

Michael Andretti (1986–) — 35

Source: Championship Auto Racing Teams

*Through 1998.

TOP 10 MEDAL-WINNING COUNTRIES*

Country	Gold	Silver	Bronze	Total
United States	795	606	522	**1,923**
Russia/U.S.S.R./C.I.S.	451	367	336	**1,154**
Germany/West Germany	198	236	244	**678**
U.K.	177	224	219	**620**
France	163	176	196	**535**
Sweden	133	151	172	**456**
Italy	155	132	133	**420**
East Germany	154	131	126	**411**
Hungary	136	124	144	**404**
Finland	100	81	118	**299**

Source: International Olympic Committee   *Through 1998 Winter Games.

SELECTED TOP OLYMPIC NOTABLES

Nadia Comaneci, gymnastics, Romania   In 1976, Nadia Comaneci was the first gymnast ever to score a perfect 10 in Olympic competition. She was fifteen. She later scored perfect 10s seven more times.

Eric Heiden, speed skating, U.S.   Eric Heiden is the only athlete to win five individual gold medals in one Olympics. He dominated the 1980 Winter Olympics by taking gold in the 500 m, 1,000 m, 1,500 m, 5,000 m, and 10,000 m (breaking the world record by more than six seconds).

Larissa Latynina, gymnastics, Soviet Union   No athlete has won more Olympic medals than this Ukrainian superstar, who won 18 between 1956 and 1964. In addition to nine gold medals—in vault (1956), floor exercise (1956, 1960, and 1964), team combined (1956, 1960, and 1964), and all-around (1956 and 1960)—Latynina won five silver and four bronze medals.

Carl Lewis, track and field, U.S.   At the age of thirty-five, Carl Lewis won the gold medal in the long jump at the 1996 Olympics. It was Lewis's fourth consecutive Olympic long jump gold and his ninth gold medal overall. Al Oerter, who won the discus from 1956 to 1968, is the only other track and field athlete to win an event in four straight Olympics. In addition to his four long jump golds, Lewis won gold in the 100 m in 1984 and 1988, the 400 m relay in 1984 and 1992, and the 200 m in 1984.

Paavo Nurmi, track and field, Finland   Paavo Nurmi won the 10,000 m in 1920 and 1928 and might have won in 1924 had he not been prevented by Finnish officials, who felt he had entered too many events. That year Nurmi had already won gold medals in the 1,500 m, the 5,000 m, the 3,000 m team race, and the individual and team cross-country races, two events he had also won in 1920. Nurmi also earned three silver medals to go with his nine golds.

Mark Spitz, swimming, U.S.   Mark Spitz set the world's record for gold medals in one Olympics in 1972 with seven. He won for the 100 m and 200 m freestyle, 100 m and 200 m butterfly, 400 m and 800 m freestyle relays, and the 400 m medley relay. These he added to the four medals he won at the 1968 Olympics: a bronze in the 100 m freestyle, a silver in the 100 m butterfly, and gold in both the 400 m and 800 m freestyle relays.

OLYMPICS CALENDAR

International Olympic Games

	2000 (Summer):	Sydney, Australia
	2002 (Winter):	Salt Lake City, UT
	2004 (Summer):	Athens, Greece
	2006 (Winter):	Top candidates: Sion, Switzerland; Turin, Italy; Poprad-Tatry, Slovakia
	2008 (Summer):	Top candidates: Boston, MA; Cincinnati, OH; Toronto, Canada

Special Olympics

1999 International Summer Games: Raleigh/Durham, NC

2001 International Winter Games: Anchorage, AK

2003 International Summer Games: Top candidate: Dublin, Ireland

TOP 10 MOST POPULAR PHYSICAL ACTIVITIES IN THE U.S.

(by number of participants)

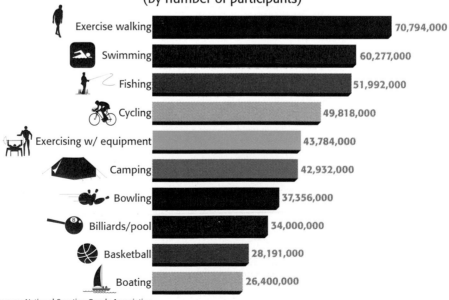

Activity	Participants
Exercise walking	70,794,000
Swimming	60,277,000
Fishing	51,992,000
Cycling	49,818,000
Exercising w/ equipment	43,784,000
Camping	42,932,000
Bowling	37,356,000
Billiards/pool	34,000,000
Basketball	28,191,000
Boating	26,400,000

Source: National Sporting Goods Association

PROFILE: HOW OUTDOOR VACATIONS ARE SPENT

Millions of outdoor vacationers who participated in the following activities from 1993–1998:

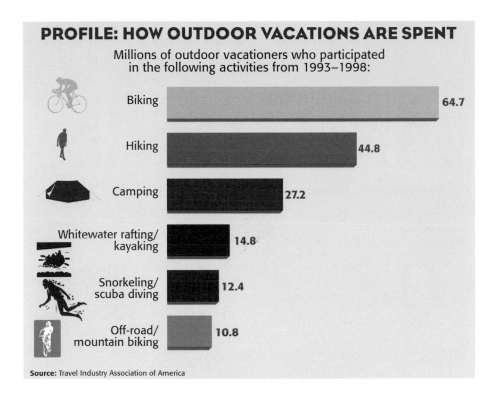

Biking — 64.7

Hiking — 44.8

Camping — 27.2

Whitewater rafting/kayaking — 14.8

Snorkeling/scuba diving — 12.4

Off-road/mountain biking — 10.8

Source: Travel Industry Association of America

FREE TIME USE IN THE U.S.

(percentage of population that participates in each activity on a regular basis)

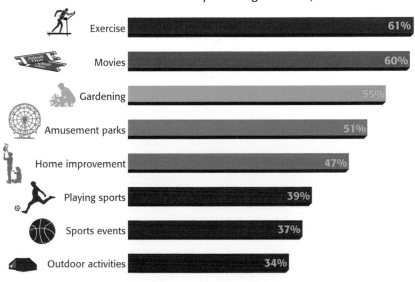

Exercise — 61%

Movies — 60%

Gardening — 55%

Amusement parks — 51%

Home improvement — 47%

Playing sports — 39%

Sports events — 37%

Outdoor activities — 34%

Source: Based on data from the U.S. Census Bureau, U.S. Department of Commerce, 1997

TELEVISION AND MOVIES

I t's Thursday night, and across the United States more than 90 million Americans are doing the same thing—tuning in prime-time television.

Television has made the country—and the world—smaller. People across the nation shared the tragedy of the Oklahoma City bombing in 1995 and the joy of Mark McGwire's and Sammy Sosa's record-shattering baseball season in 1998. Television is an extremely popular entertainment media. Nearly all U.S. households have at least one television set.

Most American homes have a videocassette recorder (VCR), too. Americans now spend more on videos each year than they do on books. But they still go to the movies.

The first permanent movie theaters opened in Paris (France), New Orleans, and Los Angeles in the late 1800s and early 1900s. People have been falling in love with movie stars ever since. Rudolph Valentino, the biggest movie star of the 1920s, has been replaced with Leonardo DiCaprio, the hero of *Titanic*.

Today the American motion picture industry is a very large one. It does more than $5 billion in business every year and releases about 400 movies. In 1988, the average cost of making a film was $18.1 million. By 1996, higher actors' salaries and greater use of special effects pushed the cost up to $39.8 million.

Yearbook

1903 *The Great Train Robbery* is one of the first successful feature movies.

1926 The British inventor J. L. Baird demonstrates a black-and-white television set. Two years later, he demonstrates color television.

1939 NBC begins its first regular television broadcast service.

1950 CATV (Community Antenna Television) cable system is introduced.

1997 *Titanic* is released; breaks many records; most expensive movie ever made; second highest in gross sales in the United States; ties with *Ben-Hur* for most Oscars.

• Notables •

Lucille Ball (1911–1989) American comedian; co-star of the *I Love Lucy* Show, one of the most popular television shows ever.

Walt Disney (1901–1966) American; creator of the first animated cartoon with sound—*Steamboat Willie*, produced in 1928. Many of Disney's works that followed became classics, including *Pinocchio*, *Fantasia*, *Bambi*, and *Peter Pan*.

Steven Spielberg (1947–   ) American movie director; created many box office blockbusters, including *E.T., the Extra-Terrestrial*, and *Jurassic Park*.

Ed Sullivan (1902–1974) American television host; helped to launch the careers of many superstar entertainers.

François Truffaut (1932–1984) French film director; leading figure in an experimental style of movie-making called "New Wave."

KEY IDEAS

animated cartoon A movie made from a series of drawings. Each drawing changes very slightly, and together they give the impression that the characters are moving. About 16 drawings are photographed in a second.

cable television A system of television reception. Signals from distant stations are picked up by a master antenna and sent by cable to people who subscribe to this service.

film noir A type of film that uses shadowy photography and disturbing music to establish an atmosphere of mystery or danger.

prime time The time period when a television audience is the largest.

sitcom Short for situation comedy. A comedy that is based on a problem or set of problems involving the main characters.

special effects Visual or sound effects that are introduced into a movie or television production, often to give viewers the sense that the events they are watching are real.

PERCENTAGE OF U.S. HOUSEHOLDS WITH AT LEAST ONE TELEVISION

A total of 97 million households have at least one television

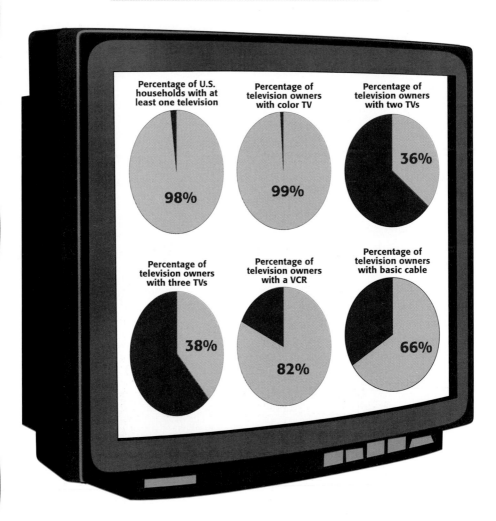

Percentage of U.S. households with at least one television
98%

Percentage of television owners with color TV
99%

Percentage of television owners with two TVs
36%

Percentage of television owners with three TVs
38%

Percentage of television owners with a VCR
82%

Percentage of television owners with basic cable
66%

Source: Based on data from *Statistical Abstract of the United States,* 1997

TOP 5 TV-OWNING COUNTRIES IN THE WORLD

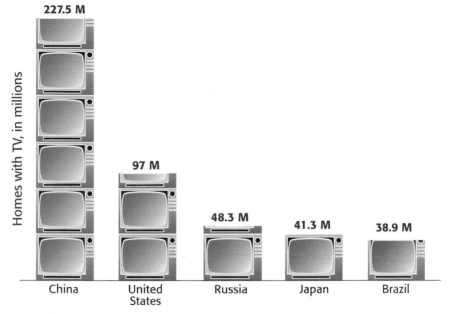

Homes with TV, in millions

227.5 M	97 M	48.3 M	41.3 M	38.9 M
China	United States	Russia	Japan	Brazil

Source: Based on data from *Statistical Abstract of the United States*, 1997

TOP 5 REGULARLY SCHEDULED NETWORK PROGRAMS, 1996–1997*
(total percentage of TV households)

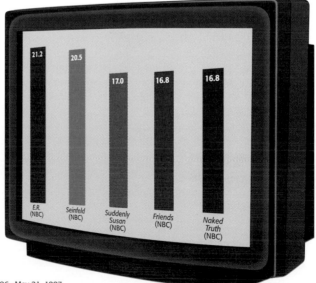

21.2	20.5	17.0	16.8	16.8
E.R. (NBC)	Seinfeld (NBC)	Suddenly Susan (NBC)	Friends (NBC)	Naked Truth (NBC)

* Season is Sept. 16, 1996–May 21, 1997.
Source: Nielsen Syndication Service National TV Ratings. Copyright 1997, Nielsen Media Research

TOP 5 TV RE-RUNS, 1996–1997 SEASON*
(by ratings)

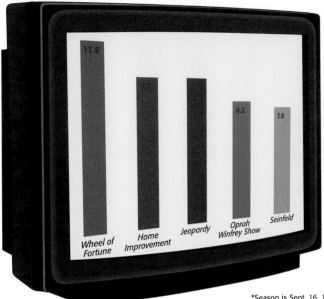

*Season is Sept. 16, 1996—May 21, 1997.

Source: Nielsen Syndication Service National TV Ratings. Copyright 1997, Nielsen Media Research

TOP 5 SPORTS SHOWS 1996–1997*
(by Nielsen rating)

 43.3

Super Bowl XXXI (Fox), New England vs. Green Bay

 33.8

Super Bowl XXXI Kickoff (Fox), New England vs. Green Bay

 30.1

NFC Championship (Fox), Carolina at Green Bay

 29.8

Super Bowl Post Game (Fox), New England vs. Green Bay

 28.5

AFC Championship Game (NBC), Jacksonville at New England

*Season is Sept. 16, 1996–May 21, 1997.

Source: Nielsen Syndication Service National TV Ratings. Copyright 1997, Nielsen Media Research.

TOP 5 U.S. "BASIC" CABLE CHANNELS*

(by number of subscribers)

ESPN — 71,100,000

CNN — 71,100,000

TNT — 70,549,000

TBS — 69,920,000

C-SPAN — 69,700,000

Source: NCTA

*Covering period January–February 1997.

TOP 5 U.S. PAY CABLE CHANNELS*

(by number of subscribers)

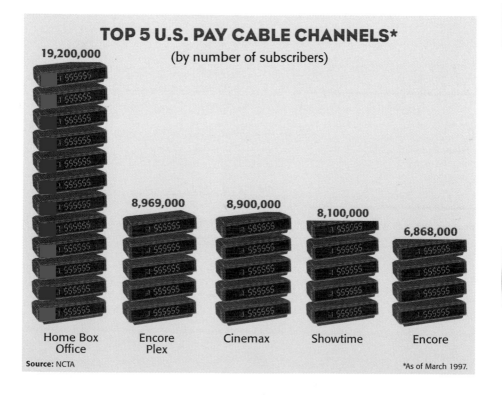

19,200,000

8,969,000

8,900,000

8,100,000

6,868,000

Home Box Office

Encore Plex

Cinemax

Showtime

Encore

Source: NCTA

*As of March 1997.

TOP 5 HIGHEST-GROSSING MOVIES OF ALL TIME, WORLDWIDE

(year of release)

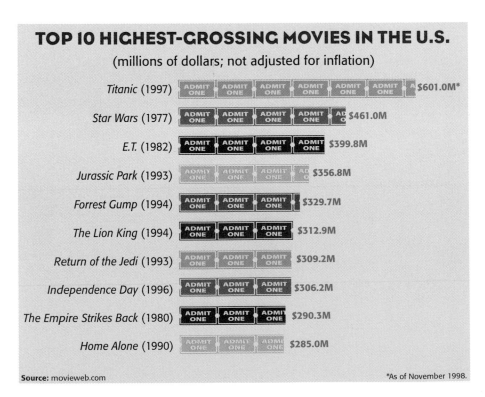

Titanic*
(1997) — **$1.8 billion***

Jurassic Park
(1993) — **$920 million**

Independence Day
(1996) — **$810 million**

Star Wars
(1977) — **$780 million**

The Lion King
(1994) — **$772 million**

Source: us.imdb.com

*As of November 1998.

TOP 10 HIGHEST-GROSSING MOVIES IN THE U.S.

(millions of dollars; not adjusted for inflation)

Titanic (1997) — **$601.0M***

Star Wars (1977) — **$461.0M**

E.T. (1982) — **$399.8M**

Jurassic Park (1993) — **$356.8M**

Forrest Gump (1994) — **$329.7M**

The Lion King (1994) — **$312.9M**

Return of the Jedi (1993) — **$309.2M**

Independence Day (1996) — **$306.2M**

The Empire Strikes Back (1980) — **$290.3M**

Home Alone (1990) — **$285.0M**

Source: movieweb.com

*As of November 1998.

TOP 5 HIGHEST-GROSSING KIDS' MOVIES OF ALL TIME, WORLDWIDE*
(in millions)

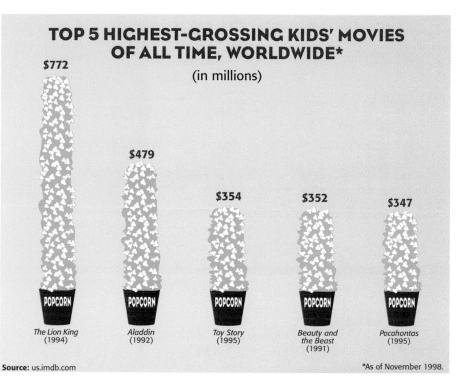

$772 — The Lion King (1994)
$479 — Aladdin (1992)
$354 — Toy Story (1995)
$352 — Beauty and the Beast (1991)
$347 — Pocahontas (1995)

Source: us.imdb.com

*As of November 1998.

TOP 6 OSCAR-WINNING MOVIES
(year of awards)

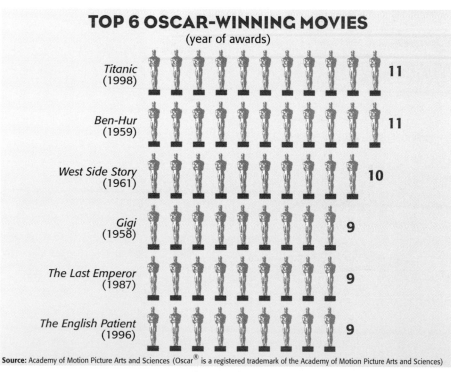

Titanic (1998) — 11
Ben-Hur (1959) — 11
West Side Story (1961) — 10
Gigi (1958) — 9
The Last Emperor (1987) — 9
The English Patient (1996) — 9

Source: Academy of Motion Picture Arts and Sciences (Oscar® is a registered trademark of the Academy of Motion Picture Arts and Sciences)

TOP 5 MOST EXPENSIVE MOVIES EVER MADE*

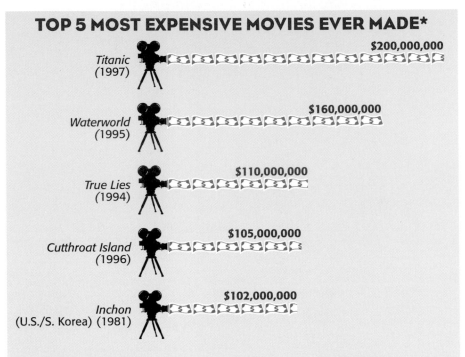

Titanic (1997) — $200,000,000

Waterworld (1995) — $160,000,000

True Lies (1994) — $110,000,000

Cutthroat Island (1996) — $105,000,000

Inchon (U.S./S. Korea) (1981) — $102,000,000

Source: entertainmentweekly.com

*All U.S.-made unless otherwise stated.

TOP 5 MOVIE-PRODUCING COUNTRIES
(average number of movies per year)

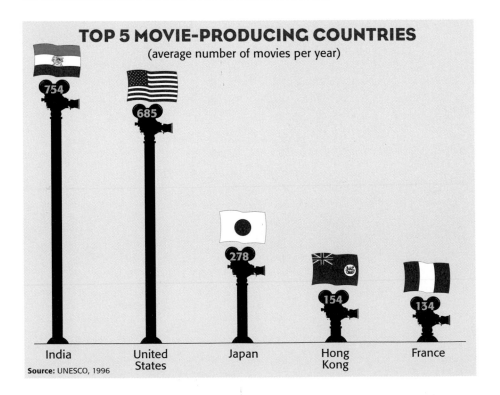

India — 754

United States — 685

Japan — 278

Hong Kong — 154

France — 134

Source: UNESCO, 1996

TOP 5 BEST-SELLING VIDEOS IN THE U.S.*
(in dollar sales)

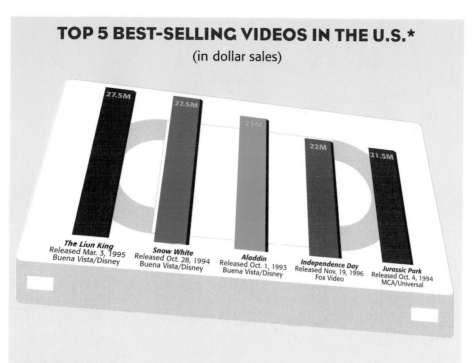

The Lion King
Released Mar. 3, 1995
Buena Vista/Disney
— 27.5M

Snow White
Released Oct. 28, 1994
Buena Vista/Disney
— 27.5M

Aladdin
Released Oct. 1, 1993
Buena Vista/Disney
— 25M

Independence Day
Released Nov. 19, 1996
Fox Video
— 22M

Jurassic Park
Released Oct. 4, 1994
MCA/Universal
— 21.5M

Source: *Video Store Magazine*

*Since 1992.

BEST-SELLING KIDS' VIDEOS OF ALL TIME
(worldwide, in millions of dollars of sales)

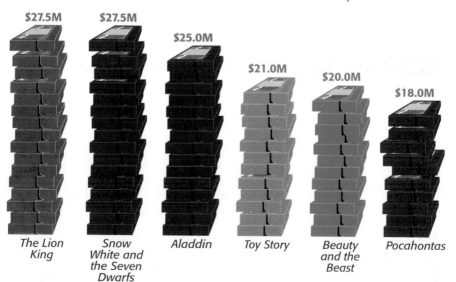

$27.5M	$27.5M	$25.0M	$21.0M	$20.0M	$18.0M
The Lion King	Snow White and the Seven Dwarfs	Aladdin	Toy Story	Beauty and the Beast	Pocahontas

Source: Based on data from *VIdeo Store Magazine*, 1997

TRANSPORTATION

Americans are on the road. More than 175 million licensed drivers log an average of almost 13,000 miles each a year, behind the wheels of nearly 200 million cars, trucks, and motorcycles. Many of those miles are over the interstate highway system, which was started in 1956 and today includes more than 42,000 miles of highway.

Nationally, more than 85 percent of commuters travel to work in private cars and vans. Only in New York City do more people use public transportation than drive to work. That makes rush hour traffic a nightmare in many areas. Los Angeles, California, has the country's worst traffic problem, followed by Washington, DC. Traffic isn't the only problem caused by America's love of cars. Automobile exhausts pollute the air, and automobile accidents claim thousands of lives each year. Automobile makers are working on these problems with improved pollution-control and safety devices.

When Americans aren't in their cars, they prefer planes for long trips. They spend $27 billion a year on air travel, more than on any other form of transportation except the automobile. Chicago's O'Hare International is the busiest airport in the world. In contrast, railroads carry a shrinking share of the nation's passengers. Almost all passenger lines are run by Amtrak, a government-subsidized corporation. High-speed rail service links East Coast cities from Washington, DC, to New York City, but many once-famous long-distance passenger trains no longer run. Railways are still important, though, especially for mass transit in urban areas and for freight.

Yearbook

3500 B.C. Egyptians use sailing ships.

A.D. 1550 Wagons run on wooden tracks in mines in the Holy Roman Empire.

1804 In Great Britain, a steam locomotive runs on iron rails. It hauls 10 tons of iron for 10 miles.

1908 Henry Ford introduces the Model T, the first inexpensive and practical car. The automobile soon becomes affordable transportation for middle-class Americans.

1952 The British-made *de Havilland Comet* is the first jet airliner to offer regular service.

• Notables •

Karl Benz (1844–1929) German engineer; in 1865 created the first design that was exclusively for an automobile. Before that, cars were converted from carriages.

John Blenkinsop (1783–1831) English inventor; designed the first practical locomotive.

Gottlieb Daimler (1834–1900) German inventor; developed the first high-speed internal combustion engine.

Robert Fulton (1765–1815) American inventor; credited with building the first practical steamboat—the *Clermont*—which helped to revolutionize American water transportation.

Wilbur (1867–1912) and Orville (1871–1948) Wright American pioneers in aviation; in 1903 they were the first people to fly a heavier-than-air craft—for 59 seconds—at Kitty Hawk, North Carolina.

KEY IDEAS

gondola Most commonly, a long, narrow, flat-bottomed boat used on the canals of the ancient Italian city of Venice. A railroad car without a top is also called a gondola, and so is the enclosed space that hangs from a hot air balloon.

internal combustion engine A heat-producing engine in which combustion takes place inside the engine instead of in a furnace. (Combustion is a chemical process that produces heat.)

jet engine An airplane engine that uses oxygen in the atmosphere to burn fuel and produces a stream of air and exhaust gases toward the rear of the plane.

monorail A train that travels on one track. Some monorails travel below the track; others, above it.

semitrailer A truck that is made up of a tractor (the cab) and a freight trailer.

NUMBER AND TYPES OF VEHICLES IN THE U.S., 1996

Mode of Transport

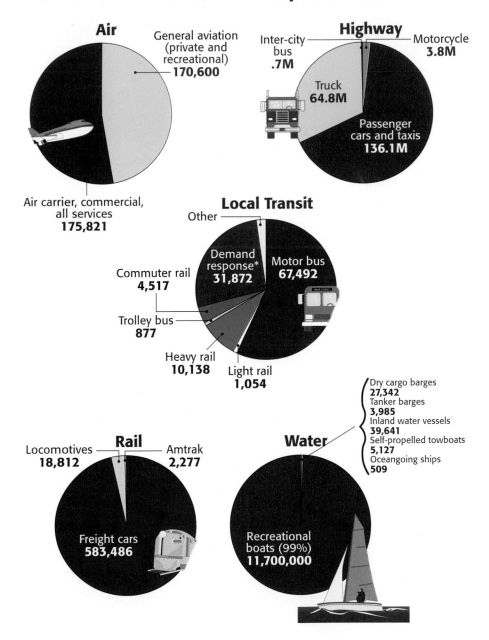

Air

General aviation (private and recreational) **170,600**

Air carrier, commercial, all services **175,821**

Highway

Inter-city bus **.7M**

Motorcycle **3.8M**

Truck **64.8M**

Passenger cars and taxis **136.1M**

Local Transit

Other

Demand response* **31,872**

Motor bus **67,492**

Commuter rail **4,517**

Trolley bus **877**

Heavy rail **10,138**

Light rail **1,054**

Rail

Locomotives **18,812**

Amtrak **2,277**

Freight cars **583,486**

Water

Dry cargo barges **27,342**
Tanker barges **3,985**
Inland water vessels **39,641**
Self-propelled towboats **5,127**
Oceangoing ships **509**

Recreational boats (99%) **11,700,000**

Source: U.S. Department of Transportation
National Transportation Statistics, 1997

Note: M = million
*Demand response = fire, ambulance, police vehicles.

HOW AMERICANS GET TO WORK

(workers 16 years old and over)

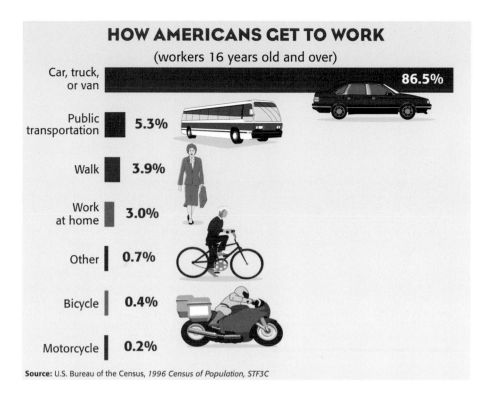

Car, truck, or van	**86.5%**
Public transportation	**5.3%**
Walk	**3.9%**
Work at home	**3.0%**
Other	**0.7%**
Bicycle	**0.4%**
Motorcycle	**0.2%**

Source: U.S. Bureau of the Census, *1996 Census of Population, STF3C*

TOP 10 BUSIEST WORLD AIRPORTS, 1996

(ranked by number of passengers)

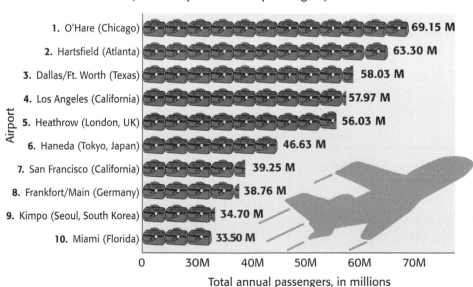

Airport	Total annual passengers
1. O'Hare (Chicago)	69.15 M
2. Hartsfield (Atlanta)	63.30 M
3. Dallas/Ft. Worth (Texas)	58.03 M
4. Los Angeles (California)	57.97 M
5. Heathrow (London, UK)	56.03 M
6. Haneda (Tokyo, Japan)	46.63 M
7. San Francisco (California)	39.25 M
8. Frankfort/Main (Germany)	38.76 M
9. Kimpo (Seoul, South Korea)	34.70 M
10. Miami (Florida)	33.50 M

Total annual passengers, in millions

Source: Airports Association Council International–North America; Air Transport Association of America

SELECTED MAJOR U.S. INTERSTATE HIGHWAYS

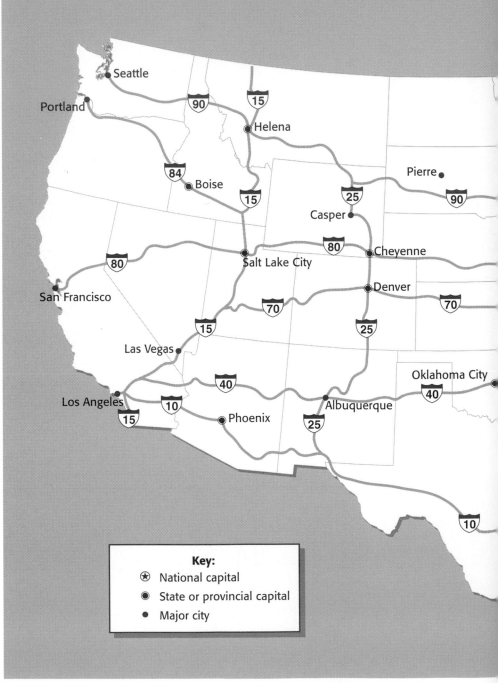

Seattle

Portland

90

15

Helena

84 Boise

15

Pierre

25 90

Casper

80 Cheyenne

Salt Lake City

Denver

80 70 70

San Francisco

70

15

Las Vegas

Oklahoma City

40 40

Los Angeles

10

Albuquerque

15 Phoenix 25

10

Key:
⊛ National capital
◉ State or provincial capital
● Major city

UNITED NATIONS

In 1945, as World War II was ending, the leaders of 51 nations agreed to a bold plan. They would form an international organization, the United Nations (U.N.), that would help keep the peace. The United Nations would be dedicated to four goals: It would work to prevent war. It would advance human rights. It would uphold treaties and international law. And it would help people in poor nations achieve a better standard of living.

These were big goals. Many people doubted that the United Nations would achieve them—or even last long. The League of Nations, a similar group formed after World War I, had collapsed in the 1930s. But the United Nations survived and grew. By 1995—its fiftieth anniversary—185 nations were members.

The United Nations plays a major role in solving disputes between nations. U.N. negotiators help arrange cease-fires and permanent peace agreements. U.N. peacekeeping troops, drawn from the armed forces of member nations, have served in trouble spots around the world. During the Korean War, troops from the United States and other nations fought under the U.N. flag. Usually, however, the United Nations uses peaceful methods, such as economic penalties, against countries that violate international law.

The United Nations has sponsored important treaties. Among them are agreements limiting the spread of nuclear weapons and protecting the environment. U.N. agencies work to fight disease, improve farming methods, and assist refugees.

Yearbook

1944 Representatives of China, the Soviet Union, the United Kingdom, and the United States meet in Washington, DC, to plan the creation of an international peacekeeping organization.

1953 The United Nations coordinates a global census to try to establish Earth's population for the first time in history. There are about 2.4 billion people.

1979 The U.N.'s World Health Organization (WHO) announces that the deadly smallpox disease has been eliminated.

1991 The United Nations mediates an end to the Persian Gulf War.

• Notables •

Dag Hammarskjöld (1905–1961)
Swedish statesman; exceptionally effective U.N. secretary-general who took part in settling crises surrounding the Suez Canal, Lebanon, and Congo.

Jeanne J. Kirkpatrick (1926–   )
First American woman to serve as ambassador to the United Nations.

John D. Rockefeller (1839–1937)
American businessman; donated $8.5 million so that the United Nations could buy a tract of land in New York City to serve as U.N. headquarters.

Eleanor Roosevelt (1884–1962)
Widow of President Franklin D. Roosevelt; served as one of the first U.N. delegates from the United States; influential in the United Nations's early efforts to protect human rights.

KEY IDEAS

General Assembly The place where the United Nations's 185 members can discuss major issues, including world peace, human rights, and the environment; is in session from September to December.

International Court of Justice (World Court) The Court issues judgments on legal issues. It is located in The Hague, Netherlands.

secretary-general The head of the Secretariat, which is where the United Nations's administrative offices are located. The secretary-general is elected by U.N. members.

Security Council The most powerful part of the United Nations. There are 15 member countries: Five are permanent and ten are elected from the General Assembly for two-year terms. The Security Council tries to resolve the most difficult international issues.

United Nations Children's Fund (UNICEF) A U.N. program that provides low-cost health services to families in developing nations.

THE UNITED NATIONS AT A GLANCE

INTERNATIONAL COURT OF JUSTICE

- Principal judicial arm of U.N.
- Headquarters at the Peace Palace in The Hague, Netherlands
- Settles matters of international law
- Contains 15 judges, each elected to nine-year terms

GENERAL ASSEMBLY

- Main deliberative organ of U.N.
- Composed of members from all member states; each has one vote
- Key decisions require two-thirds majority; others require simple majority
- Meets at world headquarters in New York City

ECONOMIC AND SOCIAL COUNCIL

- Serves as central forum for discussion of international economic and social issues; formulates policies
- Conducts studies
- Coordinates activities of special agencies around the world
- Composed of 54 members, each elected for three-year terms by the General Assembly

Includes:
UNESCO (UN Educational, Scientific, and Cultural Organization)
WHO (World Health Organization)
UNICEF (UN Children's Fund)

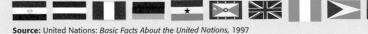

Source: United Nations: *Basic Facts About the United Nations,* 1997

Total Member States in the U.N.: 185

SECURITY COUNCIL

- 15 members; 5 permanent and 10 elected by General Assembly for two-year terms
- Responsible for maintaining international peace and security
- Representatives of each member present at U.N. headquarters at all times
- Tries to mediate and arbitrate to bring about peaceful resolutions to global conflicts
- Deploys peacekeeping forces
- Imposes economic and other sanctions
- Presidency of the council rotates by member countries

SECRETARIAT

- International staff in New York and around world that supports the other organs of the U.N.
- Members prepare studies, organize conferences, monitor U.N. activity and events, interpret speeches, work with the media and in educational areas
- Staff is made up of more than 25,000 men and women from approximately 160 countries

TRUSTEESHIP COUNCIL

- Chartered to administer and oversee issues regarding U.N. trust territories
- Suspended operation in 1994, when last remaining trust gained independence

Contact information:
United Nations
Publications
Room 1059
New York, NY 10017
212-963-1234

Web Site:
www.un.org

THE 185 MEMBER COUNTRIES
OF THE UNITED NATIONS

Afghanistan (19 Nov. 1946)
Albania (14 Dec. 1955)
Algeria (8 Oct. 1962)
Andorra (28 July 1993)
Angola (1 Dec. 1976)
Antigua and Barbuda (11 Nov. 1981)
Argentina (24 Oct. 1945)
Armenia (2 Mar. 1992)
Australia (1 Nov. 1945)
Austria (14 Dec. 1955)
Azerbaijan (9 Mar. 1992)
Bahamas (18 Sept. 1973)
Bahrain (21 Sept. 1971)
Bangladesh (17 Sept. 1974)
Barbados (9 Dec. 1966)
Belarus (24 Oct. 1945)
Belgium (27 Dec. 1945)
Belize (25 Sept. 1981)
Benin (20 Sept. 1960)
Bhutan (21 Sept. 1971)
Bolivia (14 Nov. 1945)
Bosnia and Herzegovina (22 May 1992)
Botswana (17 Oct. 1966)
Brazil (24 Oct. 1945)
Brunei Darussalam (21 Sept. 1984)
Bulgaria (14 Dec. 1955)
Burkina Faso (20 Sept. 1960)
Burundi (18 Sept. 1962)
Cambodia (14 Dec. 1955)
Cameroon (20 Sept. 1960)
Canada (9 Nov. 1945)
Cape Verde (16 Sept. 1975)
Central African Republic (20 Sept. 1960)
Chad (20 Sept. 1960)
Chile (24 Oct. 1945)
China (24 Oct. 1945)
Colombia (5 Nov. 1945)
Comoros (12 Nov. 1975)
Congo (20 Sept. 1960)
Costa Rica (2 Nov. 1945)
Côte d'Ivoire (20 Sept. 1960)
Croatia (22 May 1992)
Cuba (24 Oct. 1945)
Cyprus (20 Sept. 1960)
Czech Republic (19 Jan. 1993)
Democratic People's Republic of Korea
   (17 Sept. 1991)

Democratic Republic of the Congo
   (20 Sept. 1960)
Denmark (24 Oct. 1945)
Djibouti (20 Sept. 1977)
Dominica (18 Dec. 1978)
Dominican Republic (24 Oct. 1945)
Ecuador (21 Dec. 1945)
Egypt (24 Oct. 1945)
El Salvador (24 Oct. 1945)
Equatorial Guinea (12 Nov. 1968)
Eritrea (28 May 1993)
Estonia (17 Sept. 1991)
Ethiopia (13 Nov. 1945)
Fiji (13 Oct. 1970)
Finland (14 Dec. 1955)
France (24 Oct. 1945)
Gabon (20 Sept. 1960)
Gambia (21 Sept. 1965)
Georgia (31 July 1992)
Germany (18 Sept. 1973)
Ghana (8 Mar. 1957)
Greece (25 Oct. 1945)
Grenada (17 Sept. 1974)
Guatemala (21 Nov. 1945)
Guinea (12 Dec. 1958)
Guinea-Bissau (17 Sept. 1974)
Guyana (20 Sept. 1966)
Haiti (24 Oct. 1945)
Honduras (17 Dec. 1945)
Hungary (14 Dec. 1955)
Iceland (19 Nov. 1946)
India (30 Oct. 1945)
Indonesia (28 Sept. 1950)
Iran (Islamic Republic of) (24 Oct. 1945)
Iraq (21 Dec. 1945)
Ireland (14 Dec. 1955)
Israel (11 May 1949)
Italy (14 Dec. 1955)
Jamaica (18 Sept. 1962)
Japan (18 Dec. 1956)
Jordan (14 Dec. 1955)
Kazakhstan (2 Mar. 1992)
Kenya (16 Dec. 1963)
Kuwait (14 May 1963)
Kyrgyzstan (2 Mar. 1992)
Lao People's Democratic Republic
   (14 Dec. 1955)

Source: United Nations Press Release, 1998 (www.un.org)

Latvia (17 Sept. 1991)
Lebanon (24 Oct. 1945)
Lesotho (17 Oct. 1966)
Liberia (2 Nov. 1945)
Libyan Arab Jamahiriya (14 Dec. 1955)
Liechtenstein (18 Sept. 1990)
Lithuania (17 Sept. 1991)
Luxembourg (24 Oct. 1945)
Madagascar (20 Sept. 1960)
Malawi (1 Dec. 1964)
Malaysia (17 Sept. 1957)
Maldives (21 Sept. 1965)
Mali (28 Sept. 1960)
Malta (1 Dec. 1964)
Marshall Islands (17 Sept. 1991)
Mauritania (7 Oct. 1961)
Mauritius (24 Apr. 1968)
Mexico (7 Nov. 1945)
Micronesia (Federated States of)
   (17 Sept. 1991)
Monaco (28 May 1993)
Mongolia (27 Oct. 1961)
Morocco (12 Nov. 1956)
Mozambique (16 Sept. 1975)
Myanmar (19 Apr. 1948)
Namibia (23 Apr. 1990)
Nepal (14 Dec. 1955)
Netherlands (10 Dec. 1945)
New Zealand (24 Oct. 1945)
Nicaragua (24 Oct. 1945)
Niger (20 Sept. 1960)
Nigeria (7 Oct. 1960)
Norway (27 Nov. 1945)
Oman (7 Oct. 1971)
Pakistan (30 Sept. 1947)
Palau (15 Dec. 1994)
Panama (13 Nov. 1945)
Papua New Guinea (10 Oct. 1975)
Paraguay (24 Oct. 1945)
Peru (31 Oct. 1945)
Philippines (24 Oct. 1945)
Poland (24 Oct. 1945)
Portugal (14 Dec. 1955)
Qatar (21 Sept. 1971)
Republic of Korea (17 Sept. 1991)
Republic of Moldova (2 Mar. 1992)
Romania (14 Dec. 1955)
Russian Federation (24 Oct. 1945)
Rwanda (18 Sept. 1962)

Saint Kitts and Nevis (23 Sept. 1983)
Saint Lucia (18 Sept. 1979)
Saint Vincent and the Grenadines
   (16 Sept. 1980)
Samoa (15 Dec. 1976)
San Marino (2 Mar. 1992)
Sao Tome and Principe (16 Sept. 1975)
Saudi Arabia (24 Oct. 1945)
Senegal (28 Sept. 1960)
Seychelles (21 Sept. 1976)
Sierra Leone (27 Sept. 1961)
Singapore (21 Sept. 1965)
Slovakia (19 Jan. 1993)
Slovenia (22 May 1992)
Solomon Islands (19 Sept. 1978)
Somalia (20 Sept. 1960)
South Africa (7 Nov. 1945)
Spain (14 Dec. 1955)
Sri Lanka (14 Dec. 1955)
Sudan (12 Nov. 1956)
Suriname (4 Dec. 1975)
Swaziland (24 Sept. 1968)
Sweden (19 Nov. 1946)
Syrian Arab Republic (24 Oct. 1945)
Tajikistan (2 Mar. 1992)
Thailand (16 Dec. 1946)
The former Yugoslav Republic of Macedonia
   (8 Apr. 1993)
Togo (20 Sept. 1960)
Trinidad and Tobago (18 Sept. 1962)
Tunisia (12 Nov. 1956)
Turkey (24 Oct. 1945)
Turkmenistan (2 Mar. 1992)
Uganda (25 Oct. 1962)
Ukraine (24 Oct. 1945)
United Arab Emirates (9 Dec. 1971)
United Kingdom of Great Britain and Northern
   Ireland (24 Oct. 1945)
United Republic of Tanzania (14 Dec. 1961)
United States of America (24 Oct. 1945)
Uruguay (18 Dec. 1945)
Uzbekistan (2 Mar. 1992)
Vanuatu (15 Sept. 1981)
Venezuela (15 Nov. 1945)
Vietnam (20 Sept. 1977)
Yemen (30 Sept. 1947)
Yugoslavia (24 Oct. 1945)
Zambia (1 Dec. 1964)
Zimbabwe (25 Aug. 1980)

Note: Dates in parentheses are dates of official membership.

WEATHER

In 1897, the *Hartford Courant* wrote, "Everyone talks about the weather, but nobody does anything about it." That famous saying really isn't true. People can't control wind, rain, and the other activities in the atmosphere that we call weather. But they *can* do something about them: They can prepare for them.

Meteorologists—scientists who study weather—track changes in temperature, air pressure, winds, and humidity. They identify weather patterns and try to understand what causes storms and other weather events. Then they try to forecast the weather. Forecasts help you decide whether you need to wear a coat or carry an umbrella—but they also do much more. They alert farmers to frost so that crops can be saved. They give people time to take shelter from violent storms. National, international, and private weather services cooperate in collecting information and issuing forecasts. Radar, satellite photography, and powerful computers are among their tools. Even so, the factors that create weather are so complex that it's not unusual for forecasts to be wrong.

Long-term weather patterns determine a region's climate. Distance from the equator, height above sea level, prevailing winds, features such as mountains and oceans—these and other factors help set patterns of temperature and precipitation. Hot, cold, wet, or dry, climate affects almost every aspect of life, from clothing to housing to how people earn a living.

Yearbook

340 B.C. Aristotle's *Meteorologica* is the first complete discussion of meteorology. About 1,400 years later, it is translated into Latin.

1643 The first barometer with mercury is invented. It allows scientists to more accurately measure the pressure of the atmosphere. Barometers remain important tools for forecasting weather.

1860 The Paris Observatory publishes the first modern weather maps.

1958 Scientists warn about a possible warming of the temperature around the world, called "global warming."

• Notables •

Heinrich Dove (1803–1879) Prussian meteorologist; discovered that tropical storm winds move clockwise in the Northern Hemisphere and counterclockwise in the Southern Hemisphere.

James Espy (1785–1860) First meteorologist in the U.S government.

Joseph Gay-Lussac (1778–1850) French chemist; discovered that air at a high altitude has the same percentage of oxygen as air on the ground.

Luke Howard (1772–1864) British meteorologist; named cloud formations: cirrus, cumulus, stratus, and nimbus.

John von Neumann (1903–1957) American mathematician; produced the first computerized 24-hour weather predictions.

KEY IDEAS

Doppler radar Radio signals that are used to study storms. The radar can bounce off raindrops more than 100 miles away.

front The boundary between two different air masses.

high An air mass with higher-than-normal air pressure. This is usually a fair-weather system.

low An air mass with lower-than-normal air pressure. It is usually the center of a storm system.

mean Average; midpoint between highest and lowest.

meteorology A branch of science that deals with a planet's atmosphere, and especially Earth's. One focus of this field is the analysis and prediction of the weather.

El Niño A naturally occurring event that causes a large mass of warm water, normally located near the coast of Australia, to move east toward South America. El Niño is connected with other weather systems and can change weather patterns around the world.

TOP 5 DRIEST U.S. CITIES
(mean annual precipitation)

City	Precipitation
Yuma, Arizona	2.65" (67 mm)
Las Vegas, Nevada	4.19" (106 mm)
Bishop, California	5.61" (142 mm)
Bakersfield, California	5.72" (145 mm)
Phoenix, Arizona	7.11" (180 mm)

Source: National Climatic Data Center

TOP 5 WETTEST U.S. CITIES
(mean annual precipitation)

City	Precipitation
Quillayute, Washington	105.18" (2,672 mm)
Astoria, Oregon	66.40" (1,687 mm)
Tallahassee, Florida	65.71" (1,669 mm)
Mobile, Alabama	63.96" (1,625 mm)
Pensacola, Florida	62.25" (1,581 mm)

Source: National Weather Service

TOP 5 SNOWIEST U.S. CITIES
(mean annual snowfall)

Blue Canyon, California — 240.8" (6,116 mm)

Marquette, Michigan — 129.2" (3,282 mm)

Sault Ste. Marie, Michigan — 116.1" (2,949 mm)

Syracuse, New York — 114.0" (2,896 mm)

Caribou, Maine — 110.0" (2,794 mm)

Source: National Climatic Data Center

TOP 5 COLDEST U.S. CITIES
(average temperature)

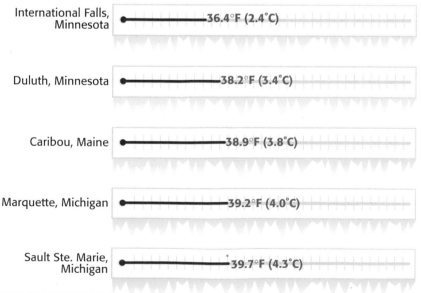

International Falls, Minnesota — 36.4°F (2.4°C)

Duluth, Minnesota — 38.2°F (3.4°C)

Caribou, Maine — 38.9°F (3.8°C)

Marquette, Michigan — 39.2°F (4.0°C)

Sault Ste. Marie, Michigan — 39.7°F (4.3°C)

Source: National Climatic Data Center

TOP 5 HOTTEST U.S. CITIES
(average temperature)

Key West, Florida ☀☀☀☀☀☀☀☀ **77.7°F (25.4°C)**

Miami, Florida ☀☀☀☀☀☀☀ **75.6°F (24.2°C)**

West Palm Beach, Florida ☀☀☀☀☀☀☀ **74.6°F (23.7°C)**

Fort Myers, Florida ☀☀☀☀☀☀☀ **73.9°F (23.3°C)**

Yuma, Arizona ☀☀☀☀☀☀☀ **73.9°F (23.3°C)**

Source: National Climatic Data Center

WORST U.S. NATURAL DISASTERS

Drought

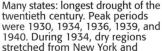

1930s Many states: longest drought of the twentieth century. Peak periods were 1930, 1934, 1936, 1939, and 1940. During 1934, dry regions stretched from New York and Pennsylvania across the Great Plains to the California coast. A great "dust bowl" covered some 50 million acres in the south central plains during the winter of 1935–1936.

Earthquake

1906 April 18, San Francisco: earthquake accompanied by fire razed more than 4 sq. mi. (10 sq. km); more than 500 dead or missing.

Flood

1889 May 31, Johnstown, PA: more than 2,200 died in the flood that caused fires, explosions, and drownings.

Hurricane

1900 August 27–September 15, Galveston, TX: more than 6,000 died from the devastating combination of high winds and a tidal wave.

Tornado

1925 March 18, Great Tri-State Tornado: Missouri, Illinois, and Indiana; 695 deaths. Eight additional tornadoes in Kentucky, Tennessee, and Alabama raised the toll to 792 dead.

Winter Storm

1888 March 11–14, East Coast: the Blizzard of 1888. Four hundred people died, as much as 5 feet (1.5 m) of snow. Damage was estimated at $20 million.

Source: National Weather Service; U.S. Department of Commerce

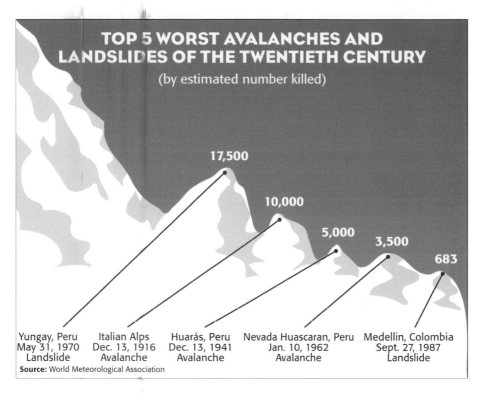

TOP 5 WORST AVALANCHES AND LANDSLIDES OF THE TWENTIETH CENTURY

(by estimated number killed)

17,500

10,000

5,000

3,500

683

Yungay, Peru	Italian Alps	Huarás, Peru	Nevada Huascaran, Peru	Medellin, Colombia
May 31, 1970	Dec. 13, 1916	Dec. 13, 1941	Jan. 10, 1962	Sept. 27, 1987
Landslide	Avalanche	Avalanche	Avalanche	Landslide

Source: World Meteorological Association

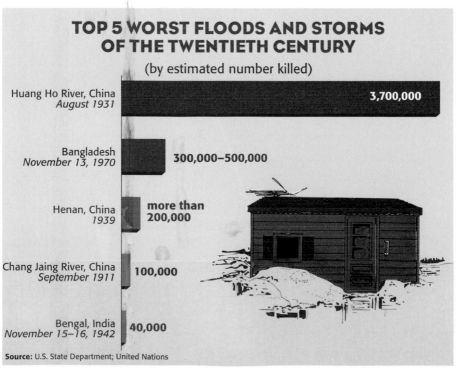

TOP 5 WORST FLOODS AND STORMS OF THE TWENTIETH CENTURY

(by estimated number killed)

Huang Ho River, China *August 1931*	**3,700,000**
Bangladesh *November 13, 1970*	**300,000–500,000**
Henan, China *1939*	**more than 200,000**
Chang Jaing River, China *September 1911*	**100,000**
Bengal, India *November 15–16, 1942*	**40,000**

Source: U.S. State Department; United Nations

WEIGHTS AND MEASURES

Weights and measures are standard units of size, weight, time, and temperature. Stone slabs from ancient Egypt show that people were using such standards as long as 5,000 years ago. Ancient measurements were based on familiar things. The Egyptians used the cubit, a unit equal to the distance from the elbow to the tip of the middle finger. The Romans used the inch (a thumb's width) and the foot (a foot's length). Our word "mile" comes from the Latin *millia passuum*, "a thousand paces."

The problem with these ancient measures was that no two people were the same size. For trade and science, people needed a single system. In 1791, a group of French scientists proposed the metric system.

Most countries use the metric system today. Units in this system are multiples of 10. For example, the basic unit of length is the meter—10 meters equal a dekameter; 10 dekameters equal a hectometer; 10 hectometers equal a kilometer; and so on.

The United States uses the customary system of measurement: 12 inches equal a foot, 3 feet equal a yard, and 1,760 yards equal a mile.

Unusual measures are used in some fields. At sea, a fathom is equal to 6 feet (2 meters), and a pica—used in the printing industry—is equal to 1/6 of an inch (.42 cm). The height of horses is measured in hands, equal to 4 inches. Gems are weighed in carats, each equal to 200 milligrams.

Yearbook

circa 1950 B.C. In Sumerica (present-day Iraq), a copper bar about 43.4 inches (110 cm) long is a standard measure.

1791 The metric system of measurement is proposed in France.

1875 An International Bureau of Weights and Measures (IBWM) is established in Sevres, France. The bureau establishes a metal bar in its possession as the official weight of the kilogram.

1960 The IBWM defines a standard meter, defined in relation to the wavelength of light that is produced when krypton gas is heated.

• Notables •

Jacques Babinet (1794–1872) French physicist; in 1827, suggested using the wavelength of light as a standard measurement. His idea was adopted more than 100 years later.

Anders Celsius (1701–1744) Swedish astronomer; first to propose the centigrade scale for measuring temperature.

Daniel Fahrenheit (1686–1736) German physicist; invented the mercury thermometer and introduced the Fahrenheit scale, used to measure temperature today in the United States and Canada.

Ole Römer (1644–1710) Danish astronomer; measured the speed of light and calculated it at 140,000 miles per second.

Pierre Vernier (1580–1637) French mathematician; in the early 1600s, invented a tool for precisely measuring length. Variations on it are still used today.

KEY IDEAS

acre An area that measures 43,560 square feet (4,046 sq. m). Originally, it was the area of land that a pair of oxen could plow in one day.

ampere (amp) A unit of electrical current.

decibel A measurement of loudness. One decibel is the smallest amount of change in a sound that a human ear can detect.

horsepower Used to measure the power of an engine, such as an automobile or steam engine. Horsepower is the power needed to lift 33,000 pounds a distance of one foot in one minute.

knot A unit of speed measurement, most commonly used in water travel; equal to 1.15 miles (1.85 km).

metric A decimal system of weights and measures based on the meter and the kilogram.

Roentgen An international unit of radiation exposure produced by an X ray.

WEIGHTS AND MEASURES

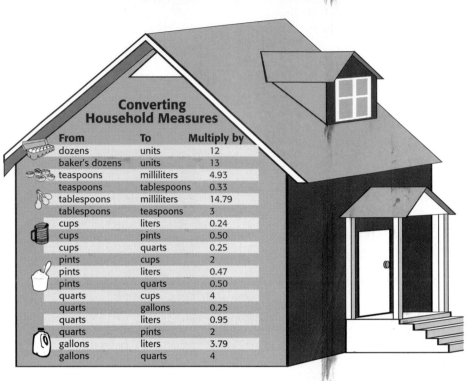

Converting Household Measures

From	To	Multiply by
dozens	units	12
baker's dozens	units	13
teaspoons	milliliters	4.93
teaspoons	tablespoons	0.33
tablespoons	milliliters	14.79
tablespoons	teaspoons	3
cups	liters	0.24
cups	pints	0.50
cups	quarts	0.25
pints	cups	2
pints	liters	0.47
pints	quarts	0.50
quarts	cups	4
quarts	gallons	0.25
quarts	liters	0.95
quarts	pints	2
gallons	liters	3.79
gallons	quarts	4

Simple Metric Conversion Table

To convert	To	Multiply by
centimeters	feet	0.0328
centimeters	inches	0.3937
cubic centimeters	cubic inches	0.0610
cubic feet	cubic meters	0.0283
degrees	radians	0.0175
feet	centimeters	30.48
feet	meters	0.3048
gallons	liters	3.785
gal. water	lb. water	8.3453
grams	ounces	0.0353
inches	centimeters	2.54
kilograms	pounds	2.205
kilometers	feet	3,280.8
kilometers	miles	0.6214
knots	miles/hour	1.151
liters	gallons	0.2642
liters	pints	2.113
meters	feet	3.281
miles	kilometers	1.609
ounces	grams	28.3495
pounds	kilograms	0.4536

Length or Distance

U.S. Customary System

1 foot (ft.)	=	12 inches (in.)		
1 yard (yd.)	=	3 feet	=	36 inches
1 rod (rd)	=	5½ yards	=	16½ feet
1 furlong (fur.)	=	40 rods	=	220 yards
	=	660 feet		
1 mile (mi.)	=	8 furlongs	=	1,760 yards
	=	5,280 feet		

An international nautical mile has been defined as 6,076.1155 feet.

Common Fractions and Their Decimal Equivalents

½	.5000	³⁄₁₁	.2727
⅓	.3333	⅘	.8000
¼	.2500	⁴⁄₇	.5714
⅕	.2000	⁴⁄₉	.4444
⅙	.1667	⁴⁄₁₁	.3636
⅐	.1429	⅚	.8333
⅛	.1250	⁵⁄₇	.7143
⅑	.1111	⅝	.6250
⅒	.1000	⁵⁄₉	.5556
¹⁄₁₁	.0909	⁵⁄₁₁	.4545
¹⁄₁₂	.0833	⁵⁄₁₂	.4167
¹⁄₁₆	.0625	⁶⁄₇	.8571
¹⁄₃₂	.0313	⁶⁄₁₁	.5455
¹⁄₆₄	.0156	⅞	.8750
⅔	.6667	⁷⁄₉	.7778
⅖	.4000	⁷⁄₁₀	.7000
²⁄₇	.2857	⁷⁄₁₁	.6364
²⁄₉	.2222	⁷⁄₁₂	.5833
²⁄₁₁	.1818	⁸⁄₉	.8889
¾	.7500	⁸⁄₁₁	.7273
⅗	.6000	⁹⁄₁₀	.9000
³⁄₇	.4286	⁹⁄₁₁	.8182
⅜	.3750	¹⁰⁄₁₁	.9091
³⁄₁₀	.3000	¹¹⁄₁₂	.9167

Six Quick Ways to Measure When You Don't Have a Ruler

1. Most credit cards are 3⅜ inches by 2⅛ inches.

2. Standard business cards are printed 3½ inches wide by 2 inches long.

3. Floor tiles are usually manufactured in 12-inch by 12-inch squares.

4. U.S. paper currency is 6⅛ inches wide by 2⅝ inches long.

5. The diameter of a quarter is approximately one inch, and the diameter of a penny is approximately three quarters of an inch.

6. A standard sheet of paper is 8½ inches wide and 11 inches long.

Temperature Conversions

Celsius		Fahrenheit
246.1	=	475°
232.2	=	450
218.3	=	425
204.4	=	400
190.6	=	375
176.7	=	350
162.8	=	325
148.9	=	300
135.0	=	275
121.1	=	250
107.2	=	225
100.0	=	**212**
43.3	=	110
40.6	=	105
37.8	=	100
35.0	=	95
32.2	=	90
29.4	=	85
26.7	=	80
23.9	=	75
21.1	=	70
18.3	=	65
15.6	=	60
12.8	=	55
10.0	=	50
7.2	=	45
4.4	=	40
1.7	=	35
0.0	=	**32**
-1.1	=	30
-3.9	=	25
-6.7	=	20
-9.4	=	15
-12.2	=	10
-15.0	=	5
-17.8	=	0
-20.6	=	-5
-23.3	=	-10
-26.1	=	-15
-28.9	=	-20
-31.7	=	-25
-34.4	=	-30
-37.2	=	-35
-40.0	=	-40
-42.8	=	-45

ZODIAC

Can the stars influence a person's life?
There is no evidence that they can. But the idea goes back thousands of years. It began with observations of the zodiac, a band of night sky filled with constellations.

In ancient times, people were keenly aware of the natural world. They noticed that the sun, stars, and planets appeared in different positions as the seasons changed. If the sun and stars could be seen at the same time, they realized, the sun would travel through 12 constellations, entering a new one every month. They named this series of constellations the zodiac, from the Greek word for life. The parts of the zodiac, or signs, were named for the constellations—Aquarius (the Water Bearer), Pisces (the Fish), Aries (the Ram), and so on.

The zodiac became the basis of the fortune-telling method known as astrology. Astrology holds that certain traits are associated with each sign. The sign under which a person is born influences his or her character and future. For example, someone born on March 10 would be influenced by Pisces. That person supposedly would be sensitive and artistic. Astrologers make their predictions by drawing, or casting, charts called horoscopes. A detailed horoscope includes information about the positions of the planets and imaginary divisions called houses. The houses represent career, health, appearance, and other aspects of life. Despite the fact that there is no scientific basis for astrology, horoscopes are extremely popular. Some people take them very seriously. Many other people simply find them fun.

Yearbook

circa 1500 B.C. Egyptians identify the constellation of Aries as a ram. They associate this animal with their most important god, Amon Ra.

410 B.C. In Chaldea (present-day Iraq), horoscopes establish the positions of planets at the time an individual is born.

circa 1400–1600 Astrology as a method of telling the future regains popularity in Renaissance Europe, largely as a result of renewed interest in astronomy and science.

1912 Chinese court astrologers are abolished.

• Notables •

Aquarius, the Water Bearer This picture of a man or boy pouring water from a jar has been identified with Zeus, the king of Greek gods. Early Greeks thought he was pouring the waters of life from the sky.

Leo the Lion In ancient China, the stars we call Leo were thought to be a horse. The Inca people of Latin America supposedly thought the stars looked like a springing puma. The Greeks claimed that the stars were the mythological Nemean Lion, which fell from the moon and destroyed the countryside until it was killed by Hercules.

Virgo The only female figure among the signs of the zodiac. The stars in Virgo have been associated with goddesses in many cultures. They include Isis, the Egyptian goddess of nature; Demeter, the Greek goddess of agriculture; and Persephone, the Roman goddess of justice.

KEY IDEAS

ascendant In astrology, this adjective refers to the heavenly body that is most important in a "house" of the zodiac at the time that a person is born.

astrological age A period of time that is identified by the name of the constellation in which the vernal equinox is located. (This is the position of the sun on the first day of spring.) We are in the Age of Aries. The famous Age of Aquarius will take place in about 600 years.

astrology A way of predicting the future based on the theory that the movements of celestial bodies—the stars, planets, sun, and moon—influence the course of human events.

horoscope A map of the heavens at the time of one's birth.

mythology Stories of gods and godlike individuals that were told by an ancient people, such as the early Greeks and Romans.

sign In astrology, one of twelve constellations that is associated with a particular month of the year.

ZODIAC SIGNS

		Planet	Element	Personality Traits
OR		Saturn	earth	serious, domineering, ambitious, blunt, loyal, persistent

Capricorn, the Goat, December 22–January 19

		Planet	Element	Personality Traits
OR ≋		Uranus	air	independent, unselfish, generous, idealistic

Aquarius, the Water Bearer, January 20–February 18

		Planet	Element	Personality Traits
OR ♓		Neptune	water	compassionate, sympathetic, sensitive, timid, methodical

Pisces, the Fishes, February 19–March 20

		Planet	Element	Personality Traits
OR ♈		Mars	fire	independent, enthusiastic, bold, impulsive, confident

Aries, the Ram, March 21–April 19

		Planet	Element	Personality Traits
OR ♉		Venus	earth	decisive, determined, stubborn, stable

Taurus, the Bull, April 20–May 20

		Planet	Element	Personality Traits
OR ♊		Mercury	air	curious, sociable, ambitious, alert, intelligent, temperamental

Gemini, the Twins, May 21–June 21

Source: Nightstar Astrology; zodiac_signs.htm

	Planet	Element	Personality Traits
OR	Moon	water	organized, busy, moody, sensitive, supportive

Cancer, the Crab, June 22–July 22

	Planet	Element	Personality Traits
OR	Sun	fire	born leader, bold, noble, generous, enthusiastic, sympathetic

Leo, the Lion, July 23–August 22

	Planet	Element	Personality Traits
OR	Mercury	earth	analytical, critical, intellectual, clever

Virgo, the Virgin, August 23–September 22

	Planet	Element	Personality Traits
OR	Venus	air	affectionate, thoughtful, sympathetic, orderly, persuasive

Libra, the Scales, September 23–October 23

	Planet	Element	Personality Traits
OR	Mars	water	intense, fearless, loyal, willful

Scorpio, the Scorpion, October 24–November 21

	Planet	Element	Personality Traits
OR	Jupiter	fire	energetic, good-natured, practical, clever

Sagittarius, the Archer, November 22–December 21

Index